THE GREAT FIRE OF LONDON

THE FIRE MONUMENT
Photograph by Lady Eardley-Wilmot

THE GREAT FIRE OF LONDON IN 1666

By WALTER GEORGE BELL, F.R.A.S.

WITH FORTY-ONE ILLUSTRATIONS INCLUD-
ING PLANS AND DRAWINGS, REPRODUCTIONS
OF ENGLISH AND FOREIGN PRINTS, AND
PHOTOGRAPHS

"If it was esteemed an honour among the Greeks to be
born in Athens, if among the Italians to be a Roman,
if among the Spaniards to be a Toledano, why should
it be a lesse honour for an Englishman to be born
in London?"—JAMES HOWEL, *Londinopolis*, 1657.

GREENWOOD PRESS, PUBLISHERS
WESTPORT, CONNECTICUT

Originally published in 1920 by John Lane,
The Bodley Head, London and
John Lane Company, New York

First Greenwood Reprinting 1971

Library of Congress Catalogue Card Number 70-114464

SBN 8371-4774-3

Printed in the United States of America

PREFACE

HERE is a substantial contribution to the history of London. For two and a half centuries the Great Fire of London has awaited an historian. In view of the vast numbers of books that have been written about the Empire's capital, it is surprising that there should have been no adequate account of the Fire. No other single incident in London's record of over a thousand years has had such influence upon its fortunes and its future. The flames which burnt through the streets in those four September days of the year 1666 destroyed almost the last vestiges of past eras when the aspect of London was predominantly that of an ecclesiastical and monastic city, with commerce gathered about the walls of the religious—vestiges which the ruthlessness of Henry VIII. failed entirely to erase. Only when rebuilt upon the ruins of the Fire London became the wholly commercial city that we know.

My sources have been largely manuscript, and for those pages which describe the measures taken for meeting the distress occasioned by the catastrophe, the temporary housing of the citizens, the restoration of trade and the vastly important work of rebuilding the destroyed City, almost entirely so. The subject had not been explored, and beyond a short paper on " The Rebuilding of London after the Great Fire of 1666," which I read before the Royal Institute of British Architects in 1918, I know of nothing printed. These later chapters, I believe, will prove the most useful ; naturally the more dramatic narrative is in the Fire itself. Perhaps because the Great Fire of London has been so little known it has undergone popular neglect ; for the destruction of the larger part of a great city by flames, leaving one hundred thousand people homeless, has possibilities which must appeal to writers of romance.

The shortcomings of this work will be known to none better than myself. None can know so well the gaps that, after the passage of centuries, I have been compelled to leave unfilled; but I offer this book, which has been a work over many years in which I have not been lacking in industry, in the belief that it will prove helpful towards a true appreciation of what the Fire of London was.

In the months that immediately followed the Fire many pamphlets and tracts were printed which professed to describe it, but the writers were more concerned in drawing a moral than in attempting to depict the scenes through which they had lived. Best of these is Thomas Vincent's *God's Terrible Voice in the City*, but of its 204 pages fourteen alone actually deal with the Fire. Waterhous's *Short Narrative* is more disappointing, however good the religious lesson read, and the proportion of facts disclosed is even smaller. The report of the Parliamentary Committee which investigated the Fire is wholly taken up with the statements of chatterboxes anxious above all things to fix the blame upon the Roman Catholics, and is only of the smallest historical value. Clarendon, Burnet, Echard, and the remaining historians of the century which succeeded the Fire devote to it a few short passages. The one vital accession to our knowledge is Pepys's *Diary* of the memorable days, disentombed from his shorthand script after a century and a half's lapse. In 1769 there was put together, under the title of *An Historical Narrative of the Great and Terrible Fire of London, Sept. 2nd, 1666*, a collection of clippings from the writers mentioned, the *London Gazette*, and a few other sources, and thereafter the subject has been allowed to rest. Dr. Lappenberg, inspired by a huge fire which occurred at Hamburg in 1842, published in that city a 32-page pamphlet, *Der Grosse Brand von London*, a hasty compilation by a serious historian that adds nothing to his reputation.

Some accepted statements have had to be revised. The flames started on Sunday, September 2nd, 1666, before daybreak, and it is represented in the *London*

Gazette that the last stage of the Fire was the second outbreak in the Temple, which began on the following Thursday night. It is probable that the official account was written by James Williamson, then editor of the *Gazette*. It is certainly wrong. Wind. Sandys, the gentleman in personal attendance on the Duke of York, says clearly in his letter, here printed in full, that the second fire in the Temple occurred on Wednesday, and that his Royal Highness remained there until one o'clock next morning when, the peril having passed, he retired to St. James's Palace for much needed rest. The writer of the letters in the Gough collection at the Bodleian also fixes Wednesday as the date. Pepys says the same. There is no contemporary who confirms the statement in the *Gazette*. Unfortunately this last has been generally followed, and the Fire has been pictured as spreading over London throughout five days, whereas in fact all the dreadful havoc it wrought was accomplished in four days, and on the Thursday nothing remained to be done but to stamp out the still smouldering embers.

No epigram is more familiar than that " The Fire of London began in Pudding Lane and ended at Pie Corner." It is probably imperishable. There is an appositeness about the two names that is attractive, but in fact the flames continued to burn and spread long after Pie Corner had been levelled with the ground. It is fortunate that, where so much was destroyed, the Church registers and records of the City Companies with but rare exceptions were saved from the Fire, and the same with the plate. There are to-day among the possessions of City churches eight cups worked by London silversmiths in the reign of Edward VI., and many other valued pieces.

I have shown in the later chapters what length of years was actually taken in rebuilding London after the conflagration. If the authenticated statement runs contrary to popular belief derived from the inscription on the Fire Monument—" three short years complete that which was considered the work of an age "—the blame must be laid upon those who made that vainglorious boast, which is as false as it is foolish.

I trust there may be no clamour against me as a detractor of Sir Christopher Wren for what is here said.

I yield to none in admiration of that great architect, but
hold that he has not been fortunate in his biographers,
and that his fame is securely based for all time upon his
matchless achievement, without need of the attribution
to him of many things of which he was not the creator.

The Guildhall has little in its archives about the Fire
itself, but its records are invaluable for the settlement
thereafter and the rebuilding of London.   It is a pleasure
to acknowledge the generous assistance I have received
from Mr. J. Craker, who acted as Records Clerk to the
Corporation during the absence on military service of
Mr. Thomas, and from Mr. Bernard Kettle, the Guildhall
Librarian.   Next in importance are the various State
papers ; but indeed the field of research is very wide.
Dr. Byvanck, the Librarian of the Royal Library at The
Hague, was good enough to deposit on loan at Guildhall
for my use the Dutch historical pamphlets in his keeping,
and I am much indebted for his great courtesy.   The
Bibliothèque Nationale in Paris proved disappointing.   A
few of the shorter foreign pamphlets upon the Fire—Dutch,
Spanish, Italian, French, German—I have printed in an
Appendix.

I should indeed be wanting in gratitude did I not
cordially acknowledge the assistance given in illustrating
this book by my friends Mr. Charles W. F. Goss, F.S.A.,
who has given me freedom of choice among his great collection of prints, and Mr. Lionel Gowing.   The latter has
photographed the surviving houses built immediately
after the Fire that are here represented.   Lady Eardley-
Wilmot kindly allows me to use her artistic photograph
of the Fire Monument which makes the frontispiece.

Various matters incidental to the Fire, topographical
or merely curious, which could not be included in the
text without undue interference with the narrative, have
been packed away in Notes at the end of the volume.

CONTENTS

LIST OF ILLUSTRATIONS

FOLDING PLATES

FULL PAGE PLATES

xi

IN THE TEXT

THE GREAT FIRE OF LONDON

THE GREAT FIRE OF
LONDON IN 1666

CHAPTER I

LONDON IN THE YEAR 1666

An asterisk (*) indicates that a note upon the subject starred will be found at the end of the volume, the reference being the page number.

SAMUEL PEPYS, who was living at the time at the Navy Office in Seething Lane, near the Tower of London, tells readers of his immortal *Diary* that on Saturday, the 1st September, 1666, certain of his maid-servants sat up late getting things ready against the feast on the Lord's Day ; at three in the morning Jane awakened the household, to inform them of a fire seen in the City. " So I rose," he writes, " and slipped on my night-gown, and went to her window, and thought it to be on the backside of Mark Lane at the farthest ; but being unused to such fires as followed, I thought it far enough off ; and so went to bed again, and to sleep."

The Great Fire, begun in Pudding Lane,* by London Bridge, had then less than two hours' growth. It seemed nothing. Could Pepys have known that no man would ever again see London as it was at that hour before dawn, doubtless he would have stayed longer, but he was little concerned by the spectacle of fire with which the populace were unhappily familiar. From the upper window the city had spread out before him—a city of narrow streets and timber-framed houses massed closely together, losing all separate identity in the mystery of the deep shadows, and against the heavens a silhouette formed of innumerable roof-gables, carried upward at a hundred points by church spires and towers.

The London that perished in the Great Fire of 1666 was not the London of Charles II., but a city much older, with mediævalism borne upon its face.   The distinction is often forgotten.   Historical events hurry by, and never in such haste as in the first half of the seventeenth century. Fifty years only had passed since Shakespeare died (the 23rd April, 1616).   In the plan of its streets and the eleva- tion of by far the greater number of its buildings, the City of London survived exactly as Shakespeare had known it.   Much had been added west ; the unceasing creep of the town westward, which the Fire was destined greatly to accelerate, had started long before that portentous event. Shakespeare's familiar Bankside was altered in character, since its theatres had ceased to attract play-loving citizens across the river.   But the old City within the wall, amidst which the Fire chiefly raged—that was the same, and in the Liberties the buildings destroyed were mostly standing in the poet's own day.

Shakespeare's London disappeared in the Fire—dis- appeared wholly save for a small area left immune about the eastern and northern wall, with relics like Crosby Hall in Bishopsgate, the Norman Tower guarding the river entrance and Barking Church near by, St. Olave, Hart Street, St. Bartholomew the Great, Smithfield, and a few others beyond the limits reached by the flames, which have survived as witnesses of what Old London was.   The fact will not diminish interest in the restoration I have attempted to make in the succeeding chapters of the London of 1666.

From any tall building, such as the tower of Gresham's Royal Exchange, an observer might have followed with his eye the complete circuit of the wall.   London was still a walled city, to be entered from the Liberties only at the gates.   Parts of the mediæval wall may be seen above ground to-day, a bastion being preserved in the church- yard of St. Giles Cripplegate, and there is an open length opposite St. Alphage, London Wall ; but the wall in 1666 was high and solid, and in most of its two miles' length was an upstanding feature—higher than these remains suggest.   In one surviving portion near The Tower, built into Barber's Bonded Warehouse, the wall is complete from foundation to rampart and bulwark, rising to a height of 35 ft. Could one again walk the streets so encompassed, much would be seen to remind one of Elizabeth and Henry VIII., much too, of Henry VI. and the great era of church building and restoration in the fifteenth century, but nothing of Charles II., whose return to the Throne had been too recent for his age to stamp its individuality upon the ancient city.

The Commonwealth had added nothing of permanence to London ; the square brick tower of Allhallows Barking, by no means a bad example of this tasteless age, alone comes to mind. Nor had the reign of Charles I., shadowed at the outset by plague and marked by broken fortunes and civil strife, lent encouragement to civic development. Of the period of James I. a good deal was standing in the Liberties—of old time " the suburbs of London," and so called in a thousand documents—but within the wall the newest buildings were chiefly Elizabethan, and a great part of the City dated back to times more remote. The streets followed the lines laid down centuries before, and were as tortuous and narrow as you may find them to-day in any Continental town where mediævalism lingers.

The Restoration enlarged a cleavage already begun in London's life. Royalists who returned with the King no longer came to dwell in the City, finding their fathers' houses diverted to other uses or unfitted for their reception. They settled by choice in more pleasant and open places nearer the Court ; about Lincoln's Inn Fields, where Inigo Jones in the previous reign had begun a great scheme of building, or farther west at Covent Garden, a quarter growing in favour with the fashionable monde. Henrietta Street bears the name of Charles the First's Consort. Some sought sites as far distant as Pall Mall, St. James's, and Soho Fields. The courtiers affected to despise the " cits " ; and the merchants, still Puritan at heart for a large part, whose interests were narrowly confined to the state of the markets and the safety of their own souls, went about their affairs little concerned with the frivolities and licentiousness of Whitehall. They were less troubled with the unrighteousness of the age than were their divines.

Greater London in 1666 loosely covered perhaps twice as much ground as at the time of James I.'s accession, but it had spread west. Within the wall it remained unaffected

by changing times and modes, an ancient city still, and was
so regarded by Londoners of that day, much as to-day we
regard Chester or York.

St. Paul's, defamed and sorely dilapidated as it was,
dominated London : its height, its mass, its position,
chosen with the intuition of genius by its first builders, all
contributed to this end. It rose clear above other buildings, the central object in the vision of London from whatever point viewed. Imagine the venerable fabric slightly
longer than Wren's cathedral, with nave and roof somewhat
higher, lacking, it is true, the majestic height reached by
the golden cross since fire in 1561 had consumed the spire ;
then, to complete the picture, reduce the scale of the
houses surrounding the present cathedral by one half.
Old St. Paul's towered above London, and around this
vast mother church, within the City's restricted area, were
grouped the belfries and spires of one hundred and nine
daughter churches.

The Dutchmen, Wencelaus Hollar and Vischer, and
the few English etchers whose engravings have faithfully
preserved the aspect of London before the Great Fire,
loved to picture it from across the river. One sees in their
drawings the artist's appreciation of a glorious skyline.
One hundred and nine parish churches stood where to-day
there are still forty-seven. They made London a city of
bell towers and spires. That is the character it bears in
every print, the first thing that enforces attention—spires
rising from all points into the sky. There is this contrast
between the two cities : London in 1666 was a town of
low buildings with churches predominant, rising above
them ; to-day piles of commercial offices, built still higher,
have shrunken and concealed the remaining churches.

London at the time of the Fire is perhaps best known
from Pepys's gossiping pages. With Pepys you live the
City's life over again. He was one of the comparatively
few men of affairs who remained a City dweller when the
vast majority had gone west. He attempts no description ;
but none the less surely the *Diary* fills in what is wanting
in the prints, which alone do not satisfy. They show the
crowded houses, framed in stout oak and tiled above the
gables, but no line on the etched plate suggests that London
was then, as it has always been, a great commercial city.

It might be empty or asleep. Pepys fills the streets with
men and women. Lombard Street and all its swinging
signs and groups of merchants are brought to mind when
Pepys visits the goldsmith bankers there. Paternoster Row,
narrow as to-day, awakens with life. It is after the Plague
has died out that Pepys drops into Bennett's, " few shops
there being yet open," to buy velvet for a coat and camelott
for a cloak for himself, or with Lady Sandwich and Mrs.
Sanderson moves among the press of fashionable coaches,
seeking " a petticoat against the Queen's coming for my
lady, of plain satin." He took his morning draught at
any of the thousand taverns with which Restoration
London abounded, and dined in the City, sometimes in-
differently ; worshipped at the numerous churches, not
always with approval of the sermon ; admired Betterton
at the Salisbury Court Theatre, Fleet Street, above all
actors. His coach, passing through the Shambles, knocked
two pieces of meat into the dirt, and Pepys thought himself
fortunate to escape from the quarrelsome butchers at the
cost of a shilling. There you realize the crush in Newgate
Market. From the boat stairs by the Bridge he took oars,
to Westminster on business or to Vauxhall for his amuse-
ment. All this is living London ; but there is no trace
that the stage scene interested him. Had it done so, we
should have had a full view of the city destroyed in the
flames.

London's restless, money-making life was grafted, with
some incongruity, upon a city that was itself the result of
the growth of centuries. On every hand were reminders
in solid masonry of other times and influences. It was to
William, bishop, in the first place, and to Godfrey, portreeve,
only in the second place, that William the Conqueror
addressed his charter to London, a slip of parchment
bearing but sixty-six words that is now a precious possession
at Guildhall. Mediæval London enjoyed a highly organized
gild life ; its merchants were its governors, and managed
its affairs free from interference by any overlord save the
King. But London's ascendancy as the commercial capital
of the kingdom was built up in what was yet an ecclesiastical
city, possessing an altogether disproportionate number of
religious foundations. The greater wealth was always
that of the Church, and it was evidenced in vast buildings,

the majesty of which is suggested in the splendid fragment
of the Augustinian Monastery that we know as St. Bartholomew the Great, Smithfield, the Carthusian House
(the Charterhouse), and the nave of Austin Friars' Church,
which to-day serves the Dutch Protestant colony in London
for worship. The gilds themselves, standing stronger by
the destruction of this rival power, were able to acquire
magnificent houses in not a few instances from the spoils
of the Church. In every principal street were to be seen
religious buildings serving a lay use. It required two
catastrophic blows, the last of which was the Great Fire,
to transform London into the wholly commercial city
that we know.

The suppression of monasticism by Henry VIII. had
done much. The great Dominican Priory at Blackfriars,
whose arrogant magnificence is bitterly recalled in Piers
Plowman's verse, the windows full of "gay glittering
glas glowyng as the sun," was brought to the ground, as
was the Carmelite Priory at Whitefriars, the little Papey
nestling within the City Wall, and much else. London
was littered with ruins for years afterwards. The dispossession of the Abbot's town mansions, followed by the
driving out of the provincial Bishops to their Sees, helped
still further to change the face of London. But the wayfarer in 1666 still found at every important crossing a
parish church confronting him, often two, sometimes
three, monuments of the piety of early citizens ; and
besides, not all the great convents had entirely disappeared.

The house of the Grey Friars in Newgate Street
had suffered little harm when, twelve years after the
Suppression, it was refitted under Edward VI.'s gift for
the education of poor children as Christ's Hospital ;
indeed, the cloistered settlement stood practically intact
when the Fire struck it. Parishioners used the chancel
of its church for worship ; the vast preaching nave filled
a utilitarian purpose as a warehouse, and there the
Stationers had stored a part of the great accumulation of
books that perished in the Fire of London. Large parts
of the Carthusian Monastery, some of great age, survive
to-day. The refectory of Austin Friars served the Pinners
Company as their hall. The chapel of Elsing Spital
became the parish church of St. Alphage, London Wall.

The church built by the Knights Templars in the twelfth
and thirteenth centuries happily stands unharmed, safe
kept by the lawyers.

The great fortress of The Tower guarded the river
approach, but this and St. Paul's apart, London's public
buildings had small distinction.   London was not, and has
never been, a magnificent city.   Indeed, the poverty of
its buildings formed the subject of slighting comment by
many travellers, accustomed to the artistic splendours of
Toledo, of Venice, of Florence and Rome.   The ancient
Guildhall, the seat of civic government, was hemmed about
with houses and hidden from sight, with no approach until
Sir Christopher Wren, after the Great Fire, cut out King
Street to open it to Cheapside.   Access before that time
was restricted to Lawrence Lane and Ironmonger Lane,
passages so mean and narrow that in neither could two
vehicles pass.   Leadenhall enjoyed a better site, as might
be expected, for there had stood a Roman building,
believed by Sir Laurence Gomme to have been the Forum,
stones of which still lie in the soil beneath the Market.
The Royal Exchange, which Queen Elizabeth, in compliment to the donor, Sir Thomas Gresham, had so named
in person, was a worthy ornament of the City.   Blackwell
Hall, the City's cloth market, and the Custom House,
dating from Elizabeth's reign, are but little known from
the writings of contemporaries, who probably found little
in them worthy of record.

Large mansions of noblemen, replacing the ecclesiastics,
remained along the Strand, extending west, with the river
frontage to their gardens.

There were, besides, considerable numbers to be found
within the City, built by nobles or wealthy merchant
adventurers ; but Aldersgate Street, where Petre House,
Thanet House, Lauderdale House, and others were situated,
almost alone remained a place of City residence of the old
noble families.   Many large mansions, after years of neglect,
had been divided into tenements, and thus helped to house
London's population, but for others, both lay and religious,
a kindlier fate had been reserved when they passed into
the possession of the Livery Companies.   This fact in its
bearing upon London at the time of the Fire has never
received the prominence it merits, for amid much else that

was drab they played no small part in giving to the City that aspect of picturesque antiquity which thereafter was lost.

Some had become corporate property by gift of wealthy members of the Companies benefited. Such was Paynter Stainers Hall in Trinity Lane, Queenhithe, which originally was the residence of Sir John Brown, Serjeant Paynter to King Henry VIII. Salters Hall had been the town mansion of the Earl of Oxford. The larger halls had been acquired by purchase, mostly after confiscation by the Crown. Drapers Hall, in Throgmorton Street,—its large garden had the last bowling green maintained in the City—was the house of Thomas Cromwell, Earl of Essex, which had fallen to the Crown upon his attainder and execution on Tower Hill. The Mercers Company took for their Hall the property of the religious College of St. Thomas of Acon, at the Poultry entrance to Cheapside, which fell into Henry VIII.'s hands at the Suppression. The Leathersellers Company fitted up as their hall the refectory of the priory of Benedictine nuns of St. Helen's, Bishopsgate.

What alone I wish now to impress is that London in 1666 still possessed numbers of its historic houses, in excellent preservation, some amongst them being the most ancient buildings in the City, and these were destroyed by the Fire. Actually only three Companies' Halls had the water frontage, but a majority lay near the Thames side or else were clustered about Guildhall. The picturesqueness of the old City which the flames devastated, consuming 13,200 houses, must not dull our sense to the fact that much of it was mean and squalid. Its tortuous ways, dark and evil-smelling, and constant obstructions to the slow moving traffic, provoked the satire of Sir William Davenant a few years before the Fire. " Sure (says he) your ancestors contrived your narrow streets in the days of wheelbarrows, before those greater engines, carts, were invented." The stranger in London, in haste to be gone, found it unsafe to use the new public hackney coaches " till the quarrel be decided whether six of your nobles, sitting together, shall stop and give way to as many barrels of beer."

London had always been crowded ; Restoration London

was densely overcrowded, even after the Plague had reduced the numbers. The wars being ended and the armies disbanded, old soldiers came to the metropolis to set up trades, their families with them. With the monarchy again firmly established, a large train of people followed the return of the Court, attending it to obtain rewards for services, preferments, and the like. There was a new era of reckless extravagance unknown in the dour days of the Commonwealth. Luxury and fashion again ran riot, and to minister to the wants of the time tradesmen in hundreds came to settle in business and take their profits out of the money now freely circulating. The Royal Exchange shops had become the City's bazaar for rare goods brought from every quarter of the world. They were never before so busy. Defoe, who was six years of age when the Great Plague broke out in 1665, and had some knowledge, computed that there were then in London above one hundred thousand more people than ever it had held before.

In this old City made up of fragments of the past, of densely packed timber-framed houses, red tiled, built about a web of cobbled streets, grown out beyond its encircling wall and badly wanting space, was carried on the greatest manufacturing and commercial business in the kingdom.

John Evelyn, the diarist, was walking one day in the well-kept grounds of Whitehall Palace when a cloud of smoke came up from the direction of London, which so invaded the Court that all the rooms, galleries and places about it were filled and infected. Men could hardly discern one another for the cloud, and none could suffer it without choking. Indignant, he wrote his *Fumifugium; or the Inconveniencie of the Aer and Smoak of London Dissipated*, proposing remedies. The King, taking him aside, warmly commended the work, and commanded him to prepare a Bill against the next session of Parliament, " being, as he said, resolved to have something done in it." The monarch was careless, the Parliament engrossed with other affairs. Five years later the Fire made way for the reform more effectively than either could have done.

The smoke cloud over London was not infrequent,

rising from the furnaces lighted by soap-boilers, dyers, brewers, and lime-burners, who pursued their noisome trades, not at distant factories or in an outer ring, but within the City itself. " It is this horrid smoke," writes Evelyn, " which obscures our churches and makes our palaces look old, which fouls our clothes and corrupts the waters, so that the very rain and refreshing dews which fall in the several seasons precipitate this impure vapour, which with its black and tenacious quality spots and contaminates whatever is exposed to it." He bitterly complains that the gardens around London no longer bore fruit, instancing especially Lord Bridgwater's orchard at Barbican and the Marquis of Hertford's in the Strand. I think it likely that Evelyn's offended sense led him to exaggerate, but the chimneys belching smoke and the soot-blackened buildings recall an aspect of industrial London at the Restoration that is seldom thought of.

In general terms, London within the Wall remained a mediæval city, displaying a good deal of the handiwork of builders of James I. and Elizabeth, but not obtrusively, for there was no violent clashing in the simple architectural styles. If individually the houses were narrow, low, and mean, as we know for the greater part they were, they formed together a wholly agreeable *mise-en-scène*. Although a jumble of shapes and heights, one and all were built for a common purpose, which gave consistency to the town— that of the private dwellings of citizens. Little survives to-day that will help us to reproduce London before the Great Fire, but four buildings may be cited as types which were duplicated a thousand times in the city destroyed by the flames. One or other will be known to every haunter of City streets. They are the timber front of Staple Inn (circa 1570), No. 17, Fleet Street (James I.), the houses with projecting plaster fronts in Middle Temple Lane, and that fine early Stuart example, the Old Dick Whittington in Cloth Fair, now no more than a pleasant memory since it was demolished in 1916.

These would be found in the better streets. A fifth type might be added—important, too, because once so numerous—in the weather-boarded shanty dwellings in Cloth Fair, but these are threatened with demolition as I write.

TYPES OF RESTORATION LONDON
Houses formerly standing in Leadenhall Street, timber built

Much had been done since James I.'s accession to encourage the use of brick, but it was still unusual within the City, save in the few recent buildings.[1] Party walls were all supposed to be of stone or brick, a precaution against the spread of fire dating back as far as FitzAlwyn's Assize in 1189 ; London's first Building Act given by London's first Mayor. The precaution was very partially observed. The house fronts were constructed of stout timber frames, raised upon a stone or brick foundation, and filled in with laths, which in turn were covered with rough plaster. The storeys projected one beyond another up to the steep gables, to afford weather protection. The plan darkened the already narrow streets, and brought opposite houses closely together. Ben Jonson illustrates this feature of the town in his play, *The Devil is an Asse*, where the lady and her lover speak softly to one another from the windows of contiguous buildings.

The City had nothing in common with what we know to-day. The substantial merchant who lived about Cornhill, Throgmorton Street, Lombard Street, and the close purlieus surrounding the Royal Exchange, or, having shipping interests, resided in Tower Street, had the apartments devoted to his counting house on the street level, and his warehouse very likely built in the rear or at the side ; he dwelt with his household in the rooms above. The mercer of Paternoster Row, and, indeed, the shopkeeper everywhere, traded indoors. Sometimes he built out a pent-house to the street, but he did not make his great display in front, nor did he expect his goods to be seen from outside. This did not mean that the streets were empty. The case was far otherwise. The apprentices were vociferous, stationed at every shop door. " What d'ye lack ? What is't ye lack, ladies ? "—their cry rang through London for centuries. Hawkers did a large and popular trade. Stalls, stools, and baskets encumbered the City streets, in such numbers that a pedestrian had often to pick his way through. They caused so much obstruction that in 1626 one Nicholas Lisle had proposed raising revenue

---

[1] Cf. *State Papers* (*Domestic*), 1624, July 5. It was not solely because of danger of fire that timber building was discouraged, but also " by reason that all great and well grown woods are much spent and wasted, so as timber for shipping waxed scarce." (*Royal Proclamation*, 1605.)

for the King's service by taxing them, and after the Fire
there was clamour for their wholesale removal in the
interests of legitimate traders.

It was not a pleasant place to live in, this City which
was more than full of people.   Where a man had business,
there his life was spent, and with him were his wife and
often a large family of children, and his assistants and
apprentices, all in one household.   This made every street
populous.   Stuart London was, too, excessively noisy.
London's vibrating note, which Lowell likened to " the
roaring loom of time," has been attuned to many keys,
but never has this been a silent city.

The streets were paved with egg-shaped cobble-stones
beaten in with sand and gravel, extending the full width
from house to house.   There were no raised side-walks.
Even the small protection to pedestrians from passing
traffic afforded by the " massy " posts which it was Dr.
Johnson's habit, in a later age, to finger nervously as he
walked down Fleet Street, was given only in a few of the
broader highways.   We know how ill-kept the City streets
were a century later ;   the paving rough and irregular by
frequent patching ;   footways, still not raised above the
road level, covered with mud and often overflowed with
water, the narrow space encroached upon by shop-windows,
show-boards, vaults and cellar doors ;   locomotion, even
in important thoroughfares, obstructed by the washing of
butts and casks [1] ;   and the conditions were worse, not
better, before the Fire.

A length of freestone before the shops was rare.   An
open kennel ran down the centre or sides of each street,
with many cross-channels, into which householders threw
their kitchen water and refuse and garbage, to be carried
along by the next shower.   It then accumulated, with
many additions swept out of the houses, till the scavengers
made a clearance, heaping the refuse high in poisonous
laystalls about the City's outskirts or along the river banks,
to rot under the influence of sun and weather.   I found
complaints at the wardmote inquests of liquid from
manure-heaps flowing out from City inn-yards to the highway, of loosened roof-gutters from which a deluge of

[1] Report by Commissioners of Sewers, 1765, Nov. 15.

filthy water after rainfall descended on passers-by, making a continual wet day after the storm was over, of broken pavements, and conditions of dirt and squalor that seem hardly conceivable.

A couple of years after the Fire a Mayoral Proclamation condemned the " intolerable foulness " of the streets in that part of the City left standing, with evil consequences to its trade, health, and government.[1] If the scavengers had done their work effectively, still they could not have cleansed the houses, the real source of every infection. Malcolm, the antiquary, has said : " This subject may be allowed to be familiar to me, and I have, perhaps, had more than common means of judging ; and I now declare it to be my full and decided opinion, that London was burnt by Government to annihilate the Plague, which was grafted in every crevice of the hateful old houses consumed in the Fire." An historian cannot accept the conclusion, but the savagery of the passage is enlightening.

Then the graveyards—one shudders to think of them ! The crowded city buried its dead in its own soil, and the harvest of victims of the Great Plague the previous year had been sown thickly till the choked ground could hold no more, and bodies were flung unceremoniously into loathsome plague-pits out in the suburbs. Even to-day the churchyards of St. Swithin's, of St. Laurence Pountney, and many others show plainly that the surface has been raised to its present height above the surrounding land by the process of finding room for additional burials.*

London in 1666 enjoyed one advantage for healthy life. It was better served with water than ever before, the New River Company's supply being distributed over a large part of the northern and central area, supplementing the services of the springs and wells, though the riverside quarter still remained dependent upon the Thames.[2] But in sewerage and general sanitation it had made little

---

[1] Guildhall archives, *Journal* 46, fo. 268*b*.

[2] After the Fire the grandchildren of the original Moris rebuilt the Thames water wheels and restored the river supply at a cost of £2,000, borrowed from future profits. The New River Company then projecting an extension of their pipes to the waterside district, they petitioned the King not to allow it, as such competition would involve ruin of their enterprise. (*State Papers, Domestic*, 1667–8, p. 112.)

advance. Lord Keeper Guilford, at his great house in Chancery Lane (in 1672) found his cellar obnoxious by reason that all the drainage of the mansion went into a small well there, and we are naively told that " when it was full a pump went to work to carry it into the open kennel of the street ! " [1] The City's rank smells were notorious. The town ditch, too nauseous for the none too fastidious sense of the Elizabethan citizen, had been filled in, but on the west, below Ludgate, there was still tolerated an uncovered sewer of outrageous filthiness in the Fleet River.

In the populous city, with its commerce, its shipping, its manufactories, its manifold activities, and its ever pressing want of space, room had to be found for the poor, always the largest numbers. Small care was given to them. The meaner dwellings, built back to back, had often a mere casing of weather boards fastened to their shaking frames. A smear of black pitch made the only water-proofing. These were the homes of thousands of London's toiling populace—two rooms, or at most three, dark, stuffy, and horribly insanitary. Narrow and filthy alleys, without pretence of paving and often ankle-deep in mud, gave the only access. Wanting even such accommodation as this, other thousands were forced to find refuge in under-ground rooms. Others, again, were herded into tenements, falling rapidly into ruin by wilful destruction and want of repair.

The overcrowding was scandalous. A small house in Dowgate Ward had been reported as accommodating eleven married couples and fifteen single persons ; another house of ten rooms in Silver Street sheltered ten families, divers of whom had lodgers. The conversion of old mansions was typified in the Whitefriars precinct, the dissolute sanctuary of Alsatia, where Sir John Parker's house stood, divided into no fewer than twenty tenements, and that of one Francis Pyke into thirty-nine tenements.[2] Fifty other examples might be cited.

Count Cominges, the French Ambassador till the war at the Court of Charles II., found London a great and wealthy city, but its large population dwelt in houses mostly

[1] North's *Life of Lord Keeper Guilford.*
[2] St. Dunstan's Wardmote Inquest Register, 1609,

only two storeys high. "However (says he), this is compensated by the existence under them of cellars so full of poor people who live only by their toil that it would be difficult to try to give their exact number." [1] He declares that the best informed spoke of a London population in 1665 of 600,000. It is difficult to estimate the actual numbers of City dwellers, excluding those west, but figures of the year 1631 afford some guidance—and bewilderment. A census of mouths to feed was then taken by Sir Robert Ducie, the Lord Mayor, by order of the Privy Council, when apprehensive of a time of approaching scarcity. It was found that there were 71,029 men, women and children dwelling within the Wall and 59,239 in the Liberties.[2] The population had enormously increased in density in the intervening thirty-five years, especially in the Liberties, by this time closely built over; otherwise how shall one account for the stark fact that in the Plague year of 1665 there were 56,558 deaths within the area of the Lord Mayor's jurisdiction ? [3] In Greater London, thinly distributed over the much larger area of Westminster City and Liberties, the enormous parish of Stepney, and the outparishes, there was another population probably equalling that of the City.

It is a popular superstition that the Fire, scorching the ground deep down, burnt out the Plague harboured in the soil, which never thereafter appeared in the metropolis. The good work that the Fire accomplished was to burn out the decaying, fever-haunted, and horribly insanitary houses, and to purge with flame the unwholesome conditions under which the citizens had been compelled to live. The London which arose under the new Building Acts was different in everything that counts for the welfare of human life. I am no enthusiast for such wholesale destruction as the Fire occasioned of historical things which later generations value, but for the health of London the Fire was a crowning mercy.

[1] *Relation de l'Angleterre en l'année* 1666 (Bibliothèque Nationale, Paris, MS. Fr. 15889). See Jusserand, " A French View of England in 1666," in *The Nineteenth Century*, April, 1914.

[2] *Notes & Queries*, 11th Ser. i, 426.

[3] Bills of Mortality, 1665. The figures are not exact for the City population, as they include deaths in the pest-houses to which many persons were brought from the out-parishes

I have shirked nothing in recapitulating the evils of the old City, full ready as it was for destruction, its dirt, overcrowding, squalor, and general unwholesomeness. When all has been admitted, London with its one hundred and nine churches rising amidst the timber-framed houses and innumerable gables, the steel-grey fortress of The Tower at the water gate and palaces beyond, was a delight to the eye. Its coarser detail, concealed in the dense masses of its buildings, only becomes known when one penetrates the narrow streets, and the vision that lingers is that of the prints—a City of shallow depth and of many spires built on rising ground along the river bank. It was essentially a City by the river; the Thames flowing by in full flood which had been the determining cause of the original foundation of London, which still we see only imperfectly out of the mists. The houses nowhere stretched far from the water. Stuart London lived dependent upon the Thames in a sense that modern citizens find it difficult to realize. Open, broad, and healthy, with hundreds of two-oared wherries at the public call, this (and not its mean streets) was London's real highway.

Contrasting Restoration London and the London of to-day, Mr. Lubbock, a recent biographer of Pepys, says truly—

It is not merely that the red roofs and gables have vanished, nor even that the clear air has become thickened and stained. It is rather that the actual point of view has shifted with the abandonment of the one great curving majestic street which old London possessed, and which, for æsthetic value, modern London has done nothing to replace. Two hundred years ago London life centred round its beautiful waterway almost as much as Venice itself, and the Thames was simply a wider and ampler Grand Canal. Its single bridge, clustered with shops, stood on a long line of narrow arches, through which the piled-up stream poured in tumultuous rapids. Above and below, the river was sprinkled with boats and barges, while on either bank London and Southwark faced each other across the water, not entrenched behind embankments or blank warehouses, but pushing out into the stream a broken fringe of dwelling houses and landing stages.

In order to understand the vast calamity of the Great Fire, there are two things always to be borne in mind in reading these pages.   The fact of momentous significance is that there was no fire insurance—nothing confronted the citizens but irreparable loss of all that the flames consumed. And the extent of that loss is not to be measured by the mere area of the City embedded in the map of London as we know it.   To the merchant of Charles II.'s age the City and its Liberties were London.

The enormous growth and imponderable, formless mass of the town that results are phenomena of a later time. A few taverns clustered about Holborn, and beyond the bars stood the George and Blue Boar—the name is still preserved—familiar in history for an intercepted letter from Charles I. to Henrietta Maria, there torn from a courier's saddle ; but it was a short line towards St. Giles, then literally " in the fields."   The town assembled more closely along the Strand to Westminster, and spread out two northern growths towards Spitalfields and Clerkenwell. These built-in areas apart, there was little else beyond open land with a few houses and the view of distant villages—Islington, Highgate, and Hampstead on the heights, and Hackney lying away north-east.   " The country mighty pleasant," says Pepys, discoursing of his coach ride with his wife to Whitechapel, Bethnal Green, Kingsland, and home by Newington Green.[1]   From Holborn grass fields were still to be seen a century after the Fire.

The destruction of London was not unexpected.   King Charles himself had frankly expressed his fears, and a year before the Great Fire (the 11th April, 1665) had written to the Lord Mayor, Recorder, and Aldermen, warning them of the peril of fire from the narrowness of the streets and alleys, and the overhanging houses built of wood.   They had his Royal authority to imprison those persons who continued to erect houses in contravention of the Building Acts, and to pull down their dwellings.[2]

The age abounded with seers, who had horrific visions of London's doom.   Through the pamphleteering literature of the Commonwealth and the early years of the Restoration there runs a vein of gloomy prognostication of impending

---

[1] *Diary*, 1664, April 25.   [2] *State Papers (Domestic)*, 1664–5, p. 303.

catastrophe, to be brought about by God's vengeance upon sinful London.

The idea lay like a nightmare over the religious feeling of the time. In conventicle and Quakers' meeting-house the pulpits had resounded with the utterances of enthusiasts, who railed in no measured terms against the monster city— the city Babylon, the bloody city, as they loved to term her—proclaiming with the fervour of fanaticism that the measure of her iniquities was full, and the day of extinction was at hand. Walter Gostelo, in a treatise printed in 1658, gave prophetic warning—

London, go on still in thy presumptuous wickedness ! put the evil day far from thee, and repent not ! do so London. But if fire make not ashes of the city, and thy bones also, conclude me a liar for ever. Oh, London ! London ! sinful as Sodom and Gomorrah ! the decree is gone out, Repent, or burn, as Sodom, as Gomorrah ! [1]

From the printed tracts I give a few passages which are not only typical, but forecast with remarkable accuracy what actually happened. Daniel Baker, after much invective against London, foresaw—

. . . a fire, a consuming fire, shall be kindled in the bowels of the earth, which will scorch with burning heat all hypocrites, unstable, double-minded workers of iniquity. . . . A great and large slaughter shall be throughout the land of darkness where the unrighteous decrees and laws have been founded. Yea, a great effusion of blood, fire and smoke shall encrease up in the dark habitations of cruelty, howling and great wailing shall be on every hand in all her streets.[2]

The Quakers were famous seers. From them all I quote only Humphrey Smith, who died in Winchester Gaol in 1662, after having endured long persecutions for the sake of his creed. His *Vision which he saw concerning London* was printed in 1660. The following passage is startling—

And as for the city, herself and her suburbs, and all that belonged to her, a fire was kindled therein ; but she knew not how, even in all her goodly places, and the kindling of it was

---

[1] *The Coming of God in Mercy, in Vengeance, beginning with Fire, to convert or consume all this so sinful City London.* London, 1658.
[2] *Certaine Warning for a Naked Heart*, Lond. 1659.

in the foundation of all her buildings, and there was none could quench it.   And the burning thereof was exceeding great, and it burned inward in a hidden manner which cannot be described. . . . All the tall buildings, and it consumed all the lofty things therein, and the fire searched out all the hidden places, and burned most of the street places.   And as I passed through her streets I beheld her state to be very miserable, and very few were those who were left in her, who were but here and there one ; and they feared not the fire, neither did the burning hurt them, but they walked as dejected, mournful people. . . . And the fire continued, for, though all the lofty part was brought down, yet there was much old stuffe, and parts of broken-down desolate walls, which the fire continued burning against.   And the vision thereof remained in me as a thing that was showed me of the Lord.

Solomon Eagle, of Defoe's Plague narrative, if not himself an historical character, was a type of others. A Quaker had been moved to pass naked through the crowds at Bartholomew Fair, in Smithfield, bearing upon his head a pan full of fire and brimstone, and warning the pleasure-loving citizens of God's impending judgment, " for which some rude people did abuse him " ; and a frenzied woman had gone to St. Paul's, a spectral figure with her face made black, and blood streaming down her dishevelled hair on to the sackcloth that constituted her only garment, some of which blood she poured upon the altar.[1]

Letters written by Roman Catholics before the Fire, of which so much was afterwards made, are worthless as evidence of a Catholic plot, but they show that adherents of the Church of Rome, though for widely divergent reasons, shared with Quakers and Nonconformists the anticipations of vengeance from Above falling upon the heretic city. After foreign enemies, French and Dutch, the popular suspicion first turned against the Nonconformists, but Protestant feeling soon found an object against which to unite the forces of calumny—the Papists.   In the campaign against the followers of Rome all other religious differences were forgotten.

The Press for years before and after the Restoration

---

[1] *A Brief Relation of the Persecutions and Cruelties that have been acted upon the People called QUAKERS in and about the City of London, etc.* Lond. 1662.

teemed with " warnings " and visions. " Most of our last
year's almanacs talked of fire in London, and one named
the month, but it was expunged by L'Estrange (who
licensed them) for fear of consequences," says the writer
of a letter in 1666.

Michael Nostradamus, more than a century earlier, is
said to have foretold the very year of the burning, but the
passage, revived after the Fire, is probably a forgery—

> Le sang du juste à Londres fera faute,
> Brûlez per foudres, de vingt-trois le six,
> La dame antique cherchera de place haute ;
> De mesme secte plusieurs seront occis.

Mother Shipton's prophecy, that London in 'sixty-six
should be burnt to ashes, was also recalled.*

These were incursions into the occult, and not lightly
dismissed in a superstitious age ; but there was remembrance of an actual peril threatened. In April, less than
five months before the Fire, John Rathbone, an old colonel
of the Parliamentary Army, had been seized for conspiracy
to kill the King and Monck, and restore the Republic.
Engaged with him in the plot were William Sanders, Henry
Tucker, Thomas Flint, Thomas Evans, John Myles, William
Wescot, and John Cole, all officers or soldiers who had
fought in the Civil War. The circumstances are detailed
in the *London Gazette*, 30th April, 1666. They had designed
to fire the City, first taking precaution to have the port-
cullises lowered at the gates, to prevent assistance being
brought in. The Horse Guards were to be seized in their
quarters and The Tower surprised, the plotters intending
to scale the walls after they had crossed the moat in boats.

The eight conspirators were tried at the Old Bailey,
convicted of high treason, and promptly executed.
September 3rd had been the date fixed for the attempt,
that being found by Lilly's Almanac, and a horoscope
constructed for the purpose, to be a lucky day, a planet
then ruling which presaged the downfall of Monarchy.
The day was also deemed fortunate by Republicans as the
anniversary of Cromwell's victories at Dunbar and
Worcester. The men's bodies were hacked and torn,
but London recalled that, almost at the hour designated
for the attempt, the burning of the City, the first part of
their contemplated work, began.

CHAPTER II

"LITTLE pityful lane!" Waterhous calls Pudding Lane in his *Short Narrative*. It is a narrow way to the waterside near London Bridge, itself insignificant, but has meant much in London's history.

A line of tottering houses ran unevenly down the steep hill towards the Thames, every one of them timber-built, old and dry. The wood was coated with pitch ; the storeys, projecting one beyond another, nearly met by the gable roofs, leaving only a thin thread of sky visible. Below went a dark, unwholesome, roughly cobbled street. The sun rarely entered this place ; the dank city smell was persistent. At night the lane was lost in black shadows, till the Fire itself lit up the neighbourhood. An occasional candle, dimly glowing through horn, was judged sufficient illumination for more important streets than this. In 1662 died John Cook, a neighbouring parishioner of St. Michael Crooked Lane. He gave by his will twenty shillings yearly to maintain a lanthorn and candle lighted, affording light to travellers passing through Thames Street and St. Michael's Lane.

A contemporary writer upon the Fire describes Pudding Lane and the neighbouring streets as the narrowest of the City, so closely built about that in some a cart could scarcely pass, and in others not at all. " The danger I did once run of my life thereabouts (says he) by the crowd of carts hath caused me many times to make reflection on the covetousness of the citizens and connivancy of magistrates, who hath suffered them from time to time to encroach upon the streets, and so to get the top of their houses so as from one side of the street to touch the other, which as it doth facilitate a conflagration, so doth it also hinder the remedy." [1]

There in the deep dark, with the Thames lapping the wharves a stone's throw distant, the Great Fire of London had its seat. The shop and house of one Farynor, the King's baker, stood in Pudding Lane, ten doors from Thames Street. By his oven, between one and two o'clock on the morning of Sunday, the 2nd September, 1666, the flames broke out. The fact does not admit of doubt. Not all the wild accusations against Papists and Frenchmen of wilfully burning the City, which fill some later pages of this book ; not Hubert's confession, upon which he was hanged, nor the disclaimers of the baker himself, affect the judgment that must result from a calm consideration of the evidence, that the Fire in its origin was due to carelessness, and was not criminal. Farynor, his day's trading done, had gone to bed, " leaving his providence with his slippers," as the writer above quoted has said.

A pile of faggots for relighting the fire was by the side of the oven (according to one statement, within the oven) and some flitches of bacon hung near ; but the baker took oath that he had drawn the oven at ten o'clock overnight ; then, having occasion to light a candle about twelve, there was not fire enough in the bakehouse to kindle the match, so he had to go into another place for that purpose. Asked whether there was no window or door that might have let in wind to fan the embers, he affirmed that was impossible. It was fixed in his mind that his house was wilfully fired.

Farynor's man was awakened by a choking sensation shortly before two o'clock, and found the house full of smoke. He roused the family. The baker looked out, and afterwards he declared that the stack of bavins (brushwood for bakers' ovens) in his yard was not then alight, and the crackling of fire already heard was far remote from the oven and chimney. With his wife and daughter he escaped through a garret window, and by means of a roof gutter reached a neighbouring house, so all three saved their lives. His man followed ; but his maidservant, not adventuring as they had done, remained behind. Left

[1] *Observations both Historical and Moral upon the Burning of London.* By Rege Sincera, 1667.

beyond reach of help, she was the first victim of the Great Fire of London.[1]

The Fire at the outset progressed slowly. An eye-witness has left on record that he watched Farynor's house burning above an hour before any other was attacked. A neighbour next door was able to get out all his goods before his house was consumed. Opposite, on Fish Street Hill, stood the Star Inn, a travellers' resort that was rebuilt after the Great Fire of London, and survived more than a century later. Its yard and outbuildings were stored with hay and other combustibles. These became ignited by scattered sparks, and thereafter the galleried inn caught fire. To those few, immediate neighbours, who first hurried out to render help, the noisy creaking of the house signs and the wind whistling among the gable roofs must have been ominous sounds.

St. Margaret Fish Street Hill was first of the churches to be attacked. Then the flames, much augmented, crossed the street, and laying hold of the timber-built houses, dry as a chip after a hot summer's long drought, burnt in parallel lines down Pudding Lane and Fish Street Hill towards the river quays. The night had the darkness that comes before dawn. London, tired with the exertions of Saturday, the busiest day of the week, had gone to bed, and the streets were deserted. Chamberlayne, a somewhat fanatical person, who wrote *The Present State of England* (1682) attributed the Fire and its spread unchecked to the drunkenness of the baker and his servants, and the sloth of the people, " filled with drink, and all in a dead sleep " ; but of this, to London's credit, there is no rag of evidence.

A hundred fires had occurred before, burning themselves out after more or less damage had been occasioned. Sir Thomas Bludworth, the Lord Mayor, was roused at his house in Maiden Lane, Aldersgate, and arrived on the scene as early as three o'clock, when few citizens were astir, and

[1] *A True and Faithfull Account, etc.*, 1667. Pepys's *Diary*, Feb. 24, 1667. Sir Edward Harley to Lady Harley, Oct. 20, 1666. (Portland MSS, *Hist. MSS. Comm.* vol. 3, p. 301.) I found incidental reference to the ill-fate of Farynor's maidservant in the letter from Sir Edward Harley to his wife, above cited, but nowhere else ; perhaps in the light of the momentous events that followed it was thought sufficiently small matter to be overlooked.

little pleased that he should himself have been disturbed. He attached no unusual importance to this particular fire.[1] It would, in all probability, never have brought about the immense conflagration that followed but for a single fact, namely, that the flames were carried down to Thames Street. There, in a more practical sense than at Pudding Lane, the Great Fire of London originated. Thames Street and the adjacent lanes immediately about the Bridge were almost monopolized by wharfingers. In cellars and sheds and warehouses were great stores of tallow, oil, spirits, hemp, and like combustible goods, brought by coasting vessels and traders from foreign ports, which came up the river to Billingsgate and Lyon Key, below the Bridge, and Queenhithe above. On the open wharves, hay, timber, and coal lay heaped, ready to blaze up when ignited by the first burning brands. It was the quarter of London favourable above all others to the spread of fire.

Fish Street Hill, which to-day is a back way, noteworthy only because the Monument is built upon it, was the highway leading direct on to old London Bridge. Carts coming over the water jostled one another in the narrow cobbled street, making the steep ascent with difficulty—it was steeper than as we know it. St. Magnus the Martyr stood at the foot of the Bridge. The lines of fire, uniting, crashed through the church. Little time availed to save anything. Happily the old registers were mostly got out, with loss of the vestry orders. The parish clerk, in haste to escape, left behind the monies received for burials since the previous Lady Day. The plate was consumed. A fierce fire burnt within the church, leaving little but shattered walls ready to fall, and the flames, bursting through the belfry stages, leapt the height of the tower, which was a conspicuous object to those crossing the bridge. They gave the first signal to London that a fire of unusual magnitude had to be met.

St. Magnus parsonage house, in the adjoining Churchyard Alley, was quickly " wasted."

London Bridge lay in the direct path of the Fire, now

---

[1] I know no reason to suppress the historical remark of Sir Thomas Bludworth, the Lord Mayor, when first he surveyed the flames of what became the Great Fire of London. " Pish ! " he said, " a woman might piss it out." (Malcolm, *Londinium Redivivum*, iv, 73.)

seething and crackling about its approaches. Old London
Bridge had been completed when King John sat on the
English throne, and even more than the Conqueror's White
Tower gave an aspect of antiquity to the city about to be
destroyed, which was so much older than Charles II. and
his age. Its long line, low upon the water, was supported
by nineteen stone arches and piers. The "starlings"
built up from the river bed made a bad obstruction to the
tide, surging down to the sea in actual rapids between
them. Narrow as was the way left for horse- and foot-
passengers on the Bridge, where for the greater length
only twelve feet divided opposite houses, there did not
remain sufficient space for the shops and buildings crowded
together on both sides. Most of these consequently projected above the river, the backs upheld by timber struts.
Over this Bridge, picturesque in its mediævalism, King
Charles had passed, riding between his brothers, the Dukes
of York and Gloucester, on his triumphant return to his
capital on the afternoon of the 29th May, 1660, with banners
waving, people cheering, and blare of trumpets; three
hundred citizens assembled there in cloth of silver doublets
and thirteen hundred more in velvet; heralds and maids
in splendid habits; the monarch preceded by Sir Thomas
Allen, the Lord Mayor, the City Mace and Marshal and
Sheriffs and Aldermen giving him attendance.

A number of houses newly built stood at the northern
end, the space having lain waste for fifteen years after a
disastrous fire on the Bridge in 1632. The carelessness of
a servant of one Briggs, a needle-maker living there, in
leaving at night a tub of hot ashes under the stairs had been
responsible for this earlier fire, which consumed forty-two
houses, and burnt for eight hours. St. Magnus Church,
though in the gravest peril, escaped on that occasion, and
in gratitude therefor a devout parishioner, Susanna
Chambers, left to the parson a yearly sum of twenty shillings
for a sermon to be preached in commemoration of God's
providence. The progress of the fire upon the Bridge was
only stayed when the flames reached the first clear space
above the water.

The flames of 1666 followed the same course, burning
through the gate-tower and laying low the new houses,
rebuilt three storeys high and again timber-framed and

timber-strutted. Overhanging portions fell into the flood below, and floated away, the rest collapsing upon their foundations. The road was thus blocked, the way being made impassable to any who might have combated the flames. Fortunately the open space which served so well in 1632 served again thirty-four years later, and there the Fire stopped. Sparks blown from the debris set alight a stable in Horse Shoe Alley, Southwark. After two houses had been involved, the Fire across the river was stayed by the pulling down of a third. No life was lost on the Bridge; but, if Walpole is right, the world lost a Holbein picture. He says—

"The father of Lord Treasurer Oxford, passing over London Bridge, was caught in a shower, and stepping into a goldsmith's shop for shelter found there a picture by Hans Holbein (who had lived in that house) and his family. He offered the goldsmith £100 for it, who consented to let him have it, but desired first to show it to some persons. Immediately after happened the Fire of London, and the picture was destroyed." [1] The anecdote is interesting, but Holbein cannot have lived in this identical house, for all those burnt on the Bridge in 1666 had been rebuilt long after the painter's death.

About one-third the length of the Bridge was cleared of the buildings encumbering it, but the damage went down. Arches and piers that had stood firm with centuries' use were left insecure when the stones had cooled. The Bridge House spent £1,500 in necessary repairs before the leaseholders could attempt to rebuild. The keyed wooden structure known as Nonsuch House, which was the wonder of the Bridge, the drawbridge, and the remaining houses towards Southwark were not touched by the Fire, and survived for Hogarth and other delineators of a later day to hand down to posterity. High above the Southwark gate-tower the impaled heads of traitors were raised beyond reach of the flames, though scorched, it may be, by live sparks drifting in the wind. The company had received new additions since King Charles's Restoration. With rope and axe the regicides had suffered death and dis-memberment, and the heads of some had been chosen for display here. Dryden, in his picture of the Fire in the

---

[1] Walpole, *Anecdotes of Painting*, ed. 1786, i, 133.

Annus Mirabilis, recalls these grisly onlookers of the scene—

> The ghosts of traitors from the Bridge descend,
> With bold fanatic spectres to rejoice;
> About the fire into a dance they bend
> And sing their sabbath notes with feeble voice.

Venner, the leader of the mad Fifth Monarchy movement, had given the last head to be impaled over the Thames.

London Bridge was flaming at eight o'clock, by which hour Pepys had risen, having slept unconcernedly after his first disturbance. Looking out at the window he saw the Fire, " not so much as it was "—the flames made less display in the daylight—and farther off: " By and by Jane comes and tells me that she hears that above 300 houses have been burned down to-night by the fire we saw, and that it is now burning down all Fish Street, by London Bridge. So I made myself ready presently, and walked to the Tower; and there got up upon one of the high places, Sir J. Robinson's little son going up with me; and there I did see the houses at that end of the bridge all on fire, and an infinite great fire on this and the other side the end of the bridge; which, among other people, did trouble me for poor little Michell and our Sarah on the bridge. So down, with my heart full of trouble, to the Lieutenant of the Tower, who tells me that it began this morning in the King's baker's house in Pudding Lane, and that it hath burned down St. Magnus Church and most part of Fish Street already. So I down to the waterside, and there got a boat, and through bridge, and there saw a lamentable fire. Poor Michell's house, as far as the Old Swan, already burnt that way, and the fire running farther." [1]

Lord Fanhope had a Thames-side mansion by London Bridge at a time when many noblemen chose the banks of the river as the most desirable dwelling place in all the capital. It had become Fishmongers Hall by purchase when, at the close of the fifteenth century, the saltfish-mongers and the stockfishmongers united, and agreed that this should be their sole meeting place. Large additions obscured the original residence, which formed barely

---

[1] Pepys's *Diary,* 1666, Sept. 2.

one-fourth of the buildings standing in 1666, west of
the bridge near its abutment.   A north-east wind blew the
flames directly towards them.   Fishmongers Hall was the
first of forty-four Companies' Halls to be destroyed in
the Great Fire of London.   A tinder box lay between it and
the bridge ; nests of dilapidated timber houses, sinking
into the last stages of decay, and crowded upon the slip of
ground below Thames Street (here the old Stockfishmonger
Row) overran the ancient fish-market quay to the water's
edge, and were intersected by foot-passages that served as
funnels to enlarge the Fire—Watergate, Churchyard Alley,
Red Cross Alley, now swept away.   These were quickly
reduced to mere foundations.

The flames set alight the high roof and lantern of the
Hall proper, built at the back of an open quadrangle, and
burnt down to the ground.   A sorry spectacle it made
amid the ruins.   The stone frontage by the river fared
better.   Hollar's drawing after the Fire shows the shell
still standing, with a lofty tower and stairway at the
western end, and a high arched gateway that gave access
to the small riverside terrace.[1]   The wings perished
with the Hall.   Apparently few, if any, of the Company's
movable possessions were saved ; at least, nothing survives
to-day, neither records nor plate, that can with certainty
be dated anterior to the Fire.   They have what is said to
be the identical dagger with which Lord Mayor Walworth,
himself a fishmonger, slew Wat Tyler—an ugly weapon,
with a twisted steel guard.   As John Stow said when
assailed by doubts, that I pass by.   Among the existing
plate is a frosted cup on baluster stem, fifteen inches high,
the bowl of which bears the inscription—

The Guift of John Owen, Esq., Prime Warden of this
Company anno dni 1668, 1669, and 1670.   In which yeares
this hall was new built, after ye dreadfull fire in 1666.

Close against the Bridge was the Thames water-house,
well known to visitors to London in Charles the Second's

---

[1] Fishmongers Hall is best shown, though on a minute scale, in Hollar's
drawing of London in 1647, and earlier in that of Hogenberg.   The hall
was rebuilt by Jerman after the Great Fire, and was demolished in 1830
to make room for the new London Bridge, west of which the present hall
stands.

reign and long after. Peter Moris, a Dutchman, had conceived the idea in 1582 of utilizing the rush of the river through the narrow arches for raising a supply to houses near the bridge foot and in Thames Street, and his wheel and engine forced the Thames water in leaden pipes over the steeple of St. Magnus Church. First one arch only, that nearest the Middlesex bank, was employed. Later five wheels creaked and groaned in the stream, with unceasing noise; their final demolition took place so late as 1822. The water was forced as far as Gracechurch Street, and ultimately to higher ground at Leadenhall, whence it was distributed. The flames of 1666 as they crossed the Bridge put the entire apparatus out of action. That was London's misfortune at the outset of the Fire.

While St. Magnus, low-lying near the river level and partly sheltered by the Bridge, was steadily burning, another church was being consumed in flame. St. Margaret Fish Street Hill, ignited from the neighbouring houses, was completely destroyed. The church was not rebuilt, and to-day the open Monument Yard occupies its site. St. Botolph Billingsgate stood in Thames Street a few paces distant from St. Magnus, and suffered a like fate when the Fire beat back against the wind. But the trend was westward; the Fire ran along the riverside hours before it made substantial progress in other directions, and only with comparative slowness burnt back from the water. The sun was southing when first the Fire assumed the form of that " bow " of flame, ever widening and enlarging, that so impressed the imagination of Pepys and other eye-witnesses.

The destruction of houses to clear a way in advance of the flames was suggested to Bludworth soon after dawn, but the cautious Lord Mayor hesitated; the cost was great. " Who shall pay the charge of rebuilding the houses ? " he asked those who so advised him,[1] little appreciating the larger charge that London must needs pay. To others who again pressed him to take this necessary course he answered, that he dare not do so without the consent of the owners.[2] Thereby he brought down upon

[1] *Relatione esattissima del' Incendio Calamitoso della citta di Londra.* Padua, 1666. (Printed in Appendix I.)
[2] Clarendon's *Life.*

himself universal blame. Wise as were so many people
after the event, they displayed little wisdom or prescience
in the actual time of crisis, none being able to realize that a
fire started in a dirty, disreputable side alley could attain
the enormous dimensions reached in its four days' onslaught.
The first impelling thought of each man was to save his
own goods ; his last thought to collaborate in steps to save
those of his neighbour. The pulling down of houses was
seriously begun before noon. It was begun too near the
Fire. The flames were quickly upon the workers, driving
them away even before a clearance could be completed.
Then, crossing the debris, flames attacked the standing
houses opposite.

London awoke that Sunday morning not greatly perturbed, rising earlier, it is true, than is now the custom.
We are told that the day was bright and sunny, with a
cloudless sky. The night—contemporary writers have
pictured its alarms. "The fire begins," says Vincent
breathlessly, "is quickly taken notice of, though in the
midst of the night. 'Fire ! fire ! fire !' doth resound the
streets ; many citizens start out of their sleep, look out of
their windows ; some dress themselves, and run to the place.
The Lord Mayor of the City comes with his officers ; a confusion there is ; counsel is taken away ; and London, so
famous for wisdom and dexterity, can now find neither
brains nor hands to prevent its ruin." [1]

Samuel Wiseman, writer of a poetic broadside, is in
the same strain—

> And now the doleful, dreadfull, hideous note
> Of Fire, is scream'd out with a deep strain'd throat ;
> Horror, and fear, and sad distracted cries
> Chide Sloth away, and bid the Sluggard rise ;
> Most direfull acclamations are let flye
> From every Tongue, tears stand in every Eye. [2]

I find nothing of this in the private letters and diaries,
which are more valuable as historical sources. It is pure
fancy. The fact is that the spectacle of fire was too
common in London for people living remote from its seat
to display much concern. It was the custom from the
nearest church belfry to ring a peal backwards to give

[1] *God's Terrible Voice in the City*, 1667.
[2] *Short Description of the Burning of London*, 1666.

alarm of fire in a City parish. Pepys, in Seething Lane, though only a quarter mile distant, slept on undisturbed. That stir and confusion prevailed in the immediate neighbourhood of the flames is no doubt true. It is equally true, and more worthy of note, that the larger area of London had no sense of its peril until the forenoon was far advanced. The churches filled with their usual congregations. The Court at Whitehall knew little of the Fire's extent till Pepys, hot-footed, arrived about eleven o'clock, "where people came about me, and I did give them an account dismayed them all." He was admitted to immediate audience of the King, and returned to the City with the first instructions to the Lord Mayor, to spare no houses, but pull down before the fire every way.

Live flakes scattered by a high wind, and the first dense volumes of smoke rolling up from the Bridge, conveyed the message of London burning. The citizens, at first merely curious, became alarmed. They flocked into the streets and on the house-roofs to see the Fire, while yet there was so little to be seen, and idle rumour enlarged the tale. The public mind was uneasy, and filled with forebodings of the war then being waged, with varying fortunes, against France and Holland. Monck, at sea, when Prince Rupert's squadron was detached to prevent a junction of the French and Dutch fleets, had attacked a greatly superior force of Dutch sail and suffered a severe reverse; but the defeat was brilliantly retrieved by a victory gained over De Ruyter on July 25th and 26th, followed by an incident of a sinister kind. A thousand sailors landed on August 8th and 9th from the English ships on the islands of Vlie and Schelling had given over the town of Brandaris to the flames, and with fire-ships sent adrift destroyed one hundred and sixty Dutch merchantmen in harbour, whose cargoes were valued at a million sterling.

The delayed news had been in London a fortnight. Monck was again at sea, and people anxiously awaited the next move in the war, fearing reprisals.

No intelligence reached our shores; only this message of London burning. "An eye for an eye, a tooth for a tooth," was the Mosaic law. The war had been brought home. Quickly panic spread. London, one man told another, had been wilfully fired! A revengeful enemy stood out in every Dutchman or Frenchman, as curious as any to know what was astir, an object of suspicion was found in each reputed Papist.   There is an interesting letter by a resident of Middle Temple,[1] who says that he knew nothing of the Fire till nine o'clock.

Then, running down to the Temple Gardens, he saw the smoke of the fires in London and Southwark, and the flames about the Bridge.   Not satisfied at that distance, he went with others into the highway.   Fleet Street was full of people, all fearful of what was happening; " for it was already imagined the design of the French and Dutch in revenge of what our forces had lately done at Brandaris upon the island Schelling.   The riding of a hot-headed fellow through the street (with more speed and fear than wit) crying ' Arm, arm ! ' had frightened most of the people out of the churches."

Dr. Taswell, afterwards Rector of Newington and of St. Mary Bermondsey, was at the time a boy in Westminster School.   In reminiscent vein he records—

" On Sunday between ten and eleven forenoon, as I was standing upon the steps which lead up to the pulpit in Westminster Abbey, I perceived some people below me running to and fro in a seeming disquietude and consternation ; immediately almost a report reached my ears that London was in a conflagration ; without any ceremony I took my leave of the preacher, and having ascended Parliament steps, near the Thames, I soon perceived four boats crowded with objects of distress.   These had escaped from the fire scarce under any other covering except that of a blanket.

" The wind blowing strong eastward, the flames at last reached Westminster (sic) ; I myself saw great flakes carried up into the air at least three furlongs ; these at last pitching upon and uniting themselves to various dry substances, set on fire houses very remote from each other in point of situation.   The ignorant and deluded mob, who upon occasion were hurried away with a kind of frenzy, vented forth their rage against the Roman Catholics and

---

[1] Three original letters from this resident of Middle Temple are in the Gough MSS. collection at the Bodleian.   They are printed by Malcolm in *Londinium Redivivum*, iv, 73–82, for which purpose they were lent by Gough.

Frenchmen ; imagining these incendiaries (as they thought) had thrown red-hot balls into the houses.

"A blacksmith in my presence, meeting an innocent Frenchman walking along the street, felled him instantly to the ground with an iron bar. I could not help seeing the innocent blood of this exotic flow in a plentiful stream down to his ankles. In another place I saw the incensed populace divesting a French painter of all the goods he had in his shop ; and, after having helped him off with many other things, levelling his house to the ground under this pretence, namely, that they thought himself was desirous of setting his own house on fire, that the conflagration might become more general." [1]

[1] *Autobiography of William Taswell, D.D.* (Camden Society), vol. 2, pp. 10, 11.

CHAPTER III

THE storm which kept apart the English and Dutch Fleets prepared for the anxiously expected engagement in the Channel, and drove some of our sloops of war in a crippled condition into port, served London badly. A fresh breeze had blown for a week. It increased in violence on Sunday, and continued with little change during the worst days of the Fire, shifting at times a point or two, but never more, and always driving the flames farther into the City. Landsmen, mystified in such matters, spoke of the wind as coming from all quarters; a sailor's knowledge here is valuable. Captain Joseph Ames, whose ship was weatherbound at Blackwall Reach, unable to get down the river, says that on the first day of the Fire the wind blew hard at east-north-east, and on the Thursday was still north-east.[1]

The City lay defenceless before the oncoming flames. Although warned by repeated fires, sometimes of considerable magnitude, the Lord Mayor and Aldermen had taken no effective steps to deal with the peril. Leathern buckets, ladders, axes, and strong iron fire-hooks were kept in each City church, usually under the tower, and at some of the Livery Companies' Halls. Many references to their use and upkeep are found in the London churchwardens' accounts of the sixteenth and early seventeenth centuries; but the provision came to be neglected. The augmentation of Peter Moris's original wheels at the Bridge, largely increasing the quantity of Thames water raised, and more especially the introduction of New River water to London, had fostered a false sense of security, or at least condoned

---

[1] Original letter of Sept. 6, 1666, at Guildhall. Printed by Welch, *History of the Monument*, pp. 64–5.

a deal of carelessness. Cocks were set up in the New River service pipes where they entered each separate ward, to be used in case of fire in place of cutting the wooden pipes, which hitherto had been the practice on such occasions, but there was no system of street fire-plugs. There had been invented by Hautsh, of Nuremberg, in 1651, an engine for throwing repeated jets of water, but such an appliance was wholly unknown in England at the time of the Great Fire of London.*

PRINT OF 1613 FROM "THE BURNING OF TIVERTON," IN BODLEIAN LIBRARY.

In the Bodleian Library is a rare book of the reign of James I., which contains a print, here reproduced, showing the whole fire service of that day at work. A fire broke out at Tiverton, Devon, in 1612, which destroyed the greater part of the ancient city, and this is a picture of Tiverton burning. The fire-hooks, here seen in use, were fixed to poles, often 20 ft. or 30 ft. in length. The hook was thrown over the ridge-beam of a burning building, there being iron rings at the end of the pole and part way up, to which cords were attached, and were dragged by

companies of men or horses till the fragile timber-built house
came clattering down. The result was bad for the house,
but this was at least an effective method of preventing the
flames spreading to adjoining premises. Old fire-hooks
are preserved at the churches of Raunds, Stanwick and
Harringworth, all in Northants, at the parish church of
Tonbridge, Kent, and the police station at Welwyn, Herts.
The " engines," so called, that were also in use in London
at the Restoration are difficult to define. The name
appears to have been given to the brass hand-squirts [1] ;
but there was also employed a portable cistern—commonly
a large cask—mounted on wheels, that could easily be
trundled to the scene of a fire.

Three of these ancient fire squirts are preserved at the
Guildhall Museum. One had belonged to the Ward of
Aldgate in 1672, the second to the parish of St. Dionis
Backchurch, and the third was used at Guildhall in 1687.
Each is a hollow cylinder, the barrel being two feet in
length, and provided with two side-handles. The nozzle
aperture is half an inch. The squirt was filled by inverting
the nozzle in water, then reversed and (when in rapid use)
held by two men, while a third operated a piston working
within. The effective delivery was less than a gallon.
With such rudimentary appliances, and nothing better, the
greatest fire ever experienced in this country was confronted.

The Thames-side above London Bridge, where the Fire
was now seated, was a rookery of stores and cellars and
low, dark dwellings, timber-built and rotting with age and
neglect, with an occasional old merchant's house, fallen
into decay and let out in tenements. A large part of the
population which gained a living upon the river crowded
into these hovels—wherrymen, stevedores, porters, carriers,
and others. A church stood here, a Livery Company's
Hall there ; and by these larger buildings a city is known,
but a hundredfold more numerous are the smaller,
unconsidered houses. They have neither history nor

[1] Two months after the destruction of the city, Nov. 8, 1666, Sir John
Robinson, Lieutenant of the Tower of London, obtained authority to
provide 400 " engines," 300 buckets, 10 ladders, and 12 hooks, for the
suppression of fire in the Tower should it occur. (*State Papers, Domestic,*
1666-7, p. 247.) Lord Berkeley, while the Fire was raging, asked for
a warrant for the delivery of all " water engines " remaining in store at
Deptford and Woolwich (*ibid.*, p. 75).

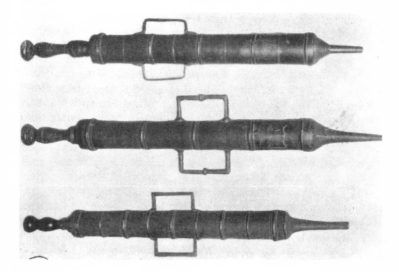

HERE BY Ϋ́ PERMISSION OF HEAVEN, HELL BROKE LOOSE
UPON THIS PROTESTANT CITY FROM THE MALICIOUS
HEARTS OF BARBAROUS PAPISTS BY Ϋ́ HAND OF THEIR
AGENT HUBERT, WHO CONFESSED, AND ON Ϋ́ RUINES
OF THIS PLACE DECLARED THE FACT FOR WHICH HE
WAS HANGED, (VIZT) THAT HERE BEGAN THAT DREDFULL FIRE, WHICH IS DESCRIBED AND PERPETUATED
ON AND BY THE NEIGHBOURING PILLAR.
Erected Anno 1681 in the Majoralite of
Sᴿ PATIENCE WARD Kᵗ.

STONE PLACED WHERE THE FIRE STARTED

Photos by Mr. Lionel Gowing

ANCIENT FIRE SYRINGES IN GUILDHALL MUSEUM
The central one bears the date 1679

remembrance. But their existence must always be kept in mind if one shall understand the terrible calamity of the Great Fire, which ultimately destroyed 13,200 houses, and left some 100,000 people homeless.

Little of that picturesque Old London which so fills the imagination was to be found by the waterside. There was but one continuous street, itself narrow and low-lying (Thames Street was raised three feet when London was rebuilt). Along it the whole of the merchandise brought by river had to pass. The way was commonly choked by carts, and the wheels rumbling on the cobble-stones and cries of the carters urging their straining horses up the steep brow of the hill into the City made the place pandemonium. On the level extending out to the river's edge, where devious alleys guided the pedestrian's footsteps to the Thames, every available inch of surface was covered by the squalid buildings, mostly weather boarded and coated with pitch, and preserving no order or plan. The wall of the Roman city had run by Thames Street, where remains of it have recently been found near the bottom of Old Fish Street towards London Bridge, and it is probable that all this land between the street and the river had been recovered from the foreshore in past centuries.

The waterside quarter was a sort of underworld of the City that rose beyond. The people, of less consequence than the goods they handled, secured a lodging begrudged to them only where space could not be more profitably utilized. To many of them, as the Fire pressed back, the broad river flowing by was the one safe refuge. Goods and furniture snatched from the flames were flung into boats, and often in desperation into the tideway itself, to float with the stream and take the chance of being salved. The Fire burnt through block after block of this choked property, with much crackling of dry wood and uprush of smoke. It is plain that the poor appliances available were not generally used at the onset of the Fire. " The engines had no liberty to play," says a chronicler, " for the narrowness of the place and the crowd of people, but some of them were tumbled down in the river, and among the rest that of Clerkenwell, esteemed one of the best." [1] Homeless families congregated about the boat-stairs and

[1] Rege Sincera, *Observations, etc.*, p. 34.

wharves, frightened by the magnitude of the Fire, looking aimlessly at the destruction, till the advancing flames drove them away. Such authority for control as existed was vested in the Lord Mayor, who displayed neither the initiative nor strength of will that the occasion urgently demanded.

Pepys gives a most valuable account of the first day's progress of the Fire, till cares for his bags of gold, his wines, and his parmesan cheese monopolized so large a part of his attention—and of his *Diary*. The picture he draws is of helpless confusion. " Everybody endeavouring to remove their goods, and flinging into the river, or bringing them into lighters that lay off ; poor people staying in their houses as long as till the very fire touched them, and then running into boats, or clambering from one pair of stairs by the waterside to another. . . Having stayed, and in an hour's time seen the fire rage every way, and nobody, to my sight, endeavouring to quench it, but to remove their goods, and leave all to the fire ; and, having seen it get as far as the Steelyard, and the wind mighty high and driving it into the City ; and everything, after so long a drought, proving combustible, even the very stones of the churches . . . I to Whitehall, with a gentleman with me, who desired to go off from the Tower, to see the fire, in my boat."

He returned by coach, and alighting at St. Paul's walked along Watling Street, " as well as I could, every creature coming away loaden with goods to save, and here and there sick people carried away in beds. Extraordinary good goods in carts and on backs "—and thus to the waterside. " River full of lighters and boats taking goods, and good goods swimming in the water." The streets were " full of nothing but people and horses and carts laden with goods, ready to run over one another, and removing goods from one burned house to another." The inexplicable nature of the Fire, sweeping right and left, and the time of its occurrence, added to the flame and noise and commotion everywhere a vague dread of foreign attack manifested in this tremendous Fire, all the more fearful in men's minds because no enemy was visible.

The diarist makes many shrewd observations that reveal the unexpected actions of people in the distress of panic. " Hardly one lighter (he notes) or boat in three that had the goods of a house in, but there was a pair of virginals in it." Why treasure the spinets when so much else was sacrificed ? The City pigeons did not escape attention. Loath to leave the shelter of the houses, they hovered about windows and balconies till, with scorched wings, they fell down.

From his boat on the river Pepys had seen the flames pass the Old Swan (still marked by Old Swan Lane and the boat-pier), attack Dyers Hall, and in an incredibly short time reach out to Coldharbour and the Steelyard. The Thames-side over the space of a quarter mile was then alight. The old Hall of the Dyers Company stood near the water, where now is Dyers Hall Wharf, an ancient building already far advanced in decay, for the Company in 1658 had contemplated taking it down and rebuilding. Little was left when the Fire had spent itself, the hall with the armour contained in it and much of the plate being consumed, though some part of the plate was saved.

Near by the Steelyard was Watermen's Hall, fated, like the halls of the Fishmongers and Dyers, to complete destruction.

The Watermen, busiest of all people in saving the property of others, seem to have shown no practical concern in saving their own. The Fire was the wherrymen's harvest time. Their boats were at every man's disposal, at rates rising to ruinous sums as the Fire progressed. It is to be suspected that so actively engaged were they upon these unconscionable bargains that few boats were available when the home of their own gild was imperilled. No plate or pictures of the Watermen's Company survived the Great Fire of London. Of the accumulated mass of papers and records dealing with the affairs of the Thames, they have to-day only three books dating before the Fire—a register of binding of apprentices, October, 1655, to June, 1665 ; a book of by-laws and orders from 1626 to 1662 ; and a volume containing Privy Council Orders. The rest were black carbon. Of all the buildings there stood intact after the Fire nothing save the stone gateway giving access to the Thames. The Hall faced the river, and had belonged in 1600 to Earl Gilbert, who destroyed the western part of the ancient building. What remained was in use by the

Watermen's Company in 1647, and probably many years before, though no date is known.

The flames, sweeping along the Thames-side, at least did good service by ridding London of Coldharbour's pestilential alleys. This, till its dissolution half a century before the Fire, had been one of the smaller sanctuaries where debtors and vagabonds herded together in a nest of foul tenements erected by the Earl of Shrewsbury when he pulled down the historic house known as Coldharbour. The sanctuary figures in many of the early plays. It was entered from Thames Street by a passage at the side of Allhallows-the-Less. That church was itself completely destroyed, and the site is marked to-day by its fragment of " God's acre." The larger Allhallows-the-More stood but a few paces distant ; an important church, with three aisles and tower, and chapels of St. Catherine and St. Barbara and Lady Chapel. This had been one of the first London churches to set up the King's arms on its walls in 1660, when Monck and Montagu, plotting the Restoration, were yet undecided.

It was so shattered by the intense heat that part of the roofless shell was afterwards blown down by wind ; the end of the fabric had to be pulled down to avoid peril of life. The steeple stood firm, and from the molten bell-metal recovered from the rubbish that strewed the floor a new bell was cast, and hung in the belfry in the year 1670.[1]

Allhallows-the-More had a cloister towards the river, already " foully defaced and ruinated " in Stow's time, its walks surrounded by a graveyard. The possession of a cloister, so entirely unexpected in a London parish church, led Sir Walter Besant to suppose there may have been some sisterhood of nuns attached to the church, to offer prayers for the safety of travellers crossing by the ferry ; and a later writer, Mr. J. Tavernor-Perry, has suggested as a more plausible theory that the cloister and the enclosing burial ground belonged to the Hanse Merchants of the neighbouring Steelyard, and had been formed by them as their *campo santo* in a foreign land.[2] It has been treated as unique, which it was not, for there were " cloysters "

[1] Churchwardens' Accounts, 1667. Vestry Minutes, 1670, Oct. 25.
[2] *The Antiquary*, New Ser. x, 125.

at various other City churches. What the term implies is not clear, but these structures seem rather to have been covered ways from the street to the church door than to have followed the well-known plan of the monastic cloister.*

More significant of the fate threatening London was the appearance of fire on Laurence Pountney Hill. The circumstances were dramatic. Till then the Fire had raged only along the Thames-side, with an arm thrust out upon the Bridge, and an ugly nucleus of flame about Fish Street Hill and the Bridge foot. St. Laurence Pountney Church, raised upon an eminence, overlooked the burning quarter by the river, as its slender tapering spire, one of the tallest in London, overlooked the whole city. Pepys saw the steeple " take fire in the very top, and there burned till it fell down." Live brands lodged by the wind had melted the lead casing and ignited the timber beneath. To another and more imaginative onlooker the fire atop of the steeple " discovered itself with so much terror, as if taking a view from that lofty place of what it intended suddenly to devour."

The apparition to a third spectator disclosed deep design. " I saw the fire," Thomas Middleton, a surgeon, told the Parliamentary Committee, " break out from the inside of Laurence Pountney steeple, when there was no fire near it. These, and such observations, begat in me a persuasion that the Fire was maintained by design." That belief was shared by many others during the dreadful days when London was burning. The fall of the steeple, with a new peal of bells placed therein not long before, completed the destruction. Late that afternoon the still blazing church, strongly fired, was visible over the whole City as far distant as the Temple Garden, a spectacle that increased the general alarm. It was not rebuilt, and the open site to-day forms a little oasis, where green bushes half conceal the tombs.

Four thousand Frenchmen and Papists were in arms, so the report ran, intending to carry with them death and destruction, and assist the conflagration. Taswell was in the streets as the news flashed along, when " every person, both in the City and suburbs, having procured some sort of weapon or other, instantly almost collected themselves together to oppose this chimerical army." The panic died down, less quickly than it had arisen, and the harassed citizens again applied themselves diligently to saving their property, not to stamping out the flames, for always, unfortunately for burning London, the care of property was the first object.

Wind driven, the Fire enlarged its scope, creeping back from the river. By noon, it had entered the courts and alleys winding up the hill from Thames Street, some of which, bearing quaint names of mediæval origin, have survived all City improvements. There is Duck's Foot Lane, near the Bridge, an interesting example of transliteration. It was the Duke's foot lane, the narrow passage way to the rear of his Grace's mansion, which Suffolk Lane, close by, keeps in remembrance. Something akin occurred with a tavern much farther west, anciently showing the sign of the Bacchanals, which had adopted the title over the door and was known to later patrons as the Bag of Nails. Suffolk House, under the shadow of St. Laurence Pountney, was consumed above ground when the flames from Thames Street and the church joined, but there was preserved intact till our time an early crypt, groined with stone ribs, and supported in the largest of its three divisions by stone pillars. This historic house, one of many ancient City dwellings that perished in the Great Fire of 1666, belonged in the fourteenth century to that famous civic magnate, Sir John Pountney, four times Lord Mayor of London, but had borne other names since that of Pountney's Inn, from successive noble owners. The Dukes of Exeter and Suffolk had lived there; then came Edward Stafford Duke of Buckingham, and afterwards Henry Courtney Earl of Devon and the Earls of Sussex. It was in Buckingham's brief day known as The Manor of the Rose, and is so referred to by Shakespeare in *King Henry VIII.*, Act 1, Sc. ii., wherein the Duke's surveyor discloses Buckingham's traitorous conversation—

> *Surv.* Not long before your highness sped to France,
> The Duke being at the Rose, within the parish
> Saint Laurence Poultney, did of me demand
> What was the speech among the Londoners
> Concerning the French journey.

The Merchant Taylors Company had acquired the larger part of the property by purchase from the Earl of Sussex

in 1561, and in the buildings established their famous
Grammar School. It was completely burnt out. John
Goad, the schoolmaster, at personal risk saved a portion
of the library, and eighteen months later collected some
of his scholars in a parish room by St. Andrew Undershaft,
as the new school buildings rose slowly. Hector Forde,
the head usher, taught in the vestry-house of St. Katherine
Cree, which escaped the Fire, undertaking to provide a
partition to prevent his boys running about the church.[1]

The City was all astir. Hasty summons had gone out
to assemble the Trained Bands. They tramped to the
Fire under command of their officers, and were posted at
their several stations, " watching at every quarter," says
Vincent, " for out-landish men, because of the general
fears and jealousies, and rumours that fire-balls were thrown
into the houses by several of them, to help on and provoke
the too furious flames." The King sent in his Guards;
the Duke of York bade Pepys tell the Lord Mayor that he
should have any more soldiers he might require; " and so,"
adds the diarist, " did my Lord Arlington [2] afterwards, as
a great secret." A spectator found a party of forty horse
of the Life Guards drawn up in Cornhill, and touring
around the edge of the Fire met some companies of the
King's regiments and of the Trained Bands marching into
the City. In Cannon Street his further progress was
stopped by the obstruction of goods and carts with which
it was filled. " Here (he adds) we met my Lord Mayor
on horseback, with a few attendants, looking like one
frightened out of his wits." [3]

In Cannon Street, not yet reached by the Fire, Pepys
first met the Lord Mayor when he returned from Whitehall
with the King's orders. His account of that bewildered
official is not more flattering—

" At last met my Lord Mayor in Canning Street, like a
man spent, with a handkercher about his neck. To the
King's message he cried, like a fainting woman, ' Lord !
what can I do ? I am spent : people will not obey me. I
have been pulling down houses ; but the fire overtakes us

[1] H. B. Wilson, *History of Merchant Taylors School;* St. Katherine
Cree Vestry Minutes, 1666.
[2] Henry Bennet Lord Arlington had been appointed Secretary of
State in 1662.
[3] Malcolm, *Londinium Redivivum,* iv, 74.

faster than we can do it.' That he needed no more soldiers ; and that for himself, he must go and refresh himself, having been up all night. So he left me, and I him, and walked home, seeing people all almost distracted, and no manner of means used to quench the fire."

None of the populace who had seen the flames speeding along by the waterside had contemplated that the Fire would spread across the City. They bundled their goods into the nearest churches, when themselves should have been quietly at devotions there, having to remove them as quickly when the Fire approached. All the morning the lanes and alleys winding up from Thames Street had been choked with people carrying household belongings on their backs away from the flames into Cannon Street, believing that safety lay there. The street ran on the ridge of the hill. In the afternoon the goods were again moved out, when the peril came near, " into Lombard Street, and farther," says Pepys, " and, among others, I saw my little goldsmith Stokes receiving some friends' goods, whose house itself was burned the day after."

The King and the Duke of York came down the river from Whitehall in the afternoon, rowed in the Royal barge, and Pepys attended them to Queenhithe. Legend tells that his Majesty watched Watermen's Hall still burning from a tall house-roof in one of the alleys by the Three Cranes in Vintry, and was so stirred by the sight, and so eager in giving directions for more houses to be pulled down in advance of the flames, that his own life was in some jeopardy. " But little was or could be done," says Pepys, " the fire coming upon them so fast. Good hopes there was of stopping it at the Three Cranes above and at Botolph's Wharf below bridge, if care be used ; but the wind carries it into the City, so as we know not by the waterside what it do there."

The Earl of Craven was one of a small band of noblemen who rendered London conspicuous service during the Fire. William Lindsay Lord Craven, after long exile on the Continent, had followed Charles II. to England at the Restoration. He had remained at his house in Drury Lane when the Court fled to Oxford on the outbreak of the Plague, and with Monck and Dean Sancroft, who also stayed, tended to the wants of the poor and the afflicted in the stricken city. His splendid activities and self-sacrificing work at great personal risk had won for him the affection of the citizens. It was, no doubt, at the burning of London that Lord Craven first acquired a passion for helping in the extinction of fires, which survived till near the end of his long life ; there is a well-known anecdote that his horse knew the smell of a fire at a great distance, and was accustomed immediately to gallop off with him to the spot.

Lord Craven, when the King and the Duke of York returned to Whitehall, was left with a Royal command to assist the Lord Mayor and magistrates,[1] and there official concern for the Fire seems to have ceased for the day. I searched the State Papers in vain for any indication of orders given on Sunday for organized action. They were plentiful enough on the following day. The catastrophe, so suddenly descending upon the capital, stupefied the authorities. Falling, too, upon a Sunday, it found the ordinary machinery of government dislocated. The Mayor and Aldermen, their authority stiffened by a few soldiers, were left to muddle through as best they might, with quite inadequate support. Confusion was everywhere ; and at times a shiver passed through the ranks of bewildered men and women, running hither and thither in the City streets, as new rumours spread, causing needless alarm of attack by French or Dutch.

The fires on Fish Street Hill and St. Laurence Pountney, for the time separate, burnt towards one another, and before they joined involved two additional churches in the common ruin. Only one short bend of Crooked Lane has survived the changes made last century, when the approaches to the new London Bridge were laid out. In this lane stood one of London's most ancient houses, " The Leaden Porch," which had belonged to Sir John Merston when Edward VI. ascended the Throne, and when the Great Fire destroyed it was a tavern with the sign of the Swan. St. Michael Crooked Lane, with its churchyard, in 1666 stood out where now is the centre of the road over which the heavy drays thunder on to the bridge. This was the third church that had occupied the site—a long building, flat roofed, with embattlements, and tower rising at the

---

[1] *London Gazette,* Aug. 30 to Sept. 3.

west end, also embattled. Walworth, that doughty Fishmonger, lay buried there with many of his brethren, for this was the Fishmongers' church. So little enduring is fame that, after his monument had been defaced in the reign of Edward VI., the Fishmongers Company, in recutting the epitaph, described him as the victor over Jack Straw ! [1] Caught by the flames at both ends, the church burnt furiously, nothing being left but the mere shell. The steeple above the tower fell upon the roof.

St. Martin Orgar, but a few paces west (" a small thing," says Stow) also perished, and the flames reached out towards Cannon Street. Frequently it becomes impossible, by reason of conflicting statements or entire absence of evidence, to say at what stage of the Fire particular places were attacked, and Vincent's assertion that " on the Lord's Day night the Fire had crept into Cannon Street, and levell'd it with the ground," must not be read literally. When dawn broke over London the flames had entered only the eastern end of Cannon Street, though so early as four o'clock on Sunday afternoon the fire on Fish Street Hill had approached within five houses of Eastcheap. In Pudding Lane at that hour only three buildings north of the Fire's original seat in the baker's shop had been destroyed.

The Fire burnt all afternoon in the Steelyard by the waterside, and far into the night—a dreadful spectacle— fed by fresh fuel in the well-stocked warehouses and detached buildings scattered about its area. The keen Hanse merchants had played an important part in founding London's commercial greatness, and they occupied a large settlement where to-day, borne on high arches, the trains run into Cannon Street station. No name in the locality bears them remembrance, but they have left in England one curious vestige of their stay. The money of the " Easterlings " was so much sought after for its good quality that a " pound Easterling," or sterling, became the recognized standard of gold coinage, and is so to-day. In 1598, when the Hansa had been ordered by Queen Elizabeth to leave her kingdom, the Steelyard was seized by the Crown and given into the keeping of the Lord Mayor, pending a decision as to its disposal. The Royal Navy

[1] Howel's *Londinopolis*, p. 92.

used a part for the storage of cordage. James I. restored the place to the Germans. There survived in 1666 the ancient guildhall of the Hanse Corporation, distinguished by its stone tower, a large structure, built with a stateliness befitting their dignity and wealth. Entrance was given by three arched gateways in Thames Street.

Though the decaying fortunes of the Hansa were shown in the decay of their buildings, they had by thrift been able to restore old houses since their eight years' dispossession. The Rhenish Winehouse in the Steelyard was a place much frequented by English merchants. Four houses had been new built in the year of the Fire.

Hoping till the last to save the property from destruction, the house-master got away with difficulty, being obliged to flee in his burning clothes. The Hamburg deputies happened then to be lodged at the Steelyard, and they also were hard pressed to escape.[1] Did they, one wonders, leave behind to the flames two of the richest works of Hans Holbein's genius, painted for the merchants in their time of prosperity, " The Triumph of Riches," and " The Triumph of Poverty " ? It is a possible explanation that, being fixed to the wall of the guildhall, these famous pictures perished with the Steelyard in the Great Fire of London. The tradition that they were conveyed to the Continent, and disappeared finally at places variously stated as Darmstadt, Paris, and in Flanders, has never satisfied.

That night a larger glare than London had known for centuries illuminated the streets. It was an accident, not provided for by City law, and still in the streets might have been noticed the tiny flare of the candles, each in its separate lantern, set out before the houses to light the traveller's way. The Fire for the greater number was as yet distant ; the citizens' duty remained—a duty emphasized by Act of Parliament four years before, which required all householders whose premises were on or near the street to show candles or light in lanterns " from such time as it shall grow dark, until nine of the clock in the evening, upon pain to forfeit the sum of one shilling for every default." [2] Two

[1] Lappenberg, *Urkundliche Geschichte des Hansischen Stahlhofes zu London.*
[2] *Stat.* 14 *Chas. II.*, c. 2.

personal impressions have been left of London burning as darkness began to fall; by the resident of Middle Temple before cited, and by Pepys, who carries the narrative further into the night.

" That evening," says the former, " I was a second time on the water, and it was then the fire appeared with all the horror and dreadfulness imaginable; the flames afforded light enough to discover themselves, the black smoke, and the buildings they so imminently threatened. The moon offered her light, too, but was overcome by this greater; which not being able (by day) to contend with that of the sun, had (as it were in spite) by smoke lessened it. I came back at eight o'clock, leaving it then at the Three Cranes, which is distant from the Bridge almost a fourth part of the space between the Temple and the Bridge. At night more of the Lifeguard and soldiers watched in the city."

Pepys hovered about the Fire like a moth round a candle, overmastered by its awesome fascination, reluctant to leave. Though compelled to attend at Whitehall in the afternoon, he was soon back, and twice took boat again on the water—

" Walked [from Whitehall] to St. James's Park, and there met my wife, and Creed, and Wood and his wife, and walked to my boat; and there upon the water again, and to the fire up and down, it still increasing, and the wind great. So near the fire as we could for smoke; and all over the Thames, with one's face in the wind, you were almost burned with a shower of fire-drops. This is very true; so as houses were burned by these drops and flakes of fire, three or four, nay, five or six houses, one from another. When we could endure no more upon the water, we to a little alehouse on the Bankside, over against the Three Cranes, and there stayed till it grew dark almost, and saw the fire grow; and, as it grew darker, appeared more and more, and in corners and upon steeples, and between churches and houses, as far as we could see up the hill of the City, in a most horrid, malicious, bloody flame, not like the fine flame of an ordinary fire. We stayed till, it being darkish, we saw the fire as one entire arch of fire from this to the other side of the bridge, and in a bow up the hill for an arch of above a mile long : it made me weep to see it. The churches, houses, and all on fire, and flaming at once, and a horrid noise the flames made, and the cracking of houses at their ruin. So home with a sad heart, and there find everybody discoursing and lamenting the fire."

The flight of homeless refugees out into the fields had as yet hardly begun. The Fire, already larger by far than any in memory, noisier, more terrible, and so full of potentialities of evil, was still a riverside fire. The greater miseries were to come. Neighbours were able to afford the shelter of a roof to many of those less fortunately circumstanced than themselves; others stayed up all night, tired but finding sleep impossible, watching the goods they had saved and stored in churches and public buildings, or heaped on the wharves at Bankside, where the great width of the river between them and the burning streets seemed to make safety assured. Pepys's household in Seething Lane was typical of many another Londoner's. He took in " poor Tom Hater," burnt out of Fish Street Hill. " We did put Mr. Hater, poor man ! to bed a little ; but he got very little rest, so much noise being in my house, taking down of goods." The wind kept the flames away from Seething Lane, and Pepys's house was never touched by the Fire ; but the excitement of the City alarmed him unduly, "the news coming every moment of the growth of the Fire."

" I kept my bed but few hours, and slept less," writes another.

The spectacle of the Fire and want of true knowledge of its progress, the City's unrest, the fears of the populace, real enough and always enlarged by false reports, attracted people to the river, where they crowded upon wherries not otherwise and better engaged in the salving of goods, a task which went on unceasingly. All through the night the Thames was alive with boats, shooting out of the darkness into the glare cast by the burning City upon the water, wherein the yellow flames were reflected in every ripple crest, lost again when the tide or the rowers' strength carried the craft beyond into the neighbouring gloom. Barges were constantly crossing from the wharves to Southwark, heaped with merchandise and household effects, trailing black shadows over the water and standing out silhouetted against the sky's artificial glow. London Bridge, itself a street of houses, stretched out a long arm from the central mass of the conflagration, its stone piers and arches radiantly white; and the smoke which rose was borne by the wind across the City and away. No living man or woman had known a fire like this.

Linked to the scene by awe, or admiration, or fear, defying sleep while watching the destruction, thousands of onlookers were still out as dawn broke after this first night when London was on fire.

Some time in the night the Boar's Head tavern in Eastcheap was consumed—first of many taverns made famous by Elizabethan wits which were lost to London in the Great Fire. Shakespeare and Burbage and Ben Jonson are said to have frequented it on their way over London Bridge to the theatres in Southwark and Bankside, and when returning after the play. Shakespeare has immortalized the house as the scene of the drunken debaucheries of Sir John Falstaff and his noisy

BOAR'S HEAD TAVERN SIGN, IN THE GUILDHALL MUSEUM.

dependants, Bardolph and Pistol, when Dame Quickly kept the reckoning, and of Doll Tearsheet's frailties. St. Magnus-the-Martyr preserves with its church plate a parcel-gilt goblet (it had belonged to the now amalgamated parish of St. Michael Crooked Lane) which an amiable legend declares to be the very cup with which Falstaff pledged Dame Quickly. That is as you will. The story seems to have arisen in the exuberant fancy of Washington Irving.

Nothing, in simple fact, survives to tell that the Boar's Head was a tavern so early as the days of Prince Hal. Possibly a tradition existed in Shakespeare's time.

The play pictures an Elizabethan tavern, otherwise Dame Quickly's bill made an unconscionable charge for sack, 5s. 8d. for two gallons. Likely enough that was a fair Elizabethan price; the liquor was sixpence a quart in Henry IV.'s reign. Moreover, sack was not then sold in taverns. The house, burnt out, was quickly rebuilt, with the carved stone sign now in the Guildhall Museum displayed over the door. A boar's head with silver tusks, believed to have fallen down with the house and taken from the ruins to Whitechapel Mount, was many years afterwards identified there—an interesting relic. The Boar's Head stood a few yards west of the spot where the statue of King William IV. from the centre of the street looks towards London Bridge.

On its western edge the Fire burnt at dark up Dowgate, then an open street leading steeply down to the water dock, not shadowed by gloom as it is to-day. The flames there consumed three more Halls of the City Companies. All closely adjacent, and away from the riverside squalor, they made together a sheltered corner of that picturesque mediæval and Tudor London, little of which survived the Great Fire. Tallow Chandlers Hall (" a handsome house " of Howel's *Londinopolis*, and certainly in existence in 1518) was typical of a merchant prince's home, the front to Dowgate Hill being shops, and between them spread an archway giving entrance to a small open court. Its three sides were built in with the Hall, court-room, beadle's room, kitchen, and offices. The Fire destroyed all, leaving blackened ruins. The fine charter by Edward VI., the records and plate were taken by the Master in his coach to Hampstead. The livery gowns, being left in a neighbouring church, were also saved. Innholders Hall has bare mention by Stow. The Company some months before had stored their plate at the Master's house (the Ram in Smithfield) and it thus escaped the Fire.

The loss to London of Skinners Hall was of more importance. The building had belonged to the Skinners Company before 1441, and incorporated the ancient Copped Hall, before which was a spacious yard; there was a parlour and ladies' parlour, a kitchen, a " pastrie," buttery and storehouse. Five shops facing Dowgate Hill stood upon the property. Nothing of these was left. The Court had assembled in Hall eleven days before the Fire, no doubt a cheerful company. The order made at their

first meeting thereafter bespeaks the desolation wrought :
" That the foundations of the Hall be dug over, and a
search made for lead, iron, pewter, etc."

The Skinners removed their plate and muniments,
first to a place of safety in Shoreditch, then into Essex
when there appeared a danger of the Fire consuming all
London. For this good service their successors are indebted to Mr. Foster, the renter warden, who at great
personal sacrifice attended to the Company's business
while his own property was burning.

The Post Office was kept at a house in Cloak Lane,
Dowgate.*   Sir Philip Frowde was Governor for the lessee
(Katharine Countess of Chesterfield, who farmed the posts
under a monopoly which gave the profits to the Duke of
York and his heirs). Frowde and his lady anxiously
watched the progress of the flames bearing towards them,
and at midnight, when the peril had become grave, they
fled for safety.   The acting postmaster, James Hickes, was
no stranger to horrors.   At hazard of life he had remained
in London throughout the previous year's Great Plague,
keeping the letter office open and attending to its business,
when neighbours were dying all around, and the red cross
and that tragic appeal, " Lord, have mercy on us ! " were
chalked on many citizens' doors.   He stayed himself this
night of the Fire till one o'clock.   Such was then the alarm
of his wife and children that they would stay no longer,
fearing lest their escape should be completely cut off.
With difficulty, and no little danger in the burning streets,
Hickes managed to reach an inn bearing the sign of the
Golden Lion in Red Cross Street, outside Cripplegate,
where he temporarily re-established the post-house. He
saved such packets as he could hastily remove, and forwarded to Williamson, Lord Arlington's secretary, the
letters of State received by the Chester and Irish mails,
with a despairing note, that " how we shall dispose of our
business only the wise God knows." [1]

Left to its fate, the Post Office was burnt out during
the night, many letters being consumed, and with them—
a loss that was more keenly felt—a complete secret
apparatus for tampering with, copying, and forging letters
in the interests of the State, that had commended itself

[1] *State Papers (Domestic),* 1666-7, p. 95.

to the devious mind of Charles II.[1] * This was the invention of the ingenious Sir Samuel Morland, who had been employed by Cromwell in espionage upon the mails, while secretly he was in communication with the exiled King. The flames had been peculiarly cruel in their onslaught. The destruction of the waterworks at London Bridge had taken from the citizens the only practical means of combating the Fire at its inception; and at the close of the first day's progress the loss of the Post Office deprived them of the one channel by which authentic news could be spread. Hickes sent his family forward to Barnet, and himself followed. From there on Tuesday, the 4th September, he addressed a circular letter to the postmasters between London and Chester, and so to Holyhead, informing them of the catastrophe. " I am commanded to tell you (he wrote) that letters from Ministers of State are to be sent hither to me, that I may convey them to the Court. When the violence of the fire is over, some place will be fixed upon for the general correspondence." [2]

The *London Gazette* published on Monday contained a dozen lines notifying the outbreak of the Fire. " It continues still with great violence," was stated. Thereafter the official sheet abruptly ceased publication. Letters to London were undelivered, and others ready for despatch were not sent out. For a whole week the postal service with the capital was completely disorganized. In the absence of news alarmist rumours spread throughout the country, and that the burning of London was due to incendiarism by foreign enemies was generally believed.

[1] See W. G. Bell, *Lond. & Midd. Arch. Soc.*, New Ser. iii, 458.
[2] Le Fleming MSS. (*Hist. MSS. Comm.*, p. 41).

CHAPTER IV

FLAMES ACROSS THE CITY

FROM Whitehall the bend of the river half concealed the burning city, but the glow of the Fire at night, and flames shooting above the highest buildings, were visible at the Palace windows. The King and his Ministers had become thoroughly alarmed, fearing that nothing could save the capital. There is a sentence in a foreign resident's letter telling how the King was awakened during the night by the noise of the Londoners crying " Fire, fire ! God and the King save us ! " [1]

As if in irony, the sun rose on Monday on a glorious day.

The Fire had already a front extending for half a mile. An area of many acres had been destroyed, but ruined houses upon it continued to burn furiously, and a large body of flame was speeding into the city north and west, travelling up Gracechurch Street and across Eastcheap and along Cannon Street, promising a conflagration that should reduce to insignificance all that had happened on the first day of the Fire. The destruction was much greater on the second day, greater still on the third, when Guildhall and St. Paul's were alight, and the Fire was in the Liberties.

The Court was no sooner astir than measures were hastily taken to retrieve the dilatoriness of Sunday, but already invaluable time had been lost. Every hour enlarged the difficulty of encircling the Fire by a cleared zone, at the edge of which the raging flames should die down for want of further fuel. The Lord Mayor was set

---

[1] *Londens Puyn-hoop.* Amsterdam, 1666.

TYPES OF RESTORATION LONDON

Houses formerly standing in Long Lane, Smithfield. The flames rapidly demolished whole
streets of inflammable timber buildings like these

aside (little more is heard of him).* He had been obstructed in the vitally important task of pulling down buildings during the early spread of the Fire by certain wealthy merchants—" tenacious and avaricious men, Aldermen, etc., would not permit, because their houses must have been the first," says Evelyn. Moreover, the ancient City law, a relic of more tumultuous days, that any man destroying another's house should be at the charge of rebuilding it, made it necessary that any decision taken at a time of such grave emergency should have the authority of the King in Council. The Duke of York assumed supreme control in the City, under the King, who nominated members of the Privy Council, noblemen and others to the charge of stations. The Earl of Manchester, the Earl of Craven, Lord Ashley (afterwards the great Earl of Shaftesbury), Lord Belasyse [1] and Lord Harrison notably were active. More troops were sent in. The justices of the peace for Middlesex appointed Ely Place, Holborn, as their meeting place, and there informal councils sat to concert measures for subduing the Fire.

A first step was the summoning of fire posts. These were spread out like a fan in advance of the flames. Westward they numbered five : at Temple Bar, Clifford's Inn Gardens, Fetter Lane, Shoe Lane, and Cow Lane, Smithfield. The parish constables were commanded to attend, each with one hundred men. Thirty foot-soldiers were attached to each post, under their officer. In addition, three gentlemen, justices of the peace, were nominated to the several posts, to direct the work of the military, constables, and civilians. Each post was provisioned with bread, cheese, and beer of the value of £5. Authority was given to reward with one shilling at the King's cost any man who was diligent at night.

Nearer the flames other posts were established at Cripplegate, in Coleman Street, and by Aldersgate. All these were maintained, not on Monday alone, but throughout the Fire. Orders were sent to the Lords-lieutenant of Middlesex, Surrey, Kent and Herts to draw in the

---

[1] Lord Belasyse, being a Catholic, years afterwards was denounced by Titus Oates for connivance in the Popish Plot, and his good services to London in the Fire did not save him the indignity of arrest and imprisonment in The Tower.

militia round London. At night the tired soldiers and citizens were relieved from this source. The most beneficial work in saving what survived of the City, and finally stamping out the Fire, was done by seamen called up from the dockyards at Deptford and Woolwich and from the fleet, who blew up with powder many houses, and being handy with rope and chain, with a strong heave and all together brought down to the ground others of the lightly-built timber structures; but so little inspired were those upon whom the responsibility rested that their services were not requisitioned till the Fire was for a large part spent.

The Londoners now appreciated the grave peril that the Fire might consume their whole City. Pepys, abroad before daybreak, found the streets filled with excited people. Like many another citizen near to the Fire, he had spent the hours snatched from sleep in getting his treasures into safety in the cellars of his house in Seething Lane, and his bags of gold and Exchequer tallies packed for removal.

" About four o'clock in the morning, my Lady Batten sent me a cart to carry away all my money and plate and best things to Sir W. Rider's, at Bednall [Bethnal] Green. Which I did, riding myself in my nightgown, in the cart; and, Lord! To see how the streets and the highways are crowded with people running and riding, and getting of carts at any rate to fetch away things. I find Sir W. Rider tired with being called up all night, and receiving things from several friends. His house full of goods, and much of Sir W. Batten's and Sir W. Pen's. I am eased at my heart to have my treasure so well secured. Then home, and with much ado to find a way, nor any sleep all this night to me nor my poor wife. But then and all this day she and I and all my people labouring to get away the rest of our things, and did get Mr. Tooker to get me a lighter to take them in, and we did carry them, myself some, over Tower Hill, which was by this time full of people's goods, bringing their goods hither; and down to the lighter, which lay at the next quay, above the Tower Dock. And here was my neighbour's wife, Mrs. ——, with her pretty child, and some few of her things, which I did willingly give way to be saved with mine;

but there was no passing with anything through the postern, the crowd was so great."

By the Thames-side the Three Cranes in Vintry was no longer standing, having been consumed in the night. Pepys in January, 1662, had " a sorry poor dinner " there, in " a narrow dog-hole of a room," though it was the best the house afforded. This was one of the oldest waterside taverns in London, timber-built no doubt, and is mentioned in a London chronicle as early as 1425, when it was The Crane in Vintry. Near at hand Vintners Hall, a fifteenth-century building,[1] met with a like fate, together with the Company's wharf and their thirteen almshouses built about the quadrangle. The latter after the Fire were removed to Mile-end Road, where they are still to be found. The Company saved their valuable plate, some pieces dating from 1518.

Three other Companies' Halls were destroyed early on Monday morning, those of the Parish Clerks and the Plumbers in Thames Street, close neighbours of the Vintners, and Joyners Hall near the water. In Parish Clerks Hall was kept the printing Press, on which were impressed the weekly bills of mortality, so valuable for their records of the Plague, and several important books in addition. It perished with the building in the Great Fire, a new press and letters being ordered in October, 1669.* The Company had taken the hall in the Vintry in or about 1562, when they moved from Bishopsgate.

Across Thames Street the flames spread to the large church of St. Martin Vintry and that of St. James Garlickhithe (the registers of the latter, dating back to 1535, were fortunately saved), and crept up the brow of the hill, burning through Whittington's pious foundation.

Richard Whittington, Lord Mayor of London in 1396, 1397, 1406, and again in 1409—he was never Sir Richard, despite the popular belief—lay buried with Alice his wife in the church of St. Michael Paternoster Royal, which he rebuilt. Twice his sepulture had been disturbed, first by a ghoulish rector, one Thomas Mountain, thinking that some great riches were coffined with him, and again in

---

[1] Vintners Hall, burnt in the Great Fire, appears to have been the house of Guy Shuldham, and is described in his will bearing date 1446. (Cf. Nichols, *Lond. and Midd. Archæol. Soc.*, iii, 446.)

Queen Mary's time by the parishioners, with the worthier object of replacing the leaden envelope, before torn from the body; " and so he resteth," adds John Stow. The marble tomb and all the church (in days of strife a popular place with devout Royalists) and Whittington's almshouses were destroyed by the Fire. College Hill, upon which St. Michael Paternoster Royal stands, takes that name from the college of priests founded by Whittington. The ecclesiastical college was suppressed, and the buildings swept away, at the spoliation of the religious houses, but the almshouses for thirteen poor men, fortunate in the protection of the Mercers Company, of which the generous donor was a member, had been allowed to survive. Left in complete ruin by the Great Fire, they were rebuilt by Sir Christopher Wren on College Hill, with the church; in 1808 the almshouses were removed to Highgate.

The Cutlers Company lost their hall in Cloak Lane, Dowgate Hill, which had been in their possession since 1451, saving only their books and plate. A cup and cover, silver gilt, bequeathed by Mr. G. Clarke in 1616, a salt in the form of an elephant, presented in 1658, and a Bible with silver clasps, dated 1541, are in their possession to-day. Down by the waterside where the Fire burnt the whole district was honeycombed with vaults and pits for the storage of brandies and wines. Its subterranean character is indicated in a name applied in mediæval times to the parish of Allhallows-the-Less—that of " Allhallows-on-the-Cellars " ; and along the river bank, too, were carried on those objectionable trades, soap-boiling, dyeing, and the like, against which John Evelyn, in *Fumifugium*, launched his thunderbolts. Steam rising from many vats floated across Thames Street, in and about which sixteen breweries were situated, largely grouped in the Ward of Vintry. All these were consumed as the flames sped along. By ten o'clock on Monday morning the Fire had reached within four houses of Queenhithe.

Few people to-day know Queenhithe, which has gone out of London's life. Once this was one-half of the Port of London !

The harbours of Billingsgate and Queenhithe served all the wants of the mediæval capital, and there all shipping was brought up.   Queenhithe in 1666 made a deep indentation of the river-bank, as it does to-day.   Behind was a market place, where still an open space is preserved. Great hopes were entertained of staying the Fire's western advance there.

The King came down the river in his barge to Queenhithe, and by his presence encouraged a squad of men who were then strenuously employed in pulling down houses and in stripping the market, in order to leave nothing that could assist the flames ; having stayed half an hour and received reports of the Fire's growth, the monarch returned to Whitehall.   All efforts were in vain. An eye-witness who watched says that " after two hours' expectation we saw all these endeavours slighted by a leap which the Fire made over twenty houses upon the turret of a house in Thames Street.'   There burning down to the ground, the flames were free to pursue their way unchecked towards Baynard's Castle.

The Fire, increasing in noise and violence, now extended in two arms, westerly along the river, and in a northerly direction up Gracechurch Street towards Lombard Street and Cornhill.   A few hours' expansion since dawn had brought the flames into the City's wealthiest quarter, where they continued to burn all day amid the rich houses of merchants and bankers.

Gracechurch Street—once Gerschereche, Gratious Street, Grasschurch Street, the various spellings bespeak its antiquity—lingered then, and lingers still, as a survival of mediæval London.   A market for herbs and fruit, with stalls out on the roadway, was held at its outspreading lower end, which had been the City's original grass-market, but long before Charles II. houses had encroached upon the open space.   Time had gone by to attempt to check the Fire there.   The old water conduit, standing out in the middle of the thoroughfare, was destroyed as the flames passed, and they broke upon St. Benet's Church, leaving only a ruin.   The mass of flame was, however, towards Lombard Street, down which it was driven by the wind with great fury.

So the larger Fire spread into the City on Monday, September 3rd—a hot, dry September day, following a succession of many similar days, with glaring sunshine ; warm enough without this work. The loudest call was for carriers, and with it came a clamour for water. The last was not forthcoming in quantities adequate for the emergency. A long drought had reduced the flow from the springs, which only in small volume reached the conduits that were placed in the principal streets—in Cornhill, Aldermanbury, Cheapside, Fleet Street and else-where—and still gave a part of London's water supply. The wells, still numerous in the City, were also low. But, worse than all, there had been criminal carelessness. In the perplexity and confusion of Sunday no man's authority was respected. Roads had been torn up, and the long trunks of elm hollowed to form pipes, which carried the New River service,* had been cut for filling the fire-buckets. The supply then ran to waste, and in sections of the City the pipes and cisterns were dry when water was most needed.

" Before the Fire (says Vincent) were pleasant and stately houses, behind ruinous and desolate heaps.'' Lombard Street, even though its buildings justified this description, was still the same narrow street, but a few feet separating the houses, that it had been when the Lombards settled there. The last Lombard merchants had quitted the country when Elizabeth reigned. They left us the familiar signs £ s. d. (*lire, soldi, denari*), and their trade as bill-brokers, bankers, and more especially insurers of the sailing fleets and cargoes upon the seas, remained about the street. Letters sent by King Henry VIII. to the City for creating a bourse at Leadenhall had failed in their object. " Merchants must be content to stand and walk in the rain, more like pedlars than mer-chants," wrote one of the number. They were brought under shelter when Sir Thomas Gresham built and gave to the City the first Royal Exchange in 1566, but without altering the quality that till to-day attaches to Lombard Street.

This was, in 1666, one of the most picturesque streets in London. Elizabethan, even mediæval, to a great extent it remained, having nothing in character with the reign of Charles II., but it was mediævalism displaying its richness, tall houses of three and four stories, stoutly

built and well kept, with large casement windows projecting out of the timber frames ; a place of patches of
strong sunlight and deep shadows, not, as in the quarter
by the riverside, mediævalism displaying its poverty and
squalor. Over the narrow causeway swung a wealth of
gilt and coloured signs of strange beasts and quaint
devices—the Unicorn, the Grasshopper, the White Horse,
the Star, the Golden Fleece, the Fox, and fifty others.

Merchants crowded into Lombard Street in its busy
hours, having their dwellings in the network of streets
and alleys north and south, where ever since has been
the financial centre of London. Lombard Street had
financed the war which the country was waging. Its
residents, when the Great Fire destroyed it, were the
wealthiest of the City men. Sir Robert Vyner, elected
Sheriff that memorable year, occupied a large house and
ground covering a quarter-acre, standing next to St.
Mary Woolnoth Church. He had providentially moved
out all his bonds and papers nearly twenty-four hours
before the Fire burnt the length of Lombard Street.[1]
He lost a fortune of £416,000 when Charles II., in 1672,
took the unconscionable course of closing the Exchequer,
leaving him an unsatisfied creditor for that amount.
Perhaps he is best remembered by an anecdote told of a
City feast in his Mayoralty, whereat the King, stealing
away to his coach in Guildhall Yard, was seized by the
hand by his host, who cried with an oath, " Sire, you
shall stay and take t'other bottle." Charles, ready in
wit, replied with the line of an old song—

" He that is drunk is as great as a King,"

and the two jovial monarchs returned to the table to
finish the carouse.

Edward Backwell, Alderman of Bishopsgate Ward,
another victim—for £290,000—of the " Merry Monarch,"
had removed his sign of the Unicorn to a shop at the
corner of Change Alley a month before the Fire.

Money could do much to purchase help, but not enough
to stay the flames. By three o'clock on Monday afternoon
the whole of Lombard Street was consumed. St. Edmund
King and Martyr, and next to the church the George Inn,

[1] *Gazette*, 1666, Sept. 3–10.

a house much resorted to by merchants (it was afterwards rebuilt) burnt at one end of Lombard Street, St. Mary Woolnoth Church at the other.   Its wealth, being largely in bonds and other securities, was easily removed, and though merchants were hard hit by their losses, and widely scattered, the Fire brought no financial panic in its train.   Evelyn, three weeks after the Fire, notes as a happy sign that not one failure was heard of.[1]   Less philosophical was a Dutch broker, whose letter to friends in Amsterdam is preserved.   " My house amongst others was burnt," he wrote ; " by God's grace my books and letters of credit are at my house at Clapham, but none know where I shall find the merchants who will pay me the moneys due."   Thomas Firmin, the philanthropist, whom his biographer describes as " a kind of almoner general of the metropolis," was amongst those burnt out of Lombard Street.   He traded there as a girdler and mercer, and some years passed before he was able to rebuild on the site of his destroyed dwelling.

The Fire threatened Cornhill in the early afternoon, having burnt through the massed houses, with intolerable heat.   Many alleys, narrow as they were in mediæval days, came out upon this busy street, and along these the wind drove the flames.   The flying people scurried away, escaping with so much of their goods as they could remove in time to safety.   In St. Michael's Alley Pasqua Rosee, fourteen years before the Great Fire, had set up the first coffee-house in London, establishing a social fashion which thereafter spread over the town.   Cornhill in 1666 was a favourite shopping place, a mart of mercers and glovers and of trade in all its variety ; even to-day it has not entirely lost that character.   It is no new thing that the press of commerce has almost concealed from view the great church of St. Michael Archangel, shops packing up to the actual porch of the tower.   The ground was so utilized in Edward the Sixth's reign.   Stow worshipped in the old church standing here, and tells much about it ; incidentally how one day the belfry was struck by lightning, and the ringers rendered prostrate.   " An ugly shapen sight appeared to them, coming in at the south window ; when the ringers came to themselves

---

[1] Letter to Sir S. Tuke, Sept. 29.

they found certain stones of the north window to be raised and scratched, as if they had been so much butter, printed with a lion's claw ; the same stones were fastened there again and so remain to this day. I have seen them oft, and have put a feather or small stick into the holes where the claws had entered three or four inches deep." The old antiquary, poking about with his feather and stick, is quite a delightful bit of self-revelation. To John Stow's father the damage done in the belfry was the work of the devil, whose form was seen in the flames.

In 1666 Cornhill was accounted a large and spacious street, though badly fulfilling such conditions as understood to-day. With the roar of the Fire at their backs, the noise ever coming nearer, soldiers and civilians were employed in pulling down the south side of the street, so as to leave a cleared open space—a dry moat beyond which the flames could not pass. It may well have been thought that the stone churches of St. Peter Cornhill * and of St. Michael Archangel would be bulwarks to resist the Fire's progress if, by vigorous use of axe and hook and chain, the inflammable timber houses could be removed in time.

The Fire destroyed both churches, leaving upstanding St. Michael's high tower, though the flames raging within it consumed the four timber stages, and the bells fell clattering to the ground.[1] The mediæval tower, built into Wren's new church, stood till 1721. A company of the King's Guards kept the throng of people back from the street. Monmouth was there on horseback among them.[2] Years afterwards, when the Duke of Monmouth landed in rebellion at Lyme Regis, it was one of the many accusations he made that James II. had caused the burning of London. He was at this time in his eighteenth year, and but recently acknowledged by Charles II. as his natural son, he had been raised to the peerage with precedence over all peers not of the Blood Royal. The favourite of fortune, young and handsome and debonair, envied by all men in the corrupt and licentious Court, he sits on horseback silhouetted for an instant against the vivid background of the Fire. Who then could have

---

[1] *Vestry Minutes*, 1667.   [2] Malcolm, *Lond. Rediv.*, iv, 75.

foretold the last pathetic scene on Tower Hill in which he was to figure ?

Monmouth was the helpless onlooker of a tragic happening. The very precautions undertaken to stay the Fire assisted its farther advance. Vincent tells of the destruction of Cornhill in one of his breathless passages : " Quickly the flames cross the way by the train of wood that lay in the streets untaken away, which had been pull'd down from houses to prevent its spreading ; and so they lick the whole street as they go : they mount up to the top of the highest houses ; they descend down to the bottom of the lowest vaults and cellars ; and march along on both sides of the way, with such a roaring noise, as never was heard in the city of London ; no stately building so great as to resist their fury."

The Fire was now in the City's heart. St. Paul's, farther west, and Guildhall, to the north, were still distant, and not as yet menaced ; but the flames on Cornhill found fresh fuel for destruction in a public building next in importance only to these. Sir Thomas Gresham's Royal Exchange had stood for a century, conspicuous in London's crowded area by its lofty square tower of stone, carrying a clock and two balconied galleries. A weather-vane fashioned as a grasshopper (the donor's house-sign and crest) swung with the wind above the ball at the summit.

The City had spent £3,737 of Elizabeth's money in acquiring and clearing the site—good measure of the spaciousness of the Exchange. Its two hundred shops, so claimed, are perhaps an exaggeration in numbers, but contemporary prints make it plain that this was one of the most striking buildings in the capital. A gateway beside the tower gave access to the open 'Change, the vaulting of its cloister walks, where the merchants congregated, being held aloft by marble pillars. Above were statues of all the English Sovereigns since the Conquest.

There had been raised on the front of the Royal Exchange an effigy of King Charles I. The Commonwealth ordered that this should be mutilated, and so stand in this public place as an example to tyrants, the head being struck off, the sceptre broken in the hand, and this inscription written, " Exit tyrannus Regum ultimus anno primo

From a Dutch Print

SIR THOMAS GRESHAM'S ROYAL EXCHANGE

restitutae libertatis Angliae 1648 " [1]—the first year of English liberty. How the calendar mocks all those who have sought to begin it anew! Later the statue was toppled down, but the inscription remained. This in turn was cut out at the Restoration. The Mercers Company, as trustees of Gresham, erected a new statue of Charles, which perished in the Great Fire.

Upper and lower pawnes, extending from the tower along Cornhill and Threadneedle Street, contained the shops and merchants' offices. In the manner of Elizabethan times these were built in stout timber frames. Gresham had brought the wood from his own estate at Battisford, in Suffolk. The Exchange pawnes formed the most fashionable shopping and loitering place in the City, stored with fanciful and artistic wares from every quarter. "Here, if anywhere," says the Rev. Samuel Rolle, " might a man have seen the glory of the world in a moment, as the Devil showed it to Christ upon a high mountain. Was it not the great storehouse, whence the nobility and gentry of England were furnished with most of those costly things wherewith they did adorn either their closets or themselves ? What artificial thing could entertain the senses and fantasies of men that was not there to be had ? Such was the delight that many gallants took in that magazine of all curious varieties that they could almost have dwelt there (going from shop to shop like bees from flower to flower). If they had but a fountain of money that could not have been drawn dry. I doubt not but a Mahomedan (who never expects other than sensible delights) would gladly have accepted of that place, and the treasures of it, for his heaven, and have thought there were none like it." [2] The Fire first seized upon the tradesmen's shops.

" The Royal Exchange itself," writes Vincent, " the glory of the merchants, is now invaded with much violence ; and when once the fire was entered, how quickly did it run down the galleries, filling them with flames ; then

[1] *State Papers* (*Domestic*), 1650, p. 261. A head of Charles I. from a broken statue is in the Guildhall Museum, and very likely is the one dissevered by the Parliament's order. Cromwell's own " picture " was set up in the Exchange during the Commonwealth, with verses under it tending much to his honour. (*Thurlow State Papers*, iii, 66.)
[2] Rolle, *Burning of London*, 1667, pt. 3, p. 45.

came down stairs, compasseth the walks, giving forth
flaming vollies, and filleth the court with sheets of fire;
by-and-by down fall all the Kings upon their faces, and
the greatest part of the stone building after them (the
founder's statue only remaining) with such a noise as was
dreadful and astonishing." The tower alone, a gaunt
and seared skeleton, and one half of a single pillar, stood
upright amid the ruin. The flames burnt down to the
crypt underground, consuming a vast quantity of im-
ported pepper and costly spices stored there by the East
India Company. Crouch, in his *Londinenses Lacrymae*,
recalls this incident in the Fire—

> Now the Imperious Element did range
> Without Controle, kept a full Ev'ning Change.
> Where the religious Spices for some Hours,
> Seem'd to burn Incense to the incensed Powers.

Sir Thomas Gresham's statue survived unbroken,
though fallen from its niche, a fact which deeply impressed the people. The Royal Exchange built by Edward
Jerman after the Great Fire of London stood till 1838,
when it was completely destroyed in a second conflagration, and again the founder's statue was preserved unharmed. In earlier days a miracle would have been
proclaimed.

Another fire was in Threadneedle Street, into which
the Royal Exchange emptied its flames, and they quickly
ignited the neighbouring church of St. Benet Fink; then
crossing the way consumed the church and entire parish
of St. Bartholomew Exchange, save only three houses
left standing in Copthall Alley. A tiny south chapel of
St. Bartholomew Exchange, called the Capel Chapel, was
but little harmed, and was used as a vestry till the destruction of the church built after the Fire in 1840. Little
shops had stood on the churchyard. They were afterwards rebuilt, and the rector was accused of appropriating
to himself the fine of £100 annual rental which hitherto
had been for the use of the poor.

Whole streets of dwellings and shops fed the raging
Fire, the timber houses burning in a bright flame which
took an orange tint in the sunlight. When night fell the
City, seen from a distance, with dark skies and dark masses
of buildings closing in upon it, presented a spectacle of

awful grandeur; but I doubt if even the Great Fire of London was impressive in these daylight hours. The flame has little notice. In letters and diaries it is the immense curtain of smoke, which at the height of the Fire covered London like a moving pall, that stimulated the imagination of writers as the most notable feature to be recalled. For four days unceasingly it rolled away, the contents of the stored warehouses continuing to burn day and night after the structures which contained them had been destroyed, giving out great volumes of dense smoke which rose above the City and were carried along by the wind.

"The yellow smoke of London (writes Vincent) ascendeth up to heaven, like the smoke of a great furnace ; a smoke so great as darkened the sun at noon-day ; if at any time the sun peeped forth, it looked red like blood." He tells of travellers out of London who rode at midday some miles together in the shadow, although no other cloud was to be seen in the sky. Evelyn computes the trailing column of smoke to have extended fifty miles in length. Far distant apparitions were seen, if strong imaginations were not overwrought ; away at Berwick-on-Tweed some soldiers witnessed " the likeness of an abundance of ships in the air." At Oxford a Mr. Locke kept an early meteorological register, and on the 4th September, 1666, it has this entry, " Dim reddish sunshine," with the further note—

This unusual colour of the Air, which without a Cloud appearing made the Sunbeams of a strange red dim Light, was very remarkable. We had then heard nothing of the Fire of *London*. But it appeared afterward to be the smoke of London then burning, which, driven this way by an Easterly wind, caused this odd Phenomenon.[1]

Since early morning Cannon Street had been laid level with the ground, from Eastcheap to its termination at St. John upon Walbrook,* where a church, newly built in 1412, stood beside the little stream that in mediæval days had flowed as an open watercourse from the fens at Moorfields, emptying into the Thames. Across the street the Fire burnt up into the City, through an area closely

---

[1] *The Observatory*, vol. 35, p. 64

packed with houses, and intersected by mere passages—
St. Clement's Lane, Nicholas Lane, Abchurch Lane, and
others. So narrow were they that nothing effectual could
be done, or attempted, to stay the progress of the flames.
In this place, as in others where the crowding was greatest,
the wind was the most destructive agent in spreading the
Fire, which started at the roofs and burnt down.   Sparks
scattered wide settled amid the dry timbers underneath
the red tiles, or in the gables, and to many an anxious
Londoner the first intimation that disaster was upon
him was that his roof was ablaze.   Where the Fire had
passed rows of brick chimney stacks stood up alone,
the timber structure of the houses about them having
been wholly consumed or fallen in debris on the ground.
" One sees in the City nothing but doorways and
chimneys standing among ruins," wrote an onlooker
afterwards.

Embedded in this confused mass of buildings were
three churches. St. Mary Abchurch evidently burnt
while its custodians were unprepared, for few relics survived the Fire, and among these is a register which still
bears the marks of the flames, as if snatched away at the
last moment.   There is also a chalice dated " Antwerp,
1581."   Rebuilt, St. Mary Abchurch stands to-day, a
red-brick Wren church, with square leaden cupola and
stunted spire ; there is, too, a church of St. Clement
Eastcheap ; but only a still open graveyard in a by-way
from Lombard Street, where land plots are perhaps the
most valuable in the world, gives reminder of the old
church dedicated to St. Nicholas, the patron of the money
changers.

To an observer centrally situated, the points of the
compass were marked by churches ablaze, throwing flames
high above their roofless walls.   London till the Great
Fire—the fact is so often emphasized in this narrative—
was still a city of a hundred towers and spires, and nowhere
were churches more thickly congregated than in this
wealthy quarter.   St. Christopher-le-Stocks lay back, soon
to be overwhelmed like the rest, St. Mildred Poultry to
the west, and southward St. Mary Woolchurch Hawe and
the cloistered church of St. Stephen Walbrook.   Let me
bespeak remembrance for Mr. Langley, churchwarden of

TIMBER BUILT VILLAGE IN POLAND BURNT BY THE RETREATING RUSSIAN ARMIES

After the Fire of London many houses showed only the stone or brick chimneys standing, after this fashion, the timber structure being consumed

St. Mary Woolchurch Hawe at this fateful time, an
exemplar to all his kind. He was clearing his house with
hired help when the sexton and some parishioners came
in hot haste to him, bearing the sacramental plate and
books from the burning church—in all a cumbersome lot
of parcels, for they included besides " the new great
bible " and " embroidered beare cloths and cushings."
He employed his men in saving the church property first,
and, awaiting their return, saw his own house and its
contents burnt over his head.

Lombard Street, Cornhill, and Threadneedle Street
were burning, with all the courts about them ; but the
most threatening, the most fateful thing for London was
not the mass of this central fire, but its slow and irresistible creep northwards. As every hour passed the Fire
presented a yet broader front to the wind blowing from
the east, the close alleys and passages, with houses crowded
within a few feet of one another, being successively involved in disaster. From the direction of the Thames
another fire burnt up Walbrook. The broad front of the
separate fires united at the Stocks Market (to-day the
Mansion House) in one great flame, which as night came
on was driven by the wind towards Cheapside, " with
such a dazzling light (says Vincent simply) and burning
heat and roaring noise by the fall of so many houses
together that was very amazing."

The Poultry lay directly in its path, and adjoining
Bucklersbury—Shakespeare's   Bucklersbury.   Falstaff,
wooing Mistress Ford, professed, " I cannot cog, and say
thou art this and that, like a many of these lisping haw-
thorn-buds, that come like women in men's apparel, and
smell like Bucklersbury in simple time."   Stow speaks of
Bucklersbury, on both sides throughout, as composed of
grocers and apothecaries. The centre of the druggists'
trade in the City it remained, almost to our own day.
The fumes from the drugs, mixing with the smell of the
burning pepper at the Royal Exchange, must have made
this a corner of peculiar horror in the Great Fire of
London.

A strong building stood in Poultry, locked and barred,
confining the prisoners committed by the Sheriffs. They
were the first of many to whom the Fire of London restored

liberty.[1] The short street was, however, chiefly notorious
for its taverns. I recall the King's Head, only because
of the story told of Charles II. and the wife of William
King, the landlord. The lady, happening to be in labour
on the great day of the Restoration, was anxious to see
the returning Sovereign, and Charles, being informed of
her wish, when passing through the Poultry good-naturedly
stopped the pageant at the tavern, that he might salute
the proud mother of his youngest subject. The house
burnt to tinder, and for years lay in ruins before being
rebuilt.[2]

The late afternoon witnessed a great extension of the
Fire westward. Towards the river lay the levelled and
blackened area cleared on Sunday, whereon spasmodic
fires burnt in cellars and buildings not wholly consumed.
From its edge a line of bright flame, thin in the sunlight,
extended from St. Swithin's Church, by London Stone,
parallel with the Thames. Already the Fire was in the
southern foot of the tributary streets which led up to
Cheapside—Cordwainer Street, Friday Street, Bread Street,
and others. St. Swithin's—the only church in London
dedicated to the rainy saint—was of early fifteenth-
century craftsmanship, a large church, with tower and
belfry and chapels of St. Katherine and St. Anne. It
had been embellished at great cost only two years before
the Fire. There is preserved an inventory of plate and
vestments, melancholy in its brevity, " which were all
that were saved out of the late Dismal Fire of London."

[1] It is testimony to the City's veneration of old customs that to this
day there is a Judge of the Compter, though the gaol has disappeared, a
fact of which London was reminded by the resignation of the late Judge
Rentoul. There were two Compters in the City, each under the control
of a Sheriff. Wood Street Compter, established in 1555, and making a
great figure in our more squalid literature, was removed to Giltspur Street
in 1791. The other Compter was in the Poultry, and both, though they
were merely lock-ups, were places of vile extortion. In each case there
was a large staff to batten on the fees, consisting of a " secondary," a
clerk of the papers, four clerk sitters, eighteen serjeants-at-mace, each
serjeant with a yeoman, a master keeper and two turnkeys. A man
might be interned for the simplest misdemeanour ; but the exactions
began at once. Was he sent to the Master's side ? That was the dearest
of all. The Knight's side was a little cheaper. If he chose to be placed
in " the hole " he probably desired to escape therefrom on the briefest
experience, and then he paid " garnish " at each door in the ascending
scale as he went up higher.—*Westminster Gazette.*
[2] Add. MSS. 5098, fo. 338.

Two large silver flagons and two gilt cups with covers are the only items of note.

The historic London Stone withstood the Fire. If Crouch be an authority (one mistrusts a versifier) then it escaped unharmed—

> All things of beauty shatter'd, lost, and gone;
> Nothing of London whole but London Stone.[1]

There is no other record that I could trace. There survives but a small fragment of what the Stone has been.

As the Fire burnt up St. Swithin's Lane it consumed Salters Hall, an ancient group of buildings formerly belonging to the Priory of Tortington, which at the Suppression had been granted by Henry VIII. to John Earl of Oxford. Little beyond ruins of this relic of monastic London was left amid the large flower garden which to this day (though much reduced in area) makes a spot of bright colour at the heart of the world's finance. Most of the records perished in the Fire. The Salters had acquired the property only in 1641.

In Trinity Lane, next Garlick Hill, Paynter-Stainers Hall had stood since early in the sixteenth century. Alderman Sir John Brown, serjeant-painter to King Henry VIII., had dwelt there, and in 1532 he conveyed his residence to his fellow paynter-stainers for their hall. The few references to it known suggest an ornate house of some importance. It was entirely destroyed. The Paynter-Stainers Company possess the only contemporary picture of the Fire of London known to be authentic, the large panel painted and presented to them by Waggoner; they have, besides, one relic of the Fire of more than passing interest—the " Binding Book " of apprentices. The pages are much stained with water, and the charred condition of the cover and sides indicate that it has been through the flames. A single youth's indentures had been entered a fortnight before the Fire, and, being new, the book had perhaps been forgotten. The *Inspeximus* of 1467, Queen Elizabeth's subsequent grant, and other valuable documents were saved unharmed, as were the plate and the pictures. Anciently the Company had the

---

[1] J. Crouch, *Londinenses Lacrymae*, 1666.

duty to seize all bad pictures and destroy them, but this difficult and invidious task they are now spared.

Out on the line of Thames Street three other churches burnt steadily, with the flare from warehouses and dwellings on fire all about them—St. Michael Queenhithe, St. Mary Somerset, and St. Mary Mounthaw. Not one of these names is to be found among City churches to-day, but the tower of St. Mary Somerset stands alone upon the street, a sphinx-like riddle to the wayfarer who comes unexpectedly upon it. He wonders what it is. This campanile is judged to be one of Sir Christopher Wren's finest works, and it was specially exempted from destruction when in 1872, under the Union of City Benefices Act, the demolition took place of the church built after the Great Fire.

" The bellowing wind," as one describes it, blew all day.

The King was repeatedly in the City during the progress of the Fire, setting an example of calm courage to the despairing people. The Duke of York was equally alert. Charles was not free from the prevailing feeling of panic, and, realizing the peril that the Fire might spread even to Westminster, prepared to send away some of his portable treasures from Whitehall, lest the flames should reach out to devour them. His bearing in the presence of the citizens concealed all trace of alarm. He mixed freely with them, assisting them in their labour, sharing their perils, and more—for the excited state of the populace, English and alien, was such that there was actual danger from the dagger of some lurking assassin. I have printed the " Short but True Account " of the Fire from the *Gazette* (see Appendix). It describes the admirable conduct of the people towards the King, but does not tell all. The inquirer who goes deeper alights upon passages that bring out with startling clearness the cowardice and greed and brutish violence that mixed with so much that was heroic in this time of appalling suffering.

London was disappearing in flames, for this was a riverside fire no longer. The flames had been driven up into the City, where now the houses of the better-class shopkeepers, prosperous merchants, and wealthy goldsmiths came crashing down. This Fire burnt like no other in men's experience. A street was alight at one end, and flames, as if spontaneously, burst out from windows twenty, thirty houses in advance of the approaching wave. Men who went late to bed at a distance from the Fire were awakened at dawn to find the roofs above them alight and smoke filling the rooms. Looking anxiously around, they saw other houses take fire, though no source from which they could have ignited was visible.[1]

Amid the roof-gables the merciless wind whistled. Flakes of fire were driving overhead. But few made use of ears or eyes, or stayed to reason. What was done by the wind they attributed to human malice. Water in many places was not to be obtained, and whole streets, with the packed courts and alleys about them, were left to the flames without effort being made to arrest their progress. By the mischance of the first hours, the Thames water raised by the wheels at the Bridge had been cut off. Bad as had been the conditions at the onset of the Fire, the shortage on this second day was being experienced in aggravated measure.

The actual cause of this I have already indicated, but the populace desired and believed a different explanation. Report spread over the town that our malignant enemies, the French and Dutch, had wilfully cut off the supply. Or else it was the work of malicious Papists, aiming at the complete destruction of the Protestant city. A story of this kind, wanting in no circumstantial detail, is told by Burnet on the authority of Bishop Lloyd, that one Grant, a Papist, had gone to the New River head at Islington, and there shut off the cocks on all the pipes that distributed the water over London, afterwards taking away the keys, so there was considerable delay in restoring the service. Like many another mendacity current at the time, it has proved to have no vestige of truth.*

The frenzy grew on Monday, strongly contrasting with the spasmodic alarms and simulated calm of the previous day, when the Fire burnt only by the river. None could now feel safe, if still distant were those long tongues of flame, for north, west, and east the flakes scattered, spreading the Fire in all directions. Frenchmen and Dutchmen were the first suspects, being avowed enemies on land and sea, but on Monday the belief hardened that

[1] Clarendon's *Life*.

the Papists, too, were giving a hand in this demoniacal work.[1] The populace turned to take vengeance on the foreigners.

Magistrates and soldiers worked strenuously to combat the Fire and clear the houses, while tumult raged about its outskirts. It is desirable to avoid exaggeration. A little knot of people eager in any pursuit quickly collects a mob, and the mob takes courage in its numbers. The search for the hapless aliens was keen. Women—viragoes of the mean streets—joined in the man-hunt, more violent, more mendacious than the men. " They had," says one Denis de Repas, a Frenchman, " their corps de garde in several streets, and did knock down several strangers for not speaking good English. Some of them were armed with spits, some with bread-staffs, and the captains with a broadsword." He blames the women alone for having caused the trouble. He was himself " half-dead by the word of killing all French and Dutch," and thanks God it had been proved that the Fire came by mere accident, or rather from the hand of God.[2]

Foreigners in London then, as at all times in this land of refuge, formed a numerous colony. " Owing to the great fire which has taken place here, I have not dared to go out," wrote a Dutchman—and he was wise. Those venturing to show themselves abroad were roughly seized and handed over to the guards by excited bystanders, who were prepared to swear they had taken them in the very act of throwing fireballs into the houses. Prisoners were apprehended having fireballs in their possession. In heated imaginations the crop grew as plentiful as mushrooms in a summer field. There was abundant evidence (if it could be believed) when everything not to be explained at a glance was held suspect. The gaols every hour received additional inmates against whom incendiarism was alleged on the flimsiest pretexts. At sight of the prisoners being marched off under guard the anger of the street mob rose, each man believing his worst suspicions to be confirmed.

A justice of the peace, Dawes Weymansel, told that a

---

[1] Clarendon's *Life*.
[2] Denis de Repas to Sir Edward Harley, Sept. 1666. Portland MSS. (*Hist. MSS. Comm.*, vol. 3, p. 298).

man he saw stopped and apprehended when entering the City at Temple Bar had his pockets stuffed with flax, tow, and such like materials for fire. Michael Marsh, a company officer of the Trained Bands, arrested a Walloon at the Nag's Head in Leadenhall Street. The foreigner was carrying a dark lantern, made (as his captor conceived) to lay a train of powder, and then containing powder. Two others of his countrymen were in his company. Three persons in unison attested that they had seen a man throw something into a house near St. Antholin's Church; immediately thereafter the place was in flames. Men handled, too, certain " black things, of a long figure " seized from a suspect, and of mysterious use, but manifestly diabolical, for none could endure to keep them in the hand by reason of their intense heat.[1]

Tales such as these ran through the choked streets, enlarging as they went. Every one became apprehensive. A poor widow hurried from the Fire through Moorfields, with chickens she had saved in the lap of her apron. She was attacked and grievously maltreated, the little fluffy things being taken to be fire-balls. Spectators in Moorfields witnessed a Frenchman assailed by a mob and almost dismembered, because he carried " balls of fire " with him in a chest. They were found to be tennis-balls after the damage to the man had been done. The King, on learning of these outrages, appointed members of the Privy Council, with guards, to various quarters of the City, with powers summarily to repress disorder. Even they thought it not safe to declare that they believed the Fire came by accident, or that it was not a plot of the Dutch and French and Papists to destroy the City. Sir Edward Southcote, passing to his country seat through London while the City was still burning, had one of his servants seized, a Frenchman, the man being overheard to speak broken English, but by explanations and gift of half-a-crown to the captors for drink obtained his release.

The excitement spread over the whole town, and ever new rumours took form as bands of alarmed refugees swarmed through the main streets, loaded with the first belongings they could hastily snatch up, and anxious only to place safety between themselves and the still advancing

[1] *A true and faithfull account, etc.*, 1667.

flames ; and boats, laden to the water's edge, made away from the Fire up river.

Far off at Westminster Cornelius Riedtveldt, a Dutch baker, lit his oven fire, for London, though its houses burn, must eat bread, and the thrifty Dutchman lose no chance of gaining good English money. Seeing smoke rising from the chimney, the people cried out that the rogue was trying to burn down that end of the town as well. They dragged him into the street, and would have left him lifeless had not, by a fortunate chance, the Duke of York happened to ride by at that moment. The baker was apprehended, and only after some days of imprisonment in Westminster Gatehouse returned to find his home plundered and his means of livelihood gone. His petition to Lord Arlington for release is in the State Papers. Himself, his wife, and certain lodgers had been committed upon a false suggestion of wicked practices that they did utterly detest and abhor. By violence of the mob their goods were taken from them, so that they had not means to subsist.

Hundreds of houses had been burnt down the previous night, but few citizens had actual need to pass the hours under the stars. Good Samaritans gave the shelter of their roofs. The churches—some, like Christ Church, Newgate Street, Austin Friars, and St. Paul's of vast size—and the Companies' Halls alone might have afforded refuge to a population greater than that left homeless. Less than a dozen such buildings in all had been reached by Sunday's flames. The flight on Monday was to the fields, few people choosing to add to their own cares and anxieties the duty of hospitality to neighbours ; and still fewer were those into whom the panic of fire had struck deep willing to trust themselves and their belongings anywhere in the burning city.

Slow progress in flight was at best possible. Often, indeed, none could be made, the multitude of carts and loads in the streets obstructing those who sought to escape, as well as hindering the few who laboured to put out the fire. Had there been a single broad, straight thoroughfare east and west, and another north, London might have emptied its population with less difficulty. The City, with its narrow, tortuous ways, seemed designed

to prevent people getting out. There was, indeed, no
great peril to life. The cause of all the confusion lay
deeply rooted in human nature, in the overmastering
desire of each man to remove as much of his goods as
could be saved from the flames, leaving the Fire to go
its own way. These first excited bands of people, making
all possible haste to leave the City for the safety of the
open country, had seen the Fire overwhelm their own
dwellings ; and they were but the forerunners of a greater
pilgrimage. The exodus which began on Monday increased
in volume as the evening approached, and lasted throughout the night. Ceaselessly it continued during Tuesday,
the worst day of panic.

In the turmoil of the Fire the City Wall became an
obstruction, blocking the way of people who were anxious
only to reach the fields.

About the gates two crowds mingled. From the edge
of the Fire and far in advance of it came a doleful stream
of humanity, men transformed into beasts of burden, led
horses equally loaded, carts piled high with household
goods ; the men hot and excited, shoving, fighting, swear-
ing. In their ears was the roar of the flames, which
behind them leapt from conquest to conquest. The thud
of falling houses added to the terrors of the flight, though
still in the daylight the Fire seemed so little spectacularly
to have accomplished so much. Women and children
bore their lesser burdens, for at such a time every shoulder
had value. There were many to whom the Fire offered
only the prospect of profit, and their greed to make the
most of the people's distress deadened the better sense
of helpfulness and pity.

" Any money is given for help," writes Vincent ;
" five, ten, twenty, and thirty pounds for a cart, to bear
forth into the fields some choice things, which were ready
to be consumed, and some of the countrymen had the
conscience to accept of the highest price which the citizens
did then offer in their extremity. I am mistaken if such
money do not burn worse than the fire out of which it was
rak'd." There is hardly a letter sent out of London
which does not condemn the extortions of these soulless
harpies. Says one writer—

" Many had paid out their all on Saturday, their pay

day, and those who had then drained themselves were
certainly put to great straits, being either forced to give
one part [of their goods] to carry away the rest or to
leave all to the fire.   The mercies of the fire were cruel to
all that it came near ; the flight from it gave opportunity
for miscarriage of thousands of pounds' worth of goods,
and to many thefts of goods lodged in open places, fields
and others, for perfect riddance out of danger and hoped
for security from it, which, as it frowardly proved, became
a removal out of the danger of fire into a den of thieves.
The riches of London and the substance of the inhabitants
thereof were as well devoured by suburban thieves and
by the countrymen's extortion for their carts and con-
veyances as by the Fire ; all of which had their respective
share in laying a load upon London's broken back, and
upon the distraction of, and within, it.   Some I hope to
have been very honest and reasonable, but into those
honest and happy hands God knows many of my goods
fell not, nor the goods of thousands more, but into the
hands of those harpies that devoured all they took, and
cried ' Give, give ! ' never to return again." [1]

Taswell's parents, whose house was consumed, lost
goods worth £40 in their hasty removal by persons who
offered their assistance as porters, but were, he declares,
in reality nothing else but downright plunderers.

The flying people pushed a way through another
stream coming into the City—labourers from parts not
yet touched, from the suburbs outside the wall, and from
the surrounding villages, the larger proportion eager for
the money which was so easily to be earned.   The men
from the country brought in their carts.   With them came
many thieves, who lurked in the abandoned shops, pilfering
and stealing among the goods which the tradesmen in
their haste had been compelled to leave behind.   They
had at least this excuse, that what they did not take the
flames would reduce to nothing.

Troops in the streets, assisted by the disciplined
Trained Bands, secured control in the immediate neighbourhood of the Fire.   Beyond its limits confusion grew
worse as the hours passed, and still the flames made headway.   The citizens accepted the presence of the military

[1] Waterhous, *Short Narrative of the Fire*, p. 30.

as relieving them of what should have been a first duty, and it became evident that for checking the spread of the Fire the authorities could rely only upon their own men, and such others as could be hired. But a problem still more grave confronted those upon whom responsibility rested. The broken roads made many places impassable, trenches being left open where the water pipes had been laid bare and cut to get at the supply. Horses plunged and fell, and at times carts loaded with salved goods had to be abandoned and burnt where they stood, owing to the impossibility of farther progress.[1] The afternoon had not far advanced when an order was given that henceforward no carts were to be admitted to the neighbourhood of the Fire.

In taking this extreme course, the magistrates sought to serve a double purpose, believing that thereby they might compel the people to assist in subduing the Fire, and at the same time avoid the entire blocking of the streets which was threatened. It failed to effect the first of these ends, and the next day was rescinded. The determination to save whatever possessions could be handled proved too strong to be overborne. The result was a return to primeval conditions. The rich became abject, the poor insolent. The brawny porter measured the capacity of his muscle and the breadth of his back to carry a load against the money-bags of the merchant citizen, and made his bargain, knowing that for once there had come into his life a moment when no longer he was the under dog. There was work for all who could give this service, the only service which counted.

[1] *Warhafftiger Bericht von der grossen Feuers-Brunst.* (Broadside), Nuremberg [? 1666].

CHAPTER V

THE Fire burnt back slowly against the strong east wind, which blew unobstructed over the open expanse of the river, protecting the stores below bridge ranged along its bank. Not until six o'clock on Monday evening did the flames reach Billingsgate, though the quays lay scarcely one hundred and fifty yards distant from the seat of the outbreak in Pudding Lane. Away from the Thames they made greater headway. The church of St. Mary-at-Hill had already been attacked, and when darkness fell was largely destroyed, with the still considerable remains of the Abbot of Waltham's inn adjoining, and all day a strenuous contest had waged for the preservation of St. Dunstan's-in-the-East.

John Dolben, Bishop of Rochester and Dean of Westminster, there gave to the frightened citizens an example of what resolute men might accomplish.

Dolben was one of those soldier priests of whom the Civil War produced many. He had joined the Royalist Forces round King Charles I.'s standard at Oxford, and while carrying the colours at Marston Moor received a musket ball in the shoulder. Later he was in York when the city was besieged by Fairfax, and a shot wound in the thigh, breaking the bone, laid him helplessly aside while the King's fortunes toppled to disaster. Often during the strife he had stood sentinel. The peril of the Fire revived the soldier spirit beneath the cassock. Assembling the Westminster School boys in a strong company, he marched at their head through the City to the eastern limits of the Fire, and there kept them hard at work for many hours fetching water from the back of St. Dunstan's. They extinguished the flames in the houses crowded closely together, and the church isolated by their efforts, and conspicuous over the City by reason of its high leaden steeple, stood after the Fire of London was out, grievously defaced, it is true, but not the mere ruin to which so many others were reduced.

St. Dionis Backchurch was left with bare walls when the Fire burnt at evening down Fenchurch Street. Burials in the littered ground shortly afterwards indicate the havoc wrought; Francis Tryon, merchant, " in the ruins of the chancel," Richard Cooke, " in the ruins of the body of the church "—there are other entries of like significance in the register. The flames consumed Turners Hall, then standing in Philpot Lane.

Leadenhall had been new built by Simon Eyre, a fifteenth-century civic magnate, and was made a storehouse for arms during the Civil War. The City apprentices in 1648 invaded Leadenhall and mastered the magazine, crying out " For God and King Charles ! " It was saved from the Fire with only its western front damaged, thanks to the enterprise of an Alderman who deserved well of the City. His name cannot be recalled. Stepping up with a hatful of money, he threw it among the people, encouraging them to renewed effort; " he alone there, under God, gave a check to the Fire," says an onlooker.[1] This was the first point at which the Fire was stopped, making no further progress ; the first definite result to be shown after forty-eight hours' conflict with the flames. Leadenhall sheltered East India House, and it stood untouched. The East India Company were, indeed, fortunate above the majority of merchants, for they lost in the Great Fire of London only their saltpetre warehouse and their pepper, all their other stores, worth in the bulk a fabulous sum, having escaped the conflagration.

Westward along the river the Fire was flaming at nine o'clock that Monday evening in Baynard's Castle, by Blackfriars, a grey fortress-palace, built by Humphrey Duke of Gloucester in 1428, which had replaced the earlier castle of Robert FitzWalter, Banneret of the City in the reign of King John. The name survives in Baynard's Castle Ward, but few people recall to-day that, until the Fire, this stronghold stood guard at the western end of

[1] John Rushworth's Letter in *Notes and Queries*, 5th ser., v, 307.

the walled City as austerely as did the Norman Tower of London at the east. Its stone turrets, pierced with windows, rose high and gaunt at the water's edge, and boat stairs stretched over the tide. King Henry VII., liking this palace by the waterside, attempted to transform its frown and render it more fitting for Royal use; but still the frown remained. Richard III., with crafty simulation of unwillingness, accepted the English Crown in Baynard's Castle—

> Alas, why would you heap these cares on me
> I am unfit for state and majesty:
> I do beseech you, take it not amiss;
> I cannot nor I will not yield to you.

Its stones were the stuff of England's history, and every one must have been known to Shakespeare, whose house in Ireland Yard, and the Blackfriars Theatre, were close by. Wolsey, not yet at the zenith of his power, pleaded before Henry VIII. at Baynard's Castle. Queen Jane lost a realm when the Council of State, assembled there, pronounced against her. Elizabeth was Lord Pembroke's guest for a water party.

"The flinty walls of Baynard's strong built castle, thought by the inhabitants that westward dwelt a powerful garrison against the flames, yield like a paper building to the Fire," wrote Wiseman.[1] It burnt all through the night, and was still ablaze at seven o'clock next morning. Baynard's Castle, with all its memories, was lost to London. The walls, broken and threatening collapse at any moment, were speedily thereafter pulled down, leaving upstanding two turrets that were substantially repaired for habitation, one of which survived until 1720, and fragments of the lower structure, built into dwelling-houses, till the beginning of last century, when the site was cleared for the premises of the Carron Iron Company.

The time of the outbreak, when darkness had already fallen, the height and mass of the building, its position at the water's edge, all combined to make the destruction of Baynard's Castle the most gorgeous spectacle of the Fire of London. Flames ran along the wide façade from window to window till all the river front was sheathed in fire, and

---

[1] Sam. Wiseman, *Short Description of the Burning of London,* 1666.

above the battlements leapt roaring into the skies, fed
from the seething cauldron below. It is a mere empty
shell that is portrayed in Hollar's engraving made after
the Fire. Imagination will fill out the sparse references
left by contemporaries ; will picture the fierce light cast
over the moving water ; the tideway crowded with boats ;
the anxious, upturned faces ; the heat and the noise ; and,
by contrast, the darkened area back from the river bank,
fogged by smoke, whereon destruction's work had been
done and there was nothing left to burn. With the turn
of the tide pools of blazing tallow and fragments of over-
toppled timber houses, still burning, floated by. Far
away beyond Billingsgate, little short of a mile distant,
bright flame again marked the Fire's eastern extremity,
and still it crept onward.

The water's edge was illuminated by isolated fires,
which burnt for days thereafter among stores of oil, coal,
tallow, and other combustible stocks brought up by the
ships.

A great curving bow, stretching from Blackfriars to
Threadneedle Street and Leadenhall, made the line of the
Fire inland. " A dreadful bow it was, such as mine eyes
never before had seen ; a bow which had God's arrow in
it with a flaming point : it was a shining bow ; not like
that in the cloud, which brings water with it, and withal
signified God's covenant not to destroy the world any more
with water : but it was a bow which had fire in it, which
signified God's anger, and his intention to destroy London
with fire." Like the pious Vincent, whose words are
quoted, many of those who watched at night saw in this
appalling conflagration the hand of a higher Power.

Only in the heart of the City was the Fire at this stage
of great depth. Its nucleus was about the Stocks Market
(to-day the Mansion House) and in the narrow ways north
and south of the Poultry and south of Cheapside, where it
burnt in one confused mass. Night had fallen almost
unnoticed by those who stayed amid the heat and swelter
to save their property, and those—fewer in number—
who still laboured to fight the flames. Light was not
wanting, for the blaze illuminated the streets like the sun
at noon. Again I turn to Vincent for an onlooker's account
of the dreadful spectacle—

" If you opened your eyes to the opening of the street, where the fire was come, you might see in some places whole streets at once in flames, that issued from the opposite windows, which folding together, were united into one great flame throughout the whole street ; and then you may see the houses tumble, tumble, tumble, from one end of the street to the other with a great crash, leaving the foundations open to the view of the heavens." He likens the noise of the Fire to the passage of a thousand iron chariots beating together upon the stones.

Evelyn describes the night sky as bearing a fiery aspect, like the top of a burning oven.

The streets were still choked with excited people, whose running to and fro, with the further obstruction of goods which had been thrust out of doors or flung from the windows, made a passage way difficult. There was work for every one who could bear a load. With goods heaped on their backs, or slung from the shoulders, men hurried away to places where carts were permitted to draw up beyond the limits of the Fire. When carts could not be obtained, they plodded along with their burdens right out of the City gates. Others came in to offer their help as porters, exacting rates of hire which every hour became more extortionate. There were places where none could approach, where the Fire consumed everything with irresistible fury, and stone walls, riven and calcined white, stood out with painful intensity amidst the yellow flames and pillars of smoke rising from the burning timber houses.

Soldiers drawn up across the streets at many points prevented both egress and access. In bewilderment the carriers plunged into the maze of narrow courts and alleys to find a means of escape from the conquering flames. The hive was in a turmoil, and as momentarily the noise of the Fire died down, there rose from the streets, loud above all other sounds, a medley of human voices. Neither the fall of night nor the east wind, still blowing freshly, brought any relief from the overpowering heat of the burning city. " The Fire," one wrote, " carried the noise of a whirlwind in it, and was so informed with terror that it surprised the eyes and hearts of men with fear, as well as their houses and goods with flame." [1]

[1] E. Waterhous, *Short Narrative*, p. 54.

LONDON BURNING BY NIGHT

From a German print in the Goss Collection

Little idea of the Fire's extent could be gained by those close at hand. It had grown so vast that a true estimate was possible only from a considerable distance. Seen from any high roof or church tower away by the City's northern wall, the panorama of flame spread out in all its appalling significance.

Masses of close buildings lay at the spectator's feet, not yet involved, but obviously awaiting destruction. No work of men's hands could stay the approach of flames like these, with the wind ever driving them on. Beyond the house roofs still intact flames shot into the sky in a long quivering line, throwing up myriads of sparks, and lighting with a weird incandescence the clouds of smoke which rolled away. A bright moon had shone during the smaller fire of Sunday night, lighting the task of Pepys as he carried his household goods at Seething Lane into his garden in readiness for removal. On Monday night the moon was no longer visible in the yellow glare.

Evelyn found language inadequate for the scene. " Oh, the miserable and calamitous spectacle ! such as haply (he writes) the world had not seen since the foundation of it, nor be outdone till the universal conflagration thereof. God grant mine eyes may never behold the like, who now saw about 10,000 houses all in one flame ! The noise and cracking and thunder of the impetuous flames, the shrieking of women and children, the hurry of people, the fall of towers, houses, and churches, was like a hideous storm ; and the air all about so hot and inflamed, that at the last one was not able to approach it, so that they were forced to stand still, and let the flames burn on, which they did, for near two miles in length and one in breadth." [1] Others, too, have described the splendid horrors of the night.

Away from the actual flames the City presented a spectacle that must have imprinted itself upon the memory of those who witnessed it. Above the general level of the house roofs, where towers and church spires rose the stone face square to the Fire reflected an intense light. So over

[1] Evelyn's *Diary*, 1666, Sept. 3. The diarist, recording his impressions, enlarges the actual facts : at no time were ten thousand houses burning together, nor did Monday's line of fire, great as it was, extend two miles in length.

London, beyond the Wall to its farthest extremity, each steeple stood up as a white lamp above the darker mass of the buildings. Far as the eye reached this illumination of the spires extended, with the visual effect, not of throwing them back, but of drawing all in close together. The larger part of a hundred towers flashed back a hundred signals to the burning City.

The Fire had already mastered nearly one-half of the City within the Wall. Fear that it could not be kept from the Liberties became acute. At midnight Lord Manchester, Lord Hollis, and other magistrates made a hasty survey of Fleet Street, beyond the Fleet River, and an hour later ordered the pulling down of some houses in Whitefriars.

New outbursts of fire disclosed where some large and important building had been attacked. A great bunch of flame rose out of Baynard's Castle, at the western extremity by the river, and burning in front of it were two churches, St. Benet Paul's Wharf and St. Peter Paul's Wharf, by Thames Street. The former contained Inigo Jones's marble monument, which was destroyed with the church. The Fire reached out to Derby House, which Queen Mary had granted in 1554 to the Heralds for their College, leaving it a blackened ruin, but thanks to the diligence of the Officers at Arms the rolls and records of chivalry were saved with insignificant loss,[1] and were given temporary lodging at Whitehall by the King.

Woodmongers' Hall, by the waterside, was alight, and on Lambeth Hill Blacksmiths' Hall belched its flames into the open churchyard of St. Mary Magdalen.

Old Fish Street burnt throughout its length, the flames continuing along Knightrider Street till they died down among the debris which covered Cannon Street, already levelled by the morning's fire. Two important churches were consumed here. St. Nicholas Cole Abbey, built upon Old Fish Street, and St. Nicholas Olave were close neighbours. Cole Abbey church, an ancient fabric, stood so low where the land by centuries' accumulation had risen about it that worshippers descended by steps to the nave. It had passed into the patronage of the Crown at the Restoration, on the attainder and execution of Colonel

[1] Petition of the Kings, Heralds and Pursuivants at Arms to the King, 1670, Dec. Pepys's *Diary*, 1666, Dec. 16.

Francis Hacker, to whom the advowson had belonged. It was to him that the warrant for the execution of Charles I. was addressed, and he had commanded the guard before Whitehall at the final scene.

The Fire was in the foot of Friday Street, whence it burnt to Cordwainers Hall, and was flaming up Bread Street towards Cheapside, leaving beneath heaped ruins the beautiful vault of Gerrard's Hall —the home of Gerrard the Giant, famous among London's fabled monsters.[1] It survived to be destroyed by vandals of the nineteenth century. Early as the days of Edward I. the bakers of London had held their market in Bread Street, being forbidden to sell bread at their houses or shops, but the custom had fallen into disuse, and at the time of the Great Fire the thoroughfare was chiefly occupied by prosperous merchants, whose signs swung out with those of many popular taverns : the Three Cups, the Star, and the George were here. Above the mass of burning houses the towers of two

TAVERN SIGN OF GERRARD THE GIANT.

churches stood out conspicuously, white in the intense light. In Allhallows Bread Street Milton was baptized. You may read the entry in the register, which was saved from the fire—

> The xxth day of December, 1608, was baptized
> John the sonne of John Milton the Scrivener.

A modern tablet erected on a block of offices marks where the church stood. Milton's father had a house in Bread Street with the sign of the Spread Eagle. It was destroyed in the Great Fire, and its site cannot now be identified, but the existence till recent years of Spread Eagle Court, near where Bread Street enters Cheapside, probably indicates the location. According to Aubrey, a contemporary, " The only inducement of several foreigners

[1] The familiar story of this London giant is told by John Stow. The tavern sign is in the Guildhall Museum.

to visit England was to see the Protector Cromwell and Mr. John Milton, and they would see the house and chamber where he was born." This was, of course, before *Paradise Lost* was written.

St. Mildred Bread Street burnt with the neighbouring church of Allhallows. The Fire, consuming the church and entire parish of St. John the Evangelist, was more cruel than the Plague, for the bills of mortality show that in the previous year this was the one City parish that escaped the infection.

Near by, at the edge of the Fire's deep " bow," flames rose from St. Mary Aldermary. That this was a large and distinguished church may be concluded from the present edifice. It is the only City church known to have been designed as a copy of that destroyed in the Great Fire, though it cannot now be told how far Wren obeyed the proviso of Henry Rogers, a benefactor who left £5000 for the rebuilding with that express direction. St. Mary's differs from every other of Wren's ecclesiastical structures. The earlier church had been built by Henry Keeble, Lord Mayor, who died in 1518. Modern street improvements have made St. Mary Aldermary, with its high tower, one of the few conspicuous churches in the City.

North of the Poultry the Fire, threatening each moment to enter Cheapside, met with a formidable obstruction of stone buildings, and for hours made no farther advance. Flame rose and fell, searching the walls and lighting the now roofless chambers of what was still a corner of monastic London, surviving the Reformation. This had been the College of St. Thomas of Acon. The religious property was acquired by the wealthy Mercers Company from King Henry VIII. at the Suppression, and they retained St. Thomas's Church, on the rear ground, as Mercers Chapel. It was a perfect example, exquisitely wrought, of a great period of ecclesiastical architecture. There, too, was kept the grammar school. Mercers Hall, standing towards Cheapside, was an early sixteenth-century structure, erected by Sir John Allen over a vaulted chapel.

The Mercers premises filled the whole space between Old Jewry and Ironmonger Lane, save where at Old Jewry corner stood St. Mary Colechurch, " builded (says Stow) upon a vault above ground, so that men are forced to ascend

up thereunto by certain steps." St. Mary's was not re-
erected after the Fire, but its name is lodged imperishably
in London annals. Peter of Colechurch (curate or chantry
priest of this church) built old London Bridge.

The Fire, confined by the stone walls and unable
for the time to conquer them, raged with the utmost
fierceness. Everything not actually of stone was consumed, the timber used in floors and roofs and the smaller
buildings feeding the flames. Leaping high into the night
sky, these dominated the lesser fires burning all around.
The Mercers Company still possess their famous Legh
Cup, presented by Sir Thomas Legh, which bears the
London hall-mark, 1499, and also their historic silver yard
measure. Much of their prized old plate was, however,
destroyed, no less than two hundred pounds of silver,
melted into shapeless masses, being afterwards dug out of
the ruins, and sold by way of commencing a fund for
rebuilding the hall. Incidentally the Great Fire shattered
the last link of the long association with the Mercers of the
sea-trading Company of Merchant Adventurers, chartered
by Edward I., whose office under Mercers Hall was consumed with the rest. A relic of the connection is preserved
in the Master's hammer, which with other arms bears those
of the Merchant Adventurers.

Pepys, passing by on Wednesday—" our feet ready to
burn, walking through the town among the hot coals "—
picked up in the street a piece of the coloured glass from
Mercers Chapel windows, prizing it as a curiosity. It lay
about in heaps, so melted and buckled by the Fire as to
look like parchment.

Across Threadneedle Street, creeping onwards in the
direction of the City wall, was the northern horn of the
crescent of bright flame which had its western extremity
in Blackfriars.

So far as the City had yet emptied itself, the rush of
people had been chiefly into Moorfields and Finsbury
Fields. These were large level spaces beyond the City's
northern wall ; incidentally the drying ground of London's
laundresses—what most impressed Sir William Davenant
about Moorfields, two or three years before the Fire, were
their " acres of old linen, making a show like the fields of
Carthagena when the five months' shifts of the whole fleet

are washt and spread." London was perilously open to attack from this ground, and traces still remained of the formidable line of military works erected there for its defence in the Civil War. More lasting than these mounds was the drainage which had been carried out to render the ground hard for the movements of artillery. Much, too, had been done by the City authorities in the reign of James I. in covering part of the soil with pleasant walks, and converting the marshes into a place of recreation for the citizens.

The advantages of all this work came to be realized when the refugees from the flames fled into Moorfields. The place offered no shelter, but otherwise was not inhospitable. A legend that John Bunyan drew inspiration for his pen picture of the Slough of Despond from the swamp north of London is probably untrue, but there is contemporary evidence of its evil condition early in the same century, when it was described as " a most noisome and offensive place, a rotten, moorish ground, burrowed and crossed with deep stinking ditches and noisome common sewers."

Homeless London camped that night wherever open ground was available, the greatest assemblage being in Moorfields and Finsbury. They were the largest spaces near at hand. Few of the fugitives had troubled to bring covering, or had, indeed, thought of it, their chief anxiety having been to save from the flames the most valuable of their movable possessions. Thousands of London's citizens lay down beside their goods, heaped anywhere on the ground, to snatch brief intervals of broken sleep under the stars. A common calamity obliterated all distinctions of rank and wealth. Rich and poor herded together. Most fortunate was the poor man, who had small loss to bemoan, and whose life had inured him to the hardship which of a sudden had become the lot of all.

Still out of the gates through the night a line of exiles continued to stream, apparently interminable, moving slowly with their hampering loads. The rough camp forming outside the City increased in area as each hour passed. No rain fell, but a wind, unnaturally heated, blew into the faces of groups of burdened men, women and children, stumbling along.

Behind them London Wall stood up, bare and unencumbered by houses, lit by the universal glare. Over its level line flames leapt high into the sky, and the dense smoke that rose, illuminated by sparks, and drifted away, gave the illusion from a distance that the entire City was on fire. All separate sounds were merged into a sullen, consistent roar, like the wash of a tremendous tide. Frequent explosions and the crash of falling walls made the effect still more impressive.

CHAPTER VI

THE DAY OF LONDON'S TRAGEDY

THE destruction of Cheapside, which began with daybreak, gave a dramatic opening to Tuesday, the 4th September, the most momentous and terrible in its results of all the days of the Fire. It witnessed the burning of St. Paul's Cathedral and of the Guildhall, and the Fire bursting through the City Wall into the Liberties ; a great body of flame, still driven onward by the relentless wind, sweeping over an area larger than that which had been cleared on the two preceding days. Lord Arlington gave expression to the general despair in a despatch sent off that morning. " The fire has burnt as far into the body of the City as St. Paul's, with such violence that no art or pains can meddle with it ; all our hopes are now, under God, in cutting off a part of the town along by Holborn Bridge, and so down to Bridewell, to see whether we can save this." [1] Hardly was the ink dry on the paper before even these slender hopes were defeated.

The Fire had been very near Cheapside all night. A temporary check was occasioned at the eastern end by the stone-built Mercers Chapel, but to the goldsmiths and other wealthy merchants of this famous thoroughfare, watching with nervous apprehension for their own fortunes, the roar told of the flames' steady approach along Friday Street, Bread Street, Soper Lane and other tributary streets to the south. And still more ominous to London were flames creeping down from the north, where there were separate small fires. Cheapside was the one wide market street of the mediæval walled city that had survived, but little changed, till Charles II.

[1] *State Papers* (*Domestic*), 1666–7, p. 99.

Wide and straight, with a bend where before St. Paul's
stood isolated the little church of St. Michael-le-Querne, its
line was continued by Newgate Street, which also had an
open market space.   A French print of the procession of
Maria de Medici on her arrival in England, here reproduced,
gives undoubtedly an exaggerated idea of the spaciousness
of Cheapside.   But the print preserves the character of
the houses in the time of Charles I., and they had changed
but little—if at all—in the succeeding thirty years till the
Fire.   Cheapside's most striking buildings were Goldsmiths' Row, ten dwelling-houses and fourteen shops
situated on the south side, a little west of Bow Church.
They had been erected by Thomas Wood, a master of the
craft, and Sheriff in 1491.   Stow declared them to be " the
most beautiful frame of fair houses and shops that be
within the walls of London, or elsewhere in England."
Four storeys high they stood, decorated towards the street
with the Goldsmiths' arms, with painted and gilt images
of " woodmen " riding upon monstrous beasts.

Cheapside was the goldsmiths' headquarters.   The
wealth of the street had impressed itself upon the imagination of Paul Hentzner, a German traveller in England in
the last years of Elizabeth's reign.   " It surpasses all the
rest (he says).   There are to be seen in this street all sorts
of gold and silver vessels exposed to sale, as well as ancient
and modern medals, as must surprise a man the first time
he sees and considers them."   It was the show street of
London, the processional way whenever the Sovereign
visited the City.   King Charles I., riding through, had
noticed that certain of the goldsmiths' shops had been
taken by milliners, booksellers, and like meaner trades,
and that goldsmiths had established themselves as far
west as Temple Bar, migrating where rents were cheaper.
Concerned for Cheapside's beauty and significance in
London, the monarch arbitrarily ordered that these
meaner tradesmen should be ejected.   Goldsmiths who
had set up elsewhere were to return, on pain of fine and
imprisonment.

The Standard, or water conduit, in Cheapside survived
till the Great Fire, to be left in ruins as the flames crossed
the street.[1]   Puritan intolerance had overturned the

---

[1] Guildhall archives, *Repertory* 74, fo. 261b.

beautiful Cross, pulled down in 1644 by order of the Long
Parliament, " a noise of trumpets sounding the while " as
the fell work was accomplished. In place of this historic
memorial of the first Edward's love for Queen Eleanor
(so rapid is the descent to the ridiculous) there stood out
another in the street. Howel, a contemporary historian,
records that upon the demolition of this ancient monument
" there was another new one popp'd up in Cheapside, hard
by the Standard, viz., a high square tabie of stone, left in
legacy by one Russel, a porter, and well-minded man, with
this distich engraven—

> God blesse the Porter who great pains doth take,
> Rest here, and welcome when thy back doth ake.

" Cheapside is all in a light fire in a few hours' time
(writes Vincent). From Soper Lane, Bow Lane, Bread
Street, Friday Street, and Old Change the fire comes up
almost together, and breaks furiously into the broad street,
and most of that side of the way was together in flames, a
dreadful spectacle ! And then partly by the fire which
came down by Mercers Chapel, partly by the fall of houses
cross the way, the other side is quickly kindled, and doth
not long stand after it." A glance at a map shows at
once the supreme importance of Cheapside in the Fire.
Could the great mass of flame burning up from the river
have been stayed on its south side and prevented from
crossing, it would have been a lesser task to save both the
northern and the western parts of the city. The opportunity was wholly neglected. When the Fire was in
Cheapside, not ten men stood by helping or calling for help.[1]
    Warned in good time the goldsmiths had mostly stored
their money and valuables in the Tower of London.[2]
Thanks to this wise precaution, their individual losses were
insignificant compared with those of other tradesmen.
Goldsmiths Hall in Foster Lane was consumed when
the Fire spread so far. The flames spared nothing that
made Cheapside famous ; but to the living generation,
not the goldsmiths' shops, not Bow Church, but the taverns
we would by choice recall, if choice there could be. What
would we not give for any substantial relic, spared by the

---

[1] John Rushworth's Letter.
[2] Lord Hothfield's MSS. (*Hist. MSS. Comm.*, p. 85).

From La Serre's "Entree Royalle," 1638

CHEAPSIDE BEFORE THE GREAT FIRE

Fire, of the old Mermaid Tavern, though it be but a single room that we might enter and find preserved just as it was when Shakespeare and Ben Jonson and Middleton and Beaumont sat there ?—

> What things have we seen
> Done at the Mermaid ! heard words that have been
> So nimble, and so full of subtle flame,
> As if that every one from whence they came,
> Had meant to put his whole wit in a jest,
> And had resolv'd to live a fool the rest
> Of his dull life ; then when there hath been thrown
> Wit able enough to justify the town
> For three days past ; wit that might warrant be
> For the whole city to talk foolishly
> Till that were cancell'd ; and when that was gone,
> We left an air behind us, which alone
> Was able to make the two next companies
> (Right witty, though but downright fools) more wise.

Francis Beaumont sent to Ben Jonson these familiar lines upon the old tavern.   Did but a single room of the Mermaid survive to-day it would, I fancy, be a place of cosmopolitan resort in London attracting more pilgrims even than visit Westminster Abbey.   Old it was even in 1666, and timber-built, no doubt, with stout oaken frames and rough plaster over laths and high roof gables, so would burn furiously, for the house is mentioned as early as 1462, and stood back from the highway, with entrances in Cheapside, Bread Street, and Friday Street.   Nothing had changed since Shakespeare had known it.   The Great Fire of London spared not a stick.   Other taverns besides, to London's irreparable loss, perished in this time—

> The Mitre in Cheapside, and then the Bull Head,
> And many like places that make noses red,

as jovial Ben Jonson's couplet describes them.   The Mitre, unlike the Mermaid, was not rebuilt.   This too, was a fifteenth-century house, standing by the Great Conduit. The Bull Head in Cheapside had its glorious day when Monck, preparing for the Restoration, made it his head-quarters : "Multitudes of people followed him there, congratulating his coming into the City, making loud shouts, bonfires, and ringing of bells."   The Half Moon in Cheapside was burnt in the Great Fire, rebuilt, and again destroyed by fire in 1821. To list all would be wearisome when the Mermaid, preserving the very spirit of Shakespeare's London, stands in memory—

> Souls of poets dead and gone,
> What Elysium have ye known,
> Happy field or mossy cavern,
> Choicer than the Mermaid Tavern ?

Much else was lost in Cheapside. The street which had signified so much in five centuries of London's history (and it would take another volume to tell all) passed out of existence in the Great Fire of 1666. It could not be recalled ; and, in truth, those who rebuilt on the ground, with plain brick and stiff formality, made no attempt to revive its ancient picturesqueness. A typical house erected immediately after the Fire still stands (No. 37) bearing upon its front a carved stone sign of the Chained Swan. I find in a sentence of a letter penned while the ruins were still hot all that is needed to convey a sense of the utter desolation wrought : " You may stand where Cheapside was, and see the Thames ! " [1]

St. Mary-le-Bow, left roofless, with the choir destroyed and tower blackened by flame and smoke when the Fire had passed,[2] represented more than a parish church— " more famous," says Stow, " than any other parish church of the whole city or suburbs." Its rank as second in importance only to the Cathedral of St. Paul itself rests upon the jurisdiction enjoyed for so many centuries by the Court of Arches established there.* To-day St. Mary-le-Bow's tall steeple, and its great dragon vane turning with every change of the wind, are known to thousands of people who would have difficulty in naming another City church. To be born within sound of Bow Bells gives the birthright to a Londoner.

The old church was but mean and low, and did not stand out to Cheapside, as does its successor. The tower rose at the south-west angle. It had served mediæval London as a beacon to guide the few solitary travellers who frequented the streets after nightfall, lamps being shown in the lantern pinnacles. The Norman crypt, from

---

[1] Le Fleming MSS. (*Hist. MSS. Comm.*, p. 41).
[2] *The Dreadful Burning of London*, by J. G., 1667.

which the church takes its name, was happily spared to us by the Fire, and by Sir Christopher Wren, whose habit when dealing with early buildings was to spare but little. It is one of the most perfect relics of ancient London that survives. The vaulting consists of a large number of intersecting arches (or " bows ") springing from fine Norman columns, and partly supported by basement walls which appear to contain still earlier work. The steeple is known in detail from its representation upon a silver church seal, bearing date 1580, which was turned up when the debris after the Great Fire was searched. It is of interest to recall that Wren designed for his new church an open stone colonnade upon Cheapside between the tower and Bow Lane, which would have

OLD BOW CHURCH TOWER, CHEAPSIDE.
(*From a silver seal.*)

been a striking architectural feature, but had not the means at disposal to take the land required from the shops.

The baptismal register (the vestry minutes were burnt) has this entry—

Kasia, ye daughter of Morgan Dandy was borne 2 Sept. 1666 (being ye day ye dreadful Fire began in London) and baptzd. in ye Country.

Two days after the flames were in Cheapside, and the infant Kasia and her suffering mother, carried on a bed through the streets surging with people, left their home to its fate.

St. Peter Chepe was not rebuilt, and its destruction in the Fire has left a little oasis of green churchyard familiar to all City men by the Wood Street corner, where a plane tree bursts into leaf in summer, and Wordsworth heard a thrush singing. The three dwarf houses standing before the plane tree are the tiniest buildings in Cheapside, and, indeed, of the whole City, for each consists of a shop and a single room above. They date from 1687, having been raised upon the site of a certain " Long Shoppe " which the parishioners obtained license so long ago as 1401 to erect in front of their church.[1]

South of Cheapside the City was in flames, and far distant as the river stores and cellars along its bank continued burning, that day, and the morrow, and for days afterwards. Add to this other bodies of fire almost as large, advancing west and north with extraordinary rapidity, a fierce roar accompanying their onrush, and one may begin to understand the appalling condition of London on the third day that it burnt—the third and greatest day of the Fire ; the mass of the Fire, treble as great as had been seen in the daylight hours of Monday, ten times as great as when the sun went down on Sunday on a city which had been roused to a state of feverish alarm, but not yet to despair. The heat, even far out on the Thames, became insupportable. Myriads of live sparks whirled in the hot air currents, and descending on dry buildings, lighted innumerable separate fires, until the one great conflagration known as the Fire of London, which it has been possible hitherto to follow in its progress, began to lose all tangible shape. The east wind, so terrible and persistent, blew harder than before. That day, on the coast, several Dutch sail were blown ashore between Deal and Walmer. It was the expiring effort of the storm before it died away to calm, and against flames driven by a raging wind, human effort could little avail.

The lighter debris carried up blackened the whole of the remaining town where it fell, laying over houses and gardens a mantle of soot and charred fragments ; and these flying witnesses of the Fire spread across a wide belt of surrounding country. A correspondent of Viscount Conway at Kensington wrote that his walks and gardens were almost covered with the ashes of papers, linen, and pieces of ceiling and plasterwork blown thither by the tempest. " Had your lordship been at Kensington you would have thought—for five days together, for so long the Fire lasted—it had been Doomsday, and that the heavens themselves had been on fire ; and the fearful cries and

---

[1] On the back wall of the houses, raised high, is a stone tablet, which those who climb may read as follows :—

<table>
<tr><td>Erected at ye sole cost and charges</td><td>WILLIAM HOWARD,</td></tr>
<tr><td>of the parish of St. Peter's Cheape</td><td>JEREMIAH TAVERNER</td></tr>
<tr><td>AoDni 1687.</td><td>Churchwardens.</td></tr>
</table>

Photo. by Mr. Lionel Gowing

THREE TINY HOUSES IN CHEAPSIDE
Built in 1687, these are the only surviving examples of " the first and least sort of building,"
of two storeys, for by-streets and lanes, authorised by the Rebuilding Act, 1667. Each
consists of two rooms only

howlings of undone people did much increase the resemblance. The loss is inestimable. I believe there was never any such desolation by fire since the destruction of Jerusalem, nor will be till the last and general conflagration." [1]

Lady Carteret told Pepys that an abundance of pieces of burnt paper were driven by the wind as far as Cranbourne, in Windsor Great Park. Among others, she took up one printed scrap whereon remained no more than the significant words, " Time is it is done." Out even to Henley and Beaconsfield little pieces of scorched silk and paper were deposited.

The King that day directed a warrant to issue for removing the Exchequer into Surrey, at Nonsuch. The Queen-Mother, anxious for her safety at Somerset House, arranged to leave at six o'clock next morning up-river for Hampton Court. Here, in the Strand, in the privacy of her apartments, the Queen-Mother was able to worship in her faith within one of the few Catholic chapels permitted in that time of persecution ; and a Spanish co-religionist, with a fervour that outstrips his accuracy, has described how the God of Hosts sheltered the place. " At this very point (says he) the onrush of the flames was suspended : and it is clear and certain that in this way the Almighty (who is Lord of all the elements) wished to rebuke the blindness of the heretics, and to show in what respect he held the sovereign Sacrament of the Altar. A hundred and forty churches of the heretics, including St. Paul's, were destroyed in the flames, but at the sight of a Catholic temple the fire acknowledged itself to be conquered. Fifty and five thousand houses were left in ruins ; it was only at the sight of one of them, one that contained within its walls sanctified memories and the worship of our holy faith, that the flaming tempest, which involved so many in the disaster, allowed itself to be subdued." [2]

The dread spread from the Palace to the most humble tenement. Overnight the Duke of York, alive to the

---

[1] This interesting letter, evidently written about Sept. 8, 1666, and to be found among the State Papers, has been printed by Timbs, *London and Westminster*, 1868, vol. 1, pp. 124–9, and more recently by Besant in his *Survey of London*, Stuart vol.

[2] *Relacion Nueva y Verdadera del formidable incendio que ha sucedido en la ciudad de Londres.* Valencia, 1666. (Printed in Appendix I.)

extreme urgency, had despatched orders to the deputy-lieutenants and justices of the peace of the adjoining counties, requiring them to summon workmen with tools to be in London by break of day. In some churches and public buildings were great hooks for pulling down houses ; these were to be brought up with haste, it having already been found that the only means of stopping the Fire was to afford it no further fuel. Lord Belasyse sent to St. Bride's for ladders, ropes, and axes. The churchwardens of St. Margaret's, Westminster, not having tools available, advanced £11 on Lord Arlington's warrant for the purchase in the parish of pickaxes and other necessaries. The stocks of ironmongers' shops were largely commandeered. One Starkey, otherwise unknown to fame, did exemplary service by providing thirteen dozen pails and sixty brooms in an emergency, " which was the means, under God, of stopping the fire at that place." [1]

While Mercers Chapel and the adjacent stone buildings offered a substantial obstruction to the Fire, the flames, searching the courts and passages north of the Poultry, at the head of Conyhope Alley broke upon Grocers Hall. Four walls stood amid ruins. The Grocers (formerly Pepperers) constituted one of the most important gilds. In the Pipe Rolls the Gilda Pipariorum is mentioned as early as 1180. They were rich enough in 1411 to acquire a permanent home, which first was the chapel, and after-wards the entire mansion, belonging to the FitzWalter family, hereditary Standard Bearers of the City. The great Hall burnt in the Fire was erected in 1427.

A single turret in the grounds, probably a remnant of the old FitzWalter mansion, survived intact amid blackened walls and smoking piles of debris. Luckily the Company's records and muniments had been deposited in this turret. Every other particle of property was destroyed. The Court met in November to receive a report from the Wardens " of the Company's plate melted in the Hall in the late violent and destructive fire, and of the melted parcels taken up and put together," and ordered that the fused silver metal, 200 lbs. in weight, should be sold to the best advantage. Grocers Hall had intimate associa-tion with the Civil War, for when Parliament had been

[1] Rugge's *Diurnal*, in Add. MSS. 10,117.

adjourned by force, the Grand Committee of Safety appointed to watch over the interests of the nation met there to hasten business for the advance of the armies.

Away on the Fire's northern edge Merchant Taylors Hall burnt, only the direction of the wind saving it from complete destruction. The Taylors had acquired the lands and house of Edmund Crepin, situate behind Thread-needle Street, in 1331; and recent excavations and repairs, disclosing the original masonry, have established the most interesting fact that it is the mediæval Hall which still stands, built in the latter half of the fourteenth century. The kitchen and crypt escaped with no serious damage, but the flames necessitated large reparation of the Hall. It becomes impossible to accept without just suspicion the statement of a Commonwealth MS., that at a City feast held under the roof rafters of Merchant Taylors Hall one thousand guests dined together, with an additional three hundred in an adjoining apartment.[1] It is curious to know that so late as 1646 the Hall floor was of earth strewn with rushes, and at that time, being found " inconvenient and oftentimes noisome," it was first paved with red tiles. North was an open garden. The Taylors almshouses on Threadneedle Street were only partially burnt. St. Martin Outwich Church, but a few paces distant, was unharmed.

All the Company's charters, account books dating from 1399, ancient deeds and much else, are preserved; they were removed to the Master's house in Seething Lane. But there was evil disaster in the Treasury, which was wholly consumed, with all its precious contents. What quantity of plate belonging to this rich Company perished, choice pieces of Elizabethan and Stuart craftsmanship, may be judged from two entries of receipts after the Fire : £286 1s. for the fused silver recovered from the debris, and a subsequent £4 19s. for more silver found " in the dust."

The mediæval foundation of St. Anthony's Hospital had stood at the corner where Broad Street turns from Threadneedle Street, possessing the curious franchise that its pigs were licensed rovers of the old City while other swine were kept within bounds; " 'Tanthony's pigs," carrying their tinkling bells, and keeping friendly relations

---

[1] *Notes and Queries*, Ser. I, v. 128.

with all who fed them, were as familiar as were the people. The chapel and sacristy of the brothers, surviving the Suppression, had been granted by the Dean and Canons of Windsor in Edward VI.'s reign to the French congregation, and became their mother church in England. It burnt, with all the houses round about, till the flames, still advancing north, reached out across Throgmorton Street and ignited Drapers Hall.

The Drapers Company, hastily seeking a place of safety for their valuables, concealed their plate in the mouth, or well, of a common sewer running beneath their gardens, and afterwards recovered it intact. The records were also removed. But no human skill could save the Hall from the fierce assault of the Fire.

Already I have indicated the historical interest of this great mansion, which had been built by Thomas Cromwell, Earl of Essex, Wolsey's pupil in statecraft, and his successor in the perilous favour of King Henry VIII. It is described in detail in a deed of the time of purchase in 1541 from the Crown. A turret gate gave admission to the paved court-yard, surrounded by the domestic buildings, and with a winding stair in one angle. An open gallery looked over ; near by was the ladies' chamber. The principal structure was the great Hall, which filled one side of the courtyard, and had two bay windows and clerestory lights, and a dark chamber with lattice windows from which guests could gaze down upon the revelry within.[1] This was a type of the luxurious Tudor house in London, rivalled by none in its magnificence.

Nothing of it withstood the flames of 1666. When the Court reassembled on the 10th September, the piled-up debris being scarcely cold, they recorded in minutes " that the Hall, parlour, and other buildings belonging thereto was all consumed to ashes by the late lamentable and dismal fire." The Renter Warden had the ill-fortune to overlook £446 left in a cupboard of the treasury, and the coin was partly fused by the fire and the rest defaced. It realized when sold only the refining value of the metal.[2]

The Drapers' gardens were on a scale generously pro-

[1] *Lond. & Midd. Archæol. Soc.*, vi, App. 60.
[2] Court Minutes, 1666, Oct. 25.

portionate to the magnificence of their buildings, and how laid out by Cromwell, John Stow has told—

This house being finished, and having some reasonable plot of ground left for a garden, he (Cromwell) caused the pales of the gardens adjoining to the north part thereof, on a sudden to be taken down ; twenty-two feet to be measured forth right into the north of every man's ground ; a line there to be drawn, a trench to be cast, a foundation laid, and a high brick wall to be built. My father had a garden there, and a house standing close to his south pale ; this house they loosed from the ground, and bare upon rollers into my father's garden twenty-two feet, ere my father heard thereof ; no warning was given him, nor other answer, when he spake to the surveyors of that work, but that their master, Sir Thomas, commanded them so to do. No man durst go to argue the matter, but each man lost his land, and my father paid his whole rent, which was 6s. 6d. the year, for that half that was left.

Unconscionable as such dealing was, Cromwell's greed served London well. The gardens so enlarged proved a turning point in the Fire. The flames swept west, where there were houses to afford fresh fuel.

The Fire burnt round the Dutch church at Austin Friars, threatening imminent destruction. The great preaching nave of the friars stands to-day, the largest and almost the sole relic of the majestic buildings with which the four chief Mendicant Orders enriched London ; [1] and near by the little church of St. Peter-le-Poore also escaped, to stand till 1788, mean in condition, built out beyond the houses and obstructing the way, " bearing the appearance of a tavern rather than a place of worship, with its clock hung out in the centre of the street, like the sign of a country inn." In their onrush west the flames consumed St. Margaret Lothbury, leaving nothing save an empty shell, and curiously a single chantry chapel, which survived uninjured, to be afterwards used as a vestry.

Founders Hall, a Tudor building erected at the head of a narrow alley from Lothbury in the troubled early years of the Reformation, was wholly consumed, and all the lands and tenements and many of the movables, books and

[1] A tiny fourteenth-century crypt of the Carmelite Priory is preserved under Brittons Court, Whitefriars, but there is not a stone in place to recall the sumptuous buildings of the Dominicans in Blackfriars, nor the Grey Friars' house in Newgate Street.

papers belonging to the Company,[1] with many merchants' houses near by. Amid the ruins left by the Fire one block stood intact. We learn of " the new buildings in Lothbury " being isolated and saved by the efforts of workmen, incited by a reward of £100 which was paid to them. At Pie Corner, where later in the day the Fire was stayed, they had £50. But such gifts were not always made. Alderman Sir Richard Browne had a chest with about £10,000 in it taken out of the fire, for which service he gave the men who ventured their lives £4. Pepys, dining the following Saturday with Sir William Batten and a great company of neighbours, had " much good discourse ; amongst others of the low spirits of some rich men in the City, in sparing any encouragement to the poor people that wrought for the saving their houses. Among others Alderman Starling,[2] a very rich man, without children, the fire at next door to him in our lane, after our men had saved his house, did give 2s. 6d. among thirty of them, and did quarrel with some that would remove the rubbish out of the way of the fire, saying that they came to steal. Sir W. Coventry told me of another this morning in Holborn, which he showed the King : that when it was offered to stop the fire near his house for such a reward that came to 2s. 6d. a man among the neighbours, he would give but 18d." [3]

Tongues of flame above the house roofs and tall wreaths of smoke ascending still higher bent with the wind. The fires joined up in one roaring conflagration, pressing onward with ever-increasing noise. Could you, standing in burning Cheapside, have looked into any of the streets running north, the same picture would have presented itself. The Fire overtook one after another in its irresistible advance. This was one of the most closely built areas in London, timber houses, their projecting upper storeys almost touching over cobbled alleys or mere foot-passages, being massed together right up to the City Wall, through which the dwellers in the honeycomb found exit into Moorfields

[1] Court Minutes, 1672, Sept. 22.
[2] Sir Samuel Starling, Alderman of Vintry Ward, " a man of good learning, solid judgment, and great courage," but fated to be better remembered for this act of incredible meanness than for his other good qualities.
[3] Pepys's *Diary*, Sept. 8.

and the Artillery Fields by Moorgate and Little Moorgate, and the postern nigh Cripplegate. These were houses in which substantial merchants lived and traded, stocked with the goods of the world, it being then a favourite merchants' quarter, as it remains to-day. Guildhall lay in the midst of the mass, and about it stood half a dozen or more of the Companies' Halls.

An advanced fire-post had been pushed out in Coleman Street, where Sir John Harmor and Colonel Fitzgerald attended, with soldiers and constables assisting. They were driven back helplessly, the Fire advancing from Lothbury engulfing the buildings, too great in magnitude by far to be stopped there, or even checked. The menacing torrent of flame was soon astride the lower end of the street, St. Stephen's Church being ablaze ; then, augmented by flames which came up from Old Jewry and the back of Mercers Chapel, broke furiously upon Guildhall, where for many hours raged the fiercest fire seen in the City's central area.

In 1666 Guildhall had no spacious square before it. The home of civic government was choked on all sides with buildings. "Fair and large," so Stow tells, St. Laurence Jewry occupied its present site. In this famous church Sir Thomas More in early manhood had delivered lectures to which resorted all the learned men of the City. A painting of the martyrdom of St. Laurence, saved out of the old church when the Fire burnt through it, hangs to-day in the vestry. Blackwell Hall, the cloth market, was opposite, and between the two a narrow passage way afforded access to a small courtyard, upon which Guildhall and the Guildhall Chapel opened. Guildhall Yard had another claim to memory, for squeezed tightly in was a famous City tavern destroyed in the Fire, the Triple Tun, commemorated in Herrick's lines to Ben Jonson :

> Ah Ben !
> Say how or when
> Shall we, thy guests
> Meet at those lyrick feasts
> Made at the Sun,
> The Dog, the Triple Tunne ;
> Where we such clusters had
> As made us nobly wild, not mad !
> And yet each verse of thine
> Outdid the meat, outdid the frolic wine.

Much of the ancient Guildhall has survived the Great Fire of London. The crypt, now thrown open to the public, and the great thickness of the walls, seen where windows pierce them, indicate the massive character of this stone structure. The Fire consumed everything above the stone floor save the actual walls; it destroyed the gallery and burst through windows and through the high-pitched roof. Gog and Magog, the City giants, burnt with the rest.[1] All that night Guildhall was raised up above the blazing city, a wonderful apparition. It appeared to Vincent " a fearful spectacle, which stood the whole body of it together in view, for several hours together, after the fire had taken it, without flames (I suppose because the timber was such solid oak) in a bright shining coal, as if it had been a palace of gold, or a great building of burnished brass."

The mediæval walls withstood the test, and they stand to-day, like native rock laved by the flames. Even part of the great oaken roof, which Vincent so picturesquely describes in the height of the Fire, kept its place in charred embers still spanning the wide hall. Wren afterwards, in the costly reconstruction of Guildhall which the Corporation undertook, raised the walls and roof twenty feet, and the new masonry still shows in contrast with the fire-marked stones below. Part of the floor, above the western crypt, was crushed in, and to-day is upheld by brick arches.

Guildhall, so richly stored with knowledge of the past, has no record of London in the Fire. It can tell you, indeed, more of London in four days of Wat Tyler's Rebellion than of those four September days in 1666 when the City burnt. It is uncertain how its precious documents were themselves preserved, but to the skilled masons, unknown and unhonoured, who laid the courses of the vaults so well and truly, there is owing something we can never repay. Little do Londoners realize the debt. We owe to them the history of London. Nothing less than its irreparable loss would have resulted had the City records been consumed, for none of them had been transcribed.

---

[1] Thomas Jordan, the City Poet, who prepared the Mayoral Pageant in 1672, speaks of his wondrous new Giants, which after the show " are to be set up in Guildhall, I hope never to be demolished by such dismal violence as happened to their predecessors "—the " dismal violence " being their destruction in the Great Fire. See also *Repertory* 77, fo. 26b. The Giants now at Guildhall were carved by Captain Richard Saunders in 1707.

John Stow, most painstaking of antiquaries, had looked into a few—and but a few. No transcript had then been made of the *Liber Albus*, the City's White Book, whereon that famous Mayor, Richard Whittington, and John Carpenter, his clerk, had laboured in the early years of the fifteenth century to compile a volume of the City's laws and precedents out of the documents they found scattered and without order ; of the *Liber Horn* and similar early records ; of the four thousand citizens' wills, dating back as early as 1226, and enrolled in the Court of Husting, which have been made available for study by the industry and scholarship of Dr. Reginald Sharpe ; of the so-called Letter Books, which in the same hands have provided historians with a vivid and detailed picture of mediæval City life ; of the Coroners' Rolls and much besides. London to-day possesses the most complete series of historical records of any capital in the world. Had the Great Fire in 1666 burnt down underground at Guildhall the history of London could not have been written, for the material had in that event perished.

I think it is plain that the records were not taken away. Their bulk and weight alone almost forbade it. There is no entry of payment or reward for such service. I found, however, mention of " the booke howses." This cannot have been a library. Whittington had given books to Guildhall to found a library, but these in the reign of Edward VI. the Protector Somerset had seized and never returned. Likely enough the reference is to the muniment rooms. The books in use and the historical records were in the custody of the Town Clerk, and would probably have been kept for safety in the vaults below his office. The fire raged through the offices and apartments, which were grouped about Guildhall with as much confusion as is the case to-day. The Council Chamber, the Lord Mayor's Court and parlour below, the Sheriff's Court, Town Clerk's offices, Hall-keeper's house—all afterwards required re-building.[1] Three days after the Fire was out the Court of Aldermen ordered that the records should be brought to Gresham House. They were fortunately intact.

The Basket Makers Company met at Guildhall, having no hall of its own. Its early history was lost in the Fire :

[1] Guildhall Library MSS., 184, fos. 1–15.

the charter (if any), minute books, and documents all perished, and there survives only a transcript of the Acts and Orders, written in 1618, and the apprentices' roll, commencing September, 1639. A brief entry in the Company's existing books dated the 10th January, 1677, tells that their room and " their chest, with carpets, cushions, silver spoons, books, writings, and other things standing in the same room, were consumed by the dreadful and lamentable fire, to the loss and detriment of the same brotherhood."

The Coopers Company, whose buildings lay immediately at the back of Guildhall, had appointed that day (Tuesday, Sept. 4) for a monthly Court. The flames were at hand ; it was resolved that instead of attending to business all members should carry away to places of safety as much as possible of the writings, plate, linen, pewter and other of the Company's property, and it is owing to this wise and praiseworthy action that the records survive. A week later, being then homeless, the Court met at the Queen's Head Tavern in Bishopsgate. The Hall, timber-built, dated from the last years of King Henry VIII.

A line of fire ran down Basinghall Street till it reached London Wall, and there burnt itself out. The toppling houses, mere flaming tinder in the ungovernable heat, were flanked by three other Halls of City Companies, each built back from the thoroughfare, with its separate court for approach. Masons Hall and Weavers Hall were entirely destroyed, and nothing survives to tell what manner of buildings they were. Girdlers Hall, a middle fifteenth-century structure, had been in John Stow's time " a very handsome building, with an open courtyard, and a garden behind it." The Fire forestalled only by a few years what must have been its inevitable fate, for in 1643 it had fallen into a ruinous condition ; the Company had no money to repair their Hall ; five years later they assessed its greatest value at £40 a year.

The whole length of Milk Street and Aldermanbury was outlined in flames, which pressed through the massed houses about Wood Street and Gutter Lane towards Aldersgate. Late that afternoon the City gate was itself environed in fire. St. Mary Aldermanbury was notable among London churches and of great age, built with a loft

LONDON BURNING BY DAY

over the porch, and possessing a cloister. All was a ruin after the Fire. In the old fabric Milton married his second wife in 1656; but it is as a London link with Shakespeare that St. Mary Aldermanbury is most warmly cherished, for in the little graveyard about Wren's later church still lie the bones of the actors Heminge and Condell, who in veneration of Shakespeare's genius and memory first collected together and edited his plays.

Some part of Wood Street survived the flames, but the Sheriff's Compter there was destroyed. The old cellars of the neighbouring Mitre Tavern are to-day in use by wine-merchants, the Fire having passed harmlessly over them. The tavern burnt, a famous house in its day. Proctor, the landlord, " the greatest vintner for some time in London for great entertainments," and his son, had perished of Plague in the previous year.[1]

Back from the street the fine Hall of the Haberdashers Company was yet another fifteenth-century building lost to London in the Great Fire. The old Hall became a Puritan centre in the City, and within its walls had been founded a flourishing Independent Church, wherein thundered William Strong, John Rowe, Theophilus Gale, Thomas Rowe, and Dr. Gibbon, all eminent divines. The Haberdashers, being rich, were bled in turn by the monarch and by Parliament, till the latter owed the Company £21,000—and never repaid it. Four treasured loving-cups of silver, one dating from 1629, are the chief salvage from the Great Fire, by which the Company suffered grievous loss both in the destruction of its home and of its rent-yielding property.

Above the flames of Wood Street's burning houses two steeples rose. St. Alban's Church stands to-day, rebuilt by Wren. St. Michael's, by Huggen Lane corner, contained one curious relic, a human head, said—on somewhat dubious authority—to be that of King James IV. of Scotland, slain at Flodden Field. Stow relates that at the battle's close the body, wrapped in lead, was brought to the Monastery of Shene, in Surrey, where after the

---

[1] Pepys's *Diary*, 1665, July 31. A house on the site (No. 9) about two hundred years in age, was demolished in 1919 for the widening of Wood Street; the carved arms of the Mercers Company borne on its front are to be reset in the new building. Whittington gave the land to his old Company, the Mercers, who have enjoyed the gift for five hundred years.

Dissolution it was thrown into a waste room among old timber and other rubbish, and he himself saw it.

Since the which time workmen there, for their foolish pleasure, hewed off his head ; and Launcelot Young, master glazier to her Majesty, feeling a sweet savour to come from thence, and seeing the same dried from all moisture, and yet the form remaining, with the hair of the head, and beard red, brought it to London to his house, in Wood Street, where for a time he kept it for the sweetness, but in the end caused the sexton of that church to bury it amongst other bones taken out of their charnel

—surely the strangest story that one may light upon in royal necrology.

The Fire was kept from Cripplegate for the time by blowing up houses with gunpowder. The expedient was first put into practice there and near The Tower. But nothing could check the immense wall of flame driven directly west by the wind, which quickly levelled with the ground the still disreputable quarter that had been allowed to grow up on the site of the dismantled sanctuary of St. Martin-le-Grand. Not a stone of the ancient church which had rung the Curfew for mediæval London was then standing. Saddlers Hall was overwhelmed ; the Company rescued what remained to them of their plate, their burial pall, and a few of their books that were in use at the time, and therefore were easily accessible, all else being lost in a confused pile of bricks, iron and melted lead that strewed the ground.

Foster Lane was the headquarters of the working goldsmiths, who toiled at their trade in the many little shops upon this narrow way. The stone church of St. Vedast offered substantial obstruction to the Fire. Its ancient tower was allowed to stand when the new church was afterwards raised, but in 1694, on account of weakness, it had to come down, and Wren's graceful steeple takes its place. Set in the steeple, unique, I believe, in London, is a clock without a face. All the works are there, and the mechanism raises the hammer of the bell which proclaims the hours, but there are no dials.

Outside the neighbouring St. Leonard's Church, a small thirteenth-century foundation, stood a monument to John

Brokeitwell, who had restored or new built the fabric, bearing this quaint verse so quaintly spelt out—

Al yat wil gud wurkes wurch
Prey for yem yat help thys Church
Geuyng almys : fur Cherite
Paternoster and Ave.

Goldsmiths Hall, in Foster Lane, rebuilt only thirty years before, stood in the Fire's path. The Parliament Committee that sequestered the estates of the Royalists conducted its long proceedings there, and with bitter memories the now dominant party must have watched the flames burning through. " Faith to tell thee, Goldsmiths Hall is damnable rich ; and informers will have the devil and all ! " says an old play.[1]   Sir Charles Doe, acting with prompt decision, obtained the keys of the treasury and took to Edmonton most of the plate, records and portable things of value, but the tables wherein the artificers' marks were struck and the books containing their names and addresses burnt, causing much confusion.   Minutes of the Company convey some idea of the ruin wrought.   Chimneys left tottering were in danger of falling if not secured ; the Warden delivered to Sir Robert Vyner parcels of molten silver and some standard pieces ; a new seal and small seal for the Company were ordered, both having been destroyed in the Fire ; in the winter the south wall fell down, breaking in the vault beneath.

Nothing withstood the fury of the Fire.   The Wax-chandlers Company suffered the loss of their Hall in Gutter Lane, near by that of the Goldsmiths, which they had been at considerable expense in rebuilding only nine years before.   Of Broderers Hall I know only that it perished, and with it most of the Company's records.   Four churches were grouped

BEFORE THE DREADFUL FIRE
ANNO DOMINI 1666
HERE STOOD THE
PARISH CHURCH
OF ST MARY, STAINING

CHURCH MEMORIAL STONE.

together within a stone's throw, and all were consumed. St. John Zachary had been a favourite burial place of the goldsmiths, and within its walls were many

---

[1] Randolph, *Hey for Honesty*, 1651.

monuments of Masters of that Company. A few stones remain. St. Mary Staining has left an open space of green churchyard to mark its site. Of St. Olave Silver Street, there is this and a further reminder, for in the wall is built a memorial stone, gruesomely decorated with a skull and crossbones, bearing the inscription here shown.

THIS WAS THE PARISH CHVRCH OF S⟨T⟩ OLAVE SILVER STREET DESTROYD BY THE DREADFVLL FIRE IN THE YEAR 1666

CHURCH MEMORIAL STONE.

St. Anne and St. Agnes, which had been nearly destroyed by fire in 1548 and rebuilt, burnt just within Aldersgate. In Noble Street, close at hand, was the house built by Serjeant Fleet, Recorder of London in the reign of Queen Elizabeth, and afterwards the residence of Robert Tichborne, Lord Mayor in 1657, who was subsequently tried and convicted of high treason. In the Great Fire, when all the houses about it were consumed, this one escaped its fury. Scriveners Hall burnt in the same street, and of its historical archives only a single folio volume, 1616–25, escaped destruction.

The flames burst through Aldersgate, but the gate itself suffered no great damage, and the Fire, being hemmed in by the stout City wall to right and left, made little headway beyond. Only about thirty houses immediately outside the gate were burnt. St. Botolph Aldersgate was scorched by the flames, wind driven across the open churchyard, as repairs afterwards made indicate. Over the street, the Hall of the Worshipful Company of Cooks stood unharmed at the edge of the Fire.

Aldersgate was no older than King James I. The Scottish monarch, early after taking possession of the British throne, entered the City by this way, beneath the ancient gate, which was much dilapidated and even dangerous. Honour was paid to him when, in 1616, the gate was pulled down and rebuilt. Its chief adornment was a colossal equestrian figure of King James, in relief,

HOUSE IN KNIGHTRIDER STREET, NEAR ST. PAUL'S
The ground floor containing the timber framing escaped destruction in the Great Fire of
London. The upper structure is *circa* 1670

over the central arch, surmounted by the quartered arms of England and Scotland, with figures of the Prophets in deep niches on the side towers.   Beneath that of Jeremiah were inscribed the words (so truly prophetic) of his 17th chapter, 25th verse: " Then shall there enter into the gates of this city kings and princes sitting upon the throne of David, riding in chariots and on horses, they, and their princes, the men of Judah, and the inhabitants of Jerusalem : and this city shall remain for ever."

Tuesday witnessed the flames which had been borne up from the river sweeping across the full length of Cheapside and along Newgate Street, and thence up to the northern Wall, till the whole City burnt from The Tower to Newgate. Dryden expresses in a sentence the extraordinary rapidity of the Fire's advance when he speaks of the flames " wading through the streets."   And far ahead of this great conflagration the Fire, devouring everything, still pressed forward along the Thames side into the Temple and up Fleet Street.

The personal service given by the King and the Duke of York on this day of London's tragedy cannot be too highly valued.   Charles was not cast in the heroic mould, nor was his Royal brother of that stamp.   The supreme peril of the capital brought out in both a display of courage which, perhaps, was little expected, and intensified the loyalty felt towards the monarch.   Undoubtedly the ascendency which the King obtained, and the sublime good sense that he manifested, against every provocation to resort to vengeful measures, did much to calm the people when, after the Fire was out, they came to realize the full measure of their distress.

The King was in the City on horseback from early morning.   He never left it that day.   He rode from place to place, an escort of Guards with him, at times unattended save by a few gentlemen, seeing that orders to man the stations were executed, passing to the very edge at which the Fire was burning, and by word and example encouraging those who toiled amid the oppressive heat to pull down houses or to throw water on the flames.   To do the King justice, he was insensible to peril.   He carried a hundred gold guineas in a pouch swung from his shoulder, and with his own hand scattered the coins among the workmen as a reward and incentive to further effort.[1] Laying regal dignity aside, the King alighted from his horse at some corner where falling buildings added to the common danger, and himself took a share in the work, handling spade and bucket and inspiring the courtiers about him to do the same. Bespattered with mud and dirt, his laced costume dripping with water, his hot face blackened with the universal fire dust but himself alert and tireless—this was another monarch than he whom his people pictured dallying with his mistresses at Whitehall. The hour had brought out the man. Never in his reign did faith in Charles stand higher in the opinion of the London populace than in the trying days of the Fire.

I brush aside the loyal panegyrists and versifiers, who were plentiful; * the truth speaks out in private letters, written with no ulterior thought of ever pleasing the Royal eye. One Henry Griffith says in his letter from London to a relative at Shrewsbury: " Some went to stealing, others to look on, but all stood to the mercy of an enraged fire, which did in three days almost destroy the metropholist (*sic*) of this our Isle, had not God of his infinite mercy stayed the fury thereof, which was done by his Majesty's and the Duke of York's singular care and pains, handling the water in buckets when they stood up to the ankles in water, and playing the engines for many hours together, as they did at the Temple and Cripplegate, which people seeing, fell to work with effect, having so good fellow labourers." [2]

Lord Conway's gossip wrote to him a few days after the Fire : " 'Tis fit your lordship should know that all that is left, both of the City and suburbs, is acknowledged, under God, to be wholly due to the King and the Duke of York, who, when the citizens had abandoned all further care of the place, and were intent chiefly upon the preservation of their goods, undertook the work themselves, and with incredible magnanimity rode up and down, giving orders for blowing up of houses with gunpowder, to make void spaces for the fire to die in, and standing still to see those orders executed, exposing their persons not only to

---

[1] Le Fleming MSS. (*Hist. MSS. Comm.*, p. 42).
[2] This interesting letter is printed in Appendix I.

the multitude, but to the very flames themselves, and the ruins of the buildings ready to fall upon them, and sometimes labouring with their own hands to give example to others : for which the people do now pay them, as they ought to do, all possible reverence and admiration." [1]

The Duke of York has other testimony to his activities equally impartial and sincere. He won the hearts of the people by his indefatigable pains day and night in helping to quench the Fire, handling buckets of water with as much diligence as the poorest man that did assist, wrote John Rushworth, a citizen, with the stinging comment, " if the Lord Mayor had done as much, his example might have gone far towards saving the City." [2] The gentleman attending the Duke of York, one Wind. Sandys, describes his long day spent in the burning streets, from five in the morning till eleven o'clock or midnight, " active and stirring in this business."

All orders signified nothing, says Sandys. " Had not the Duke been present, and forced all people to submit to his commands, by this time I am confident there had not been a house standing near Whitehall. The city [citizens] for the first rank they minded only for their own preservation ; the middle sort so distracted and amazed that they did not know what they did ; the poorer they minded nothing but pilfering ; so the city was abandoned to the fire. The Duke, on Tuesday, about twelve o'clock, was environed with fire ; the wind high, blowed such great flakes, and so far, that they fired Salisbury Court and several of the houses between that and Bridewell Dock, so the Duke was forced to fly for it, and had almost been stifled with the heat." [3]

Dockyardsmen from Woolwich and Deptford were sent in to strengthen the ranks of the soldiers and civilians, tired to exhaustion by their two days' efforts. None had before appeared ; the inspiration was that of the versatile Pepys, and his immediate object the safety of the Navy Office in Seething Lane.* A mere handful of seamen, numbering twenty-eight in all, had been employed since

---

[1] See footnote on p. 99, *ante*.

[2] *Notes and Queries*, 5th Ser., v, 307. See also letter by Robert Southwell to Cornet James Dogherty in Earl of Egmont's MSS. (*Hist. MSS. Comm.*, p. 17).

[3] Letter printed in Appendix I.

Sunday, and had done excellent work with ladders and fire-axes in bringing down houses. Lord Manchester, afterwards commending their good service, naturally made no mention of the fact that their advice had been totally disregarded. This was to use gunpowder in clearing a way before the flames, but it had been deemed too desperate a remedy, till on Tuesday, when more than one-half of the City within the Wall had been destroyed, the expedient was adopted, with entirely satisfactory results. The seamen's practice was to place a barrel full, or nearly full, of powder in each house of a row to be demolished, and ignite it by a train. The force of the explosion lifted each timber structure a yard or so ; the straining frames broke, and the building collapsed flat on the ground where it had stood, with but trifling danger to bystanders. What little fire was caused by the flame was easily stamped out. Pepys bears testimony to the efficacy of the method, though " at first it did frighten the people more than anything else."

Forty more sailors were brought into the City from the Fleet.[1] The troops in the streets were increased. Nor were there wanting considerable numbers of men, lured by the high pay offered, to assist in moving goods and in endeavours to save houses. With the larger part of the City's populace, Tuesday was a day of panic helplessness. Fearful as it had been to be in London on Monday, the second day of the Fire, to those whose homes were in its vicinity, the conditions were now still more alarming. The hot air made breathing painful. Flames sped along with almost inconceivable rapidity, razing whole streets to the ground in two or three hours. New fires broke out at far distant points. The frightened people fled in a general *sauve qui peut*, saving property where possible, in any case life, and leaving vast quantities of goods and stocks to be burnt.

The magnitude of the disaster to London is but poorly expressed by the mere devastation of streets and numbers of burnt houses ; the human element more nearly touches the imagination. In the 13,200 houses destroyed there cannot have dwelt fewer than one hundred thousand people, and to these were added in the flight thousands of

---

[1] *State Papers* (*Domestic*), 1666-7, p. 104.

others, whose sole anxiety was to seek safety when the flames were seen to be approaching their homes.   The mere mass of such numbers is stupifying.   A parade of one hundred thousand troops, drawn up compact in companies and battalions, occupies a great space—I doubt if the British Army before the European War has had such a parade. These people were marshalled in no sort of order, and consisted of those of all ages—men, women, and young children —the strong with the helpless, most of them loaded with personal belongings, and the entire disorderly rout interspersed with carts packed with goods, led horses similarly burdened, coaches and every kind of moving vehicle pressed into the service.   They went out of the City under a single impulse, not knowing whither they were going, without lodging, without shelter, without food.

Such was the exit from burning London.   The long hours dragged wearily in that slow and it might have seemed interminable procession, throughout two whole days and nights while the City emptied itself; yet the wonder is that in the time and conditions so much was accomplished.

It was no longer desirable, even had it been practicable, to keep the citizens in.   The carts were readmitted, and the confusion within the City grew worse.   The lines of refugees streaming towards the gates pressed on through the hot streets.   The rich alone could secure a vehicle, and still many were disappointed.   Half value of the goods saved was not considered too extortionate a charge for the use of a cart.   Better pay half than leave the whole to the flames, the merchant reasoned, and paid the demand. Earlier in the Fire's progress a cart had been obtained for sums ranging from 10s. up to £5.   As much as £40 and £50 was now the price, and even that was given; there is a recorded case of one wealthy householder paying £400 for his removal from the Fire.[1]   The City streets were more complicated in plan than a spider's web, and by every one the flying refugees spread outwards.   With household treasures and furniture piled high, and children seated uneasily on top, perhaps the mother with them, the cart rumbled noisily over the dreadful cobble stones ; obstructed everywhere by other carts and people crowding to get

[1] Waterhous, *Short Narrative*, 1667.

away, turned aside by the soldiers, and at times brought to a dead stop where demolished houses lay in wreckage across the roadway, or great holes gaped in its surface where pipes had been cut for water.

The head of the family trudged alongside the horse, little caring whither he went, but anywhere to get out of the doomed city. He might count himself fortunate. There were many to whom the urgent call to save the sick meant leaving all their worldly possessions to the Fire. Women were seen weeping for their children, fearful that they might be trodden down in the press, or lost in the crowd of people, or exposed to the violence of the flames ; husbands more solicitous for the safety of their wives and children than for their own ; the soldiers brusquely clearing a way with their arms when there was more need to ply buckets ; tradesmen loading their backs.[1] The faces of all men appeared ghastly in the firelight.

In the throng came some poor woman, too ill to stand, borne recumbent on a mattress through the streets. An aged man was carried the same way. " They were bringing forth their wives (some from their childbed) and their little ones (some from their sick bed) out of their houses and sending them into the country or somewhere into the fields with their goods." The strong helped the faltering steps of the weak, a common purpose uniting all. The tragedy of it touched the sympathetic heart of Vincent, whose words I quote. " Scarcely a back either of man or woman that hath strength, but had a burden on it in the streets ; it was very sad to see such throngs of poor citizens coming in, and going forth from the unburnt parts, heavy loaden with some pieces of their goods, but more heavy loaden with weighty grief and sorrow of heart, so that it is wonderful they did not quite sink under their burdens."

They left a city which seemed plainly doomed to annihilation. The flames roared in the wind, and to the sights and sounds of these awful hours was added the sharp crack of powder explosions, followed by the rattle and thud with which a shattered house fell to the ground. Those who looked back into the red heart of the Fire saw houses wreathed in flame and swaying, then toppling headlong into the roadway. The Fire sent up huge volumes of smoke as

[1] Stillingfleet's *Sermon to the House of Commons*, 1666, Oct. 10.

from some Titan's furnace, streaked with flying sparks. A feature for amazement was the great smoke arch which spanned the heavens, extending from burning London to the western horizon, a sulphurous rainbow, symbol of wrath rather than peace; and through it the sun shone red, and yet so dimly that it might be looked at with the naked eye, yielding a fainter light than in an eclipse.[1]

The feverish excitement of the flight was attended with new terrors; a false alarm, born of coward fears of attack by French and Dutch, and passing with lightning speed from group to group. "They believed that all the French in the town (which, no doubt, were a very great number) were drawn into a body, to prosecute those by the sword who were preserved by the fire; and the inhabitants of a whole street would run in a great tumult one way, upon the rumour that the French were marching at the other end of it, so terrified men were with their own apprehensions."[2] At times a new fire broke out ahead of the people, sending them scattering to find another way of escape. Their haste was quickened by a yet more dreadful peril; report spread (born, no doubt, of the noise of frequent explosions) that the Tower of London was firing its cannon into the flames to reduce the whole City, or at least to lay low all the houses about the fortress, and so isolate it.[3] Those who dwelt on the high roads near London at night as they lay in bed heard the carts continually rumbling and posting by.

Away at Enfield after dark the Fire was plainly visible. Even so far distant from London people as they passed along were heard calling out, " Forty pounds for a cart ! " and " Any money for a cart ! " to carry their goods. The light in the sky from burning London was seen at night above forty miles round about.

" As they ran they made a heart-rending murmur; one would need to have been a Nero to have watched such a spectacle without pity," says a foreign observer, describing the flight out of the London streets.[4]

Necessity sharpened men's wits. There was the man whom Vincent saw with great energy rolling a cask of oil

[1] Malcolm's *Lond. Rediv.*, iv, 80.   [2] Clarendon's *Life*.
[3] Letter to Lord Conway, *op. cit.*
[4] *Relatione esattissima del' Incendio Calamitoso, etc.*, 1666.

towards the City gates. Was it oil? One questions whether the top had not been broached for storing more valuable contents, and a form of rolling carriage thus devised older, one imagines, than the axle and wheel.

The exodus spread far. A stranger approaching London might have imagined there was before him a city which had been sacked by some conqueror and left burning. For miles around the ground was strewn with movables of all kinds, which the citizens in their flight had saved from the Fire. Moorfields and Finsbury Fields had the largest aggregation, but the rough camp spread out to Islington and Highgate on the north, to St. Giles's Fields and Soho Fields on the west. Away from the City the people still felt the intolerable heat and dry sharpness of the air, as if they had been in the area of the Fire. Those who had crossed the river in boats took refuge in St. George's Fields, whence they watched London burning. A few refugees found house room with the country people, others sought shelter in miserable huts and hovels, but the greater number —men, women, and children—lay down beside their household goods to snatch what rest they could get under the stars. Fortunately the weather remained dry and warm. " Many without a rag (says Evelyn) or any necessary utensils, bed or board, who from delicateness, riches, and easy accommodation in stately and well-furnished houses were now reduced to the extremest misery and poverty."

Dryden, though himself absent from London when disaster overwhelmed it, has in the *Annus Mirabilis* written the only poetry of value that the Fire inspired—

> Night came, but without darkness nor repose,
>   A dismal picture of the general doom ;
> Where souls, distracted, when the trumpet blows,
>   And half unready with their bodies come.
>
> Those who have homes, when home they do repair
>   To a last lodging call their wandering friends :
> Their short uneasy sleeps are broke with care,
>   To look how near their own destruction tends :
>
> Those who have none sit round where once it was,
>   And with full eyes each wonted room require,
> Haunting the yet warm ashes of the place,
>   As murdered men walk where they did expire.

Some stir up coals and watch the vestal fire,
  Others in vain from sight of ruin run.
And, while through burning labyrinths they retire,
  With loathing eye repeat what they would shun.

The most in fields like herded beasts lie down,
  To dews obnoxious on the grassy floor ;
And while their babes in sleep their sorrows drown,
  Sad parents watch the remnants of their store.

The suburbs, in every place thought to be beyond reach of the flames, were littered in like manner. Goods were heaped in Lincoln's Inn Fields, in Gray's Inn Fields and Hatton Garden, where companies of the Trained Bands were stationed to guard them, by the King's order. The open piazza of Covent Garden also did service for storage. Many of the rectors, forestalling the order contained in a Royal Proclamation of Wednesday, threw open their churches and schools for use as storehouses in the time of common calamity. Public buildings were also utilized. Pepys complained querulously that he could not find any shop in Westminster Hall at which to buy a shirt or pair of gloves, the place being stacked with people's goods.

Wild scenes took place in the burning City. Many of the lowest classes, having themselves nothing to lose, or whose little possessions were already lost, hovered about the outskirts of the Fire pilfering and stealing, always ready to attack any hapless foreigner who might come along. The flames drove from their homes many Dutchmen and Frenchmen who had found it advisable to keep concealed. At sight of them there was a hue and cry, and far too often a stern chase ended in savage brutality. English contemporary writers say little about the street disorders. Clarendon records only that in the excitement of the populace many foreigners were sorely beaten and bruised. But there are stories in these foreigners' letters one would wish not to believe, of men being hanged on signposts and afterwards cut down [1]—hanged, one must suppose, by the frenzied mob, and cut down in time by the soldiers who were in the streets to preserve order. A number of foreigners, escaping the clutches of these wretches, found refuge in the house at Barbican of the Count de Molena, the Spanish representative at King Charles's Court. It is

---

[1] *Londens Puyn-Hoop*, p. 10.

to the credit of the Catholic Ambassador's humanity that Protestant Dutchmen and Catholic Frenchmen were alike given sanctuary in this hour of their dire need.[1]

Clarendon has expressed surprise that in the general rage of the people no foreigner was assassinated outright. The magistrates cast numbers of foreign residents into prison, ostensibly on suspicion of crime, actually to keep them from the blind fury of the populace ; all were afterwards liberated. The outlying gaols were filled during the Great Fire. It would be false to suggest that only the brutish and illiterate element shared in the persecutions. That the fire came from the Lord out of Heaven was believed by some, but while London burnt it was the firm conviction of a large part of the populace that this was the hellish business of secret enemies in their midst—Frenchmen, Dutchmen and Papists—who even then were casting fireballs about to spread the conflagration still farther. A single instance may illustrate how easily the street mob was misled.

When the Fire this Tuesday afternoon was threatening Newgate Market, Lord Hollis and Lord Ashley had their station there. Near them an excited group collected, and a man was pushed out, without hat or cloak, being roughly used by his captors. The two lords recognized him as a servant of the Portuguese Ambassador. A substantial citizen was ready to take oath that he had seen this man put his hand in his pocket and throw a fireball into a shop ; immediately thereafter the house was in flames. He cried to the people to stop the man, and made haste in pursuit himself, but the villain was already taken. The people had as a first precaution seized his sword, which he was ready to draw. He did not comprehend a word of English. His pockets were searched for fireballs, but no more were found.

Lord Hollis, interpreting to the breathless and speechless man, explained the accusation. The foreigner denied that he had put his hand into his pocket ; but he remembered very well that as he walked he saw a piece of bread upon the ground. Taking it up, he had laid the bread upon a ledge in the next house. This was a custom, or superstition, among the Portuguese, so natural with them that

[1] *Relatione esattissima del' Incendio Calamitoso, etc.*, 1666.

if the King of Portugal were walking, and saw a piece of bread upon the ground, he would take it up with his own hand and keep it until he saw a place upon which to rest it.

That was, in fact, all that had happened—that, and no more. The lords and many of the people walked to the house, which was in view. There they found a piece of bread, just within the door upon a board, where the Portuguese had said he had placed it. Two doors off a house was burning—not this one. The excited citizen on the opposite side of the way, seeing the foreigner with his hand within the door, and immediately after fire breaking out, concluded that the flames were in the same house.[1]

[1] Clarendon's *Life*.

CHAPTER VII

THE Fire by Thames-side swept on from Baynard's Castle till it reached the Fleet River, then raged through the Blackfriars Precinct. A single topographical feature remains. You may pace to-day the eastern cloister walk, where black-cowled friars paced up and down centuries ago, when the most splendid convent in London covered all this land, and was a centre of religious life the influence of which spread far. Church Entry, going north into Carter Lane, follows exactly the line of the cloister walk and the passage that divided the preaching nave and choir of the conventual church. The Great Fire of London, completing the spoliation begun by Henry VIII., has left nothing else.

Queen Mary found the Priory Church already brought down ; it had been a noble structure, comparable with the existing Southwark Cathedral by London Bridge. The friars' Guest House, left standing a century after their dispossession, had passed into the hands of the Apothecaries Company in 1632, and when the Fire of London destroyed it the Company built their present Hall on the site. John Bill, the King's printer, had set up his press where to-day *The Times* is produced, and there he printed the Royal Proclamations till the Fire. The King's Printing House burnt in the flames of 1666. Close by the *London Gazette* was issued.* There is another imperishable memory of Blackfriars. The friars' upper frater, known as the Parliament Chamber, and made famous as the scene of Queen Catherine's trial before the Papal Legates, afterwards became Burbage's Blackfriars Theatre. It is, perhaps, little known that that tragedy in a Queen's life was repeated in mimic drama within the very same walls

when Shakespeare's *King Henry VIII.* was played there.[1]
The last remnants of the abandoned Blackfriars Theatre
disappeared in 1655 to make room for tenements.[2]

Noblemen, after the spoliation, had chosen the site of
the Dominican Priory, so finely situated overlooking the
Thames, for their town dwellings, and probably few of the
claustral buildings remained above ground when the Great
Fire spread into Blackfriars.   Lord Cobham entertained
Queen Elizabeth at his mansion in Blackfriars.   Lord
Hunsdon, the great Queen's Lord Chamberlain, had a house
there;   afterwards so tragically known for the "Fatal
Vespers" of the 26th October, 1623, when Father Drury
and ninety-four Catholics, secretly assembled for worship,
perished by the collapse of a floor.   The Earl and Countess
of Somerset (1615) and Lord Aubigny were other residents.
But more noteworthy is the association with Blackfriars
of Sir Anthony Vandyck.   The great painter, when he came
to settle in England, was given a house there by King
Charles I., and he died in it in 1641, being buried in Old
St. Paul's, but the Civil Wars prevented a monument
being raised.   The house had no doubt been left standing
with others of the great residences, after fashion turned
its back upon Blackfriars and streamed west.

St. Anne's Church, built for the parish after the destruction of the Dominican house, also perished, and only a bare
plot of paved churchyard survives.

Near the water by Puddle Dock the King's Wardrobe
was still kept.   Lord Sandwich, Master of the Wardrobe,
had an official residence there;   and Pepys, set down one
Lord's Day by his boatman, "went up to Jane Shore's
tower, and there W. Howe and I sang."   Cromwell's
soldiers will have spared little of such emblems of royalty
as they found, but the greater despoiler was King James I.,
upon whose memory may maledictions fall.   "In this
place," says the worthy Fuller, "were kept the ancient
clothes of our English Kings, which they wore on great
festivals, so that this Wardrobe was in effect a Library
for Antiquaries, therein to read the mode and fashion of all
ages.   These King James in the beginning of his reign gave

[1] A. W. Clapham, *Archæologia*, vol. lxiii.
[2] Notes on London Churches and Buildings, 1631–1658, Harrison's
England, vol. ii (New Shakespeare Society).

to the Earl of Dunbar, by whom they were sold, re-sold, and re-re-sold at as many hands almost as Briareus had, some gaining vast estates thereby." Wren's red-brick church of St. Andrew-in-the-Wardrobe was built where the earlier church stood till 1666.

Shakespearean associations linger about Blackfriars; there was the theatre; and Baynard's Castle; and close at hand, where Ireland Yard emerges into St. Andrew's Hill, stood the only piece of property that Shakespeare is known to have possessed in London. "I gyve, will, bequeath, and devise to my daughter Susannah Hall . . . all that messuage or tenement, with the appurtenances, wherein one John Robinson dwelleth, scituat, lying, and being in the Blackfriars in London, nere the Wardrobe "— so the will reads. Distant scarcely one hundred yards, in Carter Lane, the Bell Inn perished in the Great Fire. From this tavern, in 1598, Richard Quyney directed a letter " To my loveing good ffrend and contreymann Mr. Wm. Shackespere deliver thees," the only letter addressed to the poet that is known to exist. The original is at Stratford-on-Avon.

Blackfriars was alight many hours before the Fire threatened St. Paul's, and the flames, driven by the wind along Carter Lane and Creed Lane, gained the crest of the rising ground. Ludgate lay astride the street where the hill rose steeply from the little Fleet River. Like other gates in the City Wall, this served the double purpose of gateway and debtor's prison. King John's gate had been rebuilt in Queen Elizabeth's reign, and its single arch measured the width of the street passing through. Ludgate Hill had not attained the importance as a trading centre that it enjoyed later, when the mercers, driven from Paternoster Row by the Fire, came to settle there. It was steeper than as we know it to-day, and narrow. St. Martin's Church, with its stone tower, stood far out into what is now the roadway, and afterwards Wren, clearing the ground for his new foundations, came upon a Roman sepulchral stone bearing the figure of a soldier, one hand grasping a sword. The touching inscription is read over the centuries: " To the Departed Spirits. To Vivius Marcianus, soldier of the Second Augustan Legion, Januaria Martina, his dutiful wife, raised this memorial."

Northward the City Wall extended in a straight line to Newgate, with the Old Bailey below. The grave peril in which the entire western Liberty would lie had been foreseen if once the Fire, driven across London from the Bridge, should reach the high ground crowned by St. Paul's, and burn amidst the buildings and alleys that crowded about the Cathedral's extensive precinct. Early as Monday morning, when the Council was sitting at Ely Place, it had been proposed that the wharves and sheds about the Fleet's navigable way should be cleared and the houses on both sides pulled down, so as to make a broad open lane against the Fire from the Thames to Holborn Bridge. None, however, could comprehend that the flames should extend so far. The hopes entertained that day of setting limits to them had on Tuesday given way to despair, there being little expectation of saving anything except this western portion of the town, for which a supreme effort was made. In feverish haste soldiers and civilians, all who, by commands, threats or bribes had been persuaded to stay and give their aid, were employed in clearing a passage along the Fleet River, that should leave nothing to afford fuel for the Fire.

The same tragic thing happened that had been repeated in so many parts of London. The Fire having mastered the neighbourhood about St. Paul's, a wave of flame rose menacingly at the crest of the hill, leaping high where the Sessions House was a blazing ruin. The wind, driving through it, carried live brands and sparks high above the heads of the labourers engaged in levelling the houses about Fleet Bridge, setting buildings alight across the Fleet, and causing fires as far distant as Salisbury Court. Then breaking the bounds set by Ludgate and the City Wall, the mass of Fire advanced with bewildering speed, licked up the dry timber houses, and as an onlooker has described, " rushed like a torrent down Ludgate Hill." [1] The labourers fell back before the scorching heat; their whole day's effort was in vain. By five o'clock that afternoon Fleet Street was alight as far as the Conduit, which stood out in the roadway before Shoe Lane, and by six the flames were at the wall of the Temple. At that hour the writer whose letter I have so often quoted left the Fire

[1] Malcolm, *Lond. Rediv.*, iv, 75.

spreading, with a postcript as he looked back : " Despairing then of ever seeing this place more but in ashes, we went to Hornsey, four miles off, and in our way at Highgate we might discern with what rage and greediness it marched up Fleet Street."

Still over burning London St. Paul's, the highest, greatest, most conspicuous building of all, stood unharmed, while the Fire raged about it.   Dean Colet's famous school (the number of its one hundred and fifty-three foundation scholars is supposed to be the number of the miraculous draught of fishes) was aflame by the Cathedral's eastern end.*   The ancient bust of Colet, now at Hammersmith, is the only relic saved.   The Fire consumed the school library, with all Colet's printed books and manuscripts of grammatical learning in Hebrew, Greek, and Latin, and on divinity.   Samuel Cromleholme, the High Master, lost all his household stuff, and what hurt more deeply, his personal library, which was reputed to be the best private collection of books in London in his day.   There were many rare impressions from the presses of Aldus, Junta, Grafton, Estienne, Elzevir and others, all burnt to ashes.   " The loss of these books," says a writer mourning Cromleholme's death in 1672, " I verily believe shortened his days, for he was a great lover of his books, and spared no cost in procuring them from all parts of Europe."

It is an old legend of the Cathedral, no doubt recalled at this hour, that always a wind blows at the Dean's corner, south-west of the Churchyard ; the devil raised it by his hasty flight after St. Dunstan, the goldsmiths' patron, had tweaked his nose with his red-hot pincers. Another version is that the devil was riding on the wind to Doctors Commons, and dismounting left the wind to await him at Dean's Court.   He found the lawyers' company so congenial that the wind is waiting there still.   The Dean's house burnt, affording Sancroft opportunity for erecting the pretty house that stands to-day, though shorn of much of its pleasant garden laid out towards the river.   The statement that appears in so many works on London and St. Paul's, that the Bishop's house to the north-west (site marked by London House Yard) was also destroyed in the Great Fire is incorrect ; other despoilers had come before, and there was none left to destroy.*

WARDROBE PLACE, DOCTORS COMMONS

A charming corner of the City as rebuilt after the Great Fire, which survives to-day

Lord Burgavenny had a mansion by Amen Corner, which the Stationers Company, incorporated in the previous century, had acquired, adding to it their Hall, built " in a large timber frame." The site is held by the Company to-day; but of Lord Burgavenny's house nothing survived the Fire. The loss to the Company was very great. They had undertaken the printing of books. Not only were their buildings consumed, but also the presses and large quantities of printed volumes stored in their warehouses and in the nave of Christ Church. Happily for our knowledge of English printed books, the Stationers' registers were saved.

Where to-day the houses of the residentiary Canons of St. Paul's stand in quiet seclusion at Amen Corner was the Royal College of Physicians, Lineacre's foundation. The College had been robbed and ransacked when locked up during the previous year's Great Plague, and now was completely destroyed in the Fire, with its contents. The premises, acquired early that century, had been enlarged by the eminent Harvey, who in 1653 built a library and museum. As the flames approached, Dr. Merritt, the Harveian librarian and custos, removed to a place of safety the charters and annals, the case of surgical instruments, and the President's insignia, which still are treasured possessions of the College. The portraits of Dr. Harvey and Dr. Fox were cut from their frames and so secured. About one hundred and forty printed books from the library were all that were saved.

Mean dwellings built close against the Cathedral walls had disappeared under Laud's reforming hand, and about St. Paul's the Churchyard made a considerable open space. It seemed to the citizens a place of comparative safety. Long before the flames came round into Paternoster Row and searched the neighbouring lanes and alleys, the mercers and stationers and booksellers, whose shops elbowed one another in this vicinity, carried their goods into the church itself, and heaped other merchandise in the open Churchyard, hoping that it would there be isolated — large quantities of heavy cloth especially, and the lighter fabrics of fashionable wear. Much more went into a great strong room which it was believed no fire could force.

St. Faith under Paul's was actually in the vaults—odd

place for a parish church—a four-aisled crypt beneath the choir, ceiled with stout arches. The Cathedral floor which served for worshippers above formed also a roof for worshippers below. This was the church of the Stationers Company. London possessed no stronger place.

The booksellers moved their stocks there. Soon volumes, big and little, rose in piles from the floor, hundreds first, then thousands, each man's possessions separated, bearing his identification marks, for the booksellers would return to claim them when the Fire had beaten itself ineffectually against St. Paul's massive walls. Even should the great cathedral suffer damage, their wealth in print and bindings would be safe, for how should fire exert itself below ground ?

It seemed to many that a Divine Hand was protecting the Mother Church, the early home of Christianity in London, and that when a City in ashes should lie cold around it, still the majestic fane of St. Paul's should stand unharmed—unconquerable ! The Fire of London had swept far past.

Then, shortly before eight o'clock this Tuesday evening, when darkness fell, flames broke out on the Cathedral roof.[1]

The sentiment is false which deplores the destruction of Old St. Paul's as an irreparable loss to London. Age and association count for much ; these no new builder could replace ; but Wren has given us a better, grander fabric, more worthy in every sense of the site it surmounts and the status of the metropolitan Cathedral. Old St. Paul's was indeed vast—in length and height, and vaster even than its measurements it appeared in its deep gloom. Tall, narrow windows, with one great rose window at the east end, gave but little light to the long nave, with its heavy obstructing pillars and twelve bays. The choir, of later date, was ill adjusted ; the short tower had lost its spire, which at best was but timber covered with lead. Architecturally the Cathedral was not important. A few remains of the small cloister and of the Chapter House stand out of the ground, now converted to a garden.

If Paul's had withstood the Fire, and stood to-day, it could have taken but fourth or fifth rank when com-

[1] Taswell's *Autobiography*.

pared with the great cathedrals of the Continent, or, indeed, of our own country.   Dean Milman said truly of Old St. Paul's that it had nothing of the prodigal magnificence, the harmonious variety of Lincoln, the stately majesty of York, the solemn grandeur of Canterbury, the perfect, sky-aspiring unity of Salisbury.   It had not even one of the great conceptions which are the pride and boast of some of our other churches ;   neither the massy strength of Durham, " looking eternity " with its marvellous Galilee, nor the tower of Gloucester, nor the lantern of Ely, nor the rich picturesqueness of Beverley, nor the deep, receding, highly decorated arches of the west front of Peterborough.

And it had been misused as one hopes no other Cathedral in Christendom has suffered.   The peal of four " Jesus Bells " King Henry VIII. had gambled away to Sir Miles Partridge at a single cast of the dice.   The Knight won. Fuller quaintly tells, " Thus he brought the bells to ring in his pocket, but the ropes afterwards catched about his neck, and for some offence he was hanged in the days of King Edward VI."   Paul's Walk, the length of the long nave, had since the Reformation been a place of public passage and barter, noisy with the clatter of footsteps and cries of trade.   One recalls the last state under the Puritans, and Carlyle's biting phrase :   " Paul's Cathedral is now a Horse-guard ;   horses stamp in the Canons' stalls there ; and Paul's Cross itself, as smacking of Popery, where in fact Alablaster once preached flat Popery, is swept away altogether, with its leaden roof melted into bullets, or mixed with tin for culinary purposes."

Majestic as St. Paul's, crowning London from the hill, appeared to those who viewed it from afar, on close approach it became a pitiable monument to the rancour of Christian men.   Long neglect had occurred under Elizabeth, when the fabric was damaged by the fire of 1561, which consumed the commanding steeple.   The decay continued until the Cathedral's sorry state moved James I. to ineffectual protest—the King to whom the many ruinous or ruined cathedrals in his native land were of inauspicious omen.   Naturally, the Crown under James I. had no money for such work.   Nothing was, in fact, done until, supported by a zealous Churchman in

King Charles I., Laud, then Bishop of London, found in
the restoration of St. Paul's to something of its ancient
state a project that appealed to his ambitious mind.

" Like a great skeleton, so pitifully handled that you
might tell her ribs through her skin," the Cathedral had
then become. In Laud's own words, it was ready to sink
into its own ruins.

Inigo Jones's great Classical portico erected at the
western end, and some reparation and bad new Gothic at
the sides of the building, were all that had been accomplished when Civil War and the triumph of Puritanism
shattered to pieces the scheme of restoration, and almost
shattered the great fabric itself.

A legend that Cromwell contemplated selling St. Paul's
to the Jews is probably untrue. That it should have had
currency is testimony to the low esteem into which Erken-
wald's Cathedral had fallen. The first act of the new
masters of England was to seize all the balance remaining—
above £17,000—of the funds for repairs originally collected
by Laud. The scaffolds already raised for rebuilding the
steeple were assigned to Colonel Jephson's regiment for
£1,746 due for arrears of pay. On the scaffolding being
struck, part of the south transept and some portions of the
other roofs came down, and the ruins were left where they
fell. The lead was begged by the City to augment their
water pipes.[1] The carving of the organ loft, screen, and
stallwork, upon which skilled mediæval craftsmen had
piously laboured, was torn down. Whatever painted
glass survived in the windows was shattered. Mean shops,
let out to seamstresses and hucksters, were raised in
Inigo Jones's great portico, with chambers above and staircases leading to them. In May, 1645, all revenues of the
Dean and Chapter were forfeited by Parliament.

The place hallowed by centuries of continuous prayer
would have been silent to God's worship but for a sting to
conscience of the London Aldermen. Cornelius Burgess, a
Puritan divine who had ridden, armed with a case of pistols,
at the head of the London Militia, was on their representation appointed Lecturer, with a stipend reserved for
him of £400 a year. A part of the Cathedral's east end
was walled in as his preaching house. Save this one

---

[1] *State Papers (Domestic)*, 1655, p. 224.

enclosure, the sacred building was given over entirely to profane uses.

A chimney of a smith's forge pierced the Cathedral roof. Wooden balls and falling nine-pins clattered in the precincts. The rude soldiers of the Commonwealth rode their horses up the steps—in so doing one broke his neck— and in intervals of sport and duty battered the effigies of the dead, destroying with implacable hate every symbol that savoured to them of Papistry, or else made the offices of the Church a subject of ribald mummery. A mare having foaled in this Cathedral stable, the colt was baptized by the soldiery, with blasphemous rites too repulsive for decent print.[1]

St. Paul's was purged of its grosser abuses when Charles II. returned to the throne, and the service of the Church was resumed. But neglect and decay had left the fabric not only insecure, but dangerous. The weight of the roof had spread the walls. The tower was leaning by settlement of one of the ancient pillars. Stones were flawed and mouldering away.[2] It was not until 1666 that materials for effective restoration were available, and on the 27th August Dr. Wren—with much misgiving,—John Evelyn, Bishop Henchman, Dean Sancroft and others made an inspection, and that day they ordered plans and estimates to be prepared. Eight days later the Great Fire of London had reached Old St. Paul's, and decided its fate for ever.

Live brands carried overhead by the wind brought the Fire to the Cathedral. Martin, a bookseller in the Church-yard, saw the dread work of destruction begin, the flames rising at the edge of a board that, among others, was laid on the roof where the lead had broken away.[3] The dry timber forming the roof above the stone vaulting burnt furiously, with such a mass of flame that Taswell, the Westminster scholar, standing at the King's Bridge, the landing place at New Palace Yard more than a mile distant, was able before nine o'clock to read very clearly by the

---

[1] See a rare quarto tract, " News from Powles, Or the New Reformation of the Army : with a true Relation of a Covlt that was foaled in the Cathedrall Church of St. *Paul* in London, and how it was Publiquely *Baptized* by *Paul Hobsons* souldiers. Printed in the yeer 1649."

[2] Wren's Report, *Parentalia*, p. 174, *et seq.*

[3] Pepys's *Diary*, 1668, Jan. 14.

blaze a diminutive edition of Terence that he carried in his pocket.

Large parts of the roof, both stone and burning timber, fell in, and the cathedral became a roaring cauldron of fire. Evelyn declares that the scaffolds erected for the survey greatly contributed to the disaster. The unexpected and bewildering effect of the terrific heat upon the masses of masonry was a cause of wonderment to onlookers. Vincent writes : " The church, though all of stone outward, though naked of houses about it, and though so high above all buildings in the City, yet within a while doth yield to the violent assaults of the conquering flames, and strangely takes fire at the top ; now the lead melts and runs down, as if it had been snow before the sun ; and the great beams and massy stones, with a great noise, fall on the pavement, and break through into Faith's Church underneath ; now great flakes of stone scale, and peal off strangely from the side of the walls." [1]

" The very stones are crumbled and broken into shivers and slatts," says another. Stones split asunder with the force of an explosion, and fragments, 20 lbs., 40 lbs., and 100 lbs. in weight were broken off and hurled considerable distances.

Evelyn pictures the stones of St. Paul's flying " like grenadoes. It was astonishing (says he) to see what immense stones the heat had in a manner calcined, so that all the ornaments, columns, friezes, capitals, and projectures of massy Portland stone flew off, even to the very roof, where a sheet of lead covering a great space (no less than six acres by measure) was totally melted."

Molten lead dripped in silvery beads from the roof, raining down upon the broken stones and tombs that strewed the Cathedral floor, and there collecting, ran out into the streets in a stream. The very pavements glowed with a fiery redness, so that neither horse nor man was able to tread upon them. The debris, clattering down, had stopped all the passage ways, and no help could be applied.[2]

Part of the side walls of the aisles fell out, and by openings so made and gaping doors and windows spectators

[1] *God's Terrible Voice*, 1667.
[2] Evelyn's *Diary*, 1666, Sept. 3, 4 and 6.

in the night looked straight into the heart of the fire.
Central in the nave, towards the altar, the red flames burnt
over the tomb of Sir John Beauchamp, Constable of Dover
Castle—" the Duke Humphrey's tomb " of the unthinking
Londoners. One greater than he slept his long sleep in
the choir—" Old John of Gaunt, time-honoured Lancaster."
About the recumbent effigies of the Knight and his second
wife, Constance of Castile, the flames played, reaching up
to the helmet and spear and target covered with horn
suspended above the tomb. Half
of the memorial statue, in armour,
of Sir Nicholas Bacon, the famous
father of a more famous son, survived the Fire, the remainder
crashing to the floor ; his leaden
coffin, bearing an inscription
which recorded his twenty years'
service under Elizabeth, was unharmed. The fine old tomb
stood in St. Dunstan's Chapel of
Henry de Lacy, Earl of Lincoln,
forbear of the lawyers of
Lincoln's Inn, who still wear his
arms. Sir Christopher Hatton,
Elizabeth's dancing Chancellor,
was commemorated by a great
and garish monument in the
choir, which crushed aside the
modest tablets of Sir Philip
Sydney and his father-in-law,
Sir Francis Walsingham, hence
the couplet—

Philip and Francis have no tomb,
For great Christopher takes all the room.

Many Bishops of London,
Deans, and men of mark had
their more humble stones, and
one and all perished in the vortex
of fierce flame which St. Paul's
high walls confined. Some tombs
fell into St. Faith's beneath. Of
all the number, there are to-day

DEAN DONNE'S SHROUDED
EFFIGY.

but a few mutilated, irrecognizable fragments reverently
preserved in the crypt, and—solitary in its perfection
—the shrouded effigy of Dean Donne (died 1631)
apparently rising from his funeral urn, which alone has
come unscathed out of the Great Fire. It is told that
this was designed by the Dean's directions in his lifetime, and that he posed for the part in his own study.[1]
Isaac Walton says that an unknown friend wrote this
epitaph " with a coal " on the old Cathedral wall over his
grave—

> Reader, I am to let thee know
> Donne's body only lies below ;
> For could the grave his soul comprise,
> Earth would be richer than the skies.

The King and the Duke of York, riding on horseback
about the City, stayed to watch the destruction of the
great Cathedral, upon the restoration of which their father
had laboured. Inigo Jones's Classical portico had been
built largely at the cost of Charles I., and from its pediment
his statue had been toppled over and broken to pieces
when the Parliament seized power. The portico withstood
the fire, though greatly damaged, large flakes of stone being
split asunder, and little remaining entire. The Spanish
account I have before cited records that " In the very
sight of the King himself the fire proceeded to crown itself
the conqueror of the highest parts of the great building.
The flames seized upon the carved timber of which the
church was in places composed, licked it up in a twinkling,
and in a few hours left this marvellous building, the labour
of many years, a smoking mass of lamentable ruins." [2]

The great nave, the tower, and walls of the choir and
transepts withstood the shock of the falling roof, too stoutly
built to fall themselves. Flames burst through every
shattered window. Gaunt spaces once filled with painted
glass, through which a rosy light had fallen upon close
ranks of kneeling worshippers and gorgeous processions of
the Church, and roof open to the sky, complete the picture of
desolation which every print after the Fire presents. In

[1] Donne's effigy stood in Old St. Paul's on the north side of the Choir,
and being erect slipped down into St. Faith's after the fall of the roof had
crushed in the floor. In Wren's Cathedral the effigy, again erect, stands
in the south ambulatory wall of the Choir.

[2] *Relacion Nueva y Verdadera del formidable incendio, etc.*   1666.

Sic transit Gloria Mundi.

London

PROSPECT OF BURNING LONDON

Print by Justus Danckert, 1666, in the Goss Collection

place of a cathedral's well-ordered interior confusion was thickly strewn—with table tombs laid open and recumbent figures of alabaster fallen to the floor and broken in falling, and shields and devices by skilled mediæval carvers heaped amidst the waste [1]—the discord that only a fire can create.

Night and day St. Paul's continued burning. The scene after dawn had broken was impressed upon Taswell's memory:—

" Soon after sunrising I endeavoured to reach St. Paul's. The ground was so hot as almost to scorch my shoes; and the air so intensely warm that unless I had stopped some time upon Fleet Bridge to rest myself, I must have fainted under the extreme languor of my spirits. After giving myself a little time to breathe I made the best of my way to St. Paul's. And now let any person judge of the violent emotion I was in when I perceived the metal belonging to the bells melting; the ruinous condition of the walls; whole heaps of stone of a large circumference tumbling down with a great noise just upon my feet, ready to crush me to death. I prepared myself for returning back again, having first loaded my pockets with several pieces of bell metal. In my way home I saw several engines which were bringing up to its assistance all on fire, and those concerned with them escaping with great eagerness from the flames, which spread instantaneous almost like a wild-fire; and at last, accoutred with my sword and helmet, which I picked up among many others in the ruins, I traversed this torrid zone back again."

By the Cathedral a dreadful sight confronted him—

" I forgot to mention that near the east walls of St. Paul's a human body presented itself to me, parched up, as it were, with the flames; whole as to skin, meagre as to flesh, yellow as to colour. This was an old decrepit woman who fled here for safety, imagining the flames would not have reached her there. Her clothes were burnt, and every limb reduced to a coal."

Flames appeared on the battlements of Old St. Paul's as late as Thursday night, forty-eight hours after the outbreak.[2] Of all the vast roof, there remained in place only

---

[1] F. Wright, *A Poem ; being an Essay on the present ruins in St. Paul's Cathedral*, 1668. (Guildhall Library.)

[2] *London's Lamentations*, 1666 (Broadside).

a fragment at the east end of the choir, over the altar, the rest having fallen. The destruction was so complete that homeless people, subsequently seeking refuge in the Cathedral, could find no place in which to take shelter save with the dead in the vaults.

The Grand Duke Cosmo III., of Tuscany, a Royal guest of Charles II., passed by the pitiful ruin. " Of this stupendous fabric (he wrote) there is nothing now to contemplate except the vestiges of its ancient magnificence. One sees only a huge heap of stones, cemented together by the lead with which the church was covered ; this when melted fell among the ruins, which have entirely covered the relics of antiquity that were there formerly, and demolished many splendid monuments, both of Catholic bishops and other distinguished men, of which scarcely any trace is to be seen." [1]

The falling roof broke open the tomb within the choir and leaden coffin of Robert de Braybroke, Bishop of London and Lord Chancellor of England. In it was found entire the body laid there 262 years before, " teeth in the head, red hair on the head, beard, &c. skin and nails on the toes and fingers, without cirecloth, embalming spices, or any other condite." It was so dried up that, being set upon the feet, it stood stiff as a plank, having defied putrefaction. This some attributed to the dead man's sanctity. The prelate's remains, it is grievous to learn, being removed to the Chapter House, for years thereafter became a public show. Lord Coleraine saw them in 1675. They were in due time reinterred in Wren's vast Cathedral, but no inscription marks the Bishop's final resting place. Two other bodies so dried were discovered when the north aisle was cleared of debris.[2]

[1] Magalotti, *Travels of the Grand Duke Cosmo III.*, p. 179.
[2] This hideous story of the violation of the tomb of Dean Colet in Old St. Paul's, broken in the Great Fire of London, I should hesitate to credit were it not vouched for by John Aubrey, the antiquary, whose words I give : " After the conflagration his monument being broken, his coffin, which was lead, was full of a liquor which conserved the body. Mr. Wyld and Ralph Greatorex tasted it, and 'twas of a kind of insipid tast, something of an ironish tast. The body felt, to the probe of a stick which they thrust into a chinke, like brawne. The coffin was of lead, and layd in the wall about 2 foot ½ above the surface of the floore." (*Brief Lives*, i. 181.) The want of reverence for the dead we know from the post-mortem wanderings in Westminster Abbey of Katherine of Valois, Henry V.'s " darling

St. Faith's under Paul's is a tragic story. To protect their riches stored there, the booksellers had sought to make assurance doubly sure. When they had passed in the last volume, and books to a large part of the value of £150,000 were piled up—so much contemporaries assert the stationers' total loss to have been—they strengthened and sealed each door and window, and with great caution and prudence even the least avenue through which the smallest spark might penetrate was stopped.[1]

How it was that disaster occurred we may never know—disaster absolutely complete. Never since the burning of the great library at Alexandria had there been such a holocaust of books as in the Great Fire of London. One said that the crash of the Cathedral roof falling broke through the arches of Faith's, the heat of that inferno raging above having calcined the stones and reduced them to powder. There is a second story, told to Pepys by the booksellers Kirton and Martin in very similar words, that the merchandise laid in the Churchyard first became ignited by burning timbers from the houses on the drapers' side (Paternoster Row) falling upon it, and the fire entered through the windows of St. Faith's Church,[2] then seized upon the pews and burnt all the books within and the pillars of the church, till the roof collapsed.[3] The books continued ablaze for a week.[4] A third account is circumstantial in detail, and quite different. It is that the books survived the general conflagration; then the booksellers, anxious for their property, ventured too early to open St. Faith's, and the piled volumes, greatly heated by the Fire above them, broke into flame immediately air was admitted.[5] There is agreement only in the essential fact of destruction.

The sight of shattered tombs and broken effigies tumbled

Kate " and Consort, whose poor body, disentombed and placed in a chest, was exposed to the public gaze. One hates Pepys for the crowning indignity he cast upon it. " I had the upper part of her body in my hands, and I did kiss her mouth, reflecting upon it that I did kiss a Queen, and that this was my birthday, thirty-six years old, that I did kiss a Queen." (*Diary*, 1669, Feb. 23.)

[1] Taswell, p. 12.
[2] Pepys's *Diary*, 1666, Sept. 26, Oct. 5 ; 1668, Jan. 14.
[3] Rege Sincera, *Observations, etc.*
[4] Evelyn's *Diary*, 1666, Sept. 7.
[5] *State Papers (Domestic)*, 1666-7, p. 167. See also Clarendon.

in amid the black ashes of the books in St. Faith's vault inspired the writer of a contemporary poem, four of whose verses I give—

> See yet another Ruin ; here were laid
> Choice Authors, by the Servants of the Muses :
> And here to Sacrilegious flames betray'd
> To spare or Wit or Temples fire refuses.
>
> These half burnt Papers lying here, needs must
> Be for the Libriary of the Dead mistook :
> And for a Schollar faln himself to Dust
> Ashes of paper is a proper Book.
>
> Couldst thou not, *Pauls*, in all thy Vaults of Stone,
> Preserve these Papers from the tyrant flame ?
> When thou by Paper, and by it alone,
> Art still preserv'd to triumph o're the same.
>
> Were't not for Books where had thy Memory been ?
> But that thou art, in *Dugdales* learned Story
> And beautious Illustrations [1] to be seen,
> Thy name had been as lost as is thy Glory. [2]

Close by the Cathedral's south-west wall—seeming, indeed, to be actually attached—another church of a City parish had been built. " St. Paul's," wrote Fuller, " may be called the Mother Church indeed, having one babe in her body [St. Faith's] and another in her arms [St. Gregory's]." The little tower of St. Gregory by Paul's rose less than the height of the Cathedral nave. The church had been partially dismantled in Laud's great scheme for the improvement of the Cathedral and afterwards restored, and in the Fire of London was totally destroyed.

[1] The reference is to Sir William Dugdale's account of St. Paul's, nearly three hundred copies of which, happily only a portion of the issue, were burnt in the Great Fire of London. The edition is now very rare.

[2] F. Wright's *A Poem*, 1668, *op. cit.*

CHAPTER VIII

FIRE IN THE LIBERTIES

NOWHERE was the advance of the flames watched with keener anxiety than at Christ's Hospital. This was a nerve centre in all times of public calamity. It had been so in the previous year of the Plague. The children receiving education at the Bluecoat School of Edward VI.'s foundation comprised not only the orphans. Sons and daughters of freemen, paying scholars, came and went daily, traversing heavily infected areas of the City. Yet the school passed through the ordeal, not unscathed, but with less mortality than was common outside its walls. " God had given such a blessing to their endeavours," said the masters in a petition to the Governors, " that all this time of sickness not more than thirty-two children of the number of 260 in the house are dead of all diseases."

So, too, when the Fire began to spread through the City, in every parish were relatives anxiously concerned for the safety of their " Blue " children.

The school was gravely imperilled on Tuesday afternoon. The Governors had taken timely precautions. Boys and girls above two hundred in number were despatched to the Nagg's Head estate at Islington, a gift to the foundation four years earlier by Mr. John Browne. There they lodged the night, and afterwards were removed to another house belonging to the Hospital at Clerkenwell, where they were " dyetted " for four days, and then sent on to Ware and Hertford.

The Fire, advancing from the south-east, first struck the great church of the Grey Friars. Its high walls and roof gave effectual shelter to many of the buildings. Few people realize the immense size of these conventual churches, which till the dissolution of the religious houses were dotted about London's small area. This one was 311 feet in length, no less than three times the length of Wren's Christ Church, Newgate Street, which succeeds it. Fate had spared this thirteenth-century building from the despoiling hand of Henry VIII. The choir, which alone covered all the ground required by Wren when rebuilding after the Fire, had been given by the monarch to the parishioners for use as a parish church. The great nave made a storehouse for the reception of wine and other prizes taken from the French, and serving a useful purpose in this and like offices, it had escaped demolition. Accordingly the fabric—desecrated, indeed, and with a public passage-way driven between the choir and the nave —stood substantially unharmed in 1666, a monument of the piety of its early builders, foremost among whom was Margaret, Queen of Edward I. Beneath the stones of Christ Church, here in the heart of the City, still rest unmarked the remains of three English Queens—of Margaret herself, of Isabella, wife of Edward II., Philippa, wife of Edward III., and also of Joan, Queen of Scots.

The Grey Friars' church had sustained some injury in the earthquake which shook London on the 6th April, 1580, when a large stone was dislodged from the roof. Its fall during sermon time killed one worshipper and mortally wounded another.[1] This is thought to have been the earthquake referred to by the Nurse in *Romeo and Juliet*, Act I, Sc. 3—

> " 'Tis since the earthquake now eleven years."

Most of the priory buildings survived in 1666; in fact, this sheltered corner within the City wall, with Newgate towering near, recalled in all essentials the old conventual settlements that earlier had been so characteristic a feature of London. Only the grey-cowled friars were themselves absent. The friars' cloister, behind the church, stood erect. It enclosed a square of lawn; the plot which, paved over, still bore the name of " the Garden " when tramped by Bluecoat boys of our own generation. The claustral buildings, though protected by the church, did not escape the flames. Whittington's Library re-

[1] Wheatley, *London Past and Present*, i, 393.

mained in use till early last century, and part was standing
in 1828. It had been built over the north cloister walk
by that famous Lord Mayor in 1429. The friars' refectory,
or hall, forming the west side of the cloister, was, however,
severely damaged. The hall was found after a careful
survey in 1680 to need rebuilding. The friars' great
dorter, or dormitory, enclosing the cloister on the east,
was ruined in its upper part. Elsewhere, when the flames
had passed, was nothing but ruins, save only (a brief
school chronicle relates) " about three wards towards the
sick ward and several other rooms there, as also the wardrobe of this Hospital over the south cloister." [1] Eighty
of the children were afterwards brought back and accommodated in the fire-scarred buildings, when the cloister
was boarded up to keep them out, " being thought to be
very dangerous since the late fire." School did not re-
assemble for fourteen months.

It is impossible to tell exactly to what extent the
great church suffered in the Fire, but Wren has been
accused of unnecessary destruction of the ancient fabric.
The school chronicle speaks of " the glazed windows of
the church on that [south cloister] side being very little
damnified." Money spent by the churchwardens in clearing the church floor, removing stones, and making doorways also suggests that the main part of the fabric was
left secure. Its rebuilding by Wren was not begun till
1677. No life was lost. In commemoration of that fact
the Bluecoat boys long afterwards observed the 2nd
September, the anniversary of the Fire's outbreak, as an
annual holiday.

The quiet scholastic foundation stood against the noise
of Newgate Market—the street we know to-day as Newgate Street, an unobstructed way for the never-ceasing
traffic to and from the City, but then the Shambles, an
open meat market. Wide and straight, like Cheapside,
the street had for a great part of its length a middle row
of sheds and stalls, kept by butchers, tripe-sellers, and the

[1] Committee Minutes, 1666-9, fo. 31. A plan of Christ's Hospital
before the Fire, probably made between 1660 and 1666, was discovered
in 1901, and is reproduced in the Rev. E. H. Pearce's *Annals of Christ's
Hospital*. It shows the ground largely covered with a confused mass o
buildings and gardens. Where the great nave of the ancient church
stood is still open land, the extent of which indicates its huge proportions.

like. Country people who came in with barrows and baskets added to the confusion and rough liveliness of the place. Pepys's adventure as his coach passed in the press I recalled in an earlier chapter. Aside, in the old Stinking Lane (to-day King Edward Street) was Butchers Hall, built about 1548 upon the site of the parsonage house of St. Nicholas Shambles, a church destroyed at the Reformation, and land taken out of the churchyard. The Hall was destroyed as the Fire struck the east of Greyfriars, and Poulters Hall, but a few paces distant, suffered a like fate.

FAT BOY AT PIE CORNER.

Quickly the flames made a clearance of Newgate Market and the alleys which opened upon it from the south, and thrusting forward burst upon Newgate. The gate and prison in the City Wall then standing were largely the work of Richard Whittington, at whose cost the structure had been " re-edified "—another of his public works that had done much to ennoble his memory with the citizens. I failed to find any record of Newgate in the Fire, but its stout masonry must needs have offered considerable resistance. Repairs afterwards attempted indicate that it suffered great injury; they were, indeed, abandoned for what appears to have been complete rebuilding. The felons were marched off under escort to Southwark, but in the turmoil and confusion some of the worst characters escaped.

Through Newgate the flames turned in the direction of Smithfield, but made little headway.

" The Fire of London began in Pudding Lane and ended at Pie Corner." If so great an event can be said to have been epitomized in a sentence, this is the one; but if time be meant the legend does not bear investigation. The Fire continued to spread about Cripplegate twenty hours after Pie Corner had been razed. Pepys tells that his clerk Hewer this Tuesday had gone from

Seething Lane " to see how his mother did, and comes home late, telling us how he had been forced to remove her to Islington, her house in Pie Corner being burned." The Fire was stopped at Cock Lane, famous a century later for its ghost. At the corner, on the wall of the Fortune of War tavern, there stood till recent years the carved wooden figure of an uncommonly fat boy, bearing an inscription which told the passer-by : " This boy is in memory put up for the late Fire of London occasioned by the Sin of Gluttony, 1666." [1] As an explanation of the origin of the Fire, this is as good as some others. St. Bartholomew's Hospital and that magnificent Norman fragment, the church of St. Bartholomew the Great, were spared. This was doubly fortunate, for in the Hospital were sheltered a number of wounded and sick men from the wars.[2] Though the Hospital escaped the flames, the charity was one of the worst sufferers by the Fire, no fewer than 190 of its rent-producing houses in the City being destroyed. St. Thomas's Hospital stood at safe distance across the river in Southwark, but its City endowments underwent a like disaster, and the building itself was for a time imperilled by some thatched houses about it which took fire from flying sparks, and burnt for five hours.

In its sweep south the Fire completely enveloped St. Sepulchre's Church before Newgate.

Little in the appearance of the fabric to-day suggests the terrible ordeal through which St. Sepulchre's passed. The mediæval tower stands, with four high pinnacles, a conspicuous City landmark. From its summit one " rich Dorrington," a disappointed legal suitor, in 1600 threw himself headlong and broke his neck. The church walls

[1] The figure of the Fat Boy, now gilt, has been set in the wall of the new building which replaces the Fortune of War. The little wings shown in J. T. Smith's print of 1791 have disappeared, and a recent careful examination revealed no trace of the famous inscription. Burn (*Trades-men's Tokens*) tells that its propriety was supported by a Nonconformist divine, preaching on the anniversary of the Great Fire, who asserted " that the calamity could not have been occasioned by the sin of blasphemy, for in that case it would have begun in Billingsgate ; nor lewdness, for then Drury Lane would have been first on fire ; nor lying, for then the flames had reached the City from Westminster Hall. No, my beloved, it was occasioned by the sin of gluttony, for it began at Pudding Lane, and ended at Pie Corner."

[2] Evelyn, *Diary*, 1666, Sept. 5.

largely withstood the flames, and have been repaired and recased. But the restoration carried out in 1880 everywhere disclosed the ravages of the Fire, in remains of ancient window jambs and arches and mouldings and tracery, the stones of which were much calcined.[1] A double piscina is preserved, badly mutilated by the heat. Within the tower, still so high and strong, was a raging inferno. Heavy beams composing the different stages burnt one after another; the bells fell to the ground, and lying there melted. Afterwards the churchwardens paid £22 18s. " for cleansing the bell mettle from the dust." The sacred vessels of the church were so completely obliterated that a Mr. Willmot was employed to refine the bars cast from the pools of molten lead which had rained down from the roof, " wherein it is supposed the parish plate may be found ! " [2] The whole picture of destruction is suggested in that passage. St. Sepulchre's was so named after the Church of the Holy Sepulchre in Jerusalem, and had a grim association with Newgate, for there the execution bell was tolled when the cart started on its way to Tyburn. Simon Ford, the Royalist divine, whose hagiology is bad as his verse, writes of the Fire—

> A lofty Pile (now humbled) next appears,
> Once christ'ned 'twas Saint Sepulchers :
> Which since it felt the all-interring Flame,
> The Saint lost, kept its empty Name.
> They tell us here of One unmelted Bell
> That toll'd Condemned Felons Knell.[3]

I suspect this last was not in the belfry, but was the small hand bell, a relic snatched from the Fire, that to-day may be seen under glass in the church. It had been used by Robert Dowe, a pious Elizabethan citizen, in his self-imposed task of bringing admonition (if not comfort) to the felons, before whose cell it was his custom to stand overnight, ring his bell, and recite certain verses,[4] warning them to be prepared, for to-morrow they should die, and by timely repentance to save themselves from eternal flames.

[1] Arthur Billing, *Restoration of the Church of St. Sepulchre.*
[2] Vestry Minutes, 1666, Dec. 31.
[3] *Londini quod Reliquum,* 1667.
[4] See Note on St. Sepulchre's on page 360, *post.*

When Dowe himself died in 1605 he left £50 to St. Sepulchre's for the felons' knell to be perpetuated.

Now the Fire was in the Liberties through both the western gates, its farthest advance being along the line of Fleet Street. Ludgate is shown at evening in what is believed to be a contemporary painting, with blazing houses about it, standing dark and solid against the red background of the flames. The warders, flying for their lives, opened the cells of the debtors incarcerated there, freemen of the City who had met with adversity, and the prisoners broke gaol and scattered.[1] High above the gateway and portcullis when Ludgate was rebuilt in Elizabeth's reign a statue of the Virgin Queen had been placed, and it remained upon its niche but little harmed throughout the Fire,[2] a stiff and formal figure, with ruff and expansive farthingale, looking down the hill. The statue has been preserved, and stands to-day over the vestry door of St. Dunstan-in-the-West in Fleet Street. Other relics of Ludgate from the Fire are the ancient figures of King Lud and his sons, Androgeus and Theomantus, now at St. Dunstan's, Regent's Park. They showed indications before repair of having been much damaged by the flames.

Against Ludgate, the fifteenth-century church of St. Martin's was so far destroyed that Wren rebuilt from the foundations, designing the slender leaden steeple to direct the eye up to the huge dome of his cathedral. Part of the church's western wall rests upon the ancient City Wall. The sacred vessels were saved, 100 ozs. of gilt plate and two silver flagons weighing 124 ozs. ; in their

[1] J. Crouch, *Londinenses Lacrymae*, 1666.
[2] Evelyn's *Diary*, 1666, Sept. 7. Crouch has the following somewhat cryptic lines upon the Queen's statue at Ludgate in the Fire—

> "While good Eliza on the outside Arch,
> Fir'd into th' old Mode, stands in Yellow Starch.
> Though fancy makes not Pictures live, or love,
> Yet Pictures fancy'd may the fancy move :
> Me-thinks the Queen on White-Hall cast her Eye ;
> An Arrow could not more directly flye.
> But when she saw her Palace safe, her fears
> Vanish, one Eye drops smiles, the other tears."

The " Yellow Starch " reference doubtless is to Elizabeth's sculptured ruff.

poverty after the Fire the churchwardens twice raised money by pawning them.[1] Sir Thomas Berrie, a merchant of the Staple, had given money to provide twelve poor parishioners each week with twelve penny loaves, and his curious brass, snatched from destruction, finds a place in the new church.

A mass of flame burnt into the night on the height about Ludgate, with blazing St. Paul's the central spectacle, after myriads of sparks showered far in advance by the impetuous wind had carried the Fire west. From the crest of the hill the Liberty lay out at the spectator's feet, threaded by the narrow line of Fleet Street, whence the red roof-tiles of the timber-framed houses, packed closely together, extended to Holborn. The scene differed greatly from that within the walled City. A Royal Palace, imposing still in height and dimensions, although a Royal residence no longer, stood where the little Fleet River joined the Thames—Bridewell, of unhappy memories to King Henry VIII. Its high walls and hexagonal turrets of red Tudor brick, inset with the characteristic diaper patterns in black, as at Hampton Court, were raised around two main courts, looking strong and solid with freestone lavishly used on mullion windows and battlements and arched doorways.[2] Immediately behind spread the buildings and courtyards of the Earl of Dorset's town mansion, and on this south side of Fleet Street towards the Thames were glimpses of green trees in the Earl's garden and in the wide demesne of the Temple. Wedged in close by Dorset House, on a site where earlier had stood the private playhouse, was the Salisbury Court Theatre, a wooden structure hastily erected at the Restoration [3]—the only London playhouse burnt in the Great Fire. On its stage Betterton had played with Davenant's company. In the distant view, above the low houses, might have been picked out the Round of the Temple Church, the great gate turrets of Middle Temple, the towers of three parish churches, and astride the street Temple Bar.

[1] Vestry Minutes, 1669, Nov. 3 ; 1684, Sept. 10.
[2] I am indebted to the research of my friend, the Rev. E. J. O'Donohue, Chaplain of Bethlem and Bridewell, for much of the topography of ancient Bridewell.
[3] See the writer's *Fleet Street in Seven Centuries*, pp. 231-3.

LUDGATE IN THE GREAT FIRE
From a painting believed to be contemporary

As dusk came on, the after-glow of a red sunset and darkness increased by the heavy smoke cloud trailing far distant from London, the lights of isolated fires showed plainly and with more threatening aspect amid the confused mass of buildings, while a great flame sped along the Thames-side.

Where the ground fell below Ludgate and the Old Bailey to the Fleet River was the oldest settled quarter of London beyond the Wall. Long years back the tanners of leather had dug their curing pits by the banks of the stream towards Newgate, and to this day the district is intersected by winding alleys, bearing quaint names like Bear Alley, Seacole Lane and Turnagain Lane, which bespeak their mediæval origin. It was a fetid spot, with the Fleet River as vile and stinking as when Ben Jonson wrote the furious lines of *The Famous Voyage* upon it and the locality generally—

> Whose banks upon
> Your Fleet Lane Furies and hot Cooks do dwell,
> That with still scalding steams make the place hell

The Fire swept the ground clean, as rarely it had been before, burning along the Fleet wharves and sheds as far as Holborn Bridge, there having been time to effect only a partial clearance. Here beneath the shadow of St. Paul's lay the Fleet debtors' prison of unhappy memory, on a site partly covered to-day by the Congregational Memorial Hall, and close about it the small area of the Fleet " rules," privileged ground whereon debtors and bankrupts able to find bail and money for the wardens' extortions were permitted to live unmolested by their creditors. The Fleet Prison, sacked and burnt by Wat Tyler's rebels and rebuilt, again succumbed to the flames of 1666. Sir Jeremy Whichcote then held the wardenship under Royal Patent, a humane and estimable man, whose conduct stands out in bold relief against the prison's long record of cruel misusage. He himself took care of the homeless debtors, who had momentarily been liberated, acquired Caronne House, in South Lambeth, for their accommodation, and afterwards rebuilt the gaol at his own expense on the historic site by Fleet Ditch.[1]

[1] For the third time the Fleet Prison was burnt down when the Gordon rioters broke into it in 1780. It was finally cleared away in 1846.

The Fire thrust forward up the rise of Fleet Street, leaving Bridewell at Thames-side a roofless shell, the ground piled high with brick debris, twisted iron, and molten lead. The flames raged with such intolerable heat that the very dead in their graves were burnt. Bridewell's walls were too stoutly made to fall. This had been " a wide large house of the King's Majesty " when the young Edward VI. granted it for the foundation of Bridewell Hospital, neglected by Henry VIII. after his unhappy experience there with Queen Catherine while awaiting the divorce, and already in sad decay. The charity had few funds to spend on the fabric, and to outward appearance Bridewell remained as Henry VIII. had built it in the early years of his reign, a Royal Palace, its walls and battlements rising thirty-six feet in height, with Long Gallery and Great Chamber of Audience and all necessary offices, fitting for the lodging of the King and his Consort, and for Councils of State. The Thames front and quadrangle were hopelessly shattered, a single tower alone standing firm, but the Fire did less havoc in the northern court, separated by the chapel, and parts of the Tudor structure there, retaining their original character, were incorporated in the rebuilding and survived a century ago.

Thomas Ellwood, the Quaker, was taken a prisoner to Old Bridewell four years before the Great Fire, and in his *Autobiography* gives many particulars about it. " The hall was one of the largest I was ever in. . . . The room in length was three score feet, and had breadth proportionate. In it on the front side were very large bay windows, in which stood a large table. It had other very large tables in it with benches round, and at that time the floor was covered with rushes, against some solemn festival which I heard it was bespoken for." This clearly was Henry's palace, but little changed. Bridewell served many purposes, as a place of detention, a house of correction for vagabonds and harlots, and a school for the training of boys in useful trades ; and it was, too, the City prison for refractory apprentices, and so remains to-day. In its large unused spaces 4000 quarters of the City's corn was stored, and this was destroyed in the Fire.[1]   There

[1] Edward Atkins' Letter in *Archæologia*, xix.

was also at Bridewell the City's coal, kept for the provision
of the poor against winter. A part was removed, and
the remainder much damaged.[1] Happily for London
in the hour of its distress, the larger granary at Bridge
House, Southwark, was not reached by the flames, and
famine was not added to the other calamities suffered by
the citizens.

The dead I have mentioned. Hugh Knowling, the
chapel warden, concerned for these burnt relics of
humanity, covered them reverently with earth and sand,
an office of charity (with others) which put the Governors
in his debt, then took the questionable course of " attach-
ing " a silver communion cup, gilt, with cover, and other
pieces of plate, from which his sacrilegious fingers were
loosened only after compensation made. The children
were sent away with their art-masters, with whom they
were subsequently lodged till a new Bridewell rose out of
the ruins.[2]

A man of note lay buried before the high altar in the
neighbouring church of St. Bride—Wynkyn de Worde, who
brought the art of printing into Fleet Street. He should
ere this have been honoured by a statue if the Fleet Street
Press in the rush of life had time to think of its debt.
His tomb perished with the church, an ancient building
considerably enlarged in the fifteenth century, which met
full square the onset of the Fire ; the bells melted in the
stone tower ; part only of the church plate was saved.
There survives by the north door the vault of the Holden
family, with their coat of arms carved in stone, bearing
date 1657. Amid the houses built close against the
churchyard, all levelled with the ground, was that of
Pepys's father, in which the diarist was himself born, and
out of it was carried to his baptism in St. Bride's Church.[3]
He paid a sad visit to the ruins.

Fire had occurred at Dorset House early this fateful
Tuesday. It happened that the Duke of York, passing

---

[1] *Repertory* 72, fo. 2. An entry in the City's Accounts, 1667, " Paid
to John Bromfeild, yeoman of the woodwharf, £40 for disbursements
about preserving and removing the City's coals at Bridewell," shows that
the City in this time of distress was victimized like the rest by the extortionate rates for cartage.

[2] Bridewell Court Minutes, 1666, Sept. 14, Nov. 2.

[3] *Athenæum*, 1913, Jan. 11 ; 1914, June.

in his barge upon the Thames, had seen a live firebrand blown by the wind upon the mansion, and thanks to his prompt alarm the outbreak was quenched.[1]

"I hear that Dorset House is burnt down, but I hope it is not so," wrote Lady Thanet from Stamford to the Dowager Countess of Pembroke.[2] It was, in fact, completely burnt out when the greater Fire came up. This historic house, originally the town hostel of the Bishops of Salisbury till a forced sale in Queen Elizabeth's reign to Sir Richard Sackville, was one of the few in the City that remained a nobleman's dwelling. Many additions had been made by successive Earls of Dorset, who for a century resided in Fleet Street. Four of the Earls had been born there. The mansion, large and irregular, was of such extent that it had become divided into Great and Little Dorset House. There are, unfortunately, no family letters at Knole which touch upon the catastrophe. Dorset House was not rebuilt.

High life and low mingled here, in the manner which made strange neighbours in every crowded mediæval city. Close against the Earl's mansion and the erstwhile Royal Palace spread a nest of foul rookeries and dilapidated mansions, tinder ready for the flames—Alsatia, upper and lower, and "Sharp Island." That the sanctuary should have survived the Fire of London, and in a few years have revived in the fullness of its dissolute life depicted in Shadwell's play, *The Squire of Alsatia*, is testimony to the extraordinary tolerance of the age for such a City plague spot. The White Friars' Priory, the original sanctuary, had filled the whole space between White-friars Street and the Temple on the land falling to the Thames. Some few of its scattered buildings survived, but the greater part had been pulled down at the Dissolution, and substantial houses erected as residences for noblemen and others. These inhabitants found life intolerable in a locality infested by rogues, who maintained the ancient privilege of refuge by force rather than by any acknowledged right; and the larger houses, abandoned to decay, were divided each into as many as twenty and thirty tenements, fulfilling their part in the medley of

[1] Letter to Viscount Conway, *op. cit.*
[2] Lord Hothfield's MSS. (*Hist. MSS. Comm.*, p. 85).

dirty lodgings, dram-shops, brothels and the like which made the sanctuary all that was evil.

The Fire brought consternation to the bravos, fraudulent debtors, cheats and thieves who crowded into the mean alleys. It broke into hiding places where the King's writ had successfully been defied, and setting alight the houses from basement to roof burnt up to Fleet Street, driving the sanctuary men helter skelter in search of safety. Little of Alsatia remained that was not purged by the Fire. Its daily round has been well portrayed by Sir Walter Scott in some brilliant pages of *The Fortunes of Nigel*. Even to-day, when printing houses chiefly have replaced the fetid dens of Alsatia's hey-day, its squalid aspect comes to mind when one walks the narrow passages of Whitefriars—Hanging Sword Alley, Magpie Alley, Primrose Hill, and the rest.

A substantial wall shut off the lawyers in the Temple from their lawless neighbours of Alsatia, and the brick houses of King's Bench Walk, then newly built, gave a temporary check to the Fire's advance.[1] The Inn of the Inner Temple, stretching from near Fleet Street to the Thames, offered a broad front to the oncoming flames, and it was almost entirely burnt out. When amidst heaps of debris the Benchers of Inner Temple afterwards surveyed their property, they found standing the ancient church of the Knights Templars, which was jointly maintained by the two Societies, their hall, part of Fig Tree Court, and the gateway to Fleet Street. The last had been rebuilt in the reign of James I., with the timber-fronted house, half resting upon its stout arch, which has been preserved by the County Council as one of London's historic monuments. Substantially nothing else escaped the Fire.

The flames burnt to the boundaries of the neighbour Inn, but there were stopped, and by remarkable good fortune Middle Temple lost but a single house—Lamb Building—in the Great Fire.

As so often was the case elsewhere, the Fire of 1666 found the Templars entirely unprepared. No appliances for dealing with an extensive outbreak were provided. Water was available in abundance, the New River service

---

[1] *London Gazette*, 1666, Sept. 3–10.

having been brought to the Inn, and an unlimited quantity
was procurable from the Thames, but there were no means
at hand to turn the supply on the burning piles.   The
flames, when at length they had overcome the brick
buildings of King's Bench Walk, spread with alarming
rapidity among the older timber-framed houses of which
the Temple was largely composed.

The Benchers had two full days' warning of their
peril as the Fire swept across London from the Bridge.
They had seen the good results that attended the first
use of gunpowder in the City this same day.   Sailors from
the Fleet were sent in to assist them, with barrels of Naval
powder, and this they were able to supplement by purchase from the store of a local grocer.   In addition, the
Inn secured the services of four engineers, at a fee of a
sovereign each, to aid in the demolition of buildings.[1]
By the judicious use of gunpowder in blowing up houses,
and so leaving open spaces, it was found practicable to
check the flames in several places.[2]   But always the Fire
again obtained the mastery, fanned by a fresh wind which
drove sparks and live embers before it.

" Neither boat, barge, cart nor coach is to be had, all
the streets full of goods, and the fire flaming into the very
Temple," wrote one J. Barker, who had escaped from his
chambers with difficulty, carrying away a part of his law
books.[3]

The gravest peril to the Temple came from the north.
Fleet Street, an old highway to Westminster and perilously narrow, was built throughout its length with timber-
framed and gabled houses, some of ancient date, others
no earlier than Elizabeth and James I., that had been
erected on the lands of abbots and ecclesiastics dispossessed

---

[1] Inderwick, *Cal. Inner Temple Records*, vol. 3, pp. xii, 44.

[2] It was not at the Great Fire of 1666, but a subsequent fire which
broke out in Pump Court, Middle Temple, on the night of Sunday, the
26th January, 1679, that the famous expedient of pumping beer on the
burning houses was resorted to.   " The Thames being frozen," says
Luttrell, " there was great scarcity of water, it being so bitter a frost,
the water hung in icicles at the eves of the houses.   The engine plaid
away many barrels of beer to stop the fire : but the chief way of stopping
the fire was by blowing up the houses : in doing which many were hurt,
particularly the Earl of Faversham, whose skull was almost broken :
but he is now in some hopes of recovery."   (*Brief Relation of State Affairs*,
i, 7.)

[3] *State Papers* (*Domestic*), 1666-7, p. 99.

at the Suppression. It burnt like matchwood, the Fire passing from house to house with unprecedented speed. From Fleet Ditch to Middle Temple Gate there was not a single wide side street, and towards the river two only— Salisbury Court and Water Lane (Whitefriars Street)— were capacious enough to admit a cart. The rest were mere foot alleys giving access to the dense property built between the highway and the Temple boundaries, seldom more than seven feet dividing opposite houses. Once the Fire spread back from the highway it was left to burn itself out, for nothing could be done.

Pleydell Court thus burnt, and the advancing flames demolished Serjeants Inn. This house of the Serjeants-at-Law and of the Judges stood amid a garden adjoining Inner Temple. It had a small but ornate hall, the painted windows emblazoned with forty-three coats of arms of Fellows of the Inn,[1] and chapel and kitchen and many residential chambers. All was destroyed. Ram Alley (to-day Hare Place), an outwork of the lawless Alsatia, was alight from end to end, and flames raged in Mitre Court. The Mitre Tavern, afterwards made famous by Samuel Johnson's patronage, stood back from Fleet Street, with double yards. It escaped with no great damage, though the gallery was ignited.

Fire enveloped the Temple on two sides, and had burnt the length of King's Bench Walk, at that time its most fashionable residential quarter. The Crown Office and the King's Bench Office, both situated there, were consumed early in the night. The Alienation Office, standing in a large garden, was in flames. The worst forebodings seemed about to be realized when the mass of fire from Fleet Street, having burnt down the courts and alleys, broke upon Mitre Court Buildings, within the Temple, and raged through them. Close at hand was the Master's House. Dr. Ball, the Master of the Temple, had little more than a year before built a new residence at his own charges, and had the mortification of learning that the whole structure had been destroyed.[2]

It seemed that nothing but the intervention of Providence could save the historic church of the Knights

---

[1] Dugdale, *Origines Juridiciales.*
[2] Inderwick, *Cal. Inner Temple Records,* vol. 3, pp. 43, 44, 50.

Templars. Relief came at a most opportune hour. But those who laboured with much heat and sweat to check the flames were not idle. The peril of the stone church, itself stoutly built by mediæval craftsmen, was gravely augmented by the presence of a number of small shops which had been allowed to be raised up against its southern and western walls. Gunpowder was unsparingly used to destroy these and isolate the fabric, and although the church was very nearly touched at the south-eastern corner, it stood after the Fire was out unharmed. Lamb Building was burnt. North of the little graveyard wherein Oliver Goldsmith now lies every house was destroyed. The Exchequer Office was consumed. Even the lodges near the Thames-side had been caught by the flames. Leafless and blackened, wrecks of the fine trees then planted about King's Bench Walk swayed in the wind.

In Old Paper Buildings Selden had lodged, in rooms on the top floor with a gallery overlooking the gardens, and there he was visited, he tells delightfully in *Table Talk*, by " a lunatic person of quality, who came to my chambers in the Temple and told me he had two devils in his head." Old Paper Buildings escaped the flames.

Loss by the Fire, necessarily great in any circumstances, was aggravated by the fact that it occurred in Long Vacation, when many lawyers were away and their chambers locked. Lord Clarendon writes that " when the fire came where the lawyers had houses, as they had in many places, especially Serjeants Inn in Fleet Street, with that part of the Inner Temple that was next it and White Friars, there was scarce a man to whom those lodgings appertained who was in town ; so that whatsoever was there, their money, books and papers, besides the evidences of many men's estates deposited in their hands, were all burnt or lost, to a very great value."

Across the highway the Fire received a check, being stopped at Fetter Lane corner under singular circumstances. " Its greediness was the cause of its own destruction," says an onlooker. The flames passed over some houses in Fleet Street, setting alight a wooden one that burnt with its neighbour, and were prevented from getting farther by the obstruction of a brick house. With this fortuitous help and the assistance of a few workers there was made a wide gap by the time the main body of the Fire had advanced.[1]

The wind actually increased in violence this Tuesday evening, rising before it subsided. Fleet Street was reduced to ruins in a few hours, the flames being driven along with such impetuosity that there was despair of saving even the western end of the town. Of the large parish of St. Bride's, only sixteen houses in Great New Street, then a broad open place, were left standing. The panic spread to distant Westminster. " Nothing can be like the distraction we were in, but the Day of Judgment," wrote one afterwards. Buildings in the Strand were blown up with gunpowder in order to isolate Somerset House, the safety of which it was feared would be menaced. Lyenbergh, the Swedish Resident, fearful for his safety in Covent Garden, begged for a warrant to press four carts in which to save his goods. The fashionable residents of the Strand, having the benefit of the river, cleared the furniture from their houses into barges or any other vessels available, and despatched them upstream beyond reach of the Fire. Many dwellers on both sides of the Strand, not knowing whither to go, and scarcely conscious of what they did, fled with their families out into the streets, that they might not be within their houses when the flames fell upon them.[2]

The Court was thrown into confusion. King Charles, anxious even for Whitehall, ordered that Sir John Denham's new buildings at Scotland Yard should be unroofed and " defaced," in order to check the Fire.[3] Sir William Coventry, at St. James's, removed his goods, " as the King at Whitehall and everybody had done, and was doing," says Pepys. Clarendon turned out of Berkshire House, where he stayed while his great mansion in Piccadilly was building. " We who live in the suburbs, preparing for the same fate, fled from our lodgings, and have hardly yet recovered our goods or our wits," he wrote afterwards to Lord Winchilsea.[4]

Nearer the danger, the Benchers of Lincoln's Inn razed to the ground a tavern in Chancery Lane called the

[1] Malcolm, *Lond. Rediv.*, ii, 75.   [2] Clarendon's *Life*.
[3] *Calendar of Treasury Books*, 1667–8, p. 598.
[4] Finch MSS. (*Hist. MSS. Comm.*, p. 435).

St. John's Head, fearful lest a fire there might involve their property.[1]

Hope was almost abandoned of saving anything from the flames when late on Tuesday night salvation came to London—to what remained of London—by the fall of the wind.   At eleven o'clock messengers hastened to the Duke of York, imploring further assistance in men and tackle.   They represented that there was a prospect of stopping the Fire, the wind having then slackened.[2]   The soldiers were exhausted after the heat and labour of the day, but the new turn of events, so long and anxiously awaited, revived the spirits of all.   The wind veered to the south, and slowly its force decreased, as throughout the night the struggle was maintained, and still against fearful odds : in the Temple, north of Fleet Street, by the Fleet River to Holborn Bridge, about Cripplegate and the northern City Wall, and far distant as The Tower.   At all these places bright flame leapt to the sky, but the biggest blaze was in the choked and inaccessible property lying north of Fleet Street.

Checked by Pie Corner, Smithfield, and at Holborn Bridge, where it passed the Fleet River, the Fire out of Newgate took a southerly course.   St. Andrew Holborn thus escaped ; this church, one of the most ancient in London, was already so dilapidated that in 1682 it was found necessary to pull it down.   Only the lower portion of the old tower survives in Wren's rebuilding.   The flames crossed Shoe Lane, leaving standing at their edge the old town house of the Bishop of Bangor (then used as poor tenements), a fragment of which remained till the early years of last century.   The Fire there joined with that burning up from Fleet Street.   In Shoe Lane were rival resorts for entertainment of the town, the new cock-pit, of which Pepys gives an unpleasant account, and " a show called the Opera or Paradise," of which I know nothing save that its owner died of Plague in the previous year and the whole place was burnt out in the Fire. There, too, was claimed another victim.   Paul Lowell, a watchmaker living in Shoe Lane behind the Globe Tavern, was eighty years of age, dull of hearing, and deaf to the

[1] Add. MSS. 5067, fo. 301.   Baildon, Records of Lincoln's Inn.
[2] Wind. Sandys' Letter.

admonition of his son and his friends, who warned him of his peril. The old man declared that he would never leave his house till it fell in upon him ; and kept his word, for he sank with its ruins into the cellar, where afterwards his bones, together with his keys, were found.[1]

Eastward, against the wind, the Fire had made slower progress. In the bend of Lime Street, flames coming up from Fenchurch Street destroyed Pewterers Hall, and the Company suffered the further loss of all their City house property save only a single alley. The larger part of the records were removed in time. Preserved from the Fire, and fixed in one of the windows of the present banqueting room, is an interesting relic, a representation of a spider and fly beneath a sundial, all on the same piece of glass. Its emblematical meaning has been the subject of much speculation.

St. Gabriel Fenchurch, standing out in the street, perished, and the Fire found its limits at Clothworkers Hall, Mincing Lane, which burnt for three days and nights in one body of flame, the cellar being full of oil.[2] This was yet another Elizabethan structure lost to London, the Hall having been built in 1598 on land which " the Sheermen of London " had obtained by gift in Henry VI.'s reign, after their amalgamation with the Fullers.

The Fire entered Tower Street on Tuesday. Pepys, going there in the afternoon with Sir William Penn, " met the fire burning three or four doors beyond Mr. Howell's, whose goods, poor man, his trays and dishes, shovels, etc., were flung all along Tower Street in the kennels, and people working therewith from one end to the other ; the fire coming on in that narrow street, on both sides, with infinite fury." The labour brought little result. At night Pepys was again in Tower Street, when it was all on fire, flames burst out of the Trinity House, and the Dolphin Tavern opposite was alight.

The Custom House by the river, built by Queen Elizabeth to meet the wants of England's great age of expansion, was completely destroyed. The eastward Fire also consumed Bakers Hall, a building of much interest in Harp Lane, sometime the dwelling of John Chichele,

---

[1] Rege Sincera, *Observations*, etc., p. 14.
[2] Pepys's *Diary*, 1666, Sept. 6.

Chamberlain of London in 1437, and acquired by the Bakers Company late in the fifteenth century. The loss of these, however, would have counted as nothing had once the Tower of London been involved in the circuit of the flames, for apart from its unique place among our national possessions, the fortress was, with almost incredible folly, being used as a storehouse for the Navy's gunpowder. Evelyn had a horrific vision of what might have happened had the magazine in the White Tower exploded as the culminating act in the Fire: " It would not only have beaten down and destroyed all the bridge, but sunk and torn all the vessels in the river, and rendered the demolition beyond all expression for several miles about the country."

In fact, the powder had already been removed when the peril drew near, thanks to the energy of Sir John Robinson, the Lieutenant, and this danger at least averted. The goldsmiths' money and jewellery, valued on a rough estimate at no less than £1,200,000, were carried out to Whitehall.[1] The Fire, destroying all Mincing Lane, established itself in the foot of Mark Lane, where houses were blown to pieces to save the rest,[2] then burnt down to the Tower graff, before the Moat, alongside which were a number of old timber dwellings. It did not, however, reach them, and they stood to be afterwards pulled down as a measure of precaution. The Tower was saved by the blowing up of houses along the street from Watergate, before the Fire came so far, thus enlarging the open space. A wine-shop and warehouse were demolished by powder in Seething Lane, to prevent the flames entering there.[3]

The Fire after midnight on Tuesday came right up to Allhallows Barking Church, flames licking the stone walls and destroying the clock face on the tower. The parsonage house, immediately adjoining, was burnt to the ground. The Fire travelled no farther, and Allhallows Barking and the few houses beyond mark its extreme eastern limit. It appears from the churchwardens' accounts that the clock, chimes, and " dyall " were repaired for 20s. Pepys mentions injury to " part of the porch," but as there is

---

[1] Wind. Sandys' Letter.   [2] Add. MSS., 5063, fo. 221.
[3] Add. MSS. 5063, fo. 1.

no other entry of payment, it may be assumed that the
20*s*. represents all the damage done. The old church,
happily preserved intact, is historically the most interesting of those within the Fire area, though less known to
Londoners, probably, than to Americans, with whom it
is a place of pilgrimage by reason of its associations with
Penn, the founder of Pennsylvania.

CHAPTER IX

P EPYS, alarmed by the Fire's approach to Seething Lane, was astir before sunrise on Wednesday. The *Diary* may again be quoted for the spectacle that the City presented that day :

" About two in the morning my wife calls me up, and tells me of new cries of fire, it being come to Barking Church, which is the bottom of our lane. I up ; and finding it so, resolved presently to take her away, and did, and took my gold, which was about £2,350, W. Hewer and Jane down by Proudy's boat to Woolwich ; but Lord ! what a sad sight it was by moonlight to see the whole City almost on fire, that you might see it as plain at Woolwich as if you were by it. There, when I came, I find the gates shut but no guard kept at all ; which troubled me, because of discourses now begun, that there is a plot in it, and that the French had done it. I got the gates open, and to Mr. Sheldon's, where I locked up my gold ; and charged my wife and W. Hewer never to leave the room without one of them in it, night or day. So back again, by the way seeing my goods well in the lighters at Deptford, and watched well by people. Home, and whereas I expected to have seen our house on fire, it now being seven o'clock, it was not. But to the fire, and there find greater hopes than I expected ; for my confidence of finding our office on fire was such that I durst not ask anybody how it was, till I came and saw it was not burned. But, going to the fire, I find by the blowing up of houses, and the great help given by the workmen out of the King's yards, sent up by Sir W. Pen, there is a good stop given to it, as well at Mark Lane end as ours.

" I up to the top of Barking Steeple, and there saw the

saddest sight of desolation that I ever saw; everywhere great fires, oil cellars and brimstone and other things burning. I became afraid to stay there long, and therefore down again as fast as I could, the fire being spread as far as I could see; and to Sir W. Pen's, and there ate a piece of cold meat, having eaten nothing since Sunday but the remains of Sunday's dinner. Here I met with Mr. Young and Whistler; and having removed all my things, and received good hopes that the fire at our end is stopped, they and I walked into the town, and find Fenchurch Street, Gracious Street, and Lombard Street all in dust. The Exchange a sad sight, nothing standing there of all the statues and pillars but Sir Thomas Gresham's picture in the corner.

"Into Moorfields (our feet ready to burn walking through the town among the hot coals), and find that full of people, and poor wretches carrying their goods there, and everybody keeping his goods together by themselves; and a great blessing it is to them that it is fair weather for them to keep abroad night and day; drank there, and paid twopence for a plain penny loaf. Thence homeward, having passed through Cheapside and Newgate Market, all burned, and seen Anthony Joyce's house on fire. I also did see a poor cat taken out of a hole in a chimney joining to the wall of the Exchange, with the hair all burned off the body and yet alive. So home at night and find there good hopes of saving our office; but great endeavours of watching all night, and having men ready; and so we lodged them in the office, and had drink and bread and cheese for them. And I lay down and slept a good night about midnight; though, when I rose, I heard that there had been a great alarm of French and Dutch being risen, which proved nothing."

The sight which Pepys beheld from the church tower of Allhallows Barking an hour or two after daybreak indicated that the Fire was exhausting its strength. "Great fires" there were in various places, so many that from a distance the whole City may have seemed alight; but with the fall of the wind the Fire of London had lost its capacity for large destruction. Pepys' venturesome walk into the burnt City this Wednesday, hot and difficult as it was, would have been impossible had that been otherwise.

There was still a considerable body of flame along the City's western edge, burning noisily among the timber houses. The Duke of York was again in the streets at six o'clock. He found the Fire almost quenched on both sides of Fleet Street,[1] but it spread towards Temple Bar on the south side till stopped near Inner Temple Gate, at the spot where long afterwards the Temple Exchange Coffee House flourished. St. Dunstan's Church, opposite, escaped unharmed, though in grave peril in the narrow street. A corner house of Fetter Lane having been riven by gunpowder, the flames turned up that thoroughfare, to die down ultimately amid the destruction caused by the fire burning south from Holborn Bridge. They left standing in Fleet Street, just beyond Fetter Lane, two typical timber-framed dwellings, probably early Stuart, with balconies before the roof gables, that marked the limits to which the Fire burnt till their destruction in 1893.

A quiet haven by the corner, sheltered from the roar of the highway, maintains its ancient repose—Clifford's Inn. This is an old Inn of Chancery, sadly reduced of late years in area and picturesqueness. One seems there nearer to the Fire of London than at any other spot. A single house burnt—No. 13, the nearest to Fetter Lane—but grouped about are delightful old red-brick houses that were there while the flames raged. The row comprising Nos. 15 to 17, facing the little garden, dates from 1663 ; parts of No. 12, the oldest house in the Inn, from 1624 ; and Nos. 8 and 10, at the east end of the hall, are also of considerable antiquity.[2] Clifford's Inn Hall, in which the Fire Judges sat to adjust claims, still stands.

The Liberty of the Rolls was at the Fire's edge. Little of the ancient House for Converted Jews, of Henry III.'s foundation, can then have survived save the Rolls Chapel, the chancel of which burnt, ignited presumably by flying sparks, for the mass of the Fire never reached so far. The chancel had gone in 1667, when Hollar's drawing indicates that a new wall had been built at the east end of the nave ; and the injury done was confirmed when the fabric was finally demolished in 1896, fragments of wrought

[1] Wind. Sandys' Letter.
[2] Dr. Philip Norman, *Burlington Magazine*, i, 264.

stonework not later than the fifteenth century built into the wall bearing signs of having been exposed to fire.[1] The public records in Charles II.'s reign were widely scattered, some being at The Tower, others at Westminster, but there was a large store of them at the Rolls Chapel, mostly legal documents. These were saved without loss. The gentleman in attendance upon the Duke of York, whose letter I have before cited, tells that his Royal Highness, being satisfied that the Fire in Fleet Street was well in hand, proceeded to the Rolls, " and put the people to work there to preserve the rolls, caused all people, men, women and children that were able to work to come, and to those who refused he beat them to it ; by this means he got people to other places, as Fetter Lane, which he preserved by the assistance of some brick houses and garden walls ; likewise Shoe Lane was preserved by the same way." [2]

By the energy of all the Fire was put out, but not before several houses built upon the Rolls Gardens from Fetter Lane had been burnt down or demolished to prevent the flames spreading farther west.[3] Dutch writers, with curious persistency, assert that Temple Bar, then an old timber-built structure with steep roof, red tiled, was itself burnt ; by one account it was " reduced to ashes, all but the roof "—a topsy-turvy result, assuredly ! There is no English record of this that I know.

There was less need on Wednesday to press the people to labour than at the earlier stages of the Fire. Its progress was at length decisively checked. The wind had fallen during the night to dead calm. In all except a few scattered areas the flames were under control, and in these burnt with reduced force, dying away amid the ruins they had made. Legions of those who had flocked out of the City came back to assist in stamping out the last embers. " Now they begin to bestir themselves (writes Evelyn in his *Diary*), and not till now, who hitherto had stood as men intoxicated, with their hands across." Gunpowder was freely used in bringing down additional houses, and all about the Fire's edge the crack of explosions resounded.

---

[1] 57th Report Dep. Keeper Public Records, App., p. 23.
[2] Wind. Sandys' Letter.
[3] Fire Decrees, Guildhall, vol. i, fo. 507. Add MSS. 5063, fo. 129 ; *ibid.* 5064, fo. 258.

Fetter Lane for nearly one-half its length from Holborn was saved, the flames being stopped at the outlying burial ground of St. Dunstan's parish, a fragment of which survives at Bream's Buildings. They burnt along Dean Street on both sides. Nevill's Court was destroyed; three early Stuart timber houses there, belonging to the Goldsmiths Company, stood intact after the Fire had swept past and till our own time, protected by their large gardens —there are gardens still before the houses of this City byway. The conventicle which afterwards became the Moravian Chapel also was spared.

In the course of the morning the Fire was put out in Shoe Lane, and by noon was quenched at Holborn Bridge. It then broke out afresh in Cow Lane, Smithfield, where Alderman Sir Richard Browne, the stout Parliamentary General turned Royalist, with a party of the Trained Bands, toiled amid the heat till its extinction, having Lord Craven to help him. The whole city of ruins that day was befogged. Smoke rose in clouds from the smouldering contents of burnt warehouses, and having no wind to disperse it, hovered low.

A most troublesome and dangerous fire, involving great destruction, still raged about Cripplegate, and taxed the utmost energies of those pressed into the work of fighting it, reinforced though they were by troops and seamen relieved from duty in other parts of the City. It burnt throughout the entire day, and the night was far advanced before it was under. The Lord Mayor, Sir Thomas Bludworth, came out of the obscurity to which he had been relegated since his failure on Sunday, and with laudable energy superintended the pulling down of great numbers of houses to check its progress. Lord Manchester, Lord Ashley, and other Lords of the Council rode about the streets, having pipes opened wherever a supply of water was available, and powder brought up to assist the demolitions.[1] The Duke of York spent several hours at Cripplegate. The King joined his brother there. " I was no eye-witness," says Rolle, " but I have been informed that when the Fire came to Cripplegate His Majesty Charles II., being then and there present, did in his own person take great pains (in no less, as was told, than if he had been a poor

[1] Wind. Sandys' Letter.

Photo. by Mr. Lionel Gowing

TYPES OF RESTORATION LONDON

The Great Fire, when burning through Nevill's Court, Fetter Lane, spared these old houses, timber framed with lath and plaster fronts, which were isolated by their gardens. They were demolished in 1911

labourer) to promote the extinction of it." [1]   Many actual
eye-witnesses whom I have quoted in an earlier chapter
have testified to the King's activity.

The Fire burnt to the City Wall, making no inconsiderable addition to the damage already done to London.
John Milton lies buried in St. Giles Cripplegate, the ancient
and historical church standing outside the gate, which
bears in the basement of its tower some few traces of the
still earlier church of Alfun.   St. Giles's wholly escaped,
thanks to its isolation.   Within the City Wall the flames
found fresh fuel in the dense property which packed close
up to it, and here amid the dwellings three additional
halls of City Companies were destroyed, and a fourth
greatly injured.   Curriers Hall, which stood against the
wall, was an Elizabethan building.   The Fire consumed
the hall itself, the Company's records, and presumably the
plate as well, for nothing is found prior to 1666.   Plaisterers
Hall, in Addle Street (the Company lost all its City property
save one alley), and Brewers Hall, near by, met with a like
fate.

Elsyng Spital had been founded early in the fourteenth
century, a little east of Cripplegate, by the pious charity
of William Elsyng, for the glory of God, the good of his
soul, and the relief of one hundred poor men, by choice
those who were blind.   When the Fire came, and passed,
the brothers' chapel survived as the parish church of
St. Alphage.   The tower stands to-day, though concealed
from view, and to the belfrey stage (above which it has
been rebuilt) is the only remaining fragment of any
mediæval hospital left in London.   The flames burnt close
around, but the church was unharmed.   Elsewhere on the
Spital grounds stood Sion College, built forty years before
the Great Fire by the executors of Dr. Thomas White,
vicar of St. Dunstan-in-the-West, for a gild or fraternity
which was to consist of all the clergy of London.   The
College hall, library, offices, almshouses, and students'
chambers—all were destroyed.   Its particular pride was
a valuable collection of books, as became a company of
learned clerks, ranged in a long library, which John
Sympson, rector of St. Olave Hart Street, had added at
his own expense.   A despairing effort was made to save

[1] S. Rolle, *London's Resurrection*, 1668.

these books, a considerable portion being removed to the Charterhouse, not, however, before at least one-third had been consumed or hopelessly spoilt. The almsfolk found safe refuge in the church.[1]

West of the gate the Cripplegate fire spread to Barber Surgeons Hall, in Monkwell Street, burning a vast deal there, though much was saved. We owe the preservation of Holbein's great picture of the grant by Henry VIII. of the charter to the Barber Surgeons Company to the foresight of one Major Brooks, who when the flames drew near removed it to a place of safety.[2] It is curious to know that Pepys, having an eye to a bargain, hesitated to give £200 for the immortal work—

Aug. 28, 1668.—Harris [the actor] and I to Chyrurgeons Hall, where they are building it new very fine ; and there to see their Theatre, which stood all the Fire, and (which was our business) their great picture of Holbein's, thinking to have bought it ; I did think to give £200 for it, it being said to be worth £1000, but it is so spoiled that I have no mind to it, and it is not a pleasant though a good picture.

No trace of the damage that Pepys mentions is visible to-day.   The surgeons' theatre, " which stood all the Fire," was a detached building, erected by Inigo Jones about the year 1636.   Walpole deemed it one of the best examples of the famous architect's work ; its interior has been made familiar by a gruesome print by Hogarth.   Fire actually caught the roof of the theatre, whereupon a seaman climbed up and beat the flames out.   The Company's Hall seems to have been largely destroyed.   The old Court Room is still in use.   Most of the writings were carried out to Moorfields, but the minutes of 1666 have been lost, and the Company has no records of the Great Fire save the wardens' accounts.   Various skeletons of criminals. turned over for dissection by the surgeons after execution at Tyburn, and two stuffed human figures, popularly known as " Adam and Eve," were also among the salvage.

Flames burning through Aldersgate and at London Wall alarmed the few noble families who still dwelt in the City at Aldersgate Street.   The Countess of Thanet fled

---

[1] Waterhous, *Short Narrative*, 1667, p. 146.   Milman, *Lond. & Midd. Archæol. Soc.*, vi, 89.
[2] Wardens' Accounts.

out of London, having given crders for her house to be emptied. " I thank God," she wrote to the Dowager Countess of Pembroke at Skipton Castle, " I came well last night to Stamford, and we are all very well ; and I hear it confirmed that Thanet House is safe from the fire, and likewise Aldersgate Street, the nearest that it came to my house was Surgeons Hall, on the backside my garden, which is burnt to the ground. Whether I have a bed left at Thanet House or no I do not know. Lord Hatton doth confirm that all is burnt from Pudding Lane that is near the Bear at the Bridge foot to Temple Bar. I have sent a man up to London to Fotherby, that if my beds be carried out of the house to get some of them in again, for it is dangerous lodging for the plague and small-pox, and scarcely any lodging to be had." [1]

This fourth day of the Fire did not pass without fresh alarms. The last live embers about The Tower and the foot of Mark Lane were beaten down late in the afternoon ; [2] but at night the ruins of Shoe Lane broke into flame, and there was a violent outburst at Cripplegate, again lighting the red glare in the sky.[3]

The most serious outbreak occurred that night in the Temple, sparks from the still smouldering houses in King's Bench Walk having become lodged on some timber build-ings. These last were brought to the ground by gun-powder, but the flames were in dangerous proximity to Inner Temple Hall. Before this second fire was out what little remained standing of Inner Temple was mostly destroyed by flames and powder. The Duke of York, himself a bencher of the Inn, hurried down to the Temple on receiving the message, and remained there directing operations till one o'clock in the morning, when all danger was over. He found on arrival a crowd of people clamouring at the gates, but the lawyers refused to let them enter, fearing, with good reason, that the Inn would lose more by looting than gain by help.

Gunpowder was used unsparingly, and probably greater damage was done by its means than by the new fire. There occurred one of those farcical incidents sometimes inseparable from grim tragedy. " The Duke of York

---

[1] Lord Hothfield's MSS.   [2] Malcolm, *Lond. Rediv.*, iv, 76–7.
[3] Verney MSS. (*Hist. MSS. Comm.*, p. 485).

(says Wind. Sandys, the gentleman who attended him) found no way of saving the Temple Chapel, and the Hall by the Chapel, but blowing up the Paper house in that court, which experiment, if it had been used at first, might have saved a great many houses.   One of the Templars, seeing gunpowder brought, came to the Duke and told him it was against the rules and charter of the Temple that any should blow that house with gunpowder, upon which Mr. Germaine, the Duke's Master of the Horse, took a good cudgel and beat the young lawyer to the purpose. There is no hopes of knowing who this lawyer is, but the hope that he will bring an action of battery against Mr. Germaine." [1]

The ancient hall of Inner Temple was a precious relic of the past.   The Knights Templars had themselves raised its walls, within which took place their ceremonies and feasts.   A few remains still exist in an underground vault. It was gravely menaced by the flames, and despite the shattering of the neighbouring houses one end of the roof caught fire.   A seaman named Richard Rowe with great agility climbed the roof, and, sitting astride the ridge, beat the flames out.   His exploit, which saved the building, was celebrated in contemporary verse :

> When after one dayes rest The Temple smokes,
> And with fresh fires and fears the Strand provokes,
> But with good Conduct all was slak'd that night
> By one more valiant than a Templar Knight.
> Here a brisk rumour of afrighted gold
> Sent hundreds in ; more Covetous than bold.
> But a brave Seaman up the Tyles did skip
> As nimbly as the Cordage of a Ship.
> Bestrides the singed Hall on its highest ridge
> Moving as if he were on London Bridge,
> Or on the Narrow of a Skullers keel :
> Feels neither head nor heart nor spirits reel. [2]

The Benchers rewarded the intrepid seaman with a gift of £10 for his services.   A gift of £2 was also made to a soldier from Kingston who helped.   Either in the night fire or that which preceded it—one cannot distinguish— Inner Temple suffered additional loss by the destruction of the whole of the buildings upon the site now covered by the library, the class-rooms, the Parliament Chamber, with

---

[1] Wind. Sandys' Letter.   [2] J. Crouch, *Londinenses Lachrymae*, 1666.

the offices below, and also Tanfield Court; and a part of Fig Tree Court was blown up by gunpowder.[1] The lawyers' loss was bitter, indeed. A skeleton, and barely that, remained of all their widespread property.

This was the Fire's expiring effort, though at dawn Pepys was called up to lead the Navy men to an isolated fire in Bishopsgate, where none had previously been. He has etched for us the last scene of the Great Fire, the women hard at work in the street kennels sweeping away the water; " then they would scold for drink, and be as drunk as devils. I saw good butts of sugar broken open in the street, and people give and take handfulls out, and put into beer, and drink it." We leave the *Diary*, invaluable as it has been for its many personal touches, where Pepys takes boat to view the desolation below and above bridge, " and so to Westminster, thinking to shift myself, being all dirt from top to bottom." " A sad sight," he moralizes, " to see how the river looks; no houses nor church near it, to the Temple, where it stopped." Nights thereafter he slept uneasily, " much terrified with dreams of fire and falling down of houses."

The Great Fire of London, having burnt four days and nights, was out when the sun on Thursday rose high over the still smoking city, and the exhausted people were able to take rest. They had begun to lose count of the days, and with so much to do, so much excitement and so little sleep, it seemed a week or more since their troubles began.[2] The Fire died down almost as rapidly as it had risen. " A fire such as had not been known in Europe since the conflagration of Rome under Nero," in Macaulay's phrase, was at last conquered. No human effort alone could have subdued it under the conditions in which it raged throughout Monday and Tuesday, and only the providential fall of the wind on Tuesday night enabled its progress to be stayed. Little wonder that men of religious mind saw in this the direct intervention of the Divine Will, as if in mercy staying the flames with the command, " Thus far shalt thou go, and no farther." That was the burden of countless

---

[1] Inderwick, *Cal. Inner Temple Records*, iii, 42, 44. See also *A True and exact Relation of the Most Dreadful and Remarkable Fires*, 1666 (Broadside).

[2] Pepys's *Diary*, 1666, Sept. 5, 6, and 15.

sermons, and of printed exhortations, appeals and homilies to which the Fire of London gave rise.

The Fire was out, and a first comprehensive sight of the devastated City disclosed no majesty of ruins, but— dirt! It lay out everywhere, lying thickly about the stumps of walls and heaps of what had been houses : black dirt in the form of powdered charcoal, white and black dirt from fire-riven and calcined stones, brown dirt and yellow dirt from bricks, detritus of every source and colour deposited by the wind over the whole City and westward over Westminster, a layer left as though by a receding tide. In places it was inches thick where eddies of hot air-currents had circled. Every errant puff of wind sent the top layer of the myriads of atoms dancing. Tons of solid matter, disintegrated and changed in the intense heat of the flames, had been moved unseen. Never was there such a task of clearing up as London offered after the Fire.

Thousands of homeless citizens were in distress, camped with the goods they had salved in the open fields around London. They had escaped the flames, but were in danger of famine. Immense quantities of provisions had been consumed in the burnt houses, not being worth removal at the extortionate rates charged for cartage. In addition, the bakers, brewers and others who inhabited the unburnt parts of the town had forsaken their shops, carrying away all that was portable, and lacked the confidence or wit to return at once and fall to their occupations. In large areas spared by the fire, as well as in the fields, the people were for many hours without food.[1] The King on Wednesday issued two Royal Proclamations for their relief.

These commanded the magistrates and deputy-lieutenants in counties whence provisions were chiefly derived personally to see that as great quantities of provisions as could possibly be furnished be daily and constantly sent to London, especially of bread. For their sale and distribution markets were to be kept at Bishopsgate, at Tower Hill, and at Smithfield each day ; the wants of those refugees who had gone farther afield were to be served by the appointment of temporary markets at Clerkenwell, Islington, Finsbury Fields, Mile End Green,

[1] Clarendon's *Life*.

and Ratcliffe. All persons concerned were to resort to such places, " We having taken care," says the Proclamation, " to secure the said markets in safety, and prevent all disturbances by the refusal of payment for goods or otherwise."

Large numbers of distressed persons having preserved their goods, but not knowing how to dispose of them, it was his Majesty's pleasure that all churches, chapels, schools and other like public places should be open freely to receive such goods as might be brought to them, and the justices of Middlesex, Essex, and Surrey were commanded to see that this be done.

All cities and towns whatsoever were required, without any contradiction, to receive distressed refugees from London, and to permit them the free exercise of their manual trades, the King pledging his Royal word that when the present exigency should have passed he would take care and order that none of such persons should be a burden to the respective towns and parishes.

Thanks to the ample charity extended by all the outlying places and residents within the suburbs to ameliorate the lot of the unhappy Londoners, these first steps were successful in meeting the immediate distress, and there was no real shortage of food. The King sent biscuit from the Navy into Moorfields, but the people there, being already supplied and unaccustomed to such hard fare, made no use of it.[1]

The King himself rode out to Moorfields on Thursday (September 6) and addressed the homeless citizens gathered there. It is not difficult to reconstruct the scene : the grass fields littered with goods that had been brought out of the flaming streets ; for a background the City in ashes, the grey north Wall erect and straight, and St. Paul's the dominating ruin of a vast aggregation of ruins ; the people, rich and poor, mingled together and united in a common calamity which shattered distinctions ; and over all the blue sky of a summer day. A few gentlemen attended the King. He spoke from horseback, seeking to allay the anguish and alarm that were visible in the upturned faces around him. He told the people that the judgment which had fallen upon London was immediately from the hand of

[1] *London Gazette*, 1666, Sept. 3–10.

God, and that no plot by Frenchmen or Dutchmen or Papists had any part in bringing upon them so much misery.   Many of those who had been detained upon suspicion he had himself examined.   He assured the citizens that he found no reason to suspect connivance in burning the City.   He desired the Londoners to take no more alarm ; he had strength enough to defend them from any enemy, and assured them that he, their King, would, by the grace of God, live and die with them, and he would take a particular care of them all.[1]

Out of the exhausted inferno ominous wisps of smoke were still rising.   " I can say but this," wrote a member of Lincoln's Inn, describing the havoc, " that there is nothing but stones and rubbish, and all exposed to the open air, so that you may see from one end of the City almost to the other.   You can compare London (were it not for the rubbish) to nothing more than an open field." [2]   To another onlooker the sight of devastated London brought reminder of the broad expanses of his native Westmoreland.   " The houses are laid so flat to the ground that the city looks just like our fells, for there is nothing to be seen but heaps of stones." [3]

It was long before the full extent of the calamity could be made known, after a complete survey of the ruins.   The table given by Jonas Moore and Ralph Gatrix, the City Surveyors, needs no comment.   This was the destruction wrought and the area saved—

> 373 acres burnt within the walls, and
> 63 acres 3 roods without the walls.
> 87 parish churches, besides chapels burnt.[4]
> 13,200 houses burnt in over 400 streets and courts.
> 75 acres 3 roods still standing within the walls unburnt.
> 11 parishes without the walls yet standing.

In rough computation, the flames destroyed an area equal to an oblong with its greatest length a mile and a half, and in depth half a mile.   This does not over-estimate the destruction.   Nathanial Hardy, preaching

---

[1] Wind. Sandys' Letter.
[2] Edward Atkins' Letter.
[3] Alexander Fleming to his brother.   Le Fleming MSS. (*Hist. MSS. Comm.*, p. 41).
[4] The Surveyors' report gives eighty-nine ; but see Appendix III.

at St. Olave Hart Street, used a quaintly bookish phrase, describing the City as reduced from a volume of large folio to a decimotertio.

Dead calm succeeded the violence of the wind, and no farther extension of the Fire was to be feared ; but work remained to be done both on Thursday and Friday in beating down flames wherever they gained a new head, as happened in many places.   A detachment of two hundred soldiers was brought to London from Hertfordshire, with carts laden with pickaxes, spades, and buckets, to prevent any further outbreak and afford relief, all hands being wearied with the labour.   Similar aid was obtained from Kent, Middlesex, and Surrey, relieved by fresh bands day by day.   The King on Sunday warned the Aldermen that there was still much combustible material about the City, bavins, faggots, and the like, bearing sparks.   They were to order the owners to remove it, failing compliance to move it themselves, and meanwhile to have a good watch kept.[1]

This first Sunday after the Fire the people camped about the City's edge crowded into the surviving churches. But one was standing where there had been from five to six a week before.   Pepys attended worship at his parish church of St. Olave Hart Street.   " Our parson," he jots in the *Diary*, " made a melancholy but good sermon ; and many and most in the church cried, specially the women. The church mighty full ; but few of fashion, and most strangers."   The first rain of this fateful week fell that day.

Alarms were frequent over London for weeks afterwards, small fires continuing to burn unchecked in unopened cellars and dismantled warehouses, and places wherein coal, oil, and other inflammable goods were lodged. A newsletter, dated Sept. 29, records that on some warehouses about St. Paul's, which it was hoped were secure, being opened the goods broke into fresh flame and were consumed.[2]   Aubrey, passing the corner of Holborn Bridge on Nov. 30, saw a cellar of coals opened by labourers, " and there were burning coals which burnt ever since the Great Fire ; but being pent so close for air there was very little waste."

A deluge of rain occurred in October, descending almost

[1] *State Papers (Domestic)*, 1666–7, pp. 104, 109.
[2] *Ibid.*, p. 167.

unceasingly for ten days,[1] but it failed to put out all the
fires. Pepys made many entries in his *Diary* of the continuance of these spasmodic outbreaks :—

Dec. 1, 1666.—Walking to the Old Swan, I did see a cellar
in Tower Street in a very fresh fire, the late great winds having
blown it up. It seemed to be only of logwood, that hath kept
the fire all this while in it.

Dec. 14.—By coach to Whitehall, seeing many smokes of
the fire by the way yet.

Jan. 17, 1667.—I observe still, in many places, the smoking
remains of the late fire ; the ways mighty bad and dirty.

March 16.—The weather is now grown warm again, after
much cold ; and it is observable that within these eight days
I did see smoke remaining, coming out of some cellars, from the
late great fire, now above six months since.

A knighthood was granted by King Charles to Edmund
Berry Godfrey, who was a Justice of the Peace for Westminster—the Protestant magistrate before whom Tonge
and Oates first laid information of the famous " Popish
Plot," and whose body was thereafter found on Primrose
Hill run through with his own rapier. Godfrey received
from his Sovereign this honour and a gift of plate (the
Edmund Berry Godfrey cup *) and public acknowledgment
of his eminent service done in helping to suppress the Fire,[2]
but no others among the band of workers who had toiled
so hard to save what was left of London obtained Royal
reward.

" The dreadful fire " it is called on almost every one of
the memorial stones that mark the sites of ruined churches,
" the lamentable and dismal fire " in Acts of Parliament
and other documents. The term " Great Fire " I found
first officially used in a Royal Warrant for rebuilding the
burnt Customs House, but it was not till many years later
that the now universal name was generally adopted.

The Fire took a remarkably small toll of deaths. What
the actual numbers were has never been ascertained.
Burnet, whose sources of information were obviously in-
complete, could not learn that any one person was either
burnt or trodden to death. The King, he says, was never

---

[1] Rugge's *Diurnal*, Oct. 26. Evelyn's *Diary*, Oct. 21.
[2] *Gazette*, 1666, Sept. 18.

observed to be so much struck with anything in his whole life as with this. The *London Gazette* also asserts that no lives were lost. Eight is the largest estimate of deaths directly due to the flames.

The published Bills of Mortality indicate a death-roll of six ; but I cannot believe that these represent the actual total. Evelyn, walking amid the ruins, noticed " the stench that came from some poor creatures' bodies."

In these pages three deaths have been mentioned— Farynor's maid-servant ; the aged woman whose charred remains were seen by Taswell by the Cathedral ; and Paul Lowell, the Shoe Lane watchmaker. A fourth victim was an old man, who incautiously went to St. Paul's to save a blanket he had placed there, and being weak, the Fire overcame him.[1] Others had sunk into vaults since the Fire, as they were searching the ruins of their houses.[2] The church books of St. Botolph Aldgate record the burial of a parishioner who dropped dead on Tower Hill during the Fire, " being ffrighted."

The ruined city continued to be most dangerous by reason of concealed fires. In the burial register of St. Mary Woolnoth is an entry so late as the 18th October : " Richard Yrde, late of this Parish, being stifled in a house of office backside of deputie Canhams house, after the Cittie was burnt."

In view of the large numbers of invalids who were hastily removed from the houses and carried by boat upon the river or by carts and litters along the rough and choked streets, of pregnant women, and of the sick and frail who underwent days and nights of exposure in the open fields, it is to be feared that the deaths attributable in a secondary degree to the Great Fire of London must be estimated, not by the half-dozen, but by the hundred. One case is well known. Shirley, the poet, and his wife were driven by the flames from the house they occupied in Fleet Street, near Serjeants' Inn, and forced to take refuge with crowds of other outcasts in St. Giles's-in-the-Fields. The hardships they endured and the terror of the scenes witnessed brought on mortal illness, and the poet and his wife, dying on the same day, were buried in one grave (October 29th) in the parish churchyard there.

[1] Pepys's *Diary*, 1668, Jan. 14.　　[2] Malcolm, *Lond. Rediv.*, iv, 79.

CHAPTER X

AMID THE RUINS

SOUCHU DE RENNEFORT, a French traveller, has left in a few words a vivid impression of the ruins of London.[1] He had sailed the world as far away as the East Indies, landed at the Island of Madagascar, and on the voyage home he fell a hostage in the war which Charles II. was waging with the French King. His ship was captured by a stout Englishman, and himself held close prisoner for many weary months in the Isle of Wight. Liberated at last, he came to the capital, via Southampton and Winchester, and he first touched London at that magnificent mansion which Hyde, Earl of Clarendon and Lord Chancellor of England, had built for himself on its extreme outskirts, where now is Piccadilly. Its isolated splendour impressed him, and he recalled its origin—built, so the Chancellor's enemies maliciously asserted, out of the money Hyde received for the sale of Dunkirk. " They call it ' The Little Dunkirk,' " he learnt.

But there was much else to impress the traveller in this first sight of London. Not far away was St. James's Palace, the residence of the Duke of York. From the high ground of Piccadilly he overlooked its park, and the lawns and woodlands enforced his admiration. " It forms the most beautiful walk in London." Westminster and Whitehall—which he compares with the Louvre—loomed up massively beyond. He turned his horse down by the Royal Mews at Charing Cross and entered the Strand, passing Somerset House, where lived the Queen-Mother. The spaciousness of the Strand he remarks upon, lined as he

[1] Souchu de Rennefort, *Relation du Premier Voyage de la Compagnie des Indes Orientales en l'Isle de Madegascar ou Dauphine*, Paris, 1668, pp. 336–8.

found it with the private houses of Ambassadors. The street ended at Temple Bar, where the City commenced. Once through that gateway, the tragedy of the Great Fire burst upon him.

Thirty houses of Fleet Street were standing—thirty upon the two sides, and no more, forming of themselves a short lane abruptly terminated by ruins. Beyond this the eye saw nothing but widespread desolation.

A city swept by a cyclone of unimaginable fury would not have been levelled more effectively. Down the slight descent to where the Fleet River crossed the open panorama, up the rise to Ludgate and the city vaguely outlined beyond, and from the Thames-side sweeping wide across the traveller's path, the vision of London began and ended with ruins. Only where the northern road of Holborn made an entry by Newgate was there a bordering line of houses still erect. Souchu de Rennefort had passed the approaches—the Royal Palaces and parks, the capacious Strand, the stately mansions. This was the blackened city at which his world travels were to end !

Of course, he saw more, but he gives little detail. With his eye he measured the devastated area, lying out two miles in length, and reaching back a mile from the Thames to Moorfields ; and his estimate is wrong. To-day, where for some big new building scheme a block of houses has been laid low, and the vacant ground lies levelled, covered by loose bricks and rubbish and foundations awaiting removal, we know how desolate it looks, framed in by surrounding buildings. (I have St. Martin's-le-Grand in mind as I write.) Like this, but enlarged a thousand times, was the traveller's view of London.

Two matters especially arrested his attention—the first trifling. " There is not a single house complete (he writes), only small huts, or cabins, of the beer-sellers, which are open for the refreshment of labourers who walk from the suburbs into the City." These structures, hastily put together, stood all about the fire-swept area. He noticed that the towers and steeples, those of ninety parishes, were still upstanding, gaunt sentinels marking the ruined churches consumed by the flames. Others, too, had had their imagination stirred by this most impressive feature of the ruins. " I came directly," says the writer of a letter[1] on September 6th, " from Aldgate to Holborn over the places burnt, by direction of the Steeples remaining this day."

One sight in the desolated City was awesome.

" The great church called St. Paul's retains nothing of its former shape, except the open roof and the windows, and all the stonework has been injured by the great fire." Four Corinthian columns of Inigo Jones's immense portico at the cathedral's west door upheld, sixty-six feet aloft, the architrave on which this inscription was legible to all passers-by :—

CAROLVS. D. G. MAG. BRIT. FRAN. ET. HIB.
REX. F. D. TEMPLVM.
SANCTI. PAVLI. VETVSTATE. CONSVMPTVM.
RESTITVIT. PORTICVM. FECIT.

The King who raised this memorial to the transient glories of his Royalty lay dead, his reign ended by the stroke of the headsman's axe, and high above his capital lying in ashes the letters were preserved out of the flames, perfect where so much else had been mutilated or destroyed. Not one letter had been defaced.

John Evelyn, the diarist, had laboured in London during the height of the Fire, being entrusted by the King with the task of assisting to keep the flames from Holborn.   As soon as it was out he hurried through the streets to view the desolation wrought—

" I went this morning (Friday, September 7th) on foot from Whitehall as far as London Bridge, through the late Fleet Street, Ludgate Hill by St. Paul's, Cheapside, Exchange, Bishopsgate, Aldersgate, and out to Moorfields, thence through Cornhill, etc., with extraordinary difficulty, clambering over heaps of yet smoking rubbish, and frequently mistaking where I was : the ground under my feet so hot that it even burnt the soles of my shoes.

" I was infinitely concerned to find that goodly church, St. Paul's, now a sad ruin, and that beautiful portico (for structure comparable to any in Europe, as not long before

[1] *London's Lamentation.*   (Broadside), 1666.

repaired by the late King) now rent in pieces. The ruins
of the vaulted roof falling, broke into St. Faith's. Thus
lay in ashes that most venerable church, one of the most
ancient pieces of early piety in the Christian world, besides
near one hundred more. The lead, ironwork, bells, plate,
etc. melted, the exquisitely wrought Mercers Chapel, the
sumptuous Exchange, the august fabric of Christ Church,
all the rest of the Companies' Halls, splendid buildings,
arches, entries, all in dust ; the fountains dried up and
ruined, whilst the very waters remained boiling ; the
voragos of subterranean cellars, wells, and dungeons,
formerly warehouses, still burning in stench and dark
clouds of smoke ; so that in five or six miles traversing
about it I did not see one load of timber unconsumed, nor
many stones but what were calcined white as snow.

" The people, who now walked about the ruins, appeared
like men in some dismal desert, or rather, in some great
city laid waste by a cruel enemy ; to which was added the
stench that came from some poor creatures' bodies, beds,
and other combustible goods.

" Vast iron chains of the City streets, hinges, bars, and
gates of prisons were many of them melted and reduced to
cinders by the vehement heat. Nor was I yet able to
pass through any of the narrow streets, but kept the widest ;
the ground and air, smoke and fiery vapour, continued so
intense that my hair was almost singed, and my feet
unsufferably surbated. The by-lanes and narrow streets
were quite filled up with rubbish ; nor could one have
possibly known where he was, but by the ruins of some
church, or hall, that had some remarkable tower or
pinnacle remaining.

" I then went towards Islington and Highgate, where
one might have seen 200,000 people of all ranks and degrees
dispersed, and lying along by their heaps of what they
could save from the fire, deploring their loss ; and, though
ready to perish for hunger and destitution, yet not asking
one penny for relief, which to me appeared a stranger sight
than any I had yet beheld. His Majesty and Council,
indeed, took all imaginable care for their relief, by Proclamation for the country to come in and refresh them with
provisions.

" In the midst of all this calamity and confusion there

was, I know not how, an alarm begun that the French and Dutch, with whom we were now in hostility, were not only landed, but even entering the City.   There was, in truth, some days before great suspicion of those two nations joining ;   and now that they had been the occasion of firing the town.   This report did so terrify, that on a sudden there was such an uproar and tumult that they ran away from their goods, and taking what weapons they could come at, they could not be stopped from falling on some of those nations whom they casually met, without sense or reason.   The clamour and peril grew so excessive that it made the whole Court amazed, and they did with infinite pains and great difficulty reduce and appease the people, sending troops of soldiers and guards to cause them to retire into the fields again, where they were watched all this night.   I left them pretty quiet, and came home sufficiently weary and broken.   Their spirits thus a little calmed, and the affright abated, they now began to repair into the suburbs about the City, where such as had friends or opportunity got shelter for the present ;   to which his Majesty's Proclamation also invited them." [1]

The City's true centre is that restless area before the Mansion House, which until the subway was burrowed underneath had evil notoriety as the most dangerous street crossing in London.   The citizen of the Restoration knew it as the Stocks Market for flesh and fish, a place noisy with the cries of the dealers.   Stalls and shambles occupied the ground whereon the Lord Mayor now resides, a thin line of traffic passing at the side into the many highways that radiate from this spot.

A spectator brought up here after the Fire had five ruined churches immediately at his hand.

St. Christopher-le-Stocks was burnt out ;   the tower and walls stood, and did some service when Wren built a new church, itself destined to be demolished in 1780.   You know to-day the pretty garden court of the Bank of England, planted with shrubs and gaily coloured flowers, amidst which a fountain plays ?   That is the churchyard of St. Christopher-le-Stocks.   The last interment there was of one Jenkins, a Bank clerk.   He stood

[1] Evelyn's *Diary*, 1666, Sept. 7.

seven feet six inches high, and his burial was allowed within the Bank in order to defeat the body snatchers. The drawing office stands upon the site of the church. The Lord Mayor's stocks, wherein many a vagrom man had been held fast by the legs, were placed before this church.

Another of these Bank of England sites may opportunely be recalled. The office for changing notes occupies the ground where till the Fire stood the house of the parish squire, and the courtyard still open at the side was his courtyard.[1]

St. Mildred Poultry church, at Poultry's eastern end, perished in the Fire; and its successor, conspicuous by its tower, surmounted by a gilt ship in full sail, has since perished.

St. Stephen Walbrook, a near neighbour, suffered severely, though the bells rang in the tower after the flames had passed;[2] to this day there hangs in the new steeple one of the original bells cast by Robert Mot, who established about 1570 the foundry at Whitechapel still carried on by Messrs. Mears and Stainbank. The rebuilding gave opportunity to Sir Christopher Wren for what is recognized by architects as the most distinguished of all his City churches. The structure burnt was larger than Wren's magnificent fabric. It had been erected in the year 1439 by the great merchant family of Chichele, displacing an older church built on the opposite bank where the Walbrook stream had trickled through the City down to the Thames.

St. Mary Woolchurch Hawe, fourth of the churches about the Stocks Market, stood out in picturesque desolation, its shaking ruins being dangerous to passers-by. They were removed in February, 1668, and the materials used in the restoration of St. Mary Woolnoth. This last church had suffered least of the group in the Fire. Gay flags maintained by the Goldsmiths Company over the tomb of that stout Elizabethan Knight, Sir Martyn Bowes,

---

[1] Freshfield, *Parish Books of St. Margaret Lothbury.*

[2] Rugge's *Diurnal.* Four of Mot's bells out of a ring of six are in the peal at St. Andrew Undershaft, one of the City churches that escaped the Fire; a fifth is at St. Andrew Holborn, in the Liberties; a sixth at St. Clement Danes, just outside the City boundary; and there are two examples of the master founder's work at Westminster Abbey, both of them elaborately and fancifully decorated.

as provided under his will, were all charred; the steeple
was not burnt, and the walls, save on the north side, were
patched together, but the building survived only half a
century longer.[1] The principal charge for repairs was
advanced by Sir Robert Vyner, whose remembrance rests
less upon this pious work than upon a well-meant, if
unfortunate act of loyalty. The story has run with a
ripple of laughter.

A fine, new, larger Stocks Market was determined upon,
the site of the church and graveyard of St. Mary Woolchurch being thrown into it. Thus the market after the
Fire occupied ground now completely covered by the
Mansion House and its western approach. What more
befitting so central a position than a statue raised to the
greatness of Charles II. ? It chanced that John Sobiesky,
King of Poland, having slaughtered a vast number of
Turks and saved Vienna, his ambassador in England
ordered an equestrian statue commemorative of the
victory, and this, failing payment to the sculptor, lay boxed
up on the Tower Wharf, awaiting exportation. Vyner
purchased the statue, and disregarding the incongruities
of costume, had the head of the Polish King replaced by
that of Charles II., and the features of the Turk lying
prostrate under his horse's feet altered to those of Oliver
Cromwell. Thus manœuvred, the statue arose on this
spot in honour of the Sovereign ! It was dedicated in the
year of Vyner's Mayoralty. Walpole says that Latham
carved the head of King Charles. There is not the least
doubt about the story, which the Oriental attire and head-
dress of the betrampled Cromwell fully bear out. The
statue kept its place until the removal of the Stocks Market
to the present Farringdon Street, in 1736, when the City
fathers were puzzled to know what to do with it. Laid
aside for some years, it was presented by the Common
Council in 1779 to Robert Vyner, a descendant of the loyal
Lord Mayor, and was by him removed to his country
residence, and to-day is at Newby Hall, Ripon, the Yorkshire seat of the Vyner family.

[1] Nicholas Hawksmoor's present church of St. Mary Woolnoth, which
by reason of its situation by the Mansion House and the Royal Exchange
and its open site is the most conspicuous of all the City churches, was
consecrated on Easter Day, 1727.

A lampooner wrote these lines some years after the erection of the statue—

> Could Robert Vyner have foreseen
> The glorious triumph of his master,
> The Wool Church Statue gold had been,
> Which is now made of alabaster.
> But wise men think had it been wood,
> T'were for a bankrupt King too good.
> Those that the fabric well consider
> Do of it diversely discourse,
> Some pass their censure on the rider,
> Others their judgment on the horse;
> Most say the steed's a goodly thing,
> But all agree 'tis a lewd King.

Down Walbrook, the clearance of the ruins disclosed the burial vault of the family of Pollefexen. The mansion above (site now covered by Walbrook House, No. 37) had been destroyed in the Fire—and using the word " above " I do so literally, for, strange as it may seem, the custom of this ancient family had been to bury their dead beneath their City dwelling. The house burnt was very old, possibly preserving part of the actual residence of the Abbots of Tortington. On the wall of the vault was found a stone tablet bearing an inscription which may be read thus :

> Who lies here ? Who don't ken
> The family of Pollefexen,
> Who be they living or be they dead
> Like their own house over their head,
> That whensoever their Saviour come
> They always may be found at home.[1]

Henry Pollefexen rebuilt the house of his ancestors. He was knighted, and became Chief Justice of the Court of Common Pleas late in Charles II.'s reign.

The five churches I have recalled marked the five highways which merged at the Stocks Market, and all the roads lay in ruins : Walbrook to the Thames, the Poultry and Cheapside westward, to where the Cathedral's roofless walls and gaunt windows, the blue sky showing through, obstructed further vision ; and Lombard Street, Cornhill, and Threadneedle Street towards the east. In these long vistas of ruined London the churches were pathetic objects.

[1] White, *History of the Ward of Walbrook.*

Rolle describes them, " the outsides yet standing, their walls and steeples make such a fair show, that they who should view them at a distance would think they were just as before.   But alas ! their insides are gone ; they are fit for no use."   The fire-riven fabrics stood, but so frail and brittle were they that draymen were loth to pass them on a windy day, for fear of loosened masonry descending upon their heads.[1]

The picture of desolation was the same in whatever direction the eye turned, till in the distance upstanding houses and the few churches and Companies' Halls that survived marked the limits to which the flames burnt.   It is enough to recall that phrase written by Alexander Fleming from London to his brother in the country— " You may stand where Cheapside was, and see the Thames."   You might have stood in Cheapside and watched the boats passing on the river.

London rose out of its ashes after the Fire, not by the building of continuous streets in any part, but first here a house and there a house.   Others by degrees were joined, until at last single houses were united into whole streets, and the closely built streets again became a City.[2]   The undertaking was a stupendous one, and necessarily it made slow progress, with many setbacks.   I am at a loss to understand the inscription on the south side of the Monument, where it states, " London rises again, whether with greater speed or greater magnificence is doubtful, three short years complete that which was considered the work of an age."   It is a stupid boast.   It does not represent the facts, and they must have been well known when the words were cut.

An amiable conspiracy by historians of the succeeding century has represented the London citizens as supermen, achieving the impossible.   Oldmixon has remarked that " To the amazement of all Europe, London was, in four years' time, rebuilt with so much beauty and magnificence that they who saw it in both states, before and after the Fire, could not reflect on it without wondering where the wealth could be found to bear so vast a loss as was made

[1] S. Rolle, *Burning of London*, 1667.
[2] Sprat's *Sermon before the Sons of the Clergy*, 1678, Nov. 7.

by the Fire, and so prodigious an expense as was laid out in the rebuilding," [1] Seymour, but a trifle more modest, says the City was well nigh rebuilt in the space of four or five years. [2] A single fact may be set against these claims. St. Bartholomew Exchange parish (by the Bank of England) was so long derelict that the churchwardens, in 1670, forbade to list the names of their parish householders, " being so few inhabited in our time we thought it prudence to leave it to the succeeding churchwardens," they explained. [3]

I have set out in later chapters to show how the task was at length accomplished, and the time it occupied. London remained for a decade, and then for a second decade, a City marked all over with ruins. About them the wild flowers grew, and notably the plant *Sisymbrium Erio* flourished in such profusion that ever since the Great Fire it has borne the popular name of " London Rocket," then first given to it. Aubrey, a passing visitor, mentions particularly the *Ericoluri Neapolitana* as peeping up amidst the destroyed houses. Nature, in her mothering mood, thus toiled to cover over the work of the flames.

Four years after the Fire the area rebuilt and on which rebuilding was well advanced was little more than one-half of that over which the flames had passed. If it be sufficient that eighty-four churches destroyed in the Fire were still in ruins, no one having been rebuilt, and in few cases had even the shattered walls been cleared away ; the Guildhall, Custom House, Newgate, Ludgate, and other public buildings still unfinished ; St. Paul's a waste, wherein Wren had not yet laid the foundations of the new Cathedral ; the City Companies for a large part still without their Halls—then only can London in the year 1670 have been considered a magnificent City.

The blackened area lay out like the crater of a volcano, and as dead, broken walls leaning against rubbish heaps of loose stone and brick and charred timber. Not a roof was visible. In Hollar's view of London after the Fire there is rarely a building shown with its walls above the first floor still erect, the remainder having toppled over.

---

[1] Oldmixon, *History of London*, i, 547.
[2] Seymour's *Survey of London*, i, 70.
[3] Vestry Minutes, 1670, April 5.

Everything living had fled.   Then a wonderful thing happened.   Four days passed, and in all the fields stretching away to Highgate, Islington and Hackney, in which the homeless people, with the goods they had saved from the flaming City, had found refuge under the stars, there was scarcely a man, woman, or child to be seen.   The King in Council had ordered the churchwardens, overseers and constables to lodge such people, first in vacant houses ; then, especially the sick and women expecting child-bed, in victualling houses, inns, and places of public entertainment ; and others in private houses, taking care that such persons as had means should pay for their lodging.   For the needs of the poor his Majesty promised funds.[1]   This packing proved temporarily effective.

The common disaster awakened an abounding charity. The population closed in.   The King sent tents from the Army.   Lean-to wooden structures, hastily put together, were set up in the Artillery Ground at Finsbury, at Moorfields, in the Round at Smithfield within the rails, and on vacant land by the bridge foot at Southwark.   London Bridge was cleared at its northern end, where the houses had been levelled by the Fire, and people were permitted to settle there, the road being railed to give an unobstructed way for carts bringing food to London.

A mushroom town of sheds and tents sprang up in a few weeks, its greatest length drawn from the postern near Broad Street and outside London Wall to Moorgate, and within the Wall from Moorgate to Coleman Street. The burnt-out Londoners became for the time a gipsy population, camping in this manner about the outskirts of the fire-swept City till they could find better accommodation.   Some families raised shelters on the ruins of their own homes.   The destitute poor burrowed into vaults left secure when the buildings above had burnt, finding safe refuge from wind and rain, whence they came out to take the doles of charitable relief.   The first shops opened after the Fire appear to have been at the Royal Exchange, broken stone and bricks from the Guildhall being carted there to form a pavement for the purpose,[2] and others of the Exchange tradesmen by December had fitted up shops,

---

[1] *Privy Council Registers*, vol. 59, fos. 150–1. ; Clarendon's *Life*.
[2] *Repertory* 71, fos. 168*b*, 169, 170*b* ; *Journal* 46, fo. 117*b*.

both above and below stairs, in the already crowded precincts of Gresham House.[1]

Fear arose of plague stalking afresh through desolated London. The great annual fair at Gravesend, customarily held on October 13th, was prohibited by Royal Proclamation lest travellers thereto might bring the infection from places where it still lingered.[2]

The huge aggregation of ruins, stretching out for more than a mile, created a difficulty which left the City authorities powerless. London after the Fire was infested with thieves. Hundreds of houses had collapsed with much valuable property still in them, lying loose amid piles of charred timber and heaped bricks and stones. The flames had consumed a vast deal, but not all. Many citizens when the Fire approached had sought safety for their valuables by burying them in cellars or under the flagstones of their yards. The quantity of plate, money, jewels, household stuff, goods and merchandise discovered was very great, and much of it had been quickly misappropriated. A delegation of Aldermen waited upon Monck, and a further Royal Proclamation was published commanding all persons who either " wilfully, ignorantly, or of purpose," during the confusion had so appropriated property to bring the same within eight days to the Armoury in Finsbury Fields.[3]

" In the deluge of rich commodities," says Clarendon significantly, " there were found men ready enough to fish." Not the thieves of London alone, many as they were numbered, were attracted by the prospects of spoil and the withdrawal of the little policing that sufficed in Stuart days. The parish constables and watchmen were common sufferers with their neighbours in the Fire—all of them homeless, mostly having their own affairs claiming urgent attention. When wanted they were abroad, and the thieves made free. Bad characters from the suburbs, the outlying villages and distant towns flocked into the City, ostensibly to get work, in reality to prey upon unguarded London. The Lord Mayor issued a Proclamation on November 3rd, for the punishment " of vagrants and

[1] *Gazette*, 1666, Dec. 13–17.
[2] *Royal Proclamation*, Sept. 16.
[3] *Repertory* 71, fo. 172 ; *Royal Proclamation*, Sept. 19.

sturdy beggars, loose and idle persons, who greatly abound, wandering in and about the streets of London and amongst the ruins of this city," commanding the Aldermen forthwith to cause a substantial pair of stocks and a whipping post to be set up, each in his ward.[1]

Fires, incendiary in origin, broke out among the ruins, or in houses newly built or then building, keeping Londoners with vivid memories of the Great Fire in a state of tense nervousness.[2]   A further Mayoral Proclamation on the 24th June, 1668, recalls reports of frequent thefts and robberies committed in the devastated parts of the City. It charged the Aldermen, in his Majesty's name, to see that good and sufficient night watches be set in each ward and at the City gates.[3]   The Bridewell Governors after the Fire, as their first duty, built on their site with all speed prison rooms for men and for women—the evil characters they made their unwilling guests.[4]   There was ever present a danger from falling walls.   The tottering steeples of St. Martin Vintry and St. Margaret Moses were forthwith pulled down, and the City Surveyors were ordered to examine and certify for demolition all steeples and parts of the damaged churches that threatened to fall, to the hurt or destruction of passengers.[5]

Pepys and a party, coming home from the play a year after the Fire, found the City gates closed, as was customary after dark.   " At Newgate we find them in trouble, some thieves having this night broke open prison.   So we through, and home ; and our coachman was fain to drive hard for two or three fellows, which he said were rogues, that he met at the end of Blowbladder Street, next Cheapside."   In April, 1668, when entering into the ruins by St. Dunstan-in-the-East, he was met by two ruffians armed with clubs, who came towards him, and he describes himself

---

[1] *Journal* 46, fo. 124.

[2] " Sir John Robinson and others this day, where I was in the afternoon, do tell me of at least six or eight fires within these few days ; and continually stirs of fires, and real fires there have been, in one place or other, almost ever since the late great fire, as if there was a fate sent people for fire." (Pepys's *Diary*, 1667, May 5 ; see also 1668, June 19.)   The Insurance Office for Houses in 1680 reported ninety-seven houses burnt in the City and Liberties since the Great Fire, forty of these, however, being in the one outbreak in the Temple.

[3] *Journal* 46, fo. 231.

[4] *Bridewell Court Minutes*, 1666, Sept. 14.

[5] *Repertory*, 73, fos. 44, 109, 159b.

as wearily walking round the City Wall in order to escape the dangers within.[1]

Life itself was held in peril in these desolate streets. James Hickes, the postmaster, then lodging at Bishopsgate Street, in the fringe of the City left unburnt within the Wall, writes in a private letter three months after the Fire—

" There are many people found murdered and carried into the vaults amongst the ruins, as three last night, as I hear, and it is supposed by hasty fellows that cry ' Do you want light ? ' and carry links ; and that when they catch a man single, whip into a vault with him, knock him down, strip him from top to toe, blow out their links, and leave the persons for dead ; and an apothecary's man in Southwark, coming into Fenchurch Street, being so served and being left for dead, when these villains had done [they] struck fire with a tinder box which they took out of their pockets, lighted their links, and away, and by glimpse of their lights, as the story goes, the man perceived a dead body lying by him in the said vault. When the murderers were gone, the young man made shift to get out, from whom this relation is spread, and a woman dead in the vault was found. For want of good watches, no person dare, after the close of the evening, pass the streets amongst the ruins." [2]

The occasion demanded a victim, for the excited populace, inflamed with hostility to foreigners and Papists, and distracted by their losses, were little inclined to reason coldly. One was quickly found. Among the Frenchmen apprehended and sent to Southwark was Robert Hubert, who had been seized at Romford, in Essex, when apparently making his way to sea to fly the country. Hubert was a watchmaker, who had practised his craft in London and in his native city of Rouen, where his father was a watchmaker of good standing. The son was twenty-six years of age. Those who had worked with him at the bench both in London and Rouen regarded him as a man of disordered mind. There was nothing against him save his self-accusation.

Hubert told a remarkable story. He said that four

---

[1] *Diary*, 1667, Aug. 1 ; 1668, April 23.
[2] *State Papers* (*Domestic*), 1666–7 p. 340.

months before the Fire he left France in company with one
Stephen Peidloe, and they went into Sweden, remaining
there until they sailed together for England in the Swedish
ship *Skipper*. The vessel moored in the Thames, by St.
Katherine's Tower, below the Bridge, and he stayed on
board till the night when the Fire broke out. Peidloe
then took him ashore. They walked by the wharfs to
Pudding Lane, and arrived at Farynor's, the baker's,
Peidloe confided to him that he had brought three fire-
balls, and gave him one of them to throw into the house.

Hubert protested, but Peidloe would not listen; and
then, at his companion's instigation, Hubert said he placed
a fire-ball at the end of a long pole, and, lighting it with a
match, put it in a window, and stayed till the house was
in flames. Farynor, the baker, while confident that his
house was maliciously fired, afterwards declared there was
no such window as Hubert described, nor did the fire start
thereabouts. In this testimony he was supported by his
son and daughter.[1]

The man was tried at the Old Bailey October Sessions,
before Lord Chief Justice Kelyng, on an indictment of
felony in setting fire to the baker's house.* There he varied
his story, declaring that he had been suborned to set
London on fire when in Paris a year before. There were
three and twenty accomplices in his original narrative,
with Peidloe as chief. They dwindled to three. They had
come over together to England to put the plan into execution at the time of the Plague; but he and two of his companions went into Sweden, returning at the latter end of
August, and he then resolved to undertake it. His two
companions had escaped to France. He covered himself
with contradictions. He asserted that his sole reward for
a service of so much hazard was a pistol, but he had been
promised five pistols more when he had accomplished his
work. Obviously the man was mad.

The only remaining testimony that could be said to
bear upon the accusation was that of a French merchant,
one Graves, living in St. Mary Axe. Graves asserted that
he had full knowledge of Peidloe (who never appeared in
the flesh) and knew him to be a most debased man, apt to
any wicked design. Also he had known Hubert since a

[1] Pepys's *Diary*, 1667, Feb. 24.

child, and had observed him to be a person of mischievous inclination, fit for any villainous enterprise. He had visited Hubert in prison, and for better discovery of the truth had affected disbelief in his confession. To this Hubert replied, " Yes, sir, I am guilty, and have been brought to this pass by the instigation of Monsieur Peidloe, but not out of any malice to the English nation, but from desire of a reward which he promised me on my return to France."

The Court was clearly dissatisfied. It possessed the knowledge that Hubert's first information, delivered to Cary Harvie, the justice at Romford who examined him on his arrest, was that " when the City was on fire " Peidloe sent him ashore to throw a fire-ball near the King's Palace at Whitehall, which he did ; the story that he started the Great Fire at Pudding Lane he had enlarged when brought to London. Yet the evidence could not be put altogether aside, and a course was decided upon by which, pretty plainly, it was hoped that the self-accused man might, out of his own mouth, be made to prove himself an impostor. Hubert was asked if he could tell the place to which he first applied fire. He answered that he knew it well, and would show the house to anybody. It was directed that the prisoner should be taken near to the ruins, and asked to point out the spot.

First he was conveyed to the Thames-side, and he indicated the moorings by St. Katherine's Tower at which the Swedish ship lay. This part of his testimony was flatly contradicted by neighbouring wharfingers, who had no knowledge of any such vessel having berthed there. Incidentally, Hubert again varied his story, asserting this time that while he had himself sent one fire-ball into Farynor's house, Peidloe, using a long pole, had thrust two others through the same window.

The terrific heat of the fire had left nothing save charred timbers and debris piled high above the site of the baker's house. Pudding Lane was no longer recognizable, and without some distinguishing mark even its late residents could scarcely identify their ruined homes. It seemed likely that Hubert would fail ; instead, he withstood the test only too well for the satisfaction of his judges. A guard of substantial citizens and John Lowman, keeper of the

White Lion Gaol—the Surrey county prison—went with
the prisoner. Lowman's deposition ran :

> From thence [Thames-side] I carried the said Robert
> Hubert to Tower Hill, and did then desire him to show me the
> house that they did fire, and he said that it was near the Bridge.
> So we went along Thames Street towards the Bridge ; but
> before we came to the bridge the said Robert Hubert said, that
> the house was up there (pointing with his hand up Pudding
> Lane). So I bid him go to the place, and he went along the
> bricks and rubbish, and made a stand : Then I did ask one
> Robert Penny, a wine porter, which was the baker's house.
> and he told me that was the house where the aforesaid Robert
> Hubert stood. So I went to Robert Hubert, and stood by
> him, and turned my back towards the baker's house, and
> demanded of him which house it was that he fired, (directing
> to other houses contrary to that house) but he, turning himself
> about, said, " This was the house (pointing to the baker's
> house) that was first fired." Then by reason of his lameness,
> I set him on a horse, and carried him to several other places,
> but no other place he would acknowledge ; but rode back
> again to the baker's house, and said again " That was the
> house " (pointing to the baker's house).

Not only did the man always return to the site, but he
described how the house stood, the shape of the little yard,
and the fashion of the door and windows.

" They were surprised with wonder, and knew not
afterwards what to think," observes Clarendon. No man
accused him, but Hubert himself silenced all doubts. The
jury found him guilty, and he was hanged at Tyburn.
He died, it was said, re-asserting his guilt,[1] and, declaring
that he was a Catholic, was confessed and absolved by the
Queen's Confessor, though there is much evidence that
not only was he a Protestant, but that in a most pronounced
form—namely, a French Huguenot. The Lord Chief
Justice told the King that all his discourse was so dis-
jointed that he did not believe a word of it. Charles

---

[1] It was commonly asserted that Hubert maintained his guilt to the
last ; but the writer of a news letter to Sir Edward Mansell, 1666, Oct. 20th
(now among the State Papers), declares that he denied the fact at the
gallows. For Hubert's statement to Harvie see *London's Flames*, 1679.
Petersen's affidavit is printed in *A Protestant Monument of the Whiggs and
Dutch*, 1713 ; the evidence before the Parliamentary Committee in *A True
and Faithfull Account*, etc., 1667 ; the true bill against Hubert I have
printed in my Notes at the end of this volume.

discreetly failed to interfere. The whole episode is a melancholy example of the ineptitude of the authorities when confronted with a man who persistently protested his guilt, and of a populace, deeply moved, who saw in the ruins of London the handiwork of malicious Papists, and in this self-accused madman the instrument of their dreadful deed.

The man was hurried out of existence before the whole truth could be known ; but Hawles's statement that when the Parliamentary Committee required his evidence they found him already hanged, and so could tell no further tales, is contrary to the fact. It afterwards transpired, by testimony of Petersen, the master of the ship which brought him from Stockholm, that Hubert did not go ashore in London until two days after the Fire began, by which time the baker's house, the source of all the catastrophe, was already a public show. Clarendon wrote of him : " And though no man could imagine any reason why a man should so desperately throw away his life, which he might have saved though he had been guilty, since he was only accused upon his own confession ; yet neither the judges nor any present at the trial did believe him guilty, but that he was a poor distracted wretch, weary of his life, and chose to part with it in this way."

CHAPTER XI

THE King was greatly perturbed by the popular agitation which sought to throw responsibility for the Fire of London upon the Catholics. The Dutch war had brought him no credit. With the nation's finances in confusion, the capital lying in ashes, and large sections of his subjects gravely discontented by his own religious measures, he realized that neither the State nor the Monarchy had anything to gain from a recrudescence of violent religious strife, but much evil to fear.

In his words addressed to the homeless people camped in Moorfields, he sought to convince them that no conspiracy, whether by Frenchmen, Dutchmen or Catholics, had part in bringing upon them so much misery. All the King's energies at this time were directed to allaying the popular excitement. He sent for Sir John Kelyng, the Lord Chief Justice, to come to London and take charge of the examinations of witnesses that were at once begun, with a view to ascertaining whether the firing of the City could be attributed to any persons or faction.

On Friday night Monck, Duke of Albemarle, reached London, having left the Fleet, the command of which he had assumed in hourly expectation of an action with the Dutch; and John Rushworth saw the Lord-General next morning, " riding through the rubbish in Fleet Street." He, too, had been sent for by the King, who was anxious at this time to have about him the one man in whom, above all others, public confidence was placed. Charles

was consciously uneasy lest the most powerful agent in
his Restoration should take his recall amiss. Lord
Arlington's letter of the 4th September directing Sir
Thomas Clifford to place the Royal wishes before Monck
is phrased with the most exquisite care—

> I leave you to judge what a distraction this misfortune puts
> us to, whereof the consequences are yet more terrible to us,
> by the disorders that are likely to follow. . . . If my Lord-
> General could see the condition we are in, I am confident, and
> so is everybody else, he would think it more honour to be
> called to this occasion than to be stayed in the fleet, where it
> is possible he may not have an opportunity of fighting the
> enemy ; but here it is certain he will have it in his hands to
> give the King his kingdoms a second time, and the world see
> therein the value the King makes of him. If his Grace admits
> you to discourse the point with him, you must take pains to
> enforce it all you can, but still with this reserve and con-
> clusion, that his Majesty leaves him to make his choice
> himself.[1]

The Fire had burnt the Post House, and no mails were
sent out from London for several days. But quicker than
the delayed letters the news of the burning of London
spread throughout the country, creating general alarm.*
From West Cowes one John Lysle wrote to Williamson,
the editor of the *London Gazette :* " Since the fire of
London, both seamen and landsmen are rampant and
outrageous for revenge upon the enemy." Magistrates
arrested Frenchmen, Dutchmen and Catholics, and thrust
them into prison, without warrant or cause for such
action save that they might be concerned in a plot. The
Trained Bands were called out at Barnstaple, word having
reached the Governor " that the plot was not only for·
London, but for the destruction of the principal cities
and towns in England." The Governor of Falmouth
detained all ships from Hamburg in the harbour. Learning by report that the capital had been set on fire by
Anabaptists and other disaffected persons, the Earl of
Carlisle posted the Trained Bands of Cumberland at convenient places for the safety of the county.

In York similar measures were taken ; at Norwich,

[1] *State Papers (Domestic)*, 1666–7, p. 99.

still stricken with plague, the Mayor sent the bellman round the city, crying that none should lodge strangers before his worship had himself examined them. The Governor of Hull turned all disaffected persons out of the town, committed to close custody the Dutch prisoners who were on bail, and established a strong guard in the streets and harbour.[1]

In this first onrush of unreasoning intolerance, the Anabaptists, Fanatics, and Nonconformists generally shared with Popish recusants the public suspicion. " The Presbyterians and Fanatics look a little starched, and will have it the judgment of the Fire of London is for the sins of others not so holy as themselves," wrote one J. Fitzherbert from Bristol. " The generation of Fanatic vipers will report it God's revenge for Englishmen's valour at Vlie," said another.[2] The devout were agreed with singular unanimity that the Fire was the judgment of God, but by whose hands, and for what ends, opinions widely differed. The Catholics held it to be God's just vengeance for London's heresy ; the clergy laid the blame on schism and licentiousness ; the sectaries blamed the clergy's imposition and pride ; Quakers said it was for their persecution ; others declared it was for the murder of the late King and for the City's rebellion. The King, in his Proclamation for a public Fast, comprehensively attributed the Fire to the afflicting hand of God in judgment upon the whole nation.

Wide as the net was cast, even the Court did not escape being compromised. The Duke of York especially was singled out, as being a Papist. There were not wanting those who believed that he was criminally concerned in firing the City which in fact he had been so active in attempting to save. Some thought his countenance during the Fire had been too gay ; his look and air disclosed to others the pleasure he took in the dreadful spectacle of London in flames.[3] Others, again, blamed the King for complicity in the plot, being at heart a Papist. The Dutch issued some scandalous broadsides, and one print, which reproduced for Dutch readers the

---

[1] *State Papers (Domestic)*, 1666–7, pp. 108, 116, 119, 128, 113.
[2] *Ibid.*, pp. 149, 102.
[3] Burnet's *History of His Own Times*.

evidence taken before the Parliamentary Committee, stated that the report was published because the English Court was suspected to have caused the Fire.[1]

When calumny assailed the King and his brother, it was not to be expected that the Lords of the Council should go free. Malicious rumours were scattered abroad that the Court was so greatly prejudiced against all testimony of a conspiracy to burn London that it discountenanced witnesses to the truth. Some of the Council came to the inquiry with minds prejudiced against foreign enemies and Romanists. The Privy Council sat morning and evening examining persons brought from the prisons of Westminster and Southwark, where suspects were lodged. Evidence was taken of excited bystanders, who professed to have seen fire-balls thrown and persons caught red-handed in the act, houses in areas as yet untouched by the Fire suddenly belching forth flames from every window, in a manner which could only result from wilful firing, and much else of a like nature.

The examination was gravely forwarded to London of Edward Taylor, a boy of ten, taken by Lord Lovelace at Hurley. This little liar—an apothecary's boy—said that he was with his father, Jo Taylor, living in Covent Garden, and his uncle on the night when the Fire broke out, and in Pudding Lane they found a glass window open. They took two fire-balls, made of gunpowder and brimstone, and fired them, then flung them into the window, so setting the house alight. This was the beginning of the firing of London. From Pudding Lane, joined by two or three others, they proceeded to fire houses in Thames Street, Fleet Street, and the Royal Exchange,

---

[1] *Ondersoek van den Brand van Londen Door ordere des Parlaments van Engelandt*, 1667. The alleged Dutch plot for the burning of London can be briefly dismissed. It apparently gained some credit because of the statement at the trial of Rathbone and his fellow conspirators (*London Gazette*, 1666, April 30) that a council sat frequently in London, receiving directions from another council in Holland, by which money was distributed among the plotters. Burnet records that after the English Fleet had burnt Vlie emissaries went to De Witt offering in revenge to set London on fire, if they were assisted. De Witt rejected the proposal, saying that he would not make the breach wider, nor the quarrel irreconcilable, and made no further reflections upon it until London was burnt. Then he began to suspect there had been a design to draw him into the plot, in order that the odium might lie upon the Dutch. But he could hear no news of those who sent the proposition to him.

and went on doing like mischief two or three nights and days. His uncle hired his father for the work, and paid him £7.[1] A note made in the Secretary's office says : " The boy's age renders the whole suspected ; but it is to be put into my Lord Chief Justice's hands."

Nothing tangible resulted from all the examinations. " Many who were produced," says Clarendon, " as if their testimony would remove all doubts made such senseless relations of what they had been told, without knowing the condition of the persons who told them, or where to find them, that it was a hard matter to forbear smiling at their evidence." Old Sir Thomas Littleton, who had the reputation of being the ablest Parliament man of his time, held, too, that the charge that the Fire of London was started or continued by design failed. It is significant that not a single case was returned for trial at the Old Bailey sessions except that of Hubert, against whom there was nothing save his own confession. The prisoners were released. But already another body was at work which was to focus more effectively than anything heretofore attempted the forces of calumny that for many years to come were to oppress, under conditions even more rigorous than then existed, the unfortunate Catholics.

Parliament was not sitting when the Great Fire of London occurred. It had been prorogued in April, but was summoned to assemble at Westminster on the 18th September. " God be thanked," said the King from the Throne, prefacing a demand for money, " for our meeting together in this place. Little time hath passed since we were almost in despair of having this place left to meet in. You see the dismal ruins the fire hath made ; and nothing but a miracle of God's mercy could have preserved what is left from the same destruction." [2]

Seven days later the Commons appointed their own Committee, which ultimately was strengthened to seventy members, with Sir Robert Brook as chairman, to inquire into the causes of the Fire. They met for the first time on the 26th September, armed with powers to send for witnesses, papers, and records, and proceeded forthwith

[1] *State Papers* (*Domestic*), 1666-7, p. 110.
[2] *House of Lords' Journal*, vol. 12, p. 4.

" to receive many considerable informations from divers creditable persons about the matter wherewith they were instructed." [1]

The capacity of this first elected Parliament of Charles II. to inquire judicially into a matter arousing so much passion can best be judged by its own actions. The Commons on the 28th September voted a resolution, " That the humble thanks of this House be given to his Majesty for his great care and endeavour to prevent the burning of London " ; and thereafter, with the House of Lords, they jointly petitioned for the banishment of all Popish priests and Jesuits (who were ordered by Royal Proclamation to depart the Kingdom before the 10th December), the enforcement of the laws against Papist recusants, and the disarming of all who refused the Oaths of Allegiance and Supremacy. The King, professing that he accepted with great contentment their care for the preservation of the true religion established in his kingdom, reluctantly gave his assent. [2] A vote was also passed by the Commons that all its members should receive the Lord's Supper, on penalty that any who abstained should be taken into custody.

Sir Richard Browne dramatically produced before the Committee " some desperate daggers, fit for massacres," two hundred of which were declared to have been found in the rubbish of a house in London, wherein before the Fire two French persons lodged. [3] A general search for arms in the houses of Papists increased the popular alarm ; it was made on representations by the Committee that knowledge had reached them of intended mischief against the Protestants ; and the action of some hot-heads in casting about the streets and throwing into house-windows a venomous leaflet of verse—it was distributed even in Westminster Hall—assisted to fan the

[1] Names of the members of the Parliamentary Committee are printed in *A True and Faithfull Account*, etc., 1667. Among them figures " Mr. Pepis," but this was not the diarist.
[2] *Royal Proclamation*, 1666, Nov. 10. Lord Arlington to the Earl of Sandwich : " Your Excellency knows sufficiently the Springs upon which the animosity to the Roman Catholics rises, and how hard it is for his Majesty to forbear declaring against them, when the complaint ariseth from both Houses of Parliament."
[3] Portland MSS. (*Hist. MSS. Comm.*, vol. 3, p. 302).

flames of religious hatred.[1]   Dated the day of Gunpowder
Plot, it began with the menacing lines—

> Covre la feu, ye Hugonots,
> That have so branded us with plots ;
> For down ye must, ye Hereticks,
> For all your hopes in sixty-six.
> The hand against you is so steady,
> Your Babylon is fal'n already.
> And if you will avoid that hap,
> Return unto your Mother's lap ;
> The Devil a Mercy is for those,
> That Holy Mother-Church oppose.

The Committee's report was presented to Parliament
on the 22nd January following, and consists of evidence
alone, and only a selection of that evidence.   It made no
recommendation ; obviously it was meant to be interim.
Andrew Marvell, a Member of the Parliament for Hull,
in letters to his constituents indicates that the report
deeply impressed the House, being " full of manifest
testimony that the Fire was of a wicked design," and
proving " things of extraordinary weight which, if they
were not true, might have been thought incredible ; " [2]
but his more lively concern was in the rival inquiry into
the insolences of Popish priests.   The House ordered the
report to be taken into consideration.   Whatever finding
had been intended, Charles and his Council had already
made up their minds as to the causes of the Fire.   The
rubbish about Papistical plots and preparations—and
rubbish it is—with which the Parliamentary inquiry had
been chiefly concerned, was set aside.   The Council were
convinced, " that notwithstanding that many examinations have been taken, with great care, by the Lords of
the Council and his Majesty's Ministers, yet nothing hath
yet been found to argue it to have been other than the
hand of God upon us, a great wind, and the season so very
dry." [3]

Parliament was prorogued on the 8th February, 1667,
and the Committee itself extinguished, never to be revived.
The citizens, dissatisfied, prepared in March, 1668, a

---

[1] Rugge's *Diurnal*.
[2] Marvell to R. Franke, Mayor of Hull, Nov. 30 and Jan. 22.
[3] Memorandum by Williamson, *State Papers* (*Domestic*), 1666–7, p. 175.

Photo by Mr. Lionel Gowing

COLLEGE OF ARMS, QUEEN VICTORIA STREET

petition to lay before Parliament, praying that the inquiry might be re-opened, and fresh evidence taken for discovering the wicked instruments of the Fire ; [1] but, still harrying Papists as a godly duty, they devoted their larger energies to the better task of rebuilding the city.

Immediately the report to Parliament appeared it was seized upon as a vehicle for still further inflaming the populace against the Catholics. The presses made busy with reprints, and these were scattered broadcast about the country, bearing the title, " A true and faithfull Account of the several Informations exhibited to the Honourable Committee appointed by the Parliament to inquire into the late dreadful burning of the City of London." Five separate impressions are known to the writer. The print had the curious fate, for a Parliamentary document, of being burned at the hands of the common hangman in Westminster Palace Yard [2]—a step possibly justified by the fact that the published version contained evidence taken but not recorded in the Committee's report. Many copies were confiscated. " The book appears to have been maliciously published by some Presbyterian hand, and may do harm, being approved of by some of that party," wrote a magistrate at Rydal, who had seized several copies. The Mayor of Bristol detained a consignment of fifty, as being seditious and likely to seduce persons against the Government.[3] A " scandalous " pamphlet which I have not found, called *An Apology of the English Catholics*, having been surreptitiously printed in Jew's Lane for one Piu, a priest or Jesuit, was suppressed by the Privy Council.

The Parliamentary report is worthless as evidence of the wilful firing of London, but cannot be ignored, for it reflects the prevailing public opinion more accurately than does the calm reasoning of the Council. A large proportion of the people wished to believe, and did believe, that the destruction of the city was the work of malicious Papists. Every bit of floating calumny calculated to throw suspicion on priests and recusants and Frenchmen was carefully collected. Affidavits were sworn before

[1] *Journal* 46, fo. 219.
[2] Pepys's *Diary*, 1667, Sept. 16.
[3] *State Papers* (*Domestic*), 1667, pp. 290, 393, 401.

justices of the peace of scraps of conversation that had
passed with merchant and citizen, the confidences ex-
changed between babbling old women, and phrases caught
by some eavesdropping tavern keeper; and these were
served up to the Parliamentary Committee. I have read
the sworn evidence. It is still necessary to do so in order
to arrive at a cool judgment, for the historians of the
seventeenth and early eighteenth centuries, who have
acquitted or condemned the Catholics, or have contented
themselves with a half-hearted verdict of " Not proven "
in the charges levelled against them, obviously found it
impossible to shake themselves free from the religious
prejudices of their times. Tillotson, that godly divine,
believed that London was wilfully fired. There is nothing
in all the evidence—and certainly not Hubert's confession
—that would survive cross-examination by the least
competent lawyer.

Few extracts from the Parliamentary report will suffice
to show its quality—

Mrs. Elizabeth Styles informs, That in April last, in an
eager discourse she had with a French servant of Sir Vere Fan,
he hastily replied, " You English maids will like the Frenchmen better when there is not a house left between Temple-Bar
and London Bridge." To which she answered, " I hope your
eyes will never see that." He replied, " This will come to
pass between June and October."

Mr. Light, of Ratcliff, having some discourse with Mr.
Langhorn, of the Middle Temple, barrister (reputed a zealous
Papist) about February 15 last, after some discourse in dis-
putation about religion, he took him by the hand, and said to
him, " You expect great things in Sixty-Six, and think that
Rome will be destroyed, but what if it be London ? "

Mr. Kitely, of Barking, Essex, informs, That one Mrs.
Yazly, a Papist, of Ilford in the said county, came into his
house, August the 13th, and being in discourse with his mother,
said, " They say the next Thursday will be the hottest day
that ever was in England." She replied, " I hope the hottest
season of the year is now past." To which she answered,
" I know not whether it will be hottest for weather or action."
This Mrs. Yazly coming to the same house the week after the
Fire, Mrs. Kitely said to her with some trouble, " I have often
thought of your *hot Thursday* ; " to which she replied, " It
was not, indeed, on the Thursday, but it happened upon the
Sunday was seven-night after." Mrs. Yazly, hearing this

evidence produced against her, endeavoured to avoid her words (and so on. The woman on examination denied ever having used the words).

Then there were tales, given with much circumstantial detail, of strange incendiary weapons, devilish in their origin and their effects, and of the throwing of fire-balls:

Doctor John Packer informs, That he saw a person in the time of the Fire throw some combustible matter into a shop in the Old Bayley, which he thinks was the shop of an apothecary; and that immediately thereupon he saw a great smoke, and smelt a smell of brimstone. The person that did this immediately ran away; but upon the outcry of the people he was taken by the Guards.

Mr. Freeman, of Southwark, brewer (whose house was lately fired) informs, That . . . a paper with a ball of wildfire, containing near a pound weight wrapt in it, was found in the nave of a wheel, in a wheeler's yard, where lay a great quantity of timber.

No stranger story did the Committee listen to, with infinite patience, than that which cast suspicion upon one Belland, King Charles's firework-maker. This man, a Frenchman, lived at Marylebone, and before the Fire he had bought large quantities of pasteboard, storing twenty gross in one shop. Asked what he did with all this material, he had replied that he made fireworks for the King's pleasure. The stationer who supplied the pasteboard, being at Belland's house on one occasion, marvelled at the many thousands of fireworks that lay piled up in various sorts. " Sir," said the pyrotechnist, " do you wonder at this ? If you should see the quantity that I have made elsewhere by other men you would wonder indeed ! "

A neighbour citizen of the stationer—shrewd man no doubt he thought himself—probed the mystery of this great business to the bottom, at least to his own satisfaction.[1] It chanced that the Sunday before the Fire began Belland came down to the stationer's in great concern, because a parcel of four gross of pasteboards had not

[1] Clarendon has explained that the King's firework-maker was employed by the Office of Ordnance for making grenades of all kinds, both for hand use and for mortarpieces.

been delivered. The stationer was away from home. Belland left a message with the neighbour that he must have the pasteboards by Tuesday; after that he should have no occasion for them. What could those last words mean, " after that he should have no occasion for them " ? —uttered, too, five days before London was consumed by fire !

" Mr. Belland " (said the citizen), " what is the reason of your haste ? Have you any show suddenly before the King ? " At which he blushed and would give no answer.

Said the citizen, " What kind of fire do you make ? Only such as will crack and run ? "

Belland answered : " I make all sorts; some that will burn and make no crack at all, but will fly up in a pure body of flame higher than the top of Paul's, and waver in the air."

Said the citizen : " Mr. Belland, when you make your show, shall I see it ? "

" Yes," said Belland, " I promise you," and gave him his hand upon it.

London within a week was in flames, and the citizen, watching the dread spectacle from the Thames in a boat, saw to his amazement sundry bodies of fire burning above the fire of the houses. As high again as St. Paul's they rose, wavering in the air, just as Belland had described. So at least to one overheated imagination the pyro-technist's fireworks there disported themselves, as if in demoniacal victory, high in the air above the crackling, seething cauldron of London.

The citizen communicated with the stationer. Wise after the event—so many people were then wise—these two laid their heads together, determined to seek out Belland at his shop. On their way to Marylebone they met his two maids and his boy. These said they knew nothing of their master's whereabouts, but observing that they carried food ready dressed, the citizens concluded that they were going to him in hiding.

The two followed the servants to Whitehall. They pressed their way even into the King's Palace, where they discovered the French firework-maker had taken refuge, fearing the blind rage of the populace.

Upstairs and downstairs the servants went, on purpose

to have shaken them off, but they followed closely.   At
last one of the maids stopped at a door and knocked,
crying out that they were dogged by two men whom they
could not get rid of.   Then Belland's son appeared,
wishing the interlopers good-day.   One of them answered
him, " Both I and many thousand families more are the
worse for you ; for you, under pretence of making fireworks for the King, have destroyed a famous city, and
ruined a noble people."

At this old Belland looked from under the hangings.
I quote again the printed report—

" Sir," said he, " I hear you charge my son with suspicion
of burning the city ; I pray you speak lower " (casting his
eyes about, fearing the ladies passing by might hear), and
said, " My son doth nothing but what he hath a patent from
the King for, and shall have an order to sue any man that
shall accuse him."   And he said, " My son is no prisoner, but
lodged here, to prevent him from the rage of the common
people."   " Well," said the citizens, " you must give an
account for what you have done."   And so they shut the door
upon them.   The citizens went and inquired whose lodgings
they were ;   and were told, they belonged to the Lady
Killegrew.[1]

There the matter ends, and the Committee (mayhap
with a yawn) turned to the next equally futile deposition
of some citizen whose excitement had clouded with suspicion the most innocent action of his neighbour.   A
circumstantial narrative is given of the utterances of Mrs.
St. George, of Enfield, a Papist, on the last day of August,
" That some would hereafter be called to account for a
plot for burning the City."   The rejoinder of the garrulous
old lady's own daughter is sufficient comment upon it,
" That her mother was very apt to talk, and that she had
been fain to keep her mother within doors during the Fire,
fearing lest she should talk."   Then was told the account,
sworn on oath by eleven witnesses, of a Frenchman
brought to the White Lion, in King Street, who confessed
" that three hundred Frenchmen were in a plot or conspiracy for firing the City " ;   the testimony of a Suffolk
constable, that two days before the Fire broke out one

[1] *A True and Faithfull Account*, etc., 1667.

William Thompson, a Papist of Ipswich, had asked him, " What will you say, if you should hear that London is burnt ? " the arrival in London on the eve of the Fire of an Irishman who, with other words of mysterious purport, had uttered the phrase, *Nunc Seges est ubi Troja fuit*—but no good purpose would be served by prolonging the list.

Another Parliamentary Committee sat to certify informations " touching the insolency of Popish priests and Jesuits, and the increase of Popery." The informations, of which there were no lack, are illuminating only of the suspicious state of the public mind, and the unreasoning prejudice which existed against everybody and everything Romish. They deal with the activities of Harvey, the Queen Mother's confessor ; with threats that the Roman Catholics could raise 30,000 men, as well armed as any in Christendom, and that the next work after the .Fire would be the cutting of throats ; with reports of a recent alarming increase in Popery which men's craven fears conjured up, and like matters.

The Council found that the Fire was due to " the hand of God upon us, a great wind, and the season so very dry." That judgment has held good for two and a half centuries, and will not now be displaced.

The Monument erected by Wren that stands on Fish Street Hill, one hundred and thirty feet west of the spot where the Fire broke out, need not be described here. Associated with it is Pope's well-known couplet—

> Where London's column pointing at the skies,
> Like a tall bully, lifts the head, and lies—

but it is not always recalled that the passage which inspired this indignant protest, declaring that the Fire was " begun and carried on by the treachery and malice of the Popish faction," formed no part of the original inscription. Until June, 1681, the column properly fulfilled its purpose, as stated in the Act of Parliament that authorized its erection, " the better to preserve the memory of this direful visitation." Only after the perjuries of Titus Oates, who declared that eighty Jesuits, friars and priests had been engaged in the firing of London, and the disclosures of the so-called Popish Plot had again roused Protestant feeling in the City to frenzy, did the Common Council order the words to be engraved around the plinth of the lower pedestal. Sir Patience Ward was Lord Mayor. Though he was probably no more responsible than any other civic official, he is credited by his namesake, Thomas Ward,[1] with being their author. Oates, says the rhyme—

> swore, with flaming faggot sticks,
> In sixteen hundred sixty-six,
> That they through London took their marches,
> And burn'd the City down with torches ;
> Yet all invisible they were
> Clad in their coats of Lapland air.
> That sniffling Whig-Mayor Patience Ward,
> To this damn'd lie had such regard,
> That he his godly masons sent
> T' engrave it round the Monument.
> They did so ; but let such things pass,
> His men were fools, and he an ass.

The words were obliterated soon after the accession of James II., but were incised yet deeper when William and Mary were called to the Throne, and they were not finally removed from the Monument till the year 1830.

[1] *England's Reformation*, Hamburg, 1710.

CHAPTER XII

LOSSES IN THE FIRE

WHERE shall one find comparison with the chaos which confronted the civic authorities when at last the Fire of London had been subdued ? Cities had been sacked and burnt before and left a waste, the survivors scattering afar. London within the Wall had but a sixth part standing, and the Liberties west towards Temple Bar were burnt out. The entire population remained; but in that vast blackened area which lay open to the sky were low lying all those institutions of government which a great city, numbering souls by the hundred thousand, deems necessary for its order and welfare.

The ancient walls of Guildhall were upstanding, the floor being strewn with charred timbers from the roof and gallery, and glass fallen from gaping windows. All the surrounding buildings from which the administration of the City proceeded were heaped in ruins. The justice hall and civil courts were destroyed. Every one of the City prisons had been burnt, and the prisoners in many cases had broken gaol. London's markets, distributing food to her multitude, had been generously provided. Of them there remained Leadenhall alone. The Royal Exchange, the mart of London's great foreign trade and the gathering place of her merchants, was a medley of overturned columns and fire-riven stones.

The Fire, spreading down to the river's edge, had left few of the wharves and boat-stairs serviceable. Carriers' communications were interrupted. Letters in and out of London had stopped with the burning of the Post House. Ample food supplies came in daily from the country, and in the extremity of their distress the citizens fortunately were spared the spectre of starvation, but those who had homes still over their heads were in imminent danger of water famine, for the services from the New River and the springs, so vital to public health, ran to waste and soaked the burnt ground.

In short, there was everything to be done, and with speed. It was the City's good fortune that in that area within the Wall left unharmed, and near the Fire's edge, was standing Sir Thomas Gresham's house in Bishopsgate Street. The builder of the Royal Exchange, when growing business and social importance enabled him to move from the sign of The Grasshopper in Lombard Street, had raised for himself a considerable mansion, notable not only for its own state, but for its ample grounds. Like the Exchange, it was built in part in colonnade, the stone pillars and vaulting forming covered walks enclosing an open space. Gresham College was established there, with apartments for the seven professors, and the property was held in trust by the Corporation and Gresham's Company, the Mercers, in equal moieties. The Court of Aldermen assembled at Gresham House on Thursday, the 6th September, when London was not yet cold. Isolated fires were still burning. They decided to meet there until other provision could be made. The Lord Mayor, Sir Thomas Bludworth, had been burnt out of his house in Maiden Lane, by St. John Zachary Church, and the Sheriffs, Sir Robert Hanson and Sir William Hooker, were also homeless from the Fire. These high functionaries were invited to take lodging in Gresham House during their respective terms of office. The City Chamberlain was directed to keep his office in Gresham House. Mr. Avery, the Deputy (acting) Town Clerk, and the City Swordbearer were also accommodated with lodging there.[1]

The authority of the City officers had, in the emergency of the Fire, been displaced for that of the Lords of the Council. It was desirable that it should be restored at the earliest moment, and on the Thursday the King sent a letter to the Lord Mayor, directing him to assemble the Aldermen, magistrates, and citizens of quality, " to the end that there may be an appearance of magistracy and government " jointly with that of the Council, to take

---

[1] *Repertory* 71, fos. 169b, 170.

care for the public welfare of the City.[1] The Common
Council met on the following Monday, the 10th September,
at Gresham House, which for many months thereafter
served all the uses of a Guildhall. Its first order was to
direct the late inhabitants to clear all the streets, lanes, and
public passages of rubbish, every one before his own ground.
Until this considerable work was finished, no labour should
be permitted upon the ruins. In each ward a booth was
set up, to which occupiers of houses were required to bring
particulars of sites and area of ground covered, for record
to be made, and a register was opened of those willing to
buy or sell land.[2] * Next in urgency was the temporary
settlement of traders and craftsmen burnt out by the Fire,
so that they might carry on their occupations. A strong
committee of Aldermen and Commoners was appointed,
which met next day, with powers temporarily to apportion
sites on the City's vacant spaces among freemen whose
dwellings had been destroyed, and to consider the best
means of raising the City out of its ruins.

This last important task was ultimately left to the
entire Council, but early as the 24th September the committee had presented to the Lord Chancellor a draft of its
proposals for a Bill in Parliament, and a conference with
a committee of Parliament was immediately arranged.[3]

The covered walks and garden of Gresham House
offered facilities for the merchants, who by Royal command
met there to conduct their business. Pepys, always in-
quisitive, was with the throng, " where infinity of people,
partly through novelty to see the new place, and partly to
find out and hear what is become one man of another. I
met with many people undone, and more that have extraordinary great losses." A week after the Royal Exchange
had burnt, as many as three thousand merchants appeared
at Gresham House, and for the larger part they complied
with the demands of their foreign correspondents as if no
disaster had happened, so admirable was the spirit of
London's citizens when confronting adversity.[4] Dr. Sprat

[1] *Privy Council Registers*, vol. 59, fos. 150–1.
[2] *Gazette*, Sept. 20–24.
[3] *Journal* 46, fo. 169b. Citizens' Members of Parliament to the Lord
Mayor, Sept. 24.
[4] *Royal Proclamation*, Sept. 5 ; Pepys's *Diary*, Sept. 8 ; Le Fleming
MSS. (*Hist. MSS. Comm.*, p. 42). Evelyn to Sir S. Tuke, Sept. 29.

From Vertue's print in the Goss Collection

SIR THOMAS GRESHAM'S HOUSE IN BISHOPSGATE
After the Great Fire it was used both as Guildhall and Royal Exchange

(afterwards Bishop of Rochester) paid to them a courtly compliment. " They beheld," he wrote, " the ashes of their houses, gates and temples without the least pusillanimity. If philosophers had done this, it had well become their profession of wisdom ; if gentlemen, the nobleness of their breeding and blood would have required it ; but that such greatness of heart should have been found among the obscure multitude is no doubt one of the most honourable events that ever happened. A new City is to be built, on the most advantageous seat of all Europe for trade and command."

Alderman Backwell, the financier of Lombard Street, was by the King's command allotted rooms in Gresham House, in order that his important business with the Crown might not be interrupted. Sir Robert Vyner's great wealth in securities, money and jewels was received for safe keeping in Windsor Castle.[1] He took a house in Broad Street, where, too, Backwell and Meynell and other Lombard Street brokers migrated ; it became the financial centre while the City was rebuilding. For convenience of trade a bureau was set up in Bloomsbury, where changes of address and notice of goods lost or found could be posted.

There seems to have been an idea abroad that with the destruction of London the capital itself might be moved elsewhere, at least for a time. One from York inquired if that should be the chosen city. Not until the Thames flowed under Ouse bridge, came the reply, the Londoners being confident as ever of the supreme advantages of their port and river. The Corporation at once set an example to the citizens by taking steps for reviving communal life. Confronted with the task of restoring the public buildings, they informed the King that the City " had no common stock, nor revenue, nor any capacity to raise within itself anything considerable towards so vast an expense." [2] But much was, in fact, done by shifts and repairs while larger measures were under consideration. The Guildhall was immediately cleared of its debris in order that the courts might assemble in the places where they were anciently kept, and the Judges were able to sit there, in a wooden structure raised within the ruins, in the first week of

---

[1] *State Papers* (*Domestic*) 1666–7, pp. 112, 174.
[2] *Ibid.*, p. 469.

November. Not only had the Judges been burnt out of
their Courts, but the flames in Serjeants Inn had destroyed
their chambers as well, and the learned practitioners of
Doctors Commons, the proctors and registrars, were in a
like homeless state. Certain houses standing in the
Liberties were suggested for their lodging.[1]

It was found possible by speedy repairs to refit a portion
of the burnt-out prison at Newgate sufficiently strongly to
contain a certain number of felons. They were in sorry
plight. The gaol was without water, till in November the
Sheriffs were ordered to supply it, and in the following
March the common sewer broke into the prison ; the
Keeper had cause later to complain of the danger to health
of the prisoners and their custodians for want of rebuilding
of the ruinous parts.[2] The Keeper of Newgate, despite
all this, seems for his own profit to have made a home for
the disorderly characters let loose upon the City, for
Pepys tells " that he hath at this day made his house the
only nursery of rogues, prostitutes, pickpockets and thieves
in the world, where they were bred and entertained, and
the whole society met, and that for the sake of the Sheriffs
they durst not this day commit him, for fear of making
him let out the prisoners, but are fain to go by artifice to
deal with him." A wooden structure, as at Guildhall, was
fitted up in the ruins of the Sessions House in Old Bailey
for the gaol delivery. The ample stone porch of Guildhall
gave accommodation to the City's Court of Requests.
The provision of prisons for temporary use was a problem
of greater complexity. There were substantial structures
in the City gates, which contained rooms utilized as dwellings, and these were made fit with bolts and bars for the
purpose. The Common Crier was turned out of the
lodging which he enjoyed over Aldersgate to make place
for the prisoners from the Poultry Compter. Bishopsgate
served as substitute for the Wood Street Compter.[3]

The Royal Society had met at Gresham House since
its foundation by Charles II., in 1662, and was ejected.
Henry Howard, afterwards sixth Duke of Norfolk, a Fellow
newly elected, liberally placed at the Society's disposal a

---

[1] *Repertory* 71, fos. 171*b*, 176*b* ; 72, fo. 1.
[2] *Repertory* 72, fos. 11*b*, 95*b* ; 74, fo. 160.
[3] *Repertory* 71, fos. 171*b*, 174*b*, 177.

suite of convenient rooms in his town mansion, Arundel House in the Strand.

Other migrations were as quickly carried out. The Custom House, pending rebuilding by the Thames-side below the Bridge, was established in Lord Bayning's house in Mark Lane, where the farmers and clerks of the staffs attended. The Excise Office was removed to Southampton Fields, and that for the Hearth Tax kept in Leadenhall Street. The Post House was temporarily established in Brydges Street, Covent Garden, and a week or two later set up in Bishopsgate Street. The King's Wardrobe was removed to York House buildings. The business of Doctors Commons and of the Court of Arches was conducted in Exeter House, Strand.[1] The College of Arms, with its records and books, was by the King's command established in the Court of Requests at Westminster Hall. The Brethren of Trinity House met at Stepney. The First Fruits Office was set up in Gray's Inn. The King's Printing House was moved to the Savoy. The King's Weigh House, which had been in Cornhill, ultimately occupied the site of the consumed church of St. Andrew Hubbard.

Markets were essential for the City's continuance. There was no course open but to make the best use possible of the covered space of Leadenhall and the wider streets outside the Fire area. A Mayoral Proclamation of September 6th appointed Leadenhall as a market for flesh brought in by country butchers and for supplies by City butchers whose shops were destroyed ; and also for fish, meal, hides and leather. Stalls for herbs, roots, and like commodities were to be set in the usual place in Aldersgate Street and about the Pump in Bishopsgate Street. These supplemented the outlying markets already temporarily fixed by Royal Proclamation. Later in the year a mart for clothiers was appointed on Thursdays for the great hall in Leadenhall, for which other traders gave place, and a market was opened at Wapping.

" The citizens, instead of complaining, discourse almost of nothing but of a survey for rebuilding the City with bricks and large streets," wrote Henry Oldenburg to the

[1] *London Gazette*, 1666, Sept. 3–10 *passim*. *Privy Council Registers*, Vol. 59.

Hon. Robert Boyle on September 10th. Three days later a house-owner had already begun building at Black-friars.[1] Such enterprise was obviously undesirable, and on September 13th a Royal Proclamation was published prohibiting the rebuilding of houses until they should conform with the general regulations therein promised. The Proclamation is chiefly interesting for the proof it affords that within a week of the Fire the broad basis upon which the City was afterwards reconstructed had already been agreed upon. Charles pledged his Royal word that there should be no delay. " If any considerable number of men (for it is impossible to comply with the humour of every particular man) "—so the Proclamation runs— " shall address themselves to the Court of Aldermen, and manifest to them in what places their ground lies upon which they design to build, they shall in a short time receive such order and direction for their proceeding therein, that they shall have no cause to complain."

Charles spoke of London affectionately as " this our native city." The seat and situation of it was the most convenient and noble for the advancement of trade of any city in Europe. It was his desire, with the help of the citizens, that it should arise resplendent, " making it rather appear to the world as purged with fire (in how lamentable a manner soever) to a wonderful beauty and comeliness, than consumed by it," and in this he was encouraged by the alacrity and cheerfulness of those who had undergone the greatest loss, and seemed the most undone. An exact survey would be taken of all the ruins, and a model made for the rebuilding of the ruined places.

A single clause in the Proclamation decided the character of the new London. The woeful experience of the Fire having convinced all people of the pernicious consequences which had attended building with timber, " no man what-soever shall presume to erect any house or building, great or small, but of brick or stone."

Fleet Street, Cheapside, Cornhill, " and all other eminent and notorious streets," were to be of such a breadth as, with God's blessing, should prevent the mischief that one side might suffer if the other be on fire. No street should

[1] Le Fleming MSS. (*Hist. MSS. Comm.*, p. 42).

be so narrow as to make the passage uneasy or inconvenient, especially towards the waterside, nor should any alleys or lanes be tolerated but where, upon mature deliberation, the same be found absolutely necessary. The riverside was to be kept clear by a quay or wharf extending the length of the City. All noisome trades, those of brewers, dyers, sugar bakers, and the like, which by their continuous smoke made adjacent localities unhealthy, were to be removed and grouped in a place thereafter to be selected. On this plan London, great and glorious, should be recreated. No man's right should be sacrificed to the public convenience. Meantime, should any persons, careless of the Royal command, presume to erect buildings as they might think fit, upon pretence that the ground was their own, the Proclamation warned them that the Lord Mayor and magistrates were charged to pull down such buildings, and the refractory persons would be punished.[1] Wise as King Charles's Proclamation unquestionably was in its instant realization of the necessities of the time, and on the whole favourably received, it created some natural irritation among sections of the citizens by its interference with their liberty to do what they liked with their own property, and the arbitrary extension of the Royal prerogative.

In preparation for the survey, the Common Council, on the 9th October, directed the owners of houses that had been destroyed to clear their foundations of rubbish, and to pile up the bricks and stones within fourteen days, so that every man's property might be more exactly measured and certified. The public spirit of the citizens, responding to that of the King, was displayed in the meticulous care they took in preserving, till better times, all the machinery of parochial life. Churchwardens were elected for each City parish, though the church itself consisted of nothing but roofless and shaking walls ; Councilmen were returned, constables, beadles and scavengers appointed, and the annual beating of the bounds duly performed—the last a difficult task where the entire parish lay flat and desolate in its ruins.

Necessarily there was keen distress among the homeless

[1] The Royal Proclamation is printed by W. de Gray Birch, *Historical Charters City of London*, p. 224 *et seq.*

populace, many well-to-do traders having lost everything in the flames, and being reduced to dependence upon public charity. But the very hugeness of the disaster which had overwhelmed London itself brought a certain measure of relief. The Pewterers Company, invited in December to make a contribution to the poor, declined to do so. They replied that "In consideration of the late calamities by fire in which the Company hath been very great sufferers, and the generality of the poorer sort of people hath been in some measure gainers, it was concluded nothing should be given." [1] This decision, apparently so harsh, truthfully reflects one aspect of affairs within the City, for tradesmen who had money with which to rebuild, or land-owners money to invest, were compelled to employ it, and the labouring poor found speedy relief in the vast amount of work that was required in clearing the streets and ruins.

Immediately after the Fire, in order that the most pressing cases of want should be met, the churchwardens of every City parish were required to bring to the Lord Mayor a list of the necessitous poor in the different parishes. The Governors of hospitals and the Masters, Wardens, and Assistants of the City Companies were directed to provide their respective poor with diet, lodgings, and necessaries, though they were, both individually and corporately, amongst those most hardly hit. Many charitably disposed citizens who had themselves escaped disaster put their mansions at the disposal of the homeless people. Sir William Bateman's house in Coleman Street in this way accommodated many residents of the destroyed parish of Allhallows Bread Street.

Widespread sympathy was excited throughout the country. Lyme Regis, in Dorsetshire, within a week of the news reaching that county collected and forwarded to London a sum of £100. Lynn, in Norfolk, despatched charitable stores to London by a convoy which left under escort of the warship *Little Lion*. The town of Marlborough, Wilts, remitted £50. York at once sent its town clerk to London to express condolences with the people in their great loss, and the Lord Mayor of York wrote on the 17th September that a small sum of money, "as much as this

---

[1] Court Minutes, Welch, *Pewterers Company*, ii, 133.

poor decayed city could furnish us with," was on its way
to London for the relief of the most necessitous persons.
The benevolences of the York citizens amounted to £398.
Merchants of Leghorn collected £300 for relief.

Apart from these public benevolences were " free
gifts," which did credit to the generosity of every class of
the community. The Bishop of London received £68 5s.
for distribution from some brethren of the episcopal bench.
The Lord Chief Justice, Baron Atkins, and Mr. James
Ravenscroft jointly sent £44 17s., " being their free gifts,
whereof 2s. 6d. in bad money "—one hopes it was not the
Chief Justice's. There was, indeed, a great deal of spurious
and debased coinage in circulation at the time, and when
the full accounts came to be audited, no less than £23 18s.
had to be deducted from the total for this cause. The Dean
and Chapter of Lincoln subscribed £42 15s. The Countess
of Devonshire sent £40, and there were many more sums.[1]

In the troubled story of the relations of Ireland and
England there is no incident it is more pleasant to recall
than the offer of help voluntarily made by the warm-
hearted Irish to distressed London. Lord Ormond and
the Lords of the Council in Ireland wrote to Sir Thomas
Bludworth on the 29th September, expressing hearty
sorrow at the calamity, and desiring to assist. Money was
so scarce in Ireland that they were compelled to ask the
City to accept the greater part of such assistance as that
country could offer in cattle, alive or slaughtered. A
provision in the Bill to exclude Irish cattle then before
Parliament would be necessary. The City petitioned for
this exceptional importation, " by way of donation and
charitable loan," but December came, and the Parliament
still withheld its assent.[2] The Mayor and Council of
Londonderry sent a letter of touching affection.

It recalled how London had assisted in rebuilding that
city, devastated in the late Irish Rebellion, and asked,
" What shall we do for our once great and ever dear
Mother in this the day of her calamity ? " Deep poverty
lay upon Derry, and a general want of money was throughout all Ireland. They could perform no duty which would
be commeasurable to curing London's grievous wound.

---

[1] Guildhall Library MSS. 271.
[2] Sharpe, *London and the Kingdom*, ii, 421.

Their free voluntary subscription would be £250, to be remitted with all convenient speed, and they hoped that " tendering so freely to you our honoured Mother [it] may possibly prove a greater cordial than better compounded and more effectual medicines from greater helpers." [1]

It was self-evident, however, that the extent of distress must be such that it could only be met by an appeal over the widest possible ground. The King, while the horror of the Fire was fresh in all minds, decided that a day of fasting and humiliation should be kept, " to implore the mercies of God, that it would please him to pardon the crying sins of this nation, those especially which have drawn down this last and heavy judgment upon us, and to remove from us all other his Judgments which our sins have deserved." The Royal Proclamation fixed the 10th October next for the observance, and further commanded that collections for the aid of the sufferers in London should be taken on that day in all churches and chapels throughout England and Wales, or from house to house, and the sums received forwarded to the Lord Mayor. [2]

Dr. Sancroft, Dean of St. Paul's, preached before the King and the Court at Whitehall a remarkably bad sermon, crowded in every passage with the insufferable pedantry of the time. The King's printer has saved it from oblivion. [3] It is beyond belief that Charles consciously listened to the full two hours of it. Seth Ward, Bishop of Exeter, preached before the Lords in Westminster Abbey, and Dr. Stillingfleet, most eloquent of the three, to the House of Commons in the morning in St. Margaret's Church. Pepys went with Sir William Batten to St Margaret's, but failed to gain admittance—" so full, no standing room there ; so he and I to eat herrings at the Dog Tavern." In the afternoon there was another great crowd to hear Dr. Robert Frampton, a rising divine, afterwards the nonjuring Bishop of Gloucester—" he

---

[1] Original letter in Town Clerk's office, Guildhall. The money was never received in London, on account of the distress caused by a fire which a few months later destroyed a large part of Londonderry itself, when the City of London desired that the subscription should be devoted to the relief of sufferers thereby. (*Journal* 46, fo. 172*b*.)

[2] *Royal Proclamation*, 1666, Sept. 13.

[3] *Lex Ignea, or the School of Righteousness*, 1666.

RECEIPT FOR PUBLIC SUBSCRIPTION TOWARDS RELIEF

In the London Museum

preaches the most like an apostle that ever I heard man." [1]
The Lord Mayor and Aldermen, while burnt out of St.
Paul's, attended worship at St. Katherine Cree Church.
The special form of prayer appointed made no mention of
the Fire or of London. Its use was continued in St. Paul's
Cathedral every 2nd September so late as the year 1859,
when observance of the anniversary of the Great Fire
ceased, together with that of the State holy days abrogated
by Parliament.*

The immediate result of the church collections was a
subscription of £12,794, to which had to be added £1,077
by private gifts.

It is impossible to excite enthusiasm over the subscription. Larger contributions had been made by many
cities for losses by fire in neighbouring towns and villages
than were forwarded to London. In certain towns and
country places the collections were omitted altogether.
From others no returns were forthcoming. [2] The circumstances of the time must, however, be considered. The
country generally was poor, torn by the recent civil strife.
Sharp religious and political dissensions still divided large
sections of the populace. London lay aloof from distant
counties in those days of slow and difficult travelling. It
is certain, too, that these receipts do not fully represent
the charitable response of the country. The peculations
were scandalously large. The Earl of Essex, chairman of a
Parliamentary committee appointed for the discovery of
frauds upon the distressed Londoners, reported evidence
of thirty parishes in one large area having money in their
hands which were in default; and Sir William Bolton—
an untrustworthy witness—declared that £20,000 collected
for relief after the Fire had not been paid in. [3] Bolton, who
was Lord Mayor in succession to Sir Thomas Bludworth,
was himself subject to the disgraceful accusation of withholding money subscribed for relief, and pending inquiry
was forbidden to attend the Court of Aldermen or any
public function. After bringing a charge against the Bishop
of London, in 1668, of malfeasance of £50, and subsequently

---

[1] Pepys's *Diary*, 1666, Oct. 10th.
[2] Cf. *Royal Proclamation*, 1668, Sept. 16, in which year a second
charitable collection was made, and brought in an additional £2,306.
[3] House of Lords MSS. (*Hist. MSS. Comm.*, 9th Rep., 16a).

withdrawing it, he was himself convicted of having embezzled large sums from the subscriptions. Reduced to want, he died in obscurity, dependent upon a charitable grant which the City made to him.[1]

The subscriptions by counties are of interest. Devonshire heads the list with £1,480, Middlesex coming close with £1,474, with Yorkshire £1,184, next in order. London, despite its own plunge into poverty, sent £334, Kent £560, Surrey £642. From the far-distant border borough of Berwick-on-Tweed came £48 ; the little county of Rutland £50, Denbighshire £4 5s., and Merioneth £1 16s. Of London's contribution, the largest sums came from the Wards of Farringdon Without and Within (£77 and £38 respectively). Cornhill Ward had been swept so clean by the Fire that it is represented by only £6, and the Ward of Cheap by £4.[2]

A good deal was paid in small sums direct by the Chamber of London to widows and others for their relief, but the distribution for the first few months was mostly made by the Aldermen and Deputies of the Wards, the Bishop of London being in consultation with the Lord Mayor in apportioning the amounts. After May, 1667, where the distribution was not direct it was largely effected through the churchwardens of the various parishes. To meet the first four months' distress £3,418 had been paid out ; by the end of August, twelve months after the outbreak of the Fire, the charitable relief reached £5,887 ; and a sum nearly equal was accounted for in the second year, when the total stood at £10,611.[3] The final distribution of relief took place in October, 1669.

While still London lay in ruins the Common Council proposed that the City should buy land and build three official residences, for the Lord Mayor and the two Sheriffs.[4] Sir William Bolton, Lord Mayor-Elect, had applied to the Carpenters Company for use of their Hall, being, he represented, by occasion of the Fire destitute of a fit and convenient house in which to keep his mayoralty. The

[1] Sharpe, *London and the Kingdom,* ii, 432 ;] Pepys's *Diary,* 1667, Dec. 3 ; *Repertory* 73, fo. 61 passim ; 80, fo. 119*b*.
[2] Guildhall Library MSS., 296.
[3] Guildhall Library MSS., 271.
[4] *Journal* 46, fo. 188*b*.

Company on the 12th October, 1666, let to him the Hall
and its apartments at £100 rental, subject to indemnity
for any claims by the burnt-out Companies whom they were
temporarily housing ; and the three succeeding Lord Mayors
also leased the Hall for their mayoralties, the rent being
raised against them to £150.   At a Court of the Carpenters
Company held on the 7th October, 1670, it was resolved,
" That this Company will not let their Hall with the
appurtenances from henceforth to the Lord Mayors or to
any other person or persons under the sum of £150, and
that to be paid down before entry." [1] Evidently the
Lord Mayor's credit was not impeccable.

The City Sheriffs to this day have never enjoyed the
official houses foreshadowed so long ago. The present
Mansion House was finished in 1753, and was first occupied
by Sir Crisp Gascoyne.

There are several estimates of the losses occasioned by
the Great Fire of London. The earliest is that of the
writer using the pen-name of Rege Sincera, whose
Observations both Historical and Moral was written three
weeks after the Fire, although not printed until the following Spring. His data are necessarily inadequate—for
instance, he had not the Surveyors' report of the number
of houses burnt—but the computation is worth recalling :—

12,000 houses burnt, valued one with another at £25 a year's
rent each, which at twelve years' purchase maketh £300,
the whole amounting to £3,600,000
87 parochial churches, besides St. Paul's, the six consecrated
chapels, the Exchange, Guildhall, Custom House, the
halls of the Companies, and other public buildings,
amounting to half as much £1,800,000
The goods that every private man lost one with another,
valued at half the value of the houses £1,800,000
About 20 wharves of coals and wood valued at £1000 apiece   £20,000
About 100,000 boats and barges, 1000 cart loads, with porters
to remove the goods to and fro, as well for the houses
that were burning as for those that stood in fear of it, at
20s. a load £150,000

In all £7,370,000

Delaune, in his *Present State of London*, printed in 1681,

[1] For this information I am indebted to Sir William Soulsby, the
invaluable private secretary to so many successive Lord Mayors.

with the corrected Surveyors' figures before him, allows £3,900,000 for 13,200 houses burnt; £2,000,000 for public buildings destroyed; and a like sum for cost of removals. Also he infers that the wares, household goods, and moneys lost or spoilt by the Fire, " or pilfered away by those wicked wretches that made their gain by the common calamity," may modestly be computed above £2,000,000, making a total loss of £9,900,000.

An estimate in greater detail appears in Strype (ed. 1720) and has been repeated by the eighteenth-century historians of London.[1] It is as follows :—

	£
Houses burnt, 13,200 one with another at £25 rent at the low rate of twelve years' purchase	3,960,000
Eighty-seven parish churches [2] at £8,000 each ...	696,000
Six consecrated chapels, at £2000 each	12,000
The Royal Exchange	50,000
The Custom House	10,000
Fifty-two halls of Companies, most of which were magnificent structures and palaces, at £1,500 each ...	78,000
Three City gates at £3,000 each	9,000
Gaol of Newgate	15,000
Four stone bridges	6,000
Sessions House	7,000
Guildhall, with courts and offices belonging to it ...	40,000
Blackwell Hall	3,000
Bridewell	5,000
Poultry Compter	3,000
Wood Street Compter	3,000
Towards rebuilding St. Paul's Church, which at that time was new building, the stone-work being almost finished	2,000,000
Wares, household-stuff, monies and movable goods lost and spoilt	2,000,000
Hire of porters, carts, waggons, barges, boats, &c., for removing wares, household stuff, &c., during the Fire, and some small time after	200,000
Printed books and paper in shops and warehouses ...	150,000
Wine, tobacco, sugar, plums, &c., of which the City was at that time very full	1,500,000
Cutting a navigable river to Holborn Bridge	27,000
The Monument	14,500
The total sum ... ...£	10,788,500

[1] Elmes, in his *Sir Christopher Wren and his Times*, dictated when he was advanced in years and blind, says that this is Wren's estimate, but the statement does not appear in his larger *Memoirs*, nor have I found it elsewhere.

[2] See Appendix, " City Churches burnt in the Fire."

The sum stated takes no account of the money paid to freeholders whose ground was acquired for public purposes when the City was rebuilt, nor the cost of making wharves by the river, enlarging old streets and cutting out new streets, and providing market places, all of which added considerably to the burden borne by the people. Pepys mentions an estimate of £600,000 for loss of rents in the City. This figure, which averages every house burnt out at £45 9s. annual rental, is probably excessive. Money values were considerably higher in Stuart times than to-day, and the cost of building especially was greatly less. Where the estimate printed by Strype can be checked it is approximately near the cost, and as a rule under. The Sheriffs' Compters involved an expenditure of £8,845 and £7,705 respectively. Bridewell cost £8,523 from public funds, part being provided by charitable gifts. The expenditure on the "navigable river to Holborn Bridge"—Fleet Ditch—was not £27,000, but, including the land taken, no less than £80,532; the outlay on the Sessions House, Old Bailey, was £5,559.[1]

It was judged by contemporaries that more commodities and household stuffs were saved than perished, the Fire having given warning sufficient to allow the removal of the most valuable goods that were portable; but a vast deal had to be left behind owing to the shortage of carts. The losses among heavy goods were very large, but these again were reduced by the security given by arched cellars, which, being sealed up, in many cases withstood the flames. The booksellers, who had trusted their stocks to St. Faith's and the warehouses at Stationers Hall and Christ Church, and also the cloth merchants, were among the worst sufferers. "Some reckon roundly, and say London is ruined, England is ruined. That is too confident; yet I dare not determine how far they are out. The truth of it is, an exact computation is impossible," wrote a resident.[2]

Losses among the booksellers and stationers have been variously estimated at £150,000 and £200,000. "Many noble impressions consumed by their trusting them to the churches, which will be an extraordinary detriment to the

---

[1] Guildhall Library MSS. 184.
[2] Malcolm, *Lond. Rediv.*, iv. 78.

whole republic of learning," is Evelyn's comment.[1]   Kirton, the bookseller of St. Paul's Churchyard, had stock of the value of between £7,000 and £8,000 burnt, lost his whole fortune, and was left with debts of nearly £3,000.[2]   Almost the entire edition of the Polyglot Bible, which had just been printed after long labours by a committee of scholars, was consumed.   A large individual loss was that of Cornelius Bec, a bookseller, and his co-venturers, who had produced a work by eminent authors in nine volumes, under the title *Critici Sacri*.   The stock of 1,300 complete copies perished in the flames, whereby they lost £13,000.   It is a tradition of the book-selling trade that the exceeding rarity of the third folio of Shakespeare, printed in London in 1664, is due to the number of copies destroyed in the Fire.   Paper became so scarce that on joint petition by the Stationers Company, the King's printer, the printer of Cambridge and others, licence was given to import it from France.[3]

What authors suffered may be gathered from a letter by Sir William Dugdale, then Norroy King at Arms and the well-known writer, whose losses no doubt are typical of many others.   He wrote from London to Daniel Fleming, 1667, May 28th—

" I intended to send you books. . . . Some few were given to the judges and others, and about one hundred were disposed of into the hands of the booksellers, for which they were to account to me in Easter term.   The lamentable fire hath put an end to my determination, having consumed the whole impression,[4] which, with the plates, stood me in no less than £400 and all the remaining parts of Sir Henry Spelman's *Glossary* and *Councils*, of which not many were sold.   The paper merchant is not yet wholly paid for the paper taken up to print them.   Nearly three-hundred of my books of Paul's [Cathedral] and about 500 of my *History of Embanking and Draining*, perished also in these flames, and—what troubles me not the least—my whole copy, except thirty sheets which were printed, of the third volume of the *Monasticon Anglicanum*, through the great negligence of my printer.   You see here a sad story

[1] Letter to Sir S. Tuke, 1666, Sept. 27.
[2] Pepys's *Diary*, 1666, Sept. 26, Oct. 5.
[3] *State Papers* (*Domestic*), 1666–7, pp. 512, 527 ; 1667–8, p. 515.
[4] This was the *Origines Juridiciales*, 1666, which was just ready for publication, and very few copies were saved.

of my own losses, and somewhat of the public. There can be no thought of printing any of these for three or four years at least. There is little done as yet towards the new building of the City, all lying in rubbish and ashes. When we look back upon the transcendent wickedness thereof, it is not to be wondered at." [1]

A minor tragedy of the Fire was the burning in John Ogilby's printing house in King's Head Court, Shoe Lane, of that printer-poet's epic poem in twelve books, *Carolies*, in honour of Charles I., which consequently is unknown to the world ; "the pride, divertisement, business and sole comfort of my age," he declared. Poor, saddened old poet ! But the chastening reflection remains with me, after much reading, that the Fire of London inspired more bad poetry than happily was destroyed by it.

Large quantities of cloth had been brought to London for the Michaelmas market, in anticipation of which Blackwell Hall, by Guildhall, was stocked full by the country clothiers. All their goods were consumed when the building burnt. The loss in cloth alone was valued at £25,000.[2] The Coventry weavers lost at least £2,000, "which is a good deal as the times go," wrote one Ralph Hope from that city. Many were undone by it, their whole estate lying in London in cloth. At Norwich people were at their wits' end, not knowing how to carry on their trade by reason of the fire in the capital, where they had great business.

Alderman John Jefferies, of Bread Street Ward, and a former M.P. for Brecknockshire, had tobacco burnt of the value of £20,000.

The brewers along Thames-side petitioned for an abatement of one-half of their growing duties on excise. The stock upon which they had paid excise had taken fire ; their brewhouses were burnt down, and the intention to remove their trade from Thames Street would be still further to their detriment.[3]

The common vicissitudes of fortune are illustrated in the case of Richard Pierce, Yeoman of the King's Kitchen, and Master of the Cooks Company * a year before the Fire. His losses in the flames were between £4,000 and

---

[1] Le Fleming MSS. (*Hist. MSS. Comm.*, p. 48).
[2] Wind. Sandys' Letter.
[3] *State Papers* (*Domestic*), 1666–7, pp. 110, 133, 168, 381.

£5,000, all that he was worth, and being reduced to penury and having no other means of acquiring a livelihood for his large family, he obtained by the King's intercession leave to use Cooks Hall, left standing outside Aldersgate, for the purpose of his trade until he was in a condition to obtain a dwelling.

Thomas Catchmead, a wealthy fishmonger, lost £7,000, all his fortune, and was given license by the King to erect a little shed near the Maypole in the Strand wherein to carry on his trade.

The King himself lost his fee-farm rents in London, which could not be recovered while the City lay in ashes, and the Treasury Commissioners were directed to make good the deficiency caused thereby in the Queen's allowance from other sources. The account of the Poll Money receipts attributed a loss of £52,000 to the burning of London. Large numbers of Exchequer tallies, the cleft sticks upon which the sum of indebtedness was notched, were burnt, those in the Excise alone representing the value of £136,422, and others in the Treasurer's Remembrancer's office. Their destruction caused confusion in the accounts. Tallies for £30,000 were burnt at Guildhall. The Charter-house was so reduced that it petitioned for relief, without which it could no longer maintain its poor brethren and scholars. King Charles's Hospital of St. Margaret's, Westminster, a pious foundation by Charles I. for the up-bringing of fatherless children, lost one-half of its revenues by the Fire. Petitioners to the King became importunate. His Majesty, " often troubled with the pitiful petitions of subjects who have sustained losses by the Fire," asking for patents to make collections of alms, referred all such matters to the consideration of Sir Orlando Bridgeman, then appointed Lord Keeper on Clarendon's fall, and gave him full power to pass licences at his discretion. A sheaf of petitions went in for payments of debts owing to persons ruined by the Fire.

Sarah, widow of Francis Crofts, of London, petitioned for a grant of aid towards rebuilding houses worth £5,000 burnt down in the Fire, whereby she and her children were reduced from a plentiful condition to turn servants, and work hard for a poor livelihood.

Elizabeth Proctor, widow of William Proctor, vintner,

of London, appealed for payment of £600 due to her late husband for wine furnished on the King's account to the Prussian Ambassador four years before. She had suffered much during the Fire.

John Le Roy, jeweller, asked for speedy payment of £357, balance due for a diamond ring, value £850, for the Countess of Castlemaine, and other work ; great losses had fallen upon him by the burning of his house in the Fire.

John Gamble, one of his Majesty's wind-instrument concert, pleaded for payment of £221 10s. 4½d., arrears of his salary over four and three-quarter years. All he possessed he had lost by the dreadful Fire, and he had contracted a debt of £120, for which one of his sureties had been sent prisoner to Newgate. Ruin awaited them and their families without this payment. Twenty-two musicians on the violin made similar plaint, having had houses and goods burnt in the Fire.[1]

Yet another supplicant, in consideration of his great losses, asked for a Patent for a scheme to his own profit whereby no foreigner could remain a night without full information being available as to whence he came, where he lodged, and the like, and the same of subjects not at their own houses, that robberies, murders, and other mischiefs might be prevented. Popular resentment against aliens remained intensely strong. To some of these unfortunates writs of protection were given, entitling them to reside in the Kingdom and quietly prosecute their affairs, without molestation or acts of violence being offered to them. Magalotti, nearly three years after the Fire, found the common people of London proud, arrogant, and uncivil to foreigners, against whom, and especially the French, they cherished a profound hatred, treating such as came among them with contempt and insult. The nobility, he admits, though also proud, had not so usually the defects of the lower classes, and displayed a certain degree of politeness and courtesy towards strangers.[2]

---

[1] *State Papers (Domestic)*, 1666–7, pp. 118, 126, 161, 162, 245, 343, 405 ; *ibid.*, 1667, pp. 178, 456.

[2] *Ibid.* 1666–7, pp. 175, 106, 166 ; Magalotti, *Travels of Grand Duke Cosmo III.*

CHAPTER XIII

PLANS FOR A MODEL CITY

THE Fire was no sooner out than Christopher Wren, then Deputy Surveyor of His Majesty's Works, made a rapid survey of the devastation wrought, clambering with great difficulty over the broad plain of ashes and ruins, and at no little hazard to life.[1] Upon this groundwork he drew a plan for rebuilding a model City, which as early as September 10th was submitted to the King and Council. Evelyn also quickly had a plan ready. " Dr. Wren," he wrote to Sir Samuel Tuke, " got a start of me, but both of us did coincide so frequently that his Majesty was not displeased."

Wren's design for London sought to make all parts of it accessible by replanning the streets, and while serving this end he kept in view four principal objects : (1) to let the Royal Exchange on its existing site stand free, " the nave or centre of the town ; " (2) give to St. Paul's the significance which the metropolitan Cathedral required ; (3) improve the bad communications with London Bridge, upon which four important streets were to converge ; (4) clear the river bank from the Temple to The Tower, and construct thereon a broad public quay. The plan itself is best studied in the drawing here reproduced, and discussion could be only tedious. Let us imagine some magician having been at work, that the City as Wren would have rebuilt it had been raised in a night, and record the impressions of a wayfarer passing through.

Elizabethan Ludgate stands no longer. In its place, spanning the widened street, has been erected a triumphal arch in honour of King Charles II., the founder of New

[1] *Parentalia*, p. 265.

London.   Looking through this the whole west front of
a new St. Paul's occupies the foreground on the crest of
the hill.   It stands clear, the roadway, ninety feet broad
at the arch, widening out trumpet-shaped to give this
unrivalled view.   By the Cathedral's north and south
walls long straight roads diverge, and mounting the hill
and first glancing along the northern road one sees a
front of the Royal Exchange, and far away one of the City
gates.   That is Aldgate.   The eye then turns to the
southern road, and twice along its length piazzas open out—
to-day we might call each a circus, but there is an architectural embellishment which Finsbury Circus and Ludgate
Circus know nothing of.   In the distance, trees and bushes
on Tower Hill close the vista.

From these great arteries cross-roads run, as nearly
as may be on a rectangular plan.   They carry less traffic,
and most are but thirty feet wide.

By any of the northern ways, one soon arrives upon
another great thoroughfare of ninety feet span, commencing
at Newgate, which it is not difficult to recognize as Cheapside, although realigned.   It goes straight like an arrow
to the Royal Exchange, which terminates the view, and
there the road bends.   A little beyond Old and New
London meet, for Wren has left standing much of the
City within the eastern Wall that the Fire had spared.

If the way taken chances to be south, then one misses
the familiar Thames Street.   A quay and public walk
made forty feet broad has place at the river's edge, and
looking up-stream one notices that this fine improvement
extends as far as the Temple Gardens.   Some of the
smaller Companies' Halls front upon this river terrace,
whereabouts Baynard's Castle had stood.   There are
deep-water bays for the laden barges at Bridewell Dock,
where the purified Fleet River enters the Thames, at
Queenhithe, at Dowgate, and at Billingsgate, and the
quay is carried round these.   At the Bridge foot is a considerable open space, semi-circular, for the convenience of
the traffic converging there by the four new roads, and
beyond the new Custom House stands on its former site,
the quay continuing till it joins the Tower Wharf.

One advantage this model London enjoys is that easy
access is everywhere given to the river.   From Newgate,

NOTE TO WREN'S PLAN

Sir Christopher Wren's plan for rebuilding the burnt area laid over the existing streets indicates at a glance how completely the great architect would have destroyed the City as to-day we know it, and as it has come down to us by the growth of centuries. There is not one of the historic highways, like Cheapside, preserved; Fleet Street is irrecognizable, running straight from Ludgate to north of St. Dunstan's Church, and leaving Temple Bar and the Strand at an awkward angle; Guildhall would have had to come down; and the Royal Exchange site is moved slightly north-east.

Wren worked upon a faulty survey which cannot be brought exactly to correspond with the modern Ordnance Map, and in the folding sheet opposite some slight deviations from his plan have been made, noticeable only on careful comparison. The City gates and the bridge upon which his main roads converge are taken as fixed points. The chief changes are a shift in the angle of the north and south street system west of St. Paul's, and the placing of the reticulated system about Fleet Street several yards farther west, in order (a) to give the exit of the new Thames to Holborn highway at Hatton Garden, and (b) maintain the alignment of the new Fleet Street with St. Paul's—a basic feature of the plan. Wren's son says in *Parentalia* that his father designed to start his straight highways to Aldgate and The Tower, not from Ludgate, but from a point clear of Ludgate Prison; but this cannot be correct, as it is impossible to lay the plan on the ground with this large deviation south. For architects' views on Wren's plan see a paper by Mr. Sydney Perks, F.S.A., the City Surveyor, on "London Town-Planning Schemes in 1666," in the *Journal* for December, 1919 (Vol. 27, new series), of the Royal Institute of British Architects, and report of the subsequent discussion.

via Ludgate, a broad straight road runs direct to the Thames. Wren has cut another of his ninety-feet highways from Cripplegate across the City straight to Queenhithe ; there are others from the Moorgate via the Royal Exchange to the Bridge, and from Bishopsgate and from Aldgate to the same point. These, with the exception mentioned, are sixty-feet roads ; but the rectangular plan also affords direct access to the quay from the northern parts of the City by more than a dozen other routes. The City, too, is well provided with crossways.

Now we arrive at the Royal Exchange. A large area has been cleared for it. The building stands in the centre ; it is in Wren's grandest style, taking the shape of the Roman Forum, with double porticoes. North and south, across the broad highways, he has cut out ample space for his piazzas. On the land plots surrounding the Exchange on every side are the most important public offices of the City—the Excise Office, Post Office, Mint, Goldsmiths Hall (the goldsmiths, being the bankers of the time, were of first importance) and, a public necessity brought home by the Fire, the new Insurance Office. Around the Royal Exchange is drawn a double, and in parts treble, system of reticulated streets, so there is instant approach from all directions, and the big public buildings mostly stand four sides to the streets. The plan here is one of Wren's great achievements.

The Guildhall has been moved south-west of its historic site beyond Cheapside, having the halls of the chief Companies built in one regular square about it.

Outside the City's western Wall where the Fire burnt, the plan is somewhat different. The old, stinking Fleet Ditch is remodelled into a beautiful and useful Canal, passable by as many bridges as there are streets crossing it. Fleet Street is cut straight from the northern side of St. Dunstan's Church (leaving Temple Bar unmoved in an awkward elbow) to Ludgate, an imposing thoroughfare ninety feet wide. Central in the highway, above Shoe Lane, there opens out an enormous piazza, the largest that Wren planned. Like the Royal Exchange, this has a double system of reticulated streets, and from the piazza another ninety-feet road, perfectly straight, runs north to Holborn and Hatton Garden and south to the Thames quay. Lesser streets branch from the piazza at angles, to Smithfield, Bridewell Dock, and the Temple.

All this is the conception of a great architect, not perhaps what he would have done had entire freedom and unlimited money been at his disposal, but the best that was possible within the accepted restrictions. It is above all things an architect's town. Wren loves long vistas, and has made us love them, for, with consummate art, he has brought out all his churches conspicuously upon the principal roads, and isolated them. Down the long vistas from St. Paul's to Tower Hill and from the Cathedral to Aldgate, the full length of the City, tower and pinnacle and spire rise up to the heavens. The worst declivities of the ground have gone in a process of general levelling. All winding courts and narrow alleys have disappeared from this model City. All noisome trades have been banished to a place appointed by the Lord Mayor and Aldermen—presumably down river. Nor are there church-yards to be seen, nor green gardens, nor other " unnecessary vacuities "—so Wren deems them. The architect values too highly his space—but all I have written is of what might have been. One may imagine the loving care that Wren would have devoted, had the opportunity been given him, to the display of his churches on those long and straight highways.

One may know the City to-day and love its irregularities, but no one can see his way in it. Wren opened up the City. That, in my view, is the great merit of his plan. Two and a half centuries' experience has only emphasized the necessity for main roads north and south which Wren foresaw. This part of his plan seems to have been accepted in principle, for on the 18th October, 1666, a conference of the Privy Council's and the City Corporation's committees directed a survey to be taken for new highways from Aldersgate to the Thames, from Cripplegate through Cheapside to the Thames, and from the Royal Exchange to the Thames and back to Moorgate ; [1] but nothing came of these projects. The obvious criticism of Wren's model, all questions of cost apart, is that it made no provision for growth, and that his riverside quay, if perpetuated, would

[1] *Privy Council Registers*, vol. 59, fos. 194–7.

have shut out the enormous shipping and warehousing business, the ships and barges unloading at the water's edge direct into the warehouses, that makes the front from The Tower to Blackfriars a storehouse of the world's goods It was, too, a city for commerce and for the rich alone at a period when rich and poor were accustomed to dwell as neighbours. The greatest fault of the plan—the cardinal fault—is that the streets cross at every angle except the right angle, which is the most desirable end to be sought in town planning. Wren, having taken so much, apparently lacked courage to take all, and by accepting as fixed marks the City gates and the highways outside the burnt area and working within that limitation, he has spoilt his own conception. It is impossible that Wren, had his model plan been carried out, would have been content to build St. Paul's upon the narrow site that the angle of his main highways allows—a site insufficient for the larger City parish churches standing to-day, let alone for his vast Cathedral.

John Evelyn's ideas were quite different, though in broad outline his plan is not dissimilar to Wren's. His City is more continental in style.

Let us in fancy enter this other City by way of London Bridge, first noting that the houses built upon the Bridge have been cleared away, a proposal that Evelyn and Wren made in common. At the Bridge foot, too, there is the same piazza, or circus, but Evelyn has fewer radiating streets, one of which goes directly north across the City to a new gate made in London Wall, with a parallel street straight from Billingsgate to Bishopsgate. East to Tower Wharf and west as far as Bridewell only a river quay extends. But the Thames front—all is strange and inexplicable, till one has learnt that in levelling the roughness of the ground Evelyn has had the rubbish piled up on the mud shore to low-water mark, so that his City stands always upon the water.

The greatest care has been taken to preserve a stately river front. The long quay does away with the irregularity and deformity of the old boat stairs and wharves. Behind it, overlooking the Thames, are the rich houses of the principal merchants and some public buildings. The

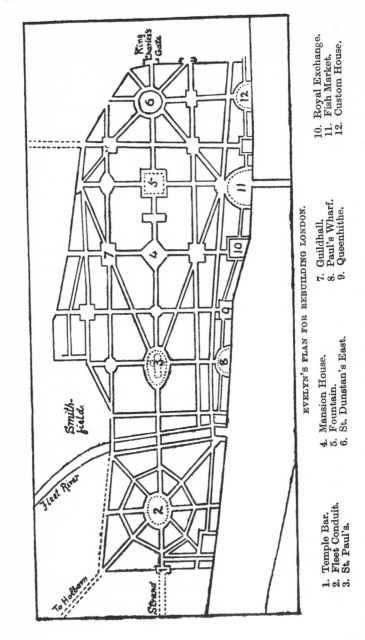

EVELYN'S PLAN FOR REBUILDING LONDON.

1. Temple Bar.
2. Fleet Conduit.
3. St. Paul's.

4. Mansion House.
5. Fountain.
6. St. Dunstan's East.

7. Guildhall.
8. Paul's Wharf.
9. Queenhithe.

10. Royal Exchange.
11. Fish Market.
12. Custom House.

warehouses are out of sight, till, glancing back, one finds them unexpectedly, ranged all along the Surrey side of the river. Had the service of the shipping made such a wholesale migration impossible, Evelyn was prepared to have had the warehouses placed behind his Middlesex quay, but fronting Thames Street; they were not to spoil his river aspect, being, as he says, " of dull and heavy appearance."

Evelyn, greatly daring. has brought the Royal Exchange down from mid-City to the waterside, where the Steelyard stood (to-day Cannon Street Station), and about it are piazzas with spacious vaults below. There is this small provision for storage. A wide road runs directly north to Moorgate. The quay continues round the little bay of Queenhithe, where Evelyn has put into practice one of his many continental ideas. The way has been cloistered to afford a covered market for the fruiterers and others —a capital suggestion. Northwards a main road, the counterpart of Wren's, leads straight from Queenhithe to Cripplegate. Paul's Wharf above Bridge, and the Custom House below, give opportunity for other riverside piazzas.

Going into the City one breaks new ground. It is curiously un-English. The Guildhall, as the headquarters of civic life, receives the prominence it deserves. No Flemish Hotel-de-Ville makes better display than this, standing before an ample square. Near where the Royal Exchange had stood is raised a stately new mansion for the Lord Mayor, also isolated. Old St. Paul's, to be preserved, receives special architectural treatment. The Churchyard has been slightly enlarged into a regular oval, and before it are built the Bishop's Palace, the Dean and Prebendaries' houses, St. Paul's School, a public library— there, too, Evelyn was in advance of his time—the Prerogative and First Fruits Offices, " all at an ample distance from the Cathedral, and with very stately fronts, in honour of that venerable pile."

Learning and religion go hand in hand, so the booksellers and stationers have their shops around the churches. Each church has its parson's house. The College of Physicians, standing isolated and conspicuous in a principal part of the town, has about it the doctors' dwellings, with

238 THE GREAT FIRE OF LONDON

those of the surgeons. The apothecaries' and druggists' shops are in neighbouring streets. It is Evelyn's idea that " all of a mistery " should be habitants of the same quarter. The better sort of shopkeepers trade in the most eminent streets and piazzas, the artificers follow their crafts in the more ordinary houses and in the intermediate and narrow passages. Taverns are placed among these, but so built as to preserve perfect uniformity.

In Evelyn's treatment of the public places the continental influence is most apparent. " In order to create variety in the streets, there should be breaks and enlargements, by spacious openings at proper distances, surrounded with piazzas, and uniformly built with beautiful fronts ; some of these openings should be square, some circular, others oval." King Charles's Gate is raised at the eastern entrance to the City from Tower Hill, not west, and all the other gates are replaced by triumphal arches adorned with statues, sculptured reliefs, and appropriate inscriptions. The principal highways are one hundred feet wide, and where openings occur—in the new Fleet Street, in the main thoroughfare west to east, and elsewhere—great fountains of water, centrally situated, are perpetually playing. St. Dunstan-in-the-East church stands isolated, the central object in a great circus. The churches and Companies' Halls are dotted about, to adorn the profile of the City in all its avenues ; but all the parish churchyards are placed in line outside the wall between Cripplegate and Aldgate—a reversion to the Roman idea. Opposite the burial grounds is found a large street with the common inns, each having its yard for country carriers, where they least encumber the town.

Clearly this plan contemplates a stone built city, whereas London was in fact rebuilt of the less costly brick. It was such a city as a Roman Emperor, rich with the plunder of conquered states, might have founded as a memorial of his triumphs ; but how it should be achieved by citizens whose fortunes had in large part been consumed by fire, and whose numbers had been decimated by plague, apparently Evelyn, in his moments of magnificence, did not stop to inquire. Admiration is enforced as much for its daring impracticability as for the plan itself—but again all I have written is of what might have been.

A third model was exhibited by Robert Hooke on the 21st September, before the Common Council.[1] Hooke, then Reader of Mathematics at Gresham College, was the most brilliant experimental philosopher of his day, and as was to be expected from such a mind as his, the design was before all things practical. London, had Hooke rebuilt it, would have been the prototype of the modern American city. The chief streets, laid out east and west, were each to run in an exact straight line, and crossing these other streets, equally straight, went north and south. All churches, public buildings, markets, and the like were to be arranged in proper and convenient places. Let us be thankful that this utilitarian scheme was not adopted, for it would have cleared from the ground as completely as marks are sponged off a slate every link with London's great and historic past. But the model seems to have been preferred by the Lord Mayor and Aldermen to those of Wren and Evelyn, and it obtained for Hooke the lucrative employment of City Surveyor. The philosopher had no use for accumulations of money. His fortune of some thousands of pounds was found, after his death at a great age, stowed away in an iron chest which had been unopened for thirty years.

Parliament was divided upon the best method of procedure in rebuilding London. There were three parties in the House of Commons, one of which favoured an entirely new arrangement of the streets, as proposed by Wren, Evelyn, and Hooke, but made no choice of plans; another desired to restore the City as before, but with brick; and the third advocated a fusion of the two projects, by raising a quay along the river, widening some of the streets, and rebuilding others on the old foundations and walls, but with brick. Colonel Birch, a member, proposed that the whole ground of London should be acquired and placed in trust, and that the trustees should sell again, giving preference to the former owners.[2] Some scheme of the kind would, indeed, have been necessary had any of the plans for a model city been carried out, but the impossibility at that time of financing an operation of such magnitude, and the hopelessness of obtaining an equitable

[1] *Journal* 46, fo. 121.   [2] Pepys's *Diary*, 1667, Sept. 24.

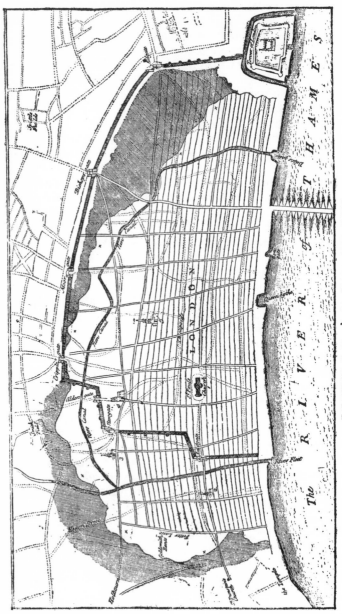

VALENTINE KNIGHT'S PROPOSED CITY CANAL.

valuation for purchase in a market where there was but a single buyer, stifled the project at its birth.

A jotting by Pepys concerning the staking out of streets has led some to believe that a start on model lines was actually made, but there is no evidence of it. The indecision of Parliament was met by the obstinate averseness of the citizens to accept any scheme for the transfer of property. They were suspicious of further loss, and moreover, fearing a westward migration of trade, were determined to keep it in the quarters to which it had been accustomed for centuries. The impracticability of rebuilding the City except on the old foundations was soon manifest, and when the Act of Parliament was framed the models were quietly set aside. They are interesting only for what might have been. Of all Wren's town-planning, London can show to-day nothing but King Street and Queen Street, designed to open up Guildhall and afford a straight road south to the river.

Mention is due of another project that had a ludicrous result. Captain Valentine Knight, of his Majesty's Service, was moved to submit proposals of his own for restoring London. The one daring novelty was a canal thirty feet wide through the City, to carry barges, with entrance from the Thames at Billingsgate, going north to Fenchurch Street, and thence west via Lothbury [1] and through the Wall between Aldersgate and Cripplegate to join the Fleet River above Holborn Bridge. It would be an interesting exercise to calculate the value of the water-covered land to-day. But the advantage claimed for the plan above all others was that of securing for the King a capital sum of £372,670 advanced by fines, and a profit revenue to the Crown for all time of no less than £223,517 per annum. Charles on receiving the document commanded the man's arrest, and himself took the occasion for a little homily to his subjects ; " as if," says the *Gazette*, " his Majesty would draw a benefit to himself from so public a calamity of his

---

[1] Could Wordsworth have had any inkling of Valentine Knight's water scheme when he wrote " The Reverie of Poor Susan " ?—

" Bright volumes of vapour through Lothbury glide,
And a river flows on through the vale of Cheapside."

people, of which his Majesty is known to have so deep
sense, that he is pleased to seek rather by all means to give
them ease under it." [1]   In gaol the reformer had leisure to
reflect upon the uncertain favour of princes.

[1] *London Gazette*, Sept. 27–Oct. 1.   Knight's printed broadsheet is in
State Papers Chas. II. (Domestic), vol. 173, no. 97 ;   there is an original
copy in the writer's possession.

CHAPTER XIV

THE greatest aid in the rebuilding of London was unquestionably that given by an Act of Parliament which has been little appreciated and understood—the Statute 18 & 19 Charles II., chap. 7, which set up the Court of Fire Judges. It was drafted to meet a situation that called for drastic measures.

The Act is short, scarce filling the two sides of a single folio printed sheet. Any three or more of his Majesty's Judges were authorized to hear and determine all differences between landlords and tenants, occupiers and others concerned, of buildings burnt or demolished in the Fire. They were to take the testimony of witnesses upon oath, the examinations of persons interested, the verdicts of jurors after inquisition upon matters of fact. They might require the attendance of parties, make orders, and their judgments were to be final, without revision by the ordinary courts of the land, writ of error or reversal, and binding upon all persons for ever. The Court should sit *sine forma et figura Judicii*—without the formalities (including fees) of courts of law or equity. The fallibility of Judges was recognized, and appeal might be made, on good cause being shown, to a Court composed of seven Judges.

The Court had powers to cancel existing agreements and covenants, to substitute for them others having equal authority, and to order new leases or extended terms of leases not exceeding forty years. The broad policy of the Act is outlined in the significant words of the Preamble—

" Whereas the greatest part of the houses in the City of London, and some in the suburbs thereof, have been burnt by the dreadful and dismal fire which happened in

September last; Many of the tenants, under-tenants, or late occupiers whereof are liable unto suits and actions to compel them to repair and rebuild the same, and to pay their rents, as if the same had not been burnt, and are not relievable therein in any ordinary course of law, and great differences are like to arise concerning the said repairs, and new building of the said houses, and payment of rents ; which if they should not be determined with all speed, and without charge, would much obstruct the re-building of the said City ; And *for that it is just, that every one concerned should bear a proportionable share of the loss*, according to their several interests, wherein in respect of the multitude of cases, varying in their circumstances, no general rule can be prescribed ; Be it therefore enacted, etc."

The Act was, in fact, the negation of all law. Indentures, covenants, penalties, forfeits by which lawyers had sought to secure the landlord in full receipt of his rents and upkeep of his property, and recovery on failure of satisfaction, and to protect the tenant during his term from ejectment, in unmolested use of the property hired ; the whole paraphernalia of parchment and signature and seal—all counted as nothing when once a case was entered in the Fire Judges' Court. Such rights as the parties enjoyed under their bond lapsed ; the Court first sought to ascertain, not upon whom the onus of rebuilding in case of fire fell under the lease, but whether landlord or tenant was best able to rebuild speedily, and acted equit-ably between the different interests. The Act took from the landlord power to compel the tenant whose fortune already was largely destroyed to restore the building— a power which, if applied, must have involved very general bankruptcy. It gave the owner impoverished by his loss, but whose estate was not wholly consumed, an incentive to rebuild his property on conditions which secured to him some return for his outlay in increased rental.

Where the landlord was without means to reinstate the tenant in his dwelling, the Court in its discretion gave the tenant leave to rebuild at his own expense, compensating him by an extension of the term of his lease and a reduction of rent.

Where the tenant was broken in fortune and with no immediate prospect of resuming his trade, the Court

would cancel his lease, perhaps on a small sum being paid
to him by the landlord for the extinction of such rights
as he enjoyed under it.

Where landlord and tenant were alike ruined and
money was not available, the interests of London were
protected by a provision made in the accompanying
Rebuilding Act, that any sites not built upon after lapse
of three years should, after nine months' notice given,
be seized by the Lord Mayor and Aldermen and sold to
such as were able to build, the proceeds being passed over
to those entitled to them.[1]

It was an Act most daringly conceived, undermining
all those sacred rights with which lawyers during past
centuries had invested property, accepted and passed by
a Parliament in which property alone was represented.
It needs the impelling force of a great calamity for law,
guarded with such jealous care and rarely altered save
with grave misgiving, to acknowledge its inadequacy.
The Act might prove successful, with the risk certainly
not less great of dire failure, for had those most concerned
shunned the Court, wanting confidence in the impartiality
of Judges by whom such far-reaching powers were exercised, there could have been nothing but popular discontent and still worse confusion. Happily for the hour,
the integrity of the judicial bench was unsullied. Sir
Matthew Hale, the Lord Chief Baron, drafted the Act and
was largely employed in its application. He enjoyed the
public confidence, and rightly, in a remarkable degree.
A man of immense industry, knowledge, and sagacity,
sternly Puritan till his death, he had been a Justice of
the Common Pleas under Cromwell, and an active agent
in the Restoration.

His was an honest, simple mind. At a trial of two

---

[1] By two subsequent Acts of Parliament the Lord Mayor and Aldermen
were forbidden to exercise their powers to seize and sell City sites not
built upon till Sept. 29, 1672, and it does not, in fact, appear that they
were ever exercised, though the threat influenced many owners to sell or
to finance building operations. (Cf. Add. MSS. 5098, fo. 338; also
Archæologia, vol. lxi, p. 394.) The statute directed the Lord Mayor to
enter such seizures and sales in a book, which should be kept as a permanent
record. There is no such book in the Guildhall archives. The staking
out of ground plots for rebuilding so late as is shown in the Surveyors'
books could not be accounted for if the Lord Mayor had exerted his
authority.

hapless women condemned for witchcraft at Bury St. Edmunds Assizes in March, 1662, over which he presided, he made no doubt at all of the existence of witches, as proved, he said simply, by the Scriptures, general consent, and Acts of Parliament. Baxter, the divine, and his great friend, has left this pen portrait of him: " He was a man most precisely just, insomuch as I believe he would have lost all he had in the world rather than do an unjust act ; patient in hearing the tediousest speech which any man had to make for himself ; the refuge of the subject who feared oppression. Every man who had a just cause was almost past fear if he could bring it before the court or assize where he sat. He was the great pillar for the rebuilding of London. By his prudence and justice he removed a multitude of grave impediments."

The operation of the Act lifted from the shoulders of the trading community the burden for the entire loss occasioned by the Fire, as well as a load of litigation, with the resulting costs and delay, that must otherwise have been almost as ruinous as the Fire itself. The Court sat in equity, but differed from all known courts in this, that in addition to the parties before it there was a third party, whose interests were confided to the safekeeping of the Judges themselves. This was the public, and in case after case the public interest in the speedy rebuilding of of the City decided the issue.[1] Humphrey Henchman,

---

[1] In some few instances an actual date was given at which rebuilding must be completed. Three typical judgments by the Court may thus be summarized :—

(a) John Tanner, petitioner, was tenant of the Cross Keys, in Fleet Street, under lease from Richard Caswell, with 49 years to run. At Lady Day, 1666, Tanner devised his leasehold interest to Robert Cotten for 21 years. Caswell, the owner, desired himself to rebuild, having other houses adjoining, and offered terms to acquire his tenant's interests. Cotten had but small enjoyment of the messuage before it was burnt down. Ordered, to the intent that the rebuilding be proceeded in without delay, that Caswell pay Tanner £100 for annulment of the lease, Cotten being discharged from all covenants, and that Caswell rebuild with all convenient speed in such manner as by the late Act of Parliament appointed (*Add. MSS.* 5063, fo. 103).

(b) Thomas Manley, petitioner, demised a house in St. Swithin's Lane to William Hickman, for 21 years from Michaelmas, 1663, at £14 annual rental and without fine, the tenant covenanting to repair. Manley also owned the adjoining house, and both were burnt. Hickman declined to accept any terms to rebuild, alleging that by reason of losses sustained by the Fire he was utterly incapacitated from so doing, and he prayed to be permitted to surrender his lease. Manley desired a contribution from his

Bishop of London, gained an unenviable reputation by his dealings with the booksellers and mercers of Paternoster Row, from whom he demanded the last penny of rent. He would promise them nothing, and when threatened with citation before the Fire Judges to compel him to a fair dealing declared that he was a Peer of Parliament, and would claim his Parliamentary privilege. Others, too, showed as little grace. But the knowledge that it was open at any time for the tenant to appear without charge before the Judges checked the rapacity of the grasping landowner, inducing him to accept terms, lest worse should befall him.

The hall of Clifford's Inn stands in which the Court sat, and its manuscript judgments, engrossed on parchment and signed by the Judges, are contained in nine particularly cumbersome volumes of " Fire Decrees " at Guildhall.[1] The Court decided some hundreds of disputes,

tenant in respect of failure to repair under the covenant. Ordered, that Hickman surrender the lease, contribute to petitioner £30 in satisfaction of his share of the loss to be borne by the Fire, to be paid within six months, and that he be discharged of all other liabilities (*Add. MSS.* 5063, fo. 318).

(c) Sarah Andrews, widow, petitioner, owned a house in Fenchurch Street let to William Phillips, apothecary, on lease for 21 years from April, 1666, at £40 rental. Phillips refused to rebuild or to pay rent, although petitioner was willing to extend the tenancy, with abatement of rent over a number of years. Phillips when before the Court offered to rebuild or to contribute one-third towards cost of rebuilding (agreed at £400) on terms. Ordered, that Sarah Andrews rebuild the house with all convenient speed, Phillips to contribute towards the charge £33 6s. 8d. within a reasonable time, £50 upon the raising of the first storey, and £50 on completion of building. Andrews to grant a new lease to Phillips for 60 years, at £40 rental, under such reasonable covenants, charges, and agreements as are usual in the lease of a house new built in London since the late dreadful Fire (*Add. MSS.* 5068, fo. 78).

This statute was the model followed in the Act of Parliament for Rebuilding Northampton passed in 1675, after a disastrous fire had consumed more than one-half of that town, the court at Northampton being composed of the judges of assize, county justices of the peace, the Mayor, and certain persons named, five constituting a quorum. Any person building a house worth £300 within seven years was to have the freedom of the town. (Cf. *Northampton Borough Records*, vol. 2, ed. J. Charles Cox, pp. 246–7.)

[1] A duplicate set of the Fire judgments, apparently the originals, is in the British Museum Library (*Add. MSS.* 5063 to 5103), bound in forty-one handy volumes. The fact that by subsequent legislation the Act was enlarged to comprise all fires happening in the City, the borough of Southwark and within the bills of mortality—in short, all London—till Sept. 30, 1670, has added to their bulk. The British Museum has an index of parishes alone, by aid of which the mass of documents is readily accessible for research.

but its well-known practice was sufficient in the larger
number of cases to bring disputants to amicable arrangement. It was in the schooling of the Fire Judges' Court
that Sir John King, a famous lawyer of the day, began
the practice which in nine years from his call brought him
to the very forefront of his profession.

London after the Fire was built upon compromise.
The Judges in the autumn had consulted together upon
the position of the tenants, whose liability where fire
began in their own or neighbours' houses was plain, but
if the destruction was the act of an enemy they were
relieved.[1] Hubert, the Frenchman, was convicted and
hanged for firing London. Here was a nice legal point,
but it was never argued, the Act of Parliament having
brushed aside all such technicalities. The operation of
the Act won general approval ; and this was the more
remarkable as grave difficulty confronted the Judges
owing to the loss of vast numbers of title deeds and leases
in the burnt houses and chambers of the lawyers. The
difficulty was met in part by a clause in the Additional
Building Act, 1670, which made proof of twenty-one
years' possession sufficient title for granting a valid lease.
The Common Council ordered full-length portraits of the
Judges to be painted by Michael Wright, at a cost of £60
each, in gratitude for their speedy settlement of disputes
and the prevention of litigation. The canvases of the
twenty-two Judges to-day hang in the Guildhall Library.*

The Fire Judges' Court, by its practice and example,
alone made the speedy restoration of London possible.
The Rebuilding Act [2] modelled the form of the new City,
while perpetuating its ancient ground plan. Few changes
in plan were made, the most important being the reserva-
tion of land forty feet wide along the whole river front
from The Tower to the Temple for a public quay, as suggested by Wren. Thames Street was widened below the
Bridge, and the whole street and the land beyond to the
water were raised at least three feet, to prevent inunda-
tions and reduce the steep acclivity from the river. Soper
Lane was transformed into Queen Street, and King Street

[1] Pepys's *Diary*, 1666, Nov. 5.
[2] *Stat.* 18 & 19 *Chas. II.*, c. 8, " An Act for the rebuilding of the City
of London."

From a drawing by Mr. F. L. Griggs in the "Burlington Magazine"
CLIFFORD'S INN HALL, FLEET STREET
In this old hall, situated on the Fire's edge, the Judges sat to determine disputes between
property owners and tenants.   The brick houses at the back date before the Fire

cut to open up the Guildhall, making together a straight new thoroughfare to the Thames. Fish Street Hill, the approach to Old London Bridge, was widened, as was Cheapside at its eastern end, the Poultry, the street east of St. Paul's to Cheapside, and Blowbladder Street (the bend joining Cheapside and Newgate Street). Newgate Market was improved by laying the Middle Row of the Shambles into the street. Water Lane (to-day White-friars Street), another way to the Thames-side, was widened. The Corporation had liberty to enlarge other streets, courts and lanes, " in such manner as there shall be cause, and by and with the approbation of his Majesty and not otherwise." [1]   An unobstructed way was given in Cheap-side, Fleet Street, Gracechurch Street and Dowgate by the demolition of the water conduits, which had stood out in the roadways and divided passing traffic, other conduits being moved to more convenient sites.

The improvements undertaken were mostly in straightening important thoroughfares, widening passages and cutting away sharp angles, in reducing acclivities and filling up hollows to the extent of a few feet. In Panyer Alley, by the north-east corner of St. Paul's, is one of the most familiar memorials of the new London, the figure carved in stone of a naked boy sitting astride a bread pannier (or basket) and with the date 1688 the couplet beneath—

> When ye have sought the City Round
> Yet still this is the highest Ground.

Thus briefly that part of the Act dealing with the ground covered may, not inadequately, be dismissed. The design of town planning failed. The sight of London in ashes had made strong appeal to Wren, Evelyn, and other men with imagination, that the opportunity afforded to lay out the City on improved lines should not un-profitably pass, but the citizens, impoverished in wealth, wholly untaught and unprepared for change, were obsti-nately averse. The large question of town building remained. By a stroke of the pen, as already said, King

---

[1] Lists of the streets improved after the Great Fire are printed by Strype. For the straightening of main thoroughfares, see Vertue's print of Leake's survey, here reproduced.

Charles converted London from a timber-built city into one of brick, and the terms of the Royal Proclamation were confirmed by the Act of Parliament, which ordered that all new buildings should be of brick or stone, with party walls, as being " not only more comely and durable, but also more safe against future perils of fire." [1]

Building Acts and Ordinances for London there had been before, but they were mainly repressive [2]; the Fire of London placed before the King and Parliament the problem of a *constructive* Act.

The new statute was drawn by men of vision. Though denied the advantages of town planning, or of any street

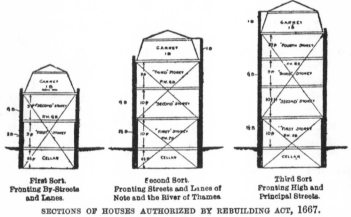

First Sort.	Second Sort.	Third Sort
Fronting By-Streets and Lanes.	Fronting Streets and Lanes of Note and the River of Thames.	Fronting High and Principal Streets.

SECTIONS OF HOUSES AUTHORIZED BY REBUILDING ACT, 1667.
By W. R. Davidge in *Journal of Royal Institute of British Architects.*

plan save that which London had inherited from mediæval times, they envisaged an entire new City, draining to the Thames, with the best houses built upon the most important highways and others of lesser quality upon streets of less note, and provided in detail for one and all in an Act which is remarkable for its comprehensiveness. The Lord Mayor, Aldermen and Common Council were charged

[1] A Commonwealth Act of 1657 for London (made void by the Restoration) forestalled this provision, directing that none should build houses save of stone or brick, "and straight up." *Acts and Ordinances of the Interregnum*, ii, 1229.

[2] See a valuable paper by Mr. W. R. Davidge, on " London's Bygone Building Acts " in the *Journal* of the Royal Institute of British Architects, 3rd Ser., vol. 21, pp. 333–369.

to determine the status of the different streets. The Act gave to London for the first time a complete code of building regulations, and so doing, did that which no Building Act before or since had attempted. " For better regulation, uniformity and gracefulness," four types of houses were allowed in the new City, and none other.

The first and least sort were to be built in by-lanes, two storeys high, irrespective (as in all cases) of cellars and garrets;

The second sort in streets and lanes of note, to be three storeys high;

The third, fronting high and principal streets, of four storeys; and

The fourth type, the merchants' mansion houses " of the greatest bigness," not built to the street front, also not to exceed four storeys.

The allotment of streets in three qualities by hard and fast rule was found impracticable, no doubt owing to the varying depth of building sites, and in carrying out the clause six streets only were classed as " high and principal streets," in which none but houses of four storeys should be permitted, all others being considered " streets and lanes of note." The clause compelling by-lanes of two-storeyed houses only as a feature of the new City was quietly laid aside, though many such houses were built. In this Act the ground floor counted as one storey.

For each type of house the thickness of brick walls, heights from floor to ceiling, depth of cellars and sufficiency of party walls, scantlings of timber and much other detail were set out in scheduled tables, to which builders were required to conform. There were sharp penalties for defaulters. The delinquent might be committed to the City gaol, and the Aldermen were empowered to demolish the unauthorized building. That man who wilfully pulled up a stake or boundary stone should have three months' imprisonment, or a fine of £10, or if a man of mean condition should be taken to the place of his offence and there whipped till the body be bloody.

The Lord Mayor was given power to prohibit noisome and perilous trades in the principal streets.

The characteristic type of house built under the Act survives to-day, and is easily distinguished by the dark weathered walls, often unadorned save by a band of protruding brick at each storey, the eaves beneath the roof, regular windows and general appearance of solidity, and steep staircases within. More will be said later. There are excellent examples in Watling Street, in Racquet Court and in Crane Court, off Fleet Street (one house bears date 1671), in Cheapside (No. 37), in Milk Street, Great Tower Street (No. 34), Knightrider Street and elsewhere in the City. Several are illustrated in this book. An old panelled house in Plough Court, Lombard Street, erected just after the Fire, in which Alexander Pope, the poet, was born, stood within memory ; it and its successor have been in unbroken occupation by the firm of Allen and Hanbury for two centuries.

As drafted, the Rebuilding Act made no financial provision. To meet the cost of public works, the City proposed a tax upon all coal brought into London, that being the least grievous burden which could be devised, borne by all classes, and the greater part falling upon the citizens themselves ; and in January, 1667, the Court of Aldermen petitioned for leave to introduce a Bill in Parliament [1] Instead, a clause was at the last moment added to the Rebuilding Act, imposing a tax of one shilling upon each chaldron or ton, the first proceeds to be devoted to compensation for land taken in enlarging streets and passages, restoring the river wharves and quays, and rebuilding the City prisons.

Long negotiations took place between the City and the Privy Council while the Act was in preparation, agitated by frequent alarms. A false rumour went abroad that the City had inserted a clause forbidding any one to engage in building who refused to abjure the Covenant.[2] The Bill was brought into the Commons by the City Members on the 29th December, 1666, and there underwent considerable amendment. Report then spread that Parliament was immediately to be prorogued. Sir John Frederick, M.P. for the City, was despatched in hot haste to Westminster, and the Lord Mayor, Sheriffs and Aldermen followed to Whitehall, with a petition to the King impressing upon him the public calamity that would

---

[1] *Repertory* 72, fos. 8, 44 ; *State Papers* (*Domestic*), 1666-7, p. 469.
[2] Sharpe, *London and the Kingdom*, ii, 430.

result if Parliament rose, London remained in ashes, and no Act for its rebuilding was upon the statute book.[1] Again in the last days of January Charles, always devious in his king-craft and at his wits' end for money, suddenly determined to prorogue Parliament, leaving the work undone, but was dissuaded therefrom by the City's urgent appeal.[2]

The problem of financing so great an undertaking as the rebuilding of London was left untouched, save for the one expedient of the Coal Tax. Thus early after the Fire, while distress was universal, it was perhaps hopeless to attempt any solution. But a not less pressing question confronted the City authorities in the anticipated shortage of labour and materials. They had first sought a short road out of the difficulty by legislation. In a draft of the Bill submitted to the Privy Council in November, they demanded that all buildings upon new foundations in all parts of the kingdom, the City of London and its Liberties excepted, be prohibited for the term of seven years, " unless the City be sooner fully rebuilt, the better to procure workmen hither." Further, that no building upon new foundations within five miles of London be permitted at any time thereafter.[3] In a Parliament composed of London members only conceivably such powers might have been granted, but in none other ; they were curtly refused.

The Fire left the City rulers in a quandary. The trade gilds, though less autocratic than in mediæval times, still exercised commanding influence in the City. But if London was to be rebuilt the gild privileges could not be retained. Labour by freemen alone was hopelessly insufficient for work which would require many thousands of skilled masons, bricklayers, carpenters, plumbers, and men of other building crafts. The time had come to take a bold decision, and cut adrift from the tradition of past centuries—either this, or London's pre-eminence as the commercial capital of the Kingdom must succumb under harassing delays. The clear vision of the merchants showed them that only by the speedy rebuilding of the

[1] *Journal* 46, fos. 135, 135b.
[2] Andrew Marvell to Mayor of Hull, 1667, Jan. 26.
[3] *Journal* 46, fos. 132b, 133.

City could the trade of London be prevented from migrating elsewhere, and that once it had gone it might never return. It was not in human nature that the gilds should surrender their rights without reluctance. The matter was eventually delegated by the Common Council to a committee, who were authorized to attend the House of Commons and do as they should think fit,[1] and a clause took its place in the Rebuilding Act which cut away the very foundation of the ancient gild law.

Its comprehensive terms were these : " All carpenters, bricklayers, masons, plasterers, joiners, and other artificers, workmen and labourers to be employed in the said buildings, who are not freemen of the said City [of London] shall for the space of seven years next ensuing, and for so long time after as until the said buildings shall be fully finished, have and enjoy such and the same liberty of working, and being set to work in the said building, as the freemen of the City of the same trades and professions have and ought to enjoy ; Any usage or custom of the City to the contrary notwithstanding. And that such artificers as aforesaid, which for the space of seven years shall have wrought in the rebuilding of the City in their respective arts, shall from and after the said seven years have and enjoy the same liberty to work as freemen of the said City for and during their natural lives."

The bells ringing backwards in the church steeples which in the first hours of the Great Fire of London had given the alarm to the citizens, rang out the knell of the old monopoly in the building crafts. The gilds, after battling successfully for centuries against the " foreigner," or non-freeman, were by a blow of adversity stripped of their powers. Craftsmen of all kinds flocked from the country to London, secure to go about their work under protection of the State, and the trade advantages of belonging to a corporation no longer able to enforce its privileges lost much of their attraction. Unable to insist on the old conditions of servitude, the London Companies were forced to find content in examining the indentures of craftsmen claiming a country apprenticeship ; and in their Halls, where but shortly

[1] *Journal* 46, fo. 138b.

before the country tradesman had presented his son to learn his trade in the town, journeymen already at work in London came forward with evidence of apprenticeship in Leicester, Beaumaris, and Carmarthen.[1] The bricklayer, mason, or plasterer obtained no right to practise other than his recognized trade, and the limitation was emphasized in the charter granted by the King to the Plaisterers Company later the same year.

This much was conceded to free labour. But Parliament foresaw, and provided against, the peril of combination and wilful withholding of work. The Act authorized any two or more Judges of the King's Bench, upon complaint by the Lord Mayor and Aldermen, to fix the rate of wages in the building industries. If any man refused to work for the wages assessed, or having begun work left it unfinished, he should suffer one month's imprisonment on conviction before a justice, or fine not exceeding £10. Similarly, the Judges were given autocratic power, should necessity arise, to fix prices of materials. They were first to call before them in conference brickmakers, tilemakers, limeburners and others trading within five miles of the Thames, with liberty to assess prices arbitrarily should these omit to attend ; and the same for the prices of carriage ; under like penalties as provided for labour. There is the suggestion of the principle of " betterment," for which the London County Council fought so strenuously more than two centuries later, in a clause of the Act which declared that houseowners who were advantaged by the rebuilding of the city, " in the value of their rents, by the liberty of the air, and free recourse for trade," should compound with the Lord Mayor for that advantage, and if any refused they should pay such sums as were assessed by a jury empanelled by the Lord Mayor for the purpose. This clause appears never to have been operative.

The Rebuilding Act passed the Commons on the 5th February, 1667, and three days later received the Royal Assent in the Lords, together with the Act for setting up the Court of Fire Judges. A few additions and amendments, of no outstanding importance, experience showed

[1] Bower Marsh, *Records of the Carpenters Company*, vol. 1, p. xi.

to be advisable, and these were comprised in a supplementary Bill which the Commons passed next year but which failed to get through the Lords, and they were incorporated in the Additional Building Act of 1670.[1] Incidentally the Carpenters Company lost their chartered privilege of providing the " Viewers " of new buildings, bricklayers being now found best fitted for the task. The Building Act of 1774 transferred the duties of the viewers to district surveyors, who still discharge them.

It was the common practice to render gifts to those able to smooth the way of public business; Pepys, the Clerk of the Acts, is engagingly frank in the *Diary* over his considerable " gettings." No scandal was occasioned or felt when Sir Edward Turner, the Speaker of the House of Commons, accepted from the Court of Aldermen the sum of £100, " as a loving remembrance for his many kind offices performed to the state of the City." One may picture in imagination the shaking figure at the Bar of the House of Commons of that man who dared approach the austere Speaker of to-day with money in his hand ; but times have changed. The Clerk of Parliaments, the Attorney-General and the Solicitor-General had each his remembrance in gold or wine.

The financial assistance given by Parliament through the Coal Dues was of the most meagre kind. The legislature either did not or would not realize the magnitude of the task confronting the citizens in restoring London from its ruins. In difficulties itself to meet the constant demands of the Crown for money, and confident in the financial strength of the City from which it had wrung so many loans, Parliament, it is plain, fully expected London to be rebuilt in less time and with less sacrifice than actually were required. The City rulers can have had no such illusions when they demanded a seven years' monopoly of new building. The Act setting up the Court of Fire Judges was to continue in force till the 31st December, 1668, " and no longer "—so says the statute. The Court's last judgment was delivered on the 29th September, 1672,

---

[1] *Stat.* 22, *Chas. II.*, c. 11 : " An Additional Act for the rebuilding of the City of London, uniting of parishes, and rebuilding of the Cathedral and Parochial Churches within the same city."

the period of the Act having twice been extended. The money contribution from the Coal Dues was ludicrously insufficient. Originally fixed at one shilling per chaldron or ton for a term limited to ten years, ending June, 1677, the tax was by the Additional Building Act, 1670, increased to three shillings and the term extended to 1687, after which it was continued and reduced to one shilling and sixpence; in fact, the tax survived over two centuries until repealed by Lord Randolph Churchill. There are coal merchants still trading who have paid the impost originally made to meet the devastation caused by the Great Fire of London.

The inscription on the Fire Monument tells that the City was restored in three years. There are many entries in the books of the Surveyors for staking out ground plots eight and ten years after the Fire; the last is so late as 1696, and by that date the towers or spires of five churches, and St. Paul's Cathedral, were still unfinished.

Even before the Rebuilding Act had passed through Parliament, Sir George Moore and other substantial landowners in Fleet Street sought approval under the Royal Proclamation of September 13th for a project to build the street, which was granted.[1] This was the first City highway to be raised out of the ruins, and disputes between landlords and tenants there were the first to be settled by the Fire Judges' Court. It was the first street in which the new paving was completed. Ludgate Hill was widened to forty-five feet, the church of St. Martin Ludgate, which had obstructed the way, being placed back in Wren's rebuilding, and a new south postern was opened in Ludgate itself for convenience of foot passengers. Fleet Street, where it narrowed to a bottle-neck from Whitefriars to Fleet Bridge, was increased to the same width, that in the words of Charles's Proclamation, " the mischief might be prevented that one side may suffer if the other be on fire." Houses which had stood back were built forward, to make the street frontage uniform. Late into the eighteenth century the Temple Exchange Coffee House stood in Fleet Street, by Inner Temple Gate,

---

[1] *Gazette*, 1666, Oct. 29.

bearing upon its front a Latin inscription carved in stone
which read—

> You see before you
> The last house of the city in flames
> The first of the city to be restored :
> May this be favourable and fortunate
> For both city and house,
> Especially for those who are auspiciously building.
> Elizabeth Moore, owner of the site,
> and
> Thomas Tuckey, tenant.[1]

A chop house in Cannon Street in after years laid
claim to be the first house built after the Fire, and no
doubt there were other claimants.

---

[1] The Latin inscription is in Malcolm's *Londinium Redivivum*, ii, 299.
Mr. Ingpen, K.C., who printed the English version in his edition of *Master
Worsley's Book*, told me that this excellent translation is the work of the
late Dr. Woods, Master of the Temple.

CHAPTER XV

I BEGIN these chapters which deal till the end of the book with the actual rebuilding of London with something in the nature of a prologue, for there is a phase of Sir Christopher Wren's great career which is peculiarly obscure. It will touch upon matters given with more detail later, but only so far as is necessary to explain the difficulties. Wren's official post after the Fire was that of "Surveyor-General and Principal Architect for rebuilding the whole City, the Cathedral Church of St. Paul, and all the principal churches, with other structures." [1] Certainly the office lacked nothing in comprehensiveness.

Wren was at the time Professor of Astronomy and Geometry at Oxford, as formerly he had been at Gresham College, London. His early years had been devoted to scientific pursuits. He had built Pembroke College Chapel, Cambridge, and had designed the Sheldonian Theatre ; he was surveyor of St. Paul's, and under Sir John Denham was assistant, or deputy, Surveyor-General of his Majesty's Works ; but the full development of his architectural genius was yet to come. He was but thirty-four when, after the Fire of London, he was called upon to undertake the greatest burden ever borne by the shoulders of a single architect.

The King, with a perspicacity for which credit should not be withheld, at once decided that Dr. Wren should be the builder of the new City. (His well-deserved knighthood did not come till 1674.) Sir John Denham stood in the way. Denham, the Cavalier poet, had held Farnham

---

[1] *Parentalia*, p. 263.

Castle for the late King in the Civil War, and through Court influence he received at the Restoration the office of Surveyor-General, despite a protest, " that though he may have, as most gentry, some knowledge of the theory of architecture, he can have none of the practice." His graceful verse on *Cooper's Hill* is his best claim to remembrance. His young wife openly became the mistress of the Duke of York, and this circumstance and her tragic death—due, rumour falsely asserted, to a poisoned cup of chocolate—and his own madness clouded his later years.

Denham being fixed in office, King Charles solved the difficulty by creating for Wren the new post. On Denham's death, in March, 1669, he succeeded as Surveyor-General of his Majesty's Works, having meantime performed the duties of which his official chief was incapable, and his commanding abilities had come under favourable notice of the King.

The difficulty confronting the inquirer, after this lapse of time, is to tell how far Wren's influence extended in the restoration of the City. I have come to the conviction, and most reluctantly, that it was slight. Wren's model plan was most hastily prepared, within a few days of the Fire, and almost as hastily was rejected. Gwynn, who reproduced Wren's plan a century later, has declared that it was approved by Parliament and " unhappily defeated by Faction." Clearly the City authorities are thereby indicated. This statement has no foundation in fact. Wren's model plan was never approved by Parliament. It was stillborn, and was so of the necessities of the time. It was impossible that it should have been carried out at a time when no financial vote in aid could be obtained from Parliament, when that great public spirit which alone could have brought to realization so gigantic a scheme was crushed under the catastrophe. Wren treated the whole of the burnt area as vacant land awaiting exploitation. (For instance, he carries one of his main highways right over the historic Guildhall.) Any attempt to have realized his plan must have involved ruinous delays, and the loss or migration elsewhere of London's trade.

It wholly lacked public support. Whatever our regrets to-day may be at its non-fulfilment, I am confident that the prevision of the merchants (in the absence of a Parliamentary vote that must have run into millions) was right.

His plan for a new model having been rejected, Wren devoted himself to the design of those public buildings reserved for his own care and attention which remain to-day as monuments of his genius, assigning to Robert Hooke, the City's Surveyor, the business of measuring, adjusting, and setting out the ground for the streets and private dwellings.[1] It is noteworthy that, although appointed " principal architect " for the rebuilding of the City, there is, with the sole exceptions of King Street and Queen Street, to open out Guildhall, and the Thames Quay, nothing of his in the lay out of the streets. His name scarcely ever occurs in the long negotiations between the City Corporation and the Privy Council; his authority is not appealed to. His reports are extraordinarily few.

A big claim has been made for Wren as the builder of the Livery Companies' Halls. Elmes, his biographer, in his last work [2] lists no fewer than thirty-six of these as his (forty-four was the total number burnt), on the principle, apparently, that the master architect did everything. The task would have taxed even Wren's indefatigable industry, for the rebuilding was quickly put in hand. The Companies' records with few exceptions survive. In that case one would have expected Wren's name repeatedly to occur in them, and constant entries of payments to him. In fact, had the Companies' records stood alone, we should hardly have known of Wren's existence, so rare and inconsequential are the few references made to him. Dr. Philip Norman, F.S.A., whose intimate study of the surviving City Companies' Halls gives weight to his opinion, finds no satisfactory evidence that Wren designed any of the Halls.[3] Nor have I discovered in the bulk of the Companies' records of this time with which I am familiar the evidence of Wren's personal design in any of the Halls.

This may seem a startling assertion to make when it

[1] *Parentalia*, p. 263.
[2] *Sir Christopher Wren and his Times.* He is so careless that he even credits Jerman's Royal Exchange to Wren.
[3] *Journal of Royal Institute of British Architects*, 1918, May.

has been the commonplace belief of one City Company after another that it possesses, or has possessed before rebuilding, a Wren Hall. The legend of Wren's creations has passed into currency almost unquestioned. None of the Companies' Halls new built after the Fire has endured as have Wren's acknowledged buildings, and those from the period which survive to-day have required reconstruction, remodelling or enlargement till they have lost their original characteristics—an unusual fate for any authentic creation of Wren's, who built for eternity.[1]

What then was Wren's part in the restoration of the commercial City ? The Custom House was the only one of his public edifices in the City brought near completion within four years of the Fire ; the repairs to Guildhall were in progress. The Royal Exchange was Edward Jerman's work. Four years passed before the erection of a single one of the churches began, eight years before the Cathedral's foundations were excavated. Meantime, one would have expected Wren, the principal architect in the rebuilding of the City, to be ever suggesting, scheming, modifying streets within the limits which the necessities of the time imposed, laying down principles upon which the citizens' houses, to be rebuilt in thousands, should be constructed. No claim in this regard is made in *Parentalia.* The Guildhall archives do not disclose these activities. If Wren did this, it is curious that the evidence of it should be destroyed. The natural inference is that he did not.

Sir Christopher Wren was born in the tradition of the Church, and was a devout Churchman. Immense as was his output, he could not do everything. He was defeated in the one great town planning project associated with his fame. We know how his advice not to attempt tinkering with the ruinous walls of Old St. Paul's, but to rebuild, was for years ignored. He designed successive plans for his Cathedral, accepting alterations against his own better judgment in order to meet the objections of lesser minds than his. In the actual building he was thwarted, and finally he was removed from the supervision of his own structure. In his matchless group of City churches,

---

[1] See Note on " Companies' Halls destroyed since the Great Fire " at the end of this volume, pp. 357, 358.

numbering fifty-one, he seems to have been left without interference, and in them he may have found consolation.

The State papers, the civic and Companies' records, and such papers as Wren himself has left do not disclose that activity in the City's reconstruction which would be expected from the principal architect for the rebuilding. I have been much impressed by its omission. But parish records do make frequent mention of visits to and consultations with Wren about the churches. The churchwardens of St. Margaret Pattens who put in their accounts the cost of refreshment " after our call upon Mr. Renn," and of a dinner after " visiting Sir Christopher Wren about our church " do not stand alone. He found time to contribute scientific papers to the Royal Society. Otherwise his mind seems to have been engrossed with his gigantic conceptions in stone, and when drawings for fourteen new churches started in the single year 1670 were required, they were ready, each one the different conception of a master. That surely is significant. Associated with Wren as the King's Commissioners for the rebuilding were Mr. Hugh May and Mr. Pratt, and the City appointed as their Surveyors Robert Hooke, Peter Mills, and Edward Jerman, with John Oliver and others under their direction as supervisors. The City work appears to have been left to the City authorities and their officers, with rarely an occasional reference to the master.

The King had proposed in the spring of 1667, and repeated his suggestion, the appointment of Sir William Bolton, the Lord Mayor, as Surveyor-General for the rebuilding of the City, but the Common Council held the opinion that there was " no use or occasion for a Surveyor-General," as the work could be well and sufficiently managed by the Surveyors already appointed.[1]

It is my belief that London as it was re-created after the Fire owed more (always apart from Wren's individual buildings, which glorified it) to King Charles II. than to Sir Christopher Wren. His was the active, agitating mind. His hand was seen everywhere. So soon as the ruins were cold, he appointed a committee of Lords of the Council, the Lord Chancellor being at its head, to

---

[1] *Journal* 46, fos. 170b, 189.

consult with the City's representatives upon the rebuilding.[1] After the Act of Parliament had passed, he desired the Lord Mayor and Aldermen, by mediation and advice, to have such things done as should contribute "to the beauty, ornament, and convenience of the City," even beyond the authority given them by the strict letter of the statute, promising them therein all assistance in his Royal power.[2] His concern for the grandeur of the principal streets led him to recommend that where end buildings of cross streets abutted on high streets, they should range in height and façade with those of the high streets.[3] The King proposed that the Halls of the lesser Companies be erected next to the Thames Quay, adding thereby to the beauty of the river frontage. He wished sufficient market space to be provided to make unnecessary any markets in the open streets.[4]

Thus frequently Charles intervened with his own suggestions. The Acts of Common Council passed in February, 1667, the King had brought before him, and a map prepared by which to trace with his finger the proposals for widening and straightening the more important streets. These generally he approved, some he enlarged, and in Fleet Street, the importance of which as an artery of the City he recognized, he recommended some such widening as is now being completed, at enormous expense.[5] The City rulers, unfortunately, were unable to accept a project by the King for continuing the Old Bailey south to the Thames, making one wide, straight street from Smithfield to the river—an improvement not less desirable to-day than two and a half centuries ago. They had, they said, no capacity to do this, forasmuch as the Act of Parliament gave no authority for cutting such a new street, nor for compensating the owners of ground taken for the purpose.

It may be, of course, that the King spoke the ideas of Wren, himself the most modest and unassuming of men, but the curious repression of Wren's personality throughout the first important years of reconstruction after the

[1] *Privy Council Registers*, vol. 59, fo. 189.
[2] Letter to the Lord Mayor, *Ibid.*, fo. 351.
[3] *Ibid.*, fo. 351.   [4] *Ibid.*, fos. 333–4.
[5] *Privy Council Registers*, vol. 59, pp. 333–4.

Photo by Mr. Lionel Gowing

"THE CROOKED BILLET," MINORIES

A typical house of the period immediately after the Great Fire, built outside the destroyed area

Fire is difficult to account for. I had expected to find much more evidence of the handiwork of the " principal architect " during that period than is available. He had to suffer many disappointments, but had always the incentive to occupy himself with that work which must have brought the greatest satisfaction to him. No particular significance need be attached to the long delay in conferring Wren's knighthood, but there is the fact.

" London rises again, whether with greater speed or greater magnificence is doubtful, three short years complete that which was considered the work of an age." This inscription is borne upon the Fire Monument, that proud column rising serene above the tide of traffic about it, which is no mean example of Wren's incomparable genius, and stands where the Fire broke out to remind London and those who come from far and near of the greatest catastrophe through which the Imperial City has passed in a thousand years of history.

The words are grotesquely false, and have done incalculable mischief, belittling the vast work undertaken in adversity in restoring the City, making it appear as nothing ; that in three years' time a new London complete, richer and more magnificent, stood on the ground ravaged by the flames. The fable has been spread broadcast. I have to tell a plain tale, extracted with much labour from surveyors' returns, from building accounts, the minutes of the City Corporation and the craft gilds, Privy Council papers and memoirs and letters, of how after long effort—and not in three years—the task was carried to completion against difficulties that might have seemed insurmountable. Only by so doing is tardy justice given to our forefathers who served London well in this most critical period, and handed on its tradition to their successors.

Let us understand the problem as it presented itself after the first week of September, 1666. Fire insurance was unknown. The fund did not exist that to-day, should a calamity of similar magnitude befall the City, would restore the buildings almost complete. In place of millions released by the liquidation of investments by the fire insurance companies was—nothing ! The flames

266   THE GREAT FIRE OF LONDON

had destroyed 436 acres of City property, the ruined
houses, mere blackened skeletons, and vast quantities of
goods consumed within them representing to the owners
a dead, irrecoverable loss. The charitable donations and
collections, at most a few thousand pounds, sufficed to
meet only the first waves of distress. The country was
waging with Holland and France a costly and unpopular
war, and the burden of taxation added to the prevailing
discontent—that war which had its last inglorious phase
when a Dutch fleet sailed up the Thames and Medway,
burnt three of our ships of the line, and over ruined
London broke the distant reverberation of the Dutch
guns bombarding Chatham ; the most humiliating moment
in our island story.

Misfortunes to London did not come singly, but fell
blow upon blow ; one would need to search far to find
another such instance of public calamity. The Great
Plague in 1665 had destroyed its population by tens of
thousands. The Great Fire next year left other thousands
of citizens homeless. Their misery was accentuated by
a winter of extraordinary severity which followed. The
drought and heat of August and September gave place
to torrential rains in October, so severe that many people
feared a famine, and water was high on the roads.[1] When
the New Year came the Thames was packed with ice,
and though the frost broke in January, it returned with
increasing rigour. Pepys declared that the 7th March,
1667, was reckoned by all people the coldest day that
ever was remembered in England. In April there was
hardly a leaf on a tree.

London all the while remained desolate in its ashes,
spotted all over with wooden sheds and shelters used as
temporary habitations, often mere roof boards thrown
across the fire-riven walls, and ringed about by the complete streets spared by the flames. Into these last the
people packed, and poverty was made the more bitter
by the enormous rise in rentals which the demand for
houses created. For a dwelling let before the Fire at
£40 the landlord claimed and obtained £150 rent. A
silkman was content to pay £50 fine and £30 per annum

[1] Evelyn, Oct. 21 ; Pepys, Oct. 18.

for the use of what had been a City housewife's closet, a little dark bedchamber, and a garret.[1]

The poor, freezing in their hovels and cellars, were compelled to buy coal at £3 to £4 a chaldron, prices having risen to heights previously unheard of. Colliers in the Thames were suspected of delaying cargoes in order to extort high freights. It had been the City law that the Livery Companies should lay in stores of coal according to their capacities, to be sold at reasonable rates in winter to the poor, and thus prevent their exploitation by dealers' rings. The wealthy Grocers were required to provide as much as 672 tons, a smaller Company like the Armourers but nineteen tons.[2] The Companies were without money, and such coal as they had already brought to London had burnt on the wharves.

The poverty and misery in the destroyed City were reflected when Sir William Bolton, the successor to Bludworth as Lord Mayor, went on 29th October to the Exchequer to be sworn, without pageant, only two or three marshals in livery cloaks riding ahead to make way for the Chief Magistrate and his attendants.[3] It grieved the heart of Pepys. " But Lord ! " he writes, " to see how meanly they now look, who upon this day used to be little lords, is a sad sight, and worthy consideration ; and everybody did reflect with pity upon the poor City, to which they are now coming to chose and swear their Lord Mayor, to what it heretofore was." Guildhall being a roofless shell, the hustings for the Lord Mayor's election were raised in Leathersellers Hall, Bishopsgate ; Dr. Frampton preached the sermon at St. Helen's Church. The Sheriffs were sworn at Gresham House. Even the customary bonfires on the 5th November for the discovery of Gunpowder Plot were not burnt, " though never," Pepys declares, " was more said of, or done against, the Papists then just at this time."

The wardmotes met as usual on St. Thomas's Day, difficult as it was to get together any representative assembly of citizens. It had been sought to obtain authority for the members of the Common Council to

[1] Pepys's *Diary*, 1666, Sept. 7 and 26.
[2] Act of Common Council, 1665, June 1.
[3] Rugge's *Diurnal*.

continue in their places for the ensuing year without election. At St. Dunstan-in-the-West, a parish half burnt out, the inquest dispensed with its customary gifts to poor prisoners and to Christ's Hospital, and instead gave its doles to distressed parishioners, as did some others.

Long years afterwards the memory of the terrible winter spent in desolated London remained little less vivid than that of the flaming horrors of the Fire itself. It was February, 1667, when the Rebuilding Act was passed; in March the City Surveyors were authorized to buy stakes for setting out the streets; in April they staked the first of the highways near St. Paul's; in May the staking out of plots for house-building began—the rigours of winter and the necessity of clearing away the enormous accumulation of debris that covered the ground having caused this delay after the legislative measures were ready. Meanwhile the chief streets had been measured, and boundary marks restored. There had been furtive attempts at rebuilding on old foundations, which at times proved too weak to support new buildings, or else threatened encroachment on newly aligned public thoroughfares; a house partly built by Leadenhall was ordered to be pulled down, as not complying with the Act.

In his Proclamation of 13th September, Charles had undertaken at once to rebuild the Custom House at his own charges, in proof of his good-will to the City and as an incentive to the citizens. It rose again on the old site by the waterside below London Bridge, after a survey had been made of the wharves to determine whether the building could not better be erected elsewhere. Wren prepared the design, and the work was completed in 1671, at a cost to the Crown of £10,000.[1] Forty-seven years later Wren's Custom House was itself destroyed by fire.

---

[1] The urgent call for economy after the Fire is evidenced in the terms of a Royal Warrant for rebuilding the Custom House. Wainscot and joiners' work were to be allowed only in the public offices called the Great Custom House and the Searchers' Office, and not above ten feet high. There should be no appointments except plain tables and benches, covered with cloth, " where the like were the same in the old Custom House before the Great Fire." Any official ordering more sumptuous provision should himself bear the expense.

On the 23rd October, 1667, the King went to the City in State, with his kettle-drums and trumpets, to lay the first stone of the first pillar of the new Royal Exchange, the funds for which were jointly provided by the Mercers Company and the Corporation, as Gresham's trustees. Flames last century again destroyed the Royal Exchange.

The City Corporation, perpetually harassed in its efforts to find money and by the general distress among the populace, attacked its stupendous task with daring enterprise. Early receipts of the Coal Dues, at the single shilling first imposed, were exhausted in payments for land taken for widening the streets. A fruitful source of revenue, used with but little scruple, was found in the large fines paid by persons to be discharged from the office of Alderman, these being devoted to the restoration of Guildhall and the Sessions House at Old Bailey. Few people probably know that the existing Mansion House was built largely out of fines paid to escape service as Sheriff. Still, the public works, though much delayed by want of funds, made such progress that the City between 1667 and 1673 was obliged to borrow £83,000 to meet its obligations.[1] The Compters (Sheriffs' prisons) at Wood Street and Poultry were quickly rebuilt. Newgate was patched up sufficiently to serve its historic purpose as a gaol until in 1670 the work of new building was begun in earnest, and nearly five years later was completed at a cost of £9,484, with the King's arms and the City arms over the portal carved by Caius Gabriel Cibber. Ludgate was repaired and its prison rebuilt between 1670 and 1673, costing £4,172. Repairs at Aldersgate, through which the flames had burst, cost £946 ; and Moorgate was rebuilt in 1673–4 at the City's charge of £1,983, Wren's new Temple Bar having at the same time been completed. Blackwell Hall, the cloth market, was ready for trade in 1671, having been rebuilt by Christ's Hospital (which enjoyed the revenues) at a cost of £10,361, this sum being afterwards refunded out of the Coal Dues.

A far larger demand upon the City's resources was made by the works at Guildhall. Wren raised the height of the historic hall by twenty feet, constructing a new roof

---

[1] Sharpe, *London and the Kingdom*, ii, 434.

and gallery, and in addition the surrounding buildings—
Council Chamber, Parlour, Town Clerk's office, Mayor's
Court, hall-keeper's house and others—were erected anew
from the foundations.   For ten years, while a new London
was growing up around it, the home of civic government
was concealed by a forest of scaffolding as the work went
on uninterruptedly till December, 1675, the expenditure
then having totalled £37,422.[1]   Wren built a flat roof over
Guildhall, intended by him as a temporary expedient.
It remained for two centuries, being replaced by the
present high-pitched, open timbered roof, in some respects
a copy of the mediæval one, in the year 1866.

In private enterprise, the Livery Companies led the
way in the rebuilding of the City.   This stands to their
lasting credit.   Never in all their long history has their
public spirit been displayed so decisively as after the Fire
of London.   The disaster fell upon the Companies with
crushing severity.   Forty-four of their Halls were burnt,
and but seven, so far as I can trace, escaped the flames.[2]
Endowed with City property by the benefactions of past
members, they had the larger part of it, if not the whole,
consumed in the Fire, the losses of individual Companies
running into many thousands of pounds, and numbers
amongst them never thereafter recovered their prosperity.
Yet the records of one Company after another bear witness
that the first practical thought of the liverymen was the
immediate restoration of their Halls, and to that task
individual members bent their energies even before their
own dwellings or warehouses could be rebuilt.   It would
be idle to conceal the fact that corporate interests were a
strong incentive.   The continued existence of the Companies depended upon the unbroken exercise of their
powers of supervision over the crafts, for once these lapsed
their authority had gone, perhaps never to be recovered.
Be that as it may, their confidence that London would
rise, great and prosperous as ever, out of its ashes, and the
boldness of their example, gave the utmost encouragement
to the citizens, then sadly needing encouragement in their
unparalleled distress.

A typical case is that of the wealthy Merchant Taylors.

[1] Guildhall Library MS. 184.
[2] For the full lists see Appendix IV.

Parts of the mediæval walls of their Hall off Threadneedle Street were left standing to be incorporated in the rebuilding. Swift hands saved from the Fire the charters, deeds, records and arras hangings, but in the debris littering the floor was fused silver of the value (as metal) of £290. This represented the Company's fine plate. Most of the adjacent buildings were destroyed ; the almshouses were partially consumed. Revenues from City rents disappeared. Wanting capital to restore the houses lost in the flames, which had brought in ground rentals of £1,400 a year, the Company were obliged to let their City sites at small rents, often at a peppercorn for the first years, in order to encourage the tenants to rebuild. Loans were outstanding, and being without income to pay the instalments falling due, they were glad to sell for £5,000 to Alderman Backwell, the financier, lands in Lombard Street and Cornhill, which the books declare they " esteemed the richest jewel of their estate."

Though stricken by poverty, the Merchant Taylors made a supreme effort to restore the gild buildings, by seeking donations from a few wealthy liverymen, small subscriptions, and loans. The Parlour was rebuilt at once, and furnished in February, 1667. A beadle's house was erected in Threadneedle Street. In the autumn of 1669 the restoration of the Hall was begun ; the whole was complete by the summer of 1671. The task, however, so exhausted the Company's finances that in ensuing years they were obliged to sell houses in Bishopsgate Street which had escaped the Fire, to suspend payments of some benefactors' grants, and to let their Hall, which for forty years was rented by the East India Company.[1]

Individual merchants, hitherto counted amongst the richest men of the City, were reduced to a mere competency, where not actually ruined. And to crown all, the Companies found themselves loaded with debt, the result of compulsory loans to the Commonwealth or to the King, which they had no means of repaying.

Those few Companies whose Halls, by good fortune, stood outside the Fire area, lent their use to distressed brethren. Carpenters Hall, by London Wall, temporarily accommodated the Goldsmiths, Drapers, Weavers, and

---

[1] Clode, *Memorials of the Merchant Taylors.*

Feltmakers. The Bricklayers, by Leadenhall Street, extended hospitality to the Coopers, the Leathersellers at Bishopsgate to the Skinners; the Saddlers met at Christ's Hospital; the Vintners assembled in public inns while their Hall by Thames-side was rebuilding, as did many others; the Merchant Taylors, Barber Surgeons, and Grocers had sufficient property left standing to house their offices during rebuilding. The Saddlers received the Dyers when their new Hall was ready.

Six months after the Fire, Barber Surgeons Hall was being repaired—" new built very fine," says Pepys—a subscription of £1,850 having been raised for that purpose, while property was sacrificed at low prices and loans were sought. Much choice City plate was sold. The Goldsmiths Company found their house rents, which before the Fire had brought in £1,271 a year, reduced to a mere £231 (money values, of course, were much higher in Restoration times than to-day), and they made up successive parcels of plate for sale, first copying the coats-of-arms and other particulars of benefactors engraved on the pieces, " to the end that such plate may be restored, and made again, when the Company shall be thereunto enabled." [1] The Founders Company sold plate to form the nucleus of a fund for rebuilding; the Coopers, Saddlers, and Girdlers did the same to discharge their debt.

In March, 1667, the Coopers Company resolved to forego fees from members till subscriptions were obtained from them for their Hall. The Pewterers Company, receiving £800 from forty additional subscriptions to the Livery, devoted that sum to the new Hall. The Paynter-Stainers pawned their plate, and members of the Court of Assistants made loans of £50 each. An assessment on members was made by the Writers of Court Hand for the cost of Scriveners Hall. This was opposed by some, and legal opinion being taken, the levy was held to be lawful.[2] Sir Robert Vyner contributed £300 to the Goldsmiths' rebuilding fund, and a silver bell and ivory hammer bearing his arms that he gave are still in use in Goldsmiths Hall.

Thanks to the enterprise and sacrifice of the Livery

[1] *Court Minutes*, 1666, Oct. 31 ;[1] 1667, July 5.
[2] Guildhall Library MS. 366, 16 (MSS. Box A).

"THE CHAINED SWAN," NO. 37 CHEAPSIDE

This old house, built *circa* 1667-8, is probably the earliest surviving of those erected immediately after the Great Fire

Companies, their Halls were the first of the larger buildings of the City to be restored, most of them being in occupation before the public structures were complete, or a single one of the demolished churches had been rebuilt. A new Butchers Hall in Pudding Lane (where the Company anciently held land), Cutlers Hall in Cloak Lane, and Innholders Hall, Dowgate, were built in 1668 ; Plaisterers Hall, Pewterers Hall, Goldsmiths Hall, and Paynter-Stainers Hall in 1669 ; the Halls of the Curriers, Stationers, Fishmongers, Watermen, and Saddlers Companies in 1670 ; Vintners Hall, Coopers Hall, and Parish Clerks Hall in 1671 ; and those of the Mercers, Founders, and Tallow Chandlers by 1672. The Mercers Company, greatly impoverished by the Fire, were glad to let their Hall at a rental for the first office of the Bank of England when that national institution was founded, and in Mercers Chapel the subscription list was opened. Grocers Hall was afterwards the home of the Bank for forty years.

If Wren did not accomplish a tithe (or any) of the Halls attributed to him, it is not less inaccurate to credit them to Edward Jerman, the City Surveyor, who died as early as November, 1668, leaving his Royal Exchange, then building, to be finished from his drawings by Cartwright, his head mason. Jerman is said to have restored Merchant Taylors Hall, and to have made designs for the Fishmongers, Haberdashers and Drapers Halls. In the few Halls built after the catastrophe of 1666 that survive, the original work has been disfigured by additions and alterations. Fire, too, has been particularly destructive in the two and a half centuries that have passed, and time's decay and the poverty into which many Companies have fallen accounts for the disappearance of others.* There stood near Billingsgate until 1906 a delightful old merchant's house, No. 32 Botolph Lane, possibly of Sir Christopher Wren's design, which tradition said was his London residence while his Cathedral and churches were building, but the tradition is unsupported by any evidence. Wren's genius is seen in his Cathedral and the City churches, but unhappily there is no adequate representation of his domestic architecture left in London.

Indeed, in all the City to-day I know only two buildings (the churches apart) that I should with confidence attribute to Wren, and possibly a third.   The Deanery of St. Paul's I feel certain is his.   It was built by Dean Sancroft under powers which enabled him to sell part of the garden land on condition that he spent not less than £2,500 on the new house ;   the work was complete by 1670, when Sancroft was released from his liability.[1] The house, with a southern wing, is much larger than the front elevation would lead one to expect.   It has a striking plan, the door opening direct into a large hall that frequently is used for diocesan meetings, and with an ante-room and the staircase well fills the whole front of that floor to the right, there being an equally large room to the left.

The second building that in all probability is Wren's design is the College of Arms, which in the cutting out of Queen Victoria Street lost the gateway with its hollow arch, by contemporaries "esteemed a curiosity." The College had no corporate funds with which to rebuild after the Fire, and an appeal made under Royal brief to the nobility and gentry produced a beggarly £700. Happily the Heralds themselves were more liberal, giving up their fees for the purpose. Sir William Dugdale, Garter, bore the expense of the north-west corner. Sir Henry St. George, Clarenceux, carrying out his predecessor's expressed intention, built up the west side and the south-west corner, and Elias Ashmole, Windsor, generously contributed.   In November, 1683, the main building of the College was finished.   No. 11 Love Lane, Aldermanbury, a merchant's house, is in Wren's style.

[1] D'Oyly's *Life of Sancroft.*

CHAPTER XVI

THE CITY RESTORED

IN the spring of 1668 Samuel Rolle estimated that there were eight hundred houses rebuilt in the flame-swept area ; some thought more. The outlook from any of them was most dispiriting for those who hoped for the speedy restoration of London. " Methinks," says the divine, " it is an ill prospect, and a ghastly sight, for those that look from the balconies or tops of their stately new houses, to see ashes and ruinous heaps on every side of them—to see ten private houses (besides churches and public halls) in the dust for one that is raised again." Where a village stands upon a great highway, most of the houses seen are inns, and so, he observes, " the major part of the houses built upon the ruins of London are let to alehouse keepers and victuallers, to entertain workmen employed about the City." In Cheapside and other centres of commerce merchants had built dwellings, but refrained from going into them till the neighbourhood be increased, fearing thieves as well as unprofitable trade.[1]

Such was the sorry state of the City nineteen months after the Fire. Two winters had passed over London's ruins. But a brighter prospect then opened, and from the spring of 1668 onwards such enterprise was shown that by the close of the year 1672 the newly built streets had become substantially continuous. When broken it was often by the open sites of churches whereon ruined walls were still standing. The City Surveyors first staked out the foundations when any house was rebuilt. Till December, 1667, this had been done in only 650 odd cases

---

[1] *London's Resurrection*, 1668, pp. 91-8.

(which would indicate that Rolle's estimate was not too small), so slow had been the recovery after the Fire. But in the first six months of 1668 a beginning was made with the erection of 1,200 houses, the progress made in new building, as might be expected, falling off towards winter.

In the spring and summer of 1669 the number of new houses under scaffolding was about 1600, a somewhat larger proportion than in the previous year.

This rate of construction was continuous until the autumn of the year 1670.

Thereafter it greatly slackened,[1] and labour, being less in demand for private dwellings, was diverted to the erection of public buildings and churches. London at this time—autumn, 1670, four years after the Fire—had not more than a dozen of its Livery Companies' Halls complete and placed in use, and Guildhall, the Custom House, Blackwell Hall, the prisons and the gates were also unfinished. Eighty-four City churches had been destroyed and not one replaced. These facts must be borne in mind in estimating the progress made in rebuilding the City as a whole. The decision to build the first of the churches was taken in 1670, and that year a start was made with fourteen of their number.[2]   St. Dunstan-in-the-East, which cannot have been greatly damaged in the Fire, was repaired by the churchwardens and the accounts passed in July, 1671, the cost having been only £1,075 ; but those on new foundations rose slowly. The citizens meantime kept their trade together by all kinds of makeshifts. Numbers of tradesmen migrated west beyond Temple Bar, to be near the fashionable world settling about Covent Garden, midway between the

---

[1] Cf. Surveys by Oliver, Mills and Hooke, Guildhall Library MS. 84 ; also Payments for staking out foundations, Guildhall Library MS. 273 to 277.   Sir William Turner, Lord Mayor 1668–9, gave such encouragement and assistance in the rebuilding that the citizens desired to pay him the signal honour of re-electing him to the Mayoralty for a second term, but this he declined.

[2] These first churches to be rebuilt were the following, given in the order in which their construction was begun, as shown in Wren's building accounts (see page 336, *post*) ; St. Christopher-le-Stocks, St. Laurence Jewry, St. Bride, St. Michael Cornhill, St. Mary-le-Bow, St. Dionis Back-church, St. Benet Fink, St. Michael Wood Street, St. Mary Aldermanbury, St. Vedast Foster Lane, St. Mary-at-Hill, St. Edmund King and Martyr, St. Mildred Poultry, St. Olave Jewry.

Court and the City, and in Henrietta Street, Charles Street and Bedford Street many City shops were re-established. Others re-opened about the New Exchange in the Strand, a rival emporium to Gresham's foundation. Pepys gossiped with a mercer there, who found receipts so good that he doubted if he and many of his trade would return, or that the City would ever regain its pre-eminence for retail shopping.[1]

The Royal College of Physicians, abandoning their ruined home by Amen Corner in 1670, rebuilt on a new site in Warwick Lane, not far distant. Wren designed the buildings around a spacious court, placing a curiously constructed dome above the lecture theatre which was visible over a great part of the City, and inspired the lines—

> A dome, majestic to the sight;
> And sumptuous arches bear its oval height;
> A golden globe plac'd high with artful skill,
> Seems, to the distant sight, a gilded pill.[2]

Westward to Trafalgar Square the physicians trekked in 1825, but Wren's City structure remained on the ground many years later, serving various purposes—" vile and unhealthy " Elmes calls them.

Sir Robert Clayton rebuilt the southern front of Christ's Hospital at a cost exceeding £10,000, in gratitude for his recovery from dangerous illness, the munificence of individual governors having made possible the restoration of other portions of the damaged school. Prominent among these donors were Sir John Moore, Erasmus Smith and Thomas Firmin.[3] The foundation itself was heavily burdened by the destruction of over one hundred of its rent-producing houses, and had no funds available for the purpose. Inner Temple, left a pitiable spectacle after fire and gunpowder had done their work, was restored from its heaped ruins largely by inducements held out to barristers to build their chambers anew on favourable terms. Dr. Ball, the Master of the Temple, erected the attractive Master's House which still stands, contributing

[1] *Diary*, 1668, June 27.
[2] Garth's *Dispensary, Canto* 1.
[3] W. Lemprière *Lond. & Midd. Arch. Soc.*, New Ser. ii, 501.

£400 to the cost and obtaining a lease for his life and thirty-one years thereafter.[1]

Sir Robert Clayton, a self-made man of vast riches, Lord Mayor in 1679, built for himself an imposing house in Old Jewry, where he and his wife, " a free-hearted woman," gave entertainments and banquets vying with those of kings. The dwelling after his death was used by successive Lord Mayors in keeping their mayoralty. An ancient house in Cheapside, No. 73 (Elkington's) has the doubtful tradition that it was designed by Wren for Sir William Turner, Lord Mayor in 1668–9, and from its use was long known as the old Mansion House ; but overlaid ornament has concealed all its original character. It was the bookseller Tegg's early last century, and still retains its remarkably fine oak staircase. The houses of the wealthier merchants mostly stood within easy compass of the Royal Exchange, and their numbers and appearance excited the enthusiasm of a writer forty years after the Great Fire, " magnificent with courts, offices and all other necessary apartments inclosed to themselves, and noble gates and frontispieces towards the streets, richly furnished within." [2] The best sur- viving examples of these mansion houses, " of the greatest bigness," are No. 34 Great Tower Street, circa 1670, which retains the pleasant features of a Georgian mer- chant's counting-house on the ground floor and has some fine carving in the salon and ante-rooms above,[3] and No. 33 Mincing Lane, of somewhat later period. These were, however, the richer adornments of what circumstances prescribed must be a plainly built City.

Labour in the building trades gravitated to London from the entire country, and enterprise elsewhere suffered in consequence ; the ship-repairing works of the Royal Dockyard at Sheerness, begun in 1665, after the Fire were brought to a standstill for lack of men. The King commanded the Lord Mayor to summon the Masters of the Masons and Bricklayers Companies, and to send to

---

[1] Inderwick, *Cal. Inner Temple Records*, iii, 42 *passim*. The east wing was added 1760, about which time, judging from the style of the archi- tecture, other alterations were carried out, but there is no record of Dr. Ball's house having been taken down and a new Master's House built.

[2] Hatton's *New View of London*, 1708.

[3] I have described this house in detail in *Unknown London*.

the Dockyard as many able workmen as were required. They were found by the expedient of the Press Gang.[1] The years that followed witnessed a revival of the conflict between the old " free " labour of the City freemen and the labour of " foreigners " who came, under protection of the Act of Parliament, to work in the rebuilding. In 1670 the Carpenters, Masons, Bricklayers, Joyners, and Plaisterers Companies petitioned the Court of Aldermen, setting forth that their ancient usages and customs were violated by the " foreigners' " practices. But the Aldermen were helpless to give redress. The clash of interests never ceased, and when the demand for labour slackened the City freemen pushed the unfree artificers out of employment, till it was complained that many hundreds of these men had been cast adrift, and fears were publicly expressed that, turning beggars in their distress, if not thieves and robbers, they would infest the country roads.[2]

That building supplies might be available, the Privy Council suspended for a term the restraint imposed by the Navigation Acts upon the free import of timber, boards, bricks, and tiles ; and thereafter the Eastland Company, which carried a large Baltic trade, obtained a grant for two years to import timber and deals for the rebuilding of London in any ships manned by English mariners. Pepys had a project with Sir William Penn for bringing deals from Scotland, believing it would yield good money. So many merchants travelled the country buying up timber, that a shortage for shipbuilding was feared. The City promoted a bill to encourage the making of brick, tile, and lime, and licensed a tenant at St. Giles-in-the-Fields to dig clay in his lands for brickmaking, notwithstanding any restrictions in his lease. Whitechapel enjoyed a thriving industry in burning bricks for the new London. Petition was made to the Privy Council for leave to fetch stone from the Portland Quarries, but this was refused except by consent of the Surveyor of the Royal Works, lest there should be insufficient for the King's undertakings at Whitehall and elsewhere. Yet

[1] *State Papers* (*Domestic*), 1667, p. 408. In the account-book of the Masons Company, 1667, is this " Item, Paid for charges for impressing men and going to Sheerness, £3 15s. 5d."
[2] *Hist. MSS. Comm.*, 8th Rep., 145.

inevitably the demand, when so much was wanting, out-stripped the supply.   The Court of the Pewterers Company, when contemplating rebuilding their Hall in October, 1667, authorized the Master "if a pennyworth of timber or other material of building come to his hand, or he can hear of," to purchase the same.[1]

I find no indication that preferential treatment in the requisitioning of materials and labour was given to the public buildings.   On the contrary, the work in London was much harassed by constant impressment by the Navy Commissioners of joiners and carpenters for the King's shipyards at Chatham and Sheerness, till Sir Richard Ford, Lord Mayor in 1670, made spirited protest that the finishing of the Royal Exchange was seriously impeded by the seizure of workmen there, and demanded that there should be no further impressment from public works in the City.   Vyner and Backwell made repre-sentations that their private buildings in Lombard Street were delayed in like manner, to the detriment of their financial business with the Crown.

Old foundations, where substantial, were often used again.   Thus one finds in the City to-day open spaces which preserve the outlines of buildings that perished in the Great Fire : Wardrobe Place is an upper court of the King's Wardrobe Palace ; Heralds' College in part pre-serves the quadrangle of Derby House ; flowers bloom in gardens within the Bank of England which mark historic sites.   At many corners in the City refreshing patches of green amid the stone and brick indicate to the passer-by where, till the Fire, some old church stood.

The King, to encourage rebuilding, remitted the Hearth Tax for seven years on houses newly built in London.[2] This was an impost levied for service of the Crown of 2s. per annum on every hearth in houses paying to Church and poor.   Land frequently passed to new ownership, or, where the freehold was retained, the building tenant was allowed a peppercorn rent for a series of years, or a reduced rent for the term of a lease.   A common basis of valuation of City land after the Great Fire was that the annual site value was one-third of the combined rental of the house

[1] C. Welch, *Pewterers Company*, ii, 134.
[2] *Royal Proclamation*, 1666, Sept. 13.   But see page 285, *post*.

and ground ; in places where street improvements gave
land lying back an important frontage its value rose
enormously, to as much as 15*s.* per foot.[1] In our own day
£50 a foot has many times been paid for freehold City
sites, and a record was made at Cornhill by a sale at £62
a foot.[2] *

Other inducements offered were less legitimate. The
coolest appropriation I know was made by the parish
authorities of St. Mary Aldermanbury. As additional
consideration for their tenant rebuilding two houses in
Love Lane, belonging to the church, they made her a gift
of a not inconsiderable slip of the churchyard for a garden,
presumably graves, tombs, and all ; the ground is to-day
covered by No. 12 Love Lane.

To find what charge was borne in rebuilding London
after the Great Fire, it is necessary to have some standard
of comparison of building costs in the time of Charles II.
and to-day. Wide divergence of views has been expressed, and some have thought that prices have advanced
three and even four times. Mr. Lawrence Weaver, F.S.A.,
at the Bodleian Library happily alighted upon Wren's
complete building accounts for the City parochial churches.[3]
He had the further good fortune to inspire Mr. William
Lunn (Messrs. Widnell and Trollope) to undertake the
laborious task of pricing all the items in the construction
of two important churches at the rates prevailing just
before the European War. This supplies the key.

The result is somewhat surprising. Wren's building
cost for St. Mary-le-Bow, Cheapside, was £15,473. The
church could be built to-day (*i.e.* in 1914) for no more
than £38,500—an addition of 150 per cent. to the original
cost. St. Stephen Walbrook cost Wren £7,652 ; to-day
the contractor's bills would amount to £15,408—an
addition of 100 per cent. to the original cost. The larger
percentage of increase in the case of St. Mary-le-Bow is
due to the more extensive use of masonry in that church.
But it is the small details of these bills, the sums paid to

[1] Pepys (*Diary*, 1667, Dec. 3), who gives Sir Richard Ford as his
authority.
[2] Sale in 1893, by Messrs. Farebrother, Ellis & Co., of freehold of
Savory's, Cornhill, 2500 feet, purchase price £155,000.
[3] See a most valuable paper in *Archæologia*, vol. lxvi, p. 1 *et seq.*

individual craftsmen and the prices of bricks, timber, plaster work, painting and carting, that are most informative upon the cost of rebuilding the citizens' houses.

Labour accounts for the larger part of the increase. The unskilled labourer of the Restoration received 1s. 6d. per working day of ten hours. To-day (meaning 1914) he would be paid 7s. 6d. Skilled craftsmen's wages were equally low. Carpenters were content with 2s. 6d. to 3s. 6d. per day, according to the work, where to-day the payment would be 11s. 8d. Bricklayers receive three times the wages paid by Wren; skilled masons slightly more. The great increase in wages has been compensated in part by cheapening in the manufacture of materials and use of machinery. Ironwork remains at about the same price, the plates, bars, and rods now turned out by rolling mills having at the Restoration to be forged by hand. Brickwork per rod has advanced from £5 10s. to £17, and bricks per M. from 14s. to £1 16s. Wren used lead very generously. Its price per cwt., with labour, has risen from 17s. 6d. to £1 10s.; plain plastering on walls, per yard, from 7d. to 1s. 2d. The only item actually less in cost to-day than in the latter half of the seventeenth century is painting, which for three oils per yard was 1s., and now is 10d., the advance in painters' wages being more than compensated by the improved manufacture of colours. All comparison rates above given are for 1914.

After the Fire the Surveyors reported 13,200 houses destroyed. Land was taken for widening streets and establishing markets, alleys were abolished. Much slum property, wooden hovels built back to back, which were unduly dignified with the name of houses, gave place to more sanitary brick dwellings. Larger buildings were favoured; and for all these reasons it is unlikely that the houses newly built in the City exceeded nine thousand in number. This total would be somewhat augmented by the new building in Inner Temple and a few other private enclosures.

The reduction is strikingly large, and indicates that the improvement of London after the Great Fire was more important than has been generally conceded—much larger, in fact, than might have been anticipated; but I have been driven to accept these figures after perusal of the accounts of payments for staking out foundations, which apparently are complete.[1] Interest was high in Charles the Second's time, eight and nine per cent. being common, and the average of twelve years' purchase for house property (excluding sites) adopted in all three contemporary estimates printed in an earlier chapter is probably not far wrong. The flaw in all calculations is the impossibility of striking any but an approximate average of the cost.[2] Taking £300 as a flat rate of the actual cost of each of nine thousand houses, and two and a quarter as an average ratio of increase in building cost in 1914, we arrive at £6,075,000 as the burden borne by the citizens in rebuilding their houses expressed in recent money values—unhappily the price would need to be doubled again in 1920.

Funds from public sources collected, like the Coal Tax, over areas larger than that swept by the Fire restored the City's public buildings that were destroyed, and with the passage of many years St. Paul's Cathedral and the City churches also. State funds met State losses, as at the Custom House and elsewhere ; the Crown from its widespread revenues made good its devastated property in London ; the corporate gilds rebuilt their Halls, though often reduced thereby to penury ; but whence came all the money for rebuilding the thousands of private houses consumed in the Fire I frankly confess I do not know, unless it be the stocking hoard. The fact of the accomplishment remains. There was no scheme of public assistance.

It was an age when large affairs of commerce were conducted without banks, without insurance, without trust of one man in another ; a time when the careful merchant stored his money bags under his own roof, jealously guarding them against theft. The reader of Pepys is kept informed how his money bags expanded in bulk and in number, the golden guineas hoarded away,

---

[1] Guildhall Library MSS. 273 to 277.

[2] In a little handbook, Phillips's *The Purchaser's Pattern*, published in 1676 for guidance of builders and investors, example is made of the third sort of house, for important street frontages like Cheapside, four storeys high with additional garrets and cellars—a house, for instance, like the " Chained Swan " in Cheapside. It says the cost of such a building cannot exceed £400.

first in hundreds, then thousands—the bags of gold that he carefully removed to Woolwich away from the peril of the Fire, as no doubt did many another City dweller when the threat came near his home.

The merchant of Charles II. resided over his shop, his apprentices and family around him ; he laboured for long hours, piling up savings methodically. He lived simply, and had no extravagant tastes. He and his wife dressed plainly, having no desire to emulate the spend-thrift courtiers in the West. Nor did the trek of wealthy City men to pleasant country houses about East London, many of which survive in now inhospitable quarters, commence till half a century later. Wealth was restricted to two classes, the landowners and the merchants, between whom the cleavage was sharp ; where the landowner spent his money in ostentatious display, the merchant saved. Time and again, as the long experience of City loans has shown, the merchants' hoard bore the national burdens, and now it came out to restore the burnt city.

What these savings aggregated we cannot know. Nor can it be told what liquid investments were available. But though trade was kept together after the Fire, every indication we have shows that London passed through a stage of poverty and great distress. The City's own treasury was filled and emptied vicariously from day to day. In November, 1668, report was made to the Common Council that so low were the finances that the utmost care and industry would be required to stave off utter decay and ruin. " For what by misemployment of the treasure in the late troubles and other ill managements, as well by the extraordinary expenses occasioned by the Plague and Fire," said the reporters, the City's debt had increased, notwithstanding that its income had been augmented by large sources of revenue which must shortly be exhausted.[1]

Loans to the King were outstanding and could not be collected. A sum of £107,000 was due, secured on the Hearth Tax and the last two subsidies. An urgent petition to Charles for reimbursement declared that the Livery Companies and City financiers who had advanced the loans " are at this juncture greatly necessitated, and

----

[1] *Journal* 46, fo. 251.

Photo by Miles and Kaye

CORNER HOUSE IN WATLING STREET

This is in many respects the best surviving example of the "second sort" of house, three storeys high, for streets and lanes of note, authorised by the Rebuilding Act, 1667. It was erected about 1674

therefore very importunate to satisfy their great debts, and that they may be enabled to rebuild their Halls and houses, and repair their other great losses occasioned by the late dreadful fire." [1] The King blamed the tax-gatherers for remissness, and by Proclamation ordered the collection to be made. Alderman Backwell gave assistance at a critical moment by taking up debts from the King to the amount of £77,400.[2] There appears in the Cash Accounts after the Restoration, and repeated in the years following the Fire, an item, " Desperate Debts, £70,810 "—apparently levies made during the Parliament's ascendancy which were never recovered.

The City found itself unable to pay the Royal Aid over three years on the burnt parts of London, which would have amounted to £144,237 ; eventually a compromise was arrived at, the Hearth Tax, which by Royal Procla-mation issued after the Fire had been remitted for seven years, was restored, and the King released the debt.[3]

The City struggled along, importunate always but happily with credit sufficiently good for a loan, and never overtook its liabilities while the Coal Dues remained at the original shilling imposed—the only financial assist-ance granted by Parliament in this hour of great need. The shilling Coal Dues to Midsummer Day, 1670, brought in only £32,630. The expenditure to be borne from this source in five years for public improvements alone amounted to £95,333, with not a penny put aside for the larger schemes awaiting fruition.[4] The impossibility of restoring London's public buildings by a local shilling tax on coal was at length borne in upon the dull intelligence of Charles's Parliament, and by the Additional Building Act of 1670 the Coal Dues were raised from 1s. to 3s. a chaldron or ton, with a resulting large increase in revenue.[5] If grimy London to-day compares unfavourably with whiter Continental cities, let us remember that in honest truth it was rebuilt on coal, on the accumulations over long years of the tax which every sack brought up the

[1] *Journal* 46, fo. 146.
[2] *Ibid.*, fo. 252.
[3] The King to the Attorney-General, 1671, July 12.
[4] Guildhall Library MS. 273.
[5] *Statute* 22, *Chas. II.*, c. 11. Two years' receipts from the enlarged Coal Dues from Midsummer, 1670, brought £76,141 to the revenues.

Thames had to bear. It was coal that paid for the straightening and widening of the streets after the Fire, for levelling the contours, for the new wharves, for prisons and markets, for the Wren churches that still are the City's outstanding glory, for the Cathedral—for all of which we of this twentieth century are the inheritors. If ever a statue be raised to the builder of the new London, surely it should be a symbolical figure of Old King Cole.

There followed the first depression after the Fire a period of a few brief years, when rebuilding made rapid progress. Robert Hooke, the Surveyor, had little rest early or late from clamorous landowners and tradesmen soliciting him to set out their ground for them at once. Busy scenes in the town are suggested by a complaint by the Court of Aldermen, of frequent hurt and mischief done to persons and buildings by the cartage of timber of extraordinary length through the streets, and better care in supervision was enjoined.[1]   London, living largely upon the capital which flowed out with such prodigality, appeared outwardly to be prosperous   But such appearances were wholly illusory.   The truth is found beneath the gloss in the evidence taken by a Parliamentary Committee which sat in 1669 to inquire into the causes of the fall of rents and the decay of trade within the kingdom ; and in the terms of a Bill for the relief of sufferers by the Fire which next year was sent up by the Commons to the Lords, but there lapsed.   In the following winter the poor debtors who crowded the gaols in and about the City petitioned the House of Lords, alleging that by reason of the Plague, the late dreadful Fire and the Dutch wars many families were ruined and had become prisoners.[2]

At the close of the period 1668–73, when rebuilding had gone so far that the commercial needs of the capital were satisfied, trade was gravely depressed.   The closing of the Exchequer in January, 1672, involved in common ruin the great goldsmiths like Vyner and Backwell and the people who had money on loan or " running cashes " with them.   Dwellings and shops were unlet, wanting tenants.   The City's " freedom," guarded with so much jealous care, itself gravely handicapped the repeopling of

[1] *Repertory* 74, fo. 306*b*.
[2] House of Lords MSS. (*Hist. MSS. Comm.*, 8th Rep. 133–4, 150, 152).

the new streets, by preventing tradesmen setting up shops except such as were freemen by servitude or purchase. Liberty for artificers employed in the building trades had been wrung from the Companies by the public necessity, but there was no like privilege for the grocer, the ironmonger, the mercer, and the stationer. Though he came from no farther than Westminster, he was banned from the City unless he paid the large fee demanded for taking up the freedom, often as much as £30, or obtained favour by some powerful influence.

It is startling to learn that there should have been in 1672 whole streets of houses new built within the City standing uninhabited, " and no person so much as asks the price of any." So asserts a public writer, who compares this state of the City with the out-parishes, where houses were occupied as soon as built, trade flourished, and rents in many cases were even higher than about the Royal Exchange.[1] A return into Guildhall in February, 1673, gave the numbers of uninhabited houses in the City as 3,423, and of those unbuilt 961. Wren himself, reporting adversely upon a proposal to build over a burial ground, instanced " the great numbers of the rebuilt houses of London which are yet uninhabited." [2]

An address by the citizens to Parliament in the year 1674 sets out that houses in the City left empty and sites yet unbuilt upon numbered three thousand, being nearly one-sixth of the total in the City and Liberties. Large sums of money formerly employed in trade had been withdrawn for building; moreover, many City traders had settled in the out-parishes, and finding the burdens there lighter would not return.[3] Already a few of the wealthiest men were seeking acquaintance with the fashionable world out west, and the Corporation found it necessary to order that every Alderman should return with his family into the City, on pain of heavy penalties.

That year, 1674, the loyal Sir Robert Vyner being Lord Mayor, the City presented its freedom to the King

---

[1] *Proposals Moderately offered for the full Peopleing and Inhabiting the City of London,* by Londinophilos, 1672.
[2] Soane Museum MS., Court Orders, fo. 51.
[3] *Reasons Humbly offered to Parliament for the Abatement of the Proportion of the Assessment upon the City of London* (Broadside, undated). See also *Journal* 48, fos. 19, 38b.

and the Duke of York.*   The extravagance of the massive
gold casket enclosing the scroll inspired a furious lyrical
onslaught from Andrew Marvell—

> Whilst their churches unbuilt, and their houses undwelt,
>   And their orphans want bread to feed 'em,
> Themselves they've bereft of the little wealth left
>   To make an offering of their freedom.

"O ye addle-brained cits!" declares Marvell, who
dismisses them contemptuously—

> And now, worshipful sirs, go fold up your furs,
>   And Vyners turn again, turn again;
> I see who e'r's freed, you for slaves are decreed,
>   Until you burn again, burn again.[1]

Historians have dismissed the Great Fire of London
with a word of justifiable pride in those who bore the
burden uncomplaining.   There must have been a good
deal of the old Puritan spirit left in men who could meet
the stroke of adversity with such fortitude.   They rebuilt
London, to their enduring honour: yet let us not forget
the many whom disaster overwhelmed—indeed, they were
very many.   These fell back into obscurity, and there is
no chronicler of their story.   Some among them, merchants of substance before the Fire, passed into the
debtors' prisons of Ludgate and the Fleet or the Marshal-
sea, to end their days in misery.   A solitary cry of distress
rises from one "Philanthropus Philagathus"—his name
is unknown—who after nine years' endurance of struggle
and penury found means to print a six-page pamphlet.
He speaks of the harsh necessities of his fellows, "these
miserably singed citizens."   They had sunk with their
losses into despair of restoration.

Many souls, he declares, still laboured and groaned
under the mortifying effects of that dismal Fire of London,
and the burden of the pamphlet is an appeal to the compassion of the King and Parliament to have thought of
their distress.   "The aforesaid sufferers are, in another

---

[1] Marvell's texts are most corrupt, owing to his satires, copied in
manuscript in his lifetime, having passed from hand to hand and been
printed only posthumously.   It is difficult to credit the author of the
graceful lines on King Charles I.'s execution with such doggerel as this.

respect, worthy objects of your help and interposition, for the stopping of the merciless fury of their creditors upon them, whereof the prisons about London are severe testimonies; as if they had been men marked out by Divine Vengeance merely to become a prey to their cruelty, and this countenanced by the Law, because of Debt, without any reflection upon the inevitable hand of God that disabled them." He asked Parliament to take into consideration the sufferings of these forlorn men, to examine into their losses by the Fire, and to afford relief by recommending to the nation either a voluntary contribution or a one or two months' tax.[1] The appeal had as little effect as water falling upon stone.

Fears that trade would go elsewhere no doubt acted as the strongest incentive with both merchants and landowners in making the heavy sacrifices required, till London, save for its Cathedral and churches and the larger public buildings still unfinished, was itself again—a London far better adapted for commerce in every way than was the old City over which the flames had driven. I think that, on the whole, this red-brick London newly built was a pretty City, though differing entirely in character from its predecessor. Every picture and print we have suggests it was so. Look, for instance, at Scott's painting in the Guildhall Art Gallery of the river front at the Fleet. Dr. Charles Patin, a visitor from Paris five years after the Great Fire, thought the newly built area of the capital its most beautiful part, with its warm coloured brick and large uniform windows, well lighting the houses; and I can understand his appreciation.[2] Houses that survive from the time do not lack grace. It was formal, and by contrast plain—by contrast, that is, with the jumble of buildings of all heights and sizes and styles, the timber-framed fronts and gabled roofs, and all that amazing variety which successive centuries'

---

[1] Parliament had passed in 1671 an Act designed to relieve and release poor prisoners for debt, which specifically mentions, *inter alia*, those impoverished by "the sad and dreadful Fire." That it was wholly ineffective is sufficiently established by this petition four years later, even were there not abundant other evidence.

[2] *Relations historiques et curieuses de Voyages en Allemagne, Angleterre Holland, Bohème, etc.* Par C[harles] P[atin]. Rouen, 1676.

growth had given to Old London, and the Fire for the larger part swept away.

A City of nine thousand houses newly built rose out of the ruins. It seems an incredible thing, that not one architect's name is identified with it. At other times architects of genius have stamped their names upon their style and generation, as Inigo Jones, Vanbrugh, and the brothers Adam, but the greatest opportunity ever afforded in domestic architecture, at least in this country, by the rebuilding of London passed without producing any notable man. Sir Christopher Wren, of course, by his great conception of St. Paul's Cathedral, the City churches in their amazing variety, and other important structures, raised himself among the immortals. But Wren, engrossed with much other work, did not build nine thousand new dwelling houses, nor does the name survive of any designer. The bewildering riddle (for our generation) of a new City growing up, taking shape with thousands of houses in hundreds of streets and courts, yet with no visible hand moulding their form, has its solution in a remark made by Professor Beresford Pite,[1] that "there being no street architecture, there were no architects."

The epigram may be stretched beyond its legitimate meaning. The architect of the individual great house, by whatever name called, has always been with us, but of that alone. In mediæval times the owner of a narrow town site called in the mason to lay the foundations, the carpenter who knew how to construct the timber framework and roof, the plasterer to fill in the rough-cast outside, the bricklayer for the chimney, the tiler—and up went the house. Inigo Jones foresaw town architecture in London when, under King Charles I., he designed the laying out of Lincoln's Inn Fields on a concerted plan, every house of which should play its part in the conception of the whole. The model of the brick house had been evolved by Inigo Jones and John Webb, whose buildings display complete mastery in the use of brickwork for plain wall surfaces, square window openings with crowning cornices, and the traditional roof of steep pitch, covered

---

[1] In discussion of a paper on "The Rebuilding of London after the Great Fire," which I read before the Royal Institute of British Architects, March 4, 1918, printed in the Institute's *Journal* for May following.

with tiles; and the general principles they set out were followed with few modifications in the streets of houses erected by builders after the Great Fire.[1]

Where ashes and desolation had been a new capital of England rose up in a few years, the subject of admiration by contemporaries, better fitted, as I have said, for its purpose than was the old town it replaced, new built upon the inspiration of a genius already dead. The London Rebuilding Act of 1667 assumes an historical importance that rarely has been given to it, for by its restrictions and careful specifications, securing uniformity never sought before, it gave birth to town architecture.

Four classes of buildings only were allowed under that Act. Order was obtained; but it is folly to imagine that the new City represented only four houses in endless repetition. There was great variety in proportions and in simple decorative treatment. Rubbed brick for window dressings, as well as for other architectural features, had been introduced about the time of the Restoration, and its use was much extended. The Lord Mayor, Aldermen and Commons, in an Order of the 8th May, 1667, instructed the Surveyors to encourage all builders, " for ornament's sake," to employ rubbed brick in their ornaments and projections on the fronts of buildings; they were to make their plain surfaces of bricks neatly wrought or rubbed at discretion. Artistic care was lavished upon decorated doorways and the detail of eaves under the roofs. Balconies stood out to the high streets from the fronts of the larger houses—they were required by the Act. The signs again swung over the footways. The pretty casement windows of the old City were restored; though the sash frame was known, its use was not general till at least five-and-twenty years later. The bow

[1] Comparison may advantageously be made of the brick houses in Clifford's Inn, Fleet Street, which (except No. 13) date before the Great Fire, with the surviving buildings in the City erected immediately after that event, several of which are illustrated in this volume. I have given the ages of some of the Clifford's Inn buildings on page 164, *ante.* In another lawyers' resort, the Temple, are to be found the largest groups standing to-day of houses raised in the period 1667-90, in King's Bench Walk, Essex Court and elsewhere. They have the characteristic façade with the string course, but being designed for the special purpose of chambers opening upon a common central staircase, the plan is not typical of the citizens' houses.

shop-windows, so admirable a feature of eighteenth-century London, came in with the Georges.

Houses rose singly, as landowners or tradesmen were able to find money. With here a finished building standing alone and next to it uncovered sites, the town for some years wore the appearance of a crazy patchwork; but the work was good. The houses keyed correctly one to another in continuous streets, precaution having been taken that all breast-summers should range of an equal height house to house, breaking only where ordered by the Surveyors. Roofs in the same way were made uniform. Disputes arising from obstructed lights, gutters, and the like were decided by arbitration of the Aldermen. From the City raised after the Fire of 1666 has developed naturally the City of London as we know it to-day, fitted wholly for commerce.

It is profitless to dream of what might have been done had public and private wealth been commensurate with the unrivalled opportunity; of the long vistas that Wren would have given through the City's extent, his incomparable church towers and steeples brought out to wide streets, forming a glorious skyline. All things considered, the accomplishment was great. The dwelling houses were built in thousands, the impoverishment of the time being evident in their very plainness, most things being made subservient to utility; yet they mark an epoch which no student of historical architecture can affect to ignore. The style of the new London raised after the Fire merges into that of William and Mary's later years, so gradually, so imperceptibly, that often the point of departure is difficult to find, and reached its fullest possibilities of development in the richer architecture characteristic of Queen Anne. The bond was broken when Georgian builders seized upon larger opportunities of freedom, and to-day the influence is dead. This let us remember to their credit, that for a full century's growth the outward form of London was moulded by these builders of Charles II.—unhonoured, unknown to us even by name—who raised a City quickly and cheaply above the ruins of the great disaster.

The Fire was destined to exert a vast influence over the future welfare of London by the new spirit of citizenship it fostered ; indeed, may be said to have created. Hitherto the limit of the individual citizen's activity and vision had been the parish or the ward, and his thoughts seldom strayed beyond. The Lord Mayor, Aldermen and Commons in Common Council assembled governed London as one entity, but local affairs were delegated to parochial authorities in a large number of separate small parishes, loosely grouped in the separate wards. London had grown up without plan ; at least, with nothing more recent than the Roman forethought which some have seen in its roughly rectangular system.[1] The narrow streets and tortuous ways which sufficed for the thirteenth and fourteenth centuries equally sufficed in the seventeenth. Till the Fire came you may search the City archives in vain for mention of a street improvement. There was none ; nor do I find that the Common Council considered itself the guardian of the pride of London. It was to private benefactors, not to civic enterprise, that even public buildings were largely due—Newgate had been rebuilt by Richard Whittington's executors ; Ludgate debtors' prison was enlarged by Dame Agnes Foster ; Leadenhall was the gift of Simon Eyre ; the Royal Exchange was the business-like speculation of Sir Thomas Gresham ; and churches like St. Benet Sherehog and others perpetuated the names of pious donors. The absence of any deeply rooted communal feeling is oppressive. I have recalled in an earlier chapter a proclamation by the Lord Mayor two years after the Fire condemning in vigorous terms the " intolerable foulness " of the City streets— the streets, be it noted, of the City of which he was himself the powerful and representative head !

With the opportunity which the Great Fire brought of building a new and improved City, pride in London had a new birth. At last there was practicability of widening the old mediæval streets, of reducing the steep acclivities of hills up from the river, of clearing away many break-neck turnings. If much was left undone, owing to the poverty of the people, much also was accomplished, and the citizen began to think of London no longer in terms of his parish, but his vision foresaw a new and

---

[1] See the late Professor Haverfield's *Ancient Town Planning*.

magnificent capital of the Kingdom. The plans of Wren, Evelyn and others for a model City were freely discussed, and though found impossible at the time they awakened public interest. It was this newly-born pride in London which led the City to expend £80,500 in converting the stinking Fleet River into a wide and navigable " New Canal," up which laden barges passed to Holborn Bridge, and to sacrifice the Thames frontage from The Tower to the Temple for the purposes of a public riverside quay.

The sanitary improvement of London which followed the Great Fire was even more beneficial to the health of the population than was the rebuilding. Hitherto each parish in the separate wards, acting through its constables, scavengers and rakers had had separate responsibility, an arrangement that with little modification had come down from mediæval times. The Rebuilding Act of 1667 changed the system by authorizing the Lord Mayor, Aldermen and Commons to nominate certain Commissioners for sewers and paving, who should exercise sole powers for seven years, or until the City's rebuilding be finished.

The amending Act of 1671 is London's sanitary charter.[1] It extended these powers in perpetuity ; it created the body so nominated the sole authority for laying out and maintaining sewers and drains, with responsibility for their scouring, and for ordering the paving and cleansing of streets ; they were to charge the cost upon all houses within the City and its Liberties in proportion to the benefits received, and to make assessments for a sanitary tax upon the several wards from time to time. London at last had an all-embracing, effective and central sanitary authority—the body favourably known for more than two centuries thereafter as the Commissioners of Sewers.[2] From that time the Fellowship of Carmen undertook the sweeping and cleansing of the streets and the carting to the laystalls of all dirt and filth. The carmen by loudly knocking a wooden clapper proclaimed their presence in the streets, whereupon residents were required to bring out to the carts all refuse from their houses. I am not

[1] *Stat.* 22 & 23, *Chas. II.*, *c.* 17, " An Act for the better paving and cleansing the streets and sewers in and about the City of London."

[2] This body, nominated by the Corporation but independent of it (more so in theory than in practice), came to an end in 1898, when certain of its powers were given back to the Corporation.

Photo by Mr. Lionel Gowing

CORNER HOUSE IN MILK STREET, CHEAPSIDE

This plain but characteristic building dates within a few years of the Great Fire

saying that the conditions prevailing after the Great Fire would be considered satisfactory to-day, but they were an immense advance upon the previous state.

Those seers who looked into the future and could find only decay were happily confounded. Trade came back into the City. Merchants flocked from Gresham House to the newly-built Royal Exchange. The mercers, having tried their fortunes west, hastened to return, and finding Paternoster Row then largely occupied by the booksellers, they swarmed like bees upon Ludgate Hill. Bucklersbury, rebuilt, was again the druggists' centre. Moorfields was covered with houses. The town, too, spread over Spitalfields, on land which had belonged to the old St. Mary's Spital, where the weavers especially congregated. A residential neighbourhood grew out towards St. Giles-in-the-Fields, and eastward to Ratcliffe. Large grounds surrounding the houses of noble families on both sides of the Strand and in Holborn after the Fire began to disappear, and streets bearing their former owners' names are with us to this day. London City had new neighbours about it, but all fears of a general exodus of trade were soon dissipated. Its accessibility to the shipping below bridge and to the Thames, which right through the Stuart era remained the chief highway of London and the carriage way of its commerce, gave to the City advantages which no other spot, then or since, could rival.

Few people realize that Wren's project of a Thames-side quay was ever carried out, still fewer how long it persisted as part of the new London. To-day's straight frontage of the Thames below Blackfriars is a consequence of the laying out of the quay, which made considerable encroachment upon the river foreshore, the land so taken being granted by the King to the City Corporation, except between Baynard's Castle and Paul's Wharf, where the gift was to St. Paul's Cathedral.[1] Most else of Wren's model plan was sacrificed, but this was retained, and the Additional Building Act of 1670 expressly directed that construction of the quay should forthwith be proceeded with, and such obstructions as already had begun to jeopardize its continuance removed. It is shown

[1] *State Papers* (*Domestic*), 1671, p. 502. In maps before the Fire a broken line of frontage is shown.

complete and clear in Ogilby's map of London in 1677. For upwards of a hundred years the quay remained a vital feature of the waterside quarter, lacking, it is true, the architectural dignity that Wren would have given to it, and not until the approach of the nineteenth century were the encroachments upon it by cranes, sheds, and brick houses at all considerable.[1] Once tolerated, they rapidly increased, till in 1821 Parliament ill-advisedly passed a short Act whitewashing the offenders, and the great conception of a public walk from The Tower to the Temple was buried for all time, though a later generation of engineers was inspired by it to lay out, farther west, the Victoria Embankment.

The Fire cleared the City of the pestilential wooden houses and general insanitary conditions that for centuries had made London the abiding place of Plague ; it brought better dwellings ; but in other respects the lessons taught were learnt but slowly. In a proposal to Parliament that the City authorities should have power to employ such and so many persons as they should think fit for the more speedy quenching of fires we have, perhaps, the germ of the London Fire Brigade. Fire plugs were for the first time inserted in the street water-pipes. An Act of Common Council in 1668 provided for better watches being kept, and larger stores of buckets, squirts, ladders, and pick-axes assembled at central places—merely the old appliances, and more of them. The Englishman showed no inventiveness. Van der Heide in 1670 devised the hose and suction pipe for the fire-engine, and the air chamber came into use by or before 1684, when it is mentioned by Perrault. Loftingh, a Dutch merchant resident in London, added the wire strengthening of the suction hose. It was not until early in the eighteenth century that Newsham in London made the first really successful fire-engine for the City's protection.

Hamburg, taught by London's experience, established its Municipal Fire Casse in 1667, but London still lagged behind. An Elizabethan craft gild at Exeter, which required payment of a penny from all members when the house of one of their number was burnt, affords perhaps

---

[1] See Horwood's Map, drawn in 1799 and engraved at the expense of the Phœnix Fire Office.

the earliest example of fire insurance. In 1635, and again
in 1638, citizens of London had petitioned King Charles I.
for a patent of monopoly to insure houses against fire;
and Wren's adoption in his model City of a site for an
insurance office showed that the subject was always in
mind. Yet nothing effectual was done for fourteen years
after the Great Fire, though furtive efforts were made
privately. Nicholas Barebone, a most active builder in
London, set up an office, " whereby," said Luttrell, " he
is likely to gain vastly," [1] and certain business men of
" the Insurance Office for Houses on the Back of the
Royal Exchange," [2] established about 1680, claimed
rivalry in having originated the idea. The Lord Mayor,

MEDAL COMMEMORATING THE PLAGUE AND THE FIRE.

Aldermen and Commons proposed in the following year a
municipal scheme to indemnify policy holders against
losses by fire at rates lower than those charged by the
private office, which were $2\frac{1}{2}$ per cent. of annual rent for
brick houses, and 5 per cent. for timber-framed houses,
the accepted valuation being that the rent represented
one-tenth the value of the fee. They designed to set
apart £100,000 for a fund. The Courts stifled the project, holding that the City charters gave no power to
transact such business. The high rates indicate the
still grave perils of fire. The Phœnix Fire Office was
located at the Rainbow Tavern in Fleet Street as early as
1682.

A medal commemorating both the Plague and the

[1] Luttrell's *Brief Relation*, i, 135.
[2] See a rare tract, " Whether it be to the Interest of the City to insure
houses from fire," 1681 (Guildhall Library, M. 4, 5).

Fire was struck, of which the only known copy is in the British Museum.*

The City raised the Fire Monument, and then, in a moment of maddened popular frenzy, inscribed upon it words attributing the conflagration of London to Popish treachery.   There had been erected on the site of Farynor's house in Pudding Lane, where the Fire started, a quite unpretentious building, which was chosen for a like distinction.   The original stone that for many years was set into the wall of the house, deeply cut so that all who passed might read, is in the Guildhall Museum, to which it was presented by Messrs. King and Son in 1876, when the relic was brought up after concealment in the cellar. Its violent message, still legible, runs—

HERE BY $\overset{E}{Y}$ PERMISSION OF HEAVEN HELL BROKE LOOSE UPON THIS PROTESTANT CITY FROM THE MALICIOUS HEARTS OF BARBAROUS PAPISTS, BY $\overset{E}{Y}$ HAND OF THEIR AGENT HUBERT, WHO CONFESSED, AND ON $\overset{E}{Y}$ RUINES OF THIS PLACE DECLARED THE FACT, FOR WHICH HE WAS HANGED, (VIZT.) THAT HERE BEGAN THAT DRED -FULL FIRE, WHICH IS DESCRIBED AND PERPETUATED ON AND BY THE NEIGHBOURING PILLAR.

ERECTED   ANNO   168 [1, I] N THE MAJORALTIE OF S^R PATIENCE WARD K^T.

CHAPTER XVII

THE CHURCH SETTLEMENT

ALTHOUGH flame overtake both fabric and parsonage, there is work for the Church which cannot cease. Death came; the parishioner had the right of burial in his parish church; and so one finds in September after the Fire, in October and November, and on into succeeding years, those repeated references which occur in the registers—at St. Bride's, Oct. 21, "Mr. Christopher Riche, in ye church porche, because ye body of ye Churche was not cleere;" at St. Magnus the Martyr, May 4, 1667, "Hanna daughter of Mr. Francis Marshall in ye North Isle of our late burnt Church;" at St. Michael Cornhill, May 31, "Thomas Kelke, brazier, by the old vestry door." Then a year later one may read—

Ann Yard was buryed in the burring place whare before the lat dreedfull fire the lat church of St. Pancras Soper Lane stood.

These though the churches were but four walls open to the sky. Weddings might be solemnized elsewhere, the baptismal rite be performed amidst brighter surroundings than the fire-scarred ruins, but the London citizen in his last resort returned to his own parish.

One observance these sad funerals lacked. Hanna Marshall being laid in the grave, the register tells that there was " no knell, the bells being all molten." London had this unaccustomed quietness for years after the Great Fire, when the churches were being rebuilt. Though in many cases the gaunt stone towers stood erect above the ruined City, the bells had crashed down, to be recovered only as broken and fused metal.

A few churches, or parts of them, by various expedients

were made serviceable. The stone walls of St. Michael Wood Street were strong and intact—strong enough to bear a temporary roof thrown across them, and the church continued to be used for divine worship. A similar use was attempted of St. Mildred Bread Street and St. Mary Magdalen Old Fish Street, but owing to weakness of the ruins the purpose had to be abandoned.[1] St. Sepulchre by Newgate, standing at the Fire's edge, was one of the few churches capable of repair. The parish is curiously situated, four parts being within the City and a fifth part in Middlesex. The Vicar, Dr. William Bell, himself spent £200 in making accommodation for his flock within the roofless walls, and he petitioned the King and Council for a benevolence. They had lost most of their rents by the Fire, and could scarcely keep their poor from starving. Other City parishes being completely burnt out, many of their poor came to St. Sepulchre's, and the burden was thus almost insupportable.[2] The churchwardens went on with repairs without waiting for the larger schemes of church building to materialize.*

The parishioners of St. Mildred Poultry found a refuge in Grocers Hall, partly left standing, though the Grocers were doubtful as to the propriety of this conversion for worship of their meeting and feasting place. They sought the advice of the Bishop of London. Learning not only that he thoroughly approved the proposal, but that the Company's acquiescence would be agreeable to the King, they readily gave their consent, and service was held there for many months thereafter. The Salters Company permitted the use by the parishioners of St. Swithin's, by London Stone, of the Long Parlour of Salters Hall, which had escaped destruction, while they were without a church. Even marriages took place there, and these continued to be solemnized in Salters Hall till 1679, when the rite was transferred to the new church.[3] The Stationers Company, having built their Hall by Ludgate Hill, granted its use for divine worship by the parishioners of St. Martin's. Brewers Hall, in Addle Street, served a like purpose for the parish of St. Mary Aldermanbury.

[1] *Victoria County Hist. London*, i, 340.
[2] *State Papers* (*Domestic*), 1666–7, p. 172.
[3] St. Swithin's Marriage Registers, 1667, April 16, *passim*.

A Christian city must needs rebuild its churches, and projects for this end were elaborated contemporaneously with those for restoring the City; but the whole matter was extremely complicated. Pious donors in mediæval times had served God by multiplying churches, with the consequence that the City and its Liberties were divided into no fewer than one hundred and nine parishes. The excessive number of churches and small area of the parishes made administration difficult. There were rights of patrons, of impropriators, rectors, vicars, the jurisdiction of ecclesiastical courts, all in a confused tangle. The thirteen " Peculiars " in the City of London acknowledged the jurisdiction, not of London, but of Canterbury. Wren, perhaps dismayed, as well he might be, proposed to cut the knot by ignoring vested rights, by placing the patronage of City churches in the Lord Mayor and Corporation, and reducing the number of parishes to thirty-nine by amalgamating those of smallest area. He would have built few but magnificent churches.[1] A scheme on these lines was drafted, but the project was broken by the powerful interests whose rights it assailed.

The number of thirty-nine new churches was retained in the Rebuilding Act which became law in 1667, but the ecclesiastical clauses of that statute were never operative. The Act had one fatal omission. It did not decide what churches should be rebuilt, leaving instead a choice to be made with the advice and consent of the Archbishop of Canterbury and the Bishop of London. A list of proposed churches was drawn up. But the clash of conflicting interests and jealousies of neighbouring parishes made any amicable settlement impossible. No one was satisfied. Protest meetings were held; the aid of the Corporation was invoked; and an organized campaign took place in the winter of 1669, as a result of which a committee of parishioners consulted the Bishop of London concerning the drafting of a new bill.[2] The fruits of the agitation are to be seen in the City to-day. Fifty-one churches were built under the Additional Building Act of 1670 instead of thirty-nine, and the churches were named in the statute. Each parish without a church was annexed to a church

[1] Tanner MSS., Bodleian Lib. 142, fos. 118–20.
[2] *Journal* 46, fo. 132b.

parish, but for ecclesiastical purposes only. The full number of parishes was retained, each with its separate churchwardens and officers. In our own time the destruction of several of Wren's churches has made amalgamation still closer, and so it comes about that to-day Prebendary Ingram, Rector of St. Margaret Lothbury, has the assistance of sixteen churchwardens—a congregation in itself—for he is not only rector of St. Margaret's, but of seven other annexed parishes.

Four years thus passed before a settlement of Church affairs was reached, and still the question of tithe was outstanding. Lacking a controlling authority, the City churchyards became almost derelict, especially those where rebuilding of the church was abandoned. Such sheltered spots by night were a resort for thieves and footpads ; by day the City housewives hung out their washing over the graves.* The Archbishop of Canterbury and Lords of the Council wrote to the Lord Mayor complaining that smiths' forges and other artificers' shops, and even alehouses, were kept within the sacred ruins of the burnt churches. Many thefts had taken place in the confusion of the Fire, and the Lord Mayor and Aldermen were required to obtain inventories of all communion plate, vestments, records, and movable goods that remained to each parish. The plate, books, bells, and lead of St. Michael Paternoster Royal were purloined by the churchwardens after the Fire. At St. Pancras Soper Lane a churchwarden disappeared with the plate. Sir Joseph Childs seized part of the site of the east end of St. Botolph Billingsgate, and defied ejectment. A mason rebuilding by St. Thomas the Apostle encroached on part of the parsonage land.[1]

The City possessed in St. Paul's a Cathedral, woefully riven and torn, but still capable of temporary use. Wren, at the King's command, hastily fitted up a choir and auditory within the desolate ruins.[2] The west end by the great portico was chosen as the safest place ; the east of the Cathedral and the high altar had been left a mass of tumbled wreckage where the floor fell into St. Faith's, and the walls threatened collapse. The great architect foresaw that a new Cathedral must be built, and at once prepared

[1] *Victoria County Hist. London*, i, 342.
[2] Order in Council, 1667, Jan. 15.

plans. Against his advice and strong protests, a patching of the venerable fabric went on under the direction of a Commission appointed for repairs. But Wren's prevision was soon justified. Sancroft, on the 25th April, 1668, summoned him hurriedly to London from Oxford. "What you whispered in my ear," wrote the Dean, "at your last coming hither, is now come to pass. Our work at the west end of St. Paul's is fallen about our ears. Your quick eye discerned the walls and pillars gone off their perpendiculars, and I believe other defects, too, which are now exposed to every common observer. The third pillar from the west, at the south side, which they had new cased with stone, fell with a sudden crash ; the next, bigger than the rest, stood alone, certain to fall, yet so unsafe that they dared not venture to take it down. In short, the whole work of Inigo Jones was so overloaded as to threaten a total wreck." [1]

In this temporary chapel Dean Sancroft preached before the King a sermon on the Fire on the anniversary of 1667. St. Paul's had become perilous to life, and as a place of worship had to be abandoned. Still courage was lacking to take the decision to build a new Cathedral, and five more years passed before Letters Patent were issued for that purpose. The fabric rose slowly, dominating London with more majesty than ever Old St. Paul's, the work of many periods and influences, had done. Much stone material of the mediæval building is incorporated in Wren's Cathedral.[2] Its cost was £747,600, five-sixths of which was borne by the Coal Dues, so the grime of London which since has clustered thickly about it has but come home. Wren accepted the trust in a spirit of humble piety, without thought of reward ; there is a familiar story of Sarah Duchess of Marlborough, annoyed at a bill of charges, reminding her architect sharply that the great Dr. Wren was content to be dragged up in a basket three or four times a week to the top of St. Paul's, and at hazard of life, for a fee of £200 a year. This was, in fact, all that he

[1] Elmes, *Memoirs of Wren*, p. 245.
[2] This was plainly disclosed in the repairs undertaken of recent years on the great piers of St. Paul's. Behind the facing of Portland stone of the pier of the south transept arch is a core of small rubble of Kentish rag, chalk, and five or six other kinds of stone evidently taken from the ruins after the Great Fire.

received for his Cathedral, but for his City churches his fees were £13,000, a small enough sum for so superb an amount of work.

When industries and population returned to the river-side, the parishioners of Allhallows-the-More solved the problem of facilities for worship by building in August, 1669, upon their ample churchyard, what was described as "a shed or tabernacle." It was the forerunner of a system that became general in the ruined areas. For the purpose, £100 of trust money and the proceeds of the sale of melted lead and bell-metal were employed, the intention being that in the tabernacle the parishioners and their neighbours should worship God till such time as a new church was ready. A door made in the churchyard wall gave entrance; there were pews for the churchwardens, sidesmen, and constables, and forms for seating the con-gregation. The tabernacle was used for worship and as a vestry room for years thereafter.[1]

Another source remained from which the State Church might be served when the rebuilding and repopulation of the City far outpaced the progress made with the churches. It had troubled the French Ambassador Cominges, himself a devout Catholic and Knight of the Holy Ghost, to under-stand how the State should tolerate sixty religions. "To mention all the sects with which the realm is infested would be impossible," says he in the *Relation*. "Studying this question with a very clever man, who had been formerly a Professor at Leyden, called Soudan, we numbered sixty different ones; hence in the City of London those several places where people meet and pray God, each according to how the Devil inspires him, although these poor fanatics attribute all their unruly movements to the inspiration of the Holy Ghost." [2] King Charles had no qualms of con-science in their repression.

The law against conventicles had been little observed in the general distress after the Fire, for it was deemed hard to hinder men suffering under a common affliction from worshipping God in any way they chose, when there were no churches, and in many cases no ministers remaining to tend to their welfare. The law was strengthened by

[1] *Vestry Minutes*, 1669, *Aug.* 3, passim.
[2] *Relation de l'Angleterre en l'année* 1666.

the Conventicles Act of 1670.   Its arbitrary powers were barbarously carried out in London by a military force, to the terror of many people and the death of some.[1]   The dissenters were scattered and their meeting houses confiscated, and by an Order in Council of the 15th June, 1670, eight conventicles were listed, which thenceforward were utilized for divine worship by the Established Church, until such time as the parish churches were ready.   Humphrey Henchman, Bishop of London, was authorized to appoint an orthodox minister to each, and acted with such expedition that worship commenced on the following Sunday.

These converted churches were as follows :—

1. Fisher's Folly, in Bishopsgate Street.[2]

2. In Hand Court, Bishopsgate Street, a meeting house built for Vincent's Congregation.

3. A large room built in St. Michael's Alley, Cornhill.

4. Mr. Doolittle's meeting house in Mugwell Street.

5. Cockpit in Jewin Street, used as Grimes's meeting house.

6. Mr. Wood's meeting house in Blackfriars.

7. Four rooms in Salisbury Court, Fleet Street, in possession of John Fowl, schoolmaster.

8. In New Street, four rooms, with pews and benches.

Of these eight conventicles, only the last (rebuilt in 1748) survives to-day as the Moravian Chapel in Fetter Lane.[3]   The original entrance was by Goldsmith Court, Great New Street.   The conventicle belonged to the wife of the Rev. John Turner, who had been ejected in 1662 from the living of Sudbury, in Middlesex, and afterwards preached at his wife's chapel, ministering to his congregation there throughout both the Plague and the Fire.

[1] Burnet's *History of His Own Times*.

[2] So called mockingly after Jasper Fisher, citizen and goldsmith, a man of no particular birth or fortune, and encumbered by debt, who built for himself this sumptuous dwelling-house.   It afterwards became the residence of the Earl of Oxford, and later of the Earl of Devonshire, whose name is still preserved in Devonshire Square, which occupies the site.

[3] The Stamford Street Chapel and Blackfriars Mission (the Rev. J. W. Piggott, pastor) to-day maintains unbroken the tradition of another of the conventicles existing at the time of the Great Fire, being an amalgamation of Nathaniel Vincent's congregation in 1666 at Farthing Alley, Southwark, afterwards St. Thomas's Chapel, and the Princes Street Chapel, Westminster, where Thomas Cawton preached in 1670.

Turner was driven out by the bishop, and not until many years later was the chapel restored to its rightful owners.

The needs of the Church in London, however, were but inadequately served by this method of robbing the dissenting Peter to pay the Established Paul. A majority of these seized conventicles lay about the fringe of the fire-swept area. A Commission consisting of the Archbishop of Canterbury, the Bishop of London and the Lord Mayor appointed by the Act of 1670, decided as a first step to give temporary accommodation by raising ten tabernacles. The parishes chosen were St. Michael Queenhithe, St. Bride, Allhallows-the-More (already built, the money being repaid), St. Michael Crooked Lane, Christ Church, St. Alban Wood Street, St. Margaret Lothbury, St. Anne and St. Agnes, St. Margaret New Fish Street, and St. Mary Magdalen Old Fish Street. The scheme was financed by a grant from the Coal Dues. The tabernacles were estimated to cost £150 each, and in October, 1670, a sum of £1500 was allotted for the purpose. The actual cost greatly varied; at St. Mary Abchurch it was £265, at St. Pancras Soper Lane £50 only.

Where two or more parishes were united, the tabernacles were commonly erected on the site of an abandoned church, failing this in a churchyard. They were timber built on a brick base, and in some cases were tiled and paved, the fittings being quite simple, in harmony. Pulpit and canopy at St. Mary Aldermary were furnished for £5, communion table £1, and reading desk and Clerk's desk £2 10s. The provision of a tabernacle at St. Michael Queenhithe was delayed owing to the piles of materials which " the scandalous demeanour " of the churchwardens permitted to encumber the ground. So well did these structures serve their purpose that ultimately twenty more were raised in other parishes. Few people who accept the somewhat contemptuous term " tin tabernacle " for a makeshift church as a modern witticism know that the name had its origin in these temporary structures built for the worship of London citizens after the Great Fire.

The clergy's maintenance was a problem that in the same year was pressing for solution. Fault for the bitterness it entailed cannot be attributed to exactions demanded by the clergy themselves. At the time of the Great Fire the London parochial clergy were receiving their incomes under an Act of 1545, a reduced tithe being paid proportionate to the rental value of property in the parishes. A commutation of tithe was accepted in principle, a schedule being proposed by the clergy themselves which would, in fact, have brought them less income than was agreed upon at a conference of the Aldermen and City parsons at Guildhall in December.[1] Both scales, however, made an advance on the payments before the Fire ; the parishioners were the poorer by that calamity, and they had reason for grave discontent over the manner in which the City cures were served. The Great Ejectment of 1662 drove from the Church many of the most earnest and devout of her ministers. Fifty-five of the clergy of City parishes alone surrendered their offices rather than submit in a matter of conscience. Pluralists and placemen crowded to accept the vacant livings, and when the Fire overwhelmed London there was scarcely a City rector or vicar who had not duties to fulfil elsewhere that extra emoluments might be earned. For periods—and often long periods—the entire care of the City parish was left to an underpaid curate, whose lean habit and threadbare coat testified to the gnawing poverty which was the lot of the less favoured servants of the Church.

Dr. Brydoke, one of the worst of the pluralists, while holding the City living of St. Bartholomew Exchange, value £199, was also Dean of Salisbury, rector of Stands, Lancashire, value £400, and Prebendary of Windsor. Dr. Cartwright, who received £72 with the living of St. Thomas the Apostle, also held a living at Barking, Essex, worth £400 a year. The parson of St. Antholin's held two livings in distant Yorkshire ; Mr. Booker, with St. Michael Queenhithe (£60) had as well a living in Norfolk ; Dr. Robert Breton, of St. Martin Ludgate (£136) was also vicar of Deptford. Dr. Thomas Hodges triplicated the parts of Dean of Hereford, Vicar of Kensington, and rector of St. Peter Cornhill. The last brought in £155, and it was complained against him that he allowed a very worthy minister only £30 a year and the perquisites for officiating for him at St. Peter's.

[1] See printed broadside in *State Papers Chas. II.*, Vol. 280, No. 152.

Still grosser was the scandal of the appropriated livings. Allhallows-the-Less, value £72 a year, was held by impropriators, two maiden ladies who allowed but £8 a year to the minister. St. Gregory by Paul's, for its misfortune, had as impropriators the Minor Canons of St. Paul's. They took the complete tithe, £80, in fine and rent, not allowing a penny for a preacher, whom the parishioners had to find and pay.[1]

As is customary in such matters, the settlement effected by the London Clergy Act of 1671 was a compromise.[2] That Act dealt only with the consumed parishes, then regrouped around fifty-one churches still to be built. In no case did rector or vicar receive more than £200 a year ; only in six parishes—St. Dunstan-in-the-East, St. Sepulchre, Allhallows-the-More, Christ Church, St. Mary-at-Hill, and St. Mary-le-Bow—was that sum paid ; in thirty-two others the income was less than £150 ; in eight parishes it was but £100. Rector or vicar received this fixed annual sum, assessed on all properties within his parish, in commutation of the tithe hitherto paid by householders (or owners). Glebe and perquisite gifts were not touched. The fact that appeal lay to the Lord Mayor and Aldermen alone did not conduce to the smooth working of the Act. Its inequity was apparent before long. The continuous increase in the value of City properties made the burden ever lighter to the parishioners, and the reduced purchasing power of money ever more prejudicial to the City parson, till a protesting rector of St. Michael Bassishaw could say truthfully that the Act " does not place a clergyman, in point of income, on a level with a clerk in a counting-house, or a foreman in a reputable shop, and scarce raises him above the mechanic who maintains himself by the labour of his hands." So grave became the injustice that in the year 1804 the sums given in commutation of tithe were readjusted by Parliament,[3] no incumbent thereafter receiving less than £200 a year, and the highest income

---

[1] *A Brief Account of the Maintenances arising by Tithe, Glebe, and other Profits to the Several Ministers of the Parish Churches demolished by the late Dreadful Fire in London.* 1670. (Broadside.)

[2] *Stat.* 22 & 23 *Chas. II.*, c. 15 : " An Act for the better settlement of the Maintenance of the Parsons, Vicars, and Curates in the parishes of the City of London burnt in the late dreadful Fire there."

[3] *Stat.* 44, *Geo. III.*, c. 89.

NO. 34 GREAT TOWER STREET

Circa 1670.   A fine example near The Tower of the fourth sort of building, or
City merchant's mansion house "of the greatest bigness," authorised by the
Rebuilding Act. 1667

paid was £366. A parish with City property, St. Mary Aldermanbury, derives sufficient income from this one source to relieve the parishioners of any charge.

It has proved unfortunate that the arrangements made after the Fire did not comprise the unconsumed City parishes, although the clergy sought their inclusion. As a consequence, tithe disputes still occasionally arise.

The Dutch community in London found their church at Austin Friars unharmed, but suffered much from the Fire and persecution; diminished collections at their worship indicate how severe were their losses.[1] The French Church in Threadneedle Street was entirely destroyed. Lewis Herault, the pastor, petitioned the King to grant him the next vacant prebend at Windsor or Westminster; he was grown old, and his flock was brought so low by the Fire that they could no longer afford him the small allowance on which he and his family had subsisted.[2] The French Protestant congregation, finding the nave and tower of St. Martin Orgar, by Cannon Street, capable of repair, obtained a lease of the ruin, which was confirmed by Act of Parliament, and converted it into a place of worship for their use. Charles, quite gratuitously, offered the church of St. Nicholas Cole Abbey to the Lutherans in London, to be rebuilt for their congregation, but this being a parish church appointed to continue, the Court of Aldermen referred the Swedish Resident back to the King, and instead a grant of Holy Trinity-the-Less was made.[3]

Long before the Fire the Jews had drifted East from the neighbourhood to which, in mediæval times, they had given the name that survives in Old Jewry and in the Church of St. Laurence Jewry, and their residential quarter and synagogues in Leadenhall Street and St. Helen's were beyond the area reached by the flames.[4]

The year 1670 witnessed a commencement being made with the great task of rebuilding the City churches, the impost upon coal, which originally had been quite inadequate and was then trebled, providing substantially

[1] Moens, *Registers of Dutch Church at Austin Friars*.
[2] *State Papers (Domestic)*, 1666–7, pp. 385, 461.
[3] *Ibid.*, 1668–9, p. 369. *Repertory*, 74, fo. 105.
[4] A Dutch writer (*Londens Puyn-Hoop*) mentions a Jews' synagogue in Coleman Street which escaped the Fire, but no record of this survives in the community.

the whole of the cost.   Fourteen churches were begun that year, and of these St. Vedast Foster Lane preserves much of the walls that stood throughout the Great Fire ; they were recased with Portland stone.   St. Christopher-le-Stocks (afterwards removed to give place to the Bank of England) was treated in a like manner.   But in most cases the demolition begun by the flames was completed, and Wren's fabrics rose from new foundations.   Exceptions were St. Mary-le-Bow, which stands in part upon the old Norman crypt, St. Michael Queenhithe and St. Olave Jewry ; and from what is visible of St. Bride below ground I fancy that there, too, Wren utilized portions of the mediæval lower courses.   Materials from the old churches were largely used in the rebuilding.

Fourteen churches had been completed by January, 1678, apart from St. Sepulchre's and St. Mary Woolnoth, repaired.   Five others were far advanced.   St. Mary-le-Bow, St. Olave Jewry, and St. Nicholas Cole Abbey were " near paid off ; " at St. Laurence Jewry by Guildhall, St. Magnus the Martyr, a conspicuous landmark by London Bridge,[1] St. Bride and St. Stephen Walbrook work was still being done on the towers ; the rebuilding of Christ Church and five others had been begun.[2]   The co-operation of the parishioners was sought.   Each parish was required to raise and deposit with the Commissioners a sum of £500 before the building contract was given out, this money being ultimately repaid.

In a few instances large sums were forthcoming as donations.   The construction of St. Mary-le-Bow, Cheapside, was accelerated by a gift made by Lady Williamson of £2,000, and with other gifts the subscription was £2,385. For rebuilding the nave of St. Mary Aldermary, Henry Rogers left £5,000 in his will ; the present tower was afterwards added, when Wren utilized the lower courses left undisturbed, the stones of which still bear on their surface marks of the Fire.   Sir John Langham gave £500 towards

---

[1] A clause in the Additional Building Act was drafted in the Lords for converting the sites of the riverside churches and churchyards of St. Magnus, St. Michael Queenhithe, St. Botolph Billingsgate, and Allhallows the More and Less into public store-yards for coal and other fuel, the parishes having power to acquire burial places at a convenient distance from the City ; but this was not accepted.

[2] *Victoria County Hist. London*, p. 342.

St. Michael Cornhill. At St. Stephen Walbrook the Grocers Company, patrons of the living, provided the wainscoting and pews—against the wishes of Wren, be it said. The Court of Aldermen found the guarantee money for St. Laurence Jewry and other churches. St. Benet Fink had a benefactor giving £1000. There were gifts to the Church in kind, like that by a Tredegar ironmaster, William Morgan, whose contribution towards St. Mildred Poultry was one ton of iron.

By the year 1683 London possessed twenty-five of its new churches, which were in use for worship, seventeen others were nearly finished.[1] Often the progress made in building overran the funds available, and money had to be borrowed at high rates of interest on the security of the Coal Dues; for St. Paul's no less a sum than £83,744 was paid as interest on loans. Seventeen years had then passed since the Great Fire, and in addition to three churches but lately begun there were still six others—St. Margaret Lothbury, Allhallows Lombard Street, St. Andrew-by-the-Wardrobe, St. Michael Paternoster Royal, St. Mary Somerset, and St. Margaret Pattens—awaiting to be commenced from the foundations. Facts like these, added to what has been said concerning the time required for the public buildings and streets of new houses, make ridiculous the claim set out upon the Fire Monument, that the City was restored complete in a state of greater magnificence than before in the short space of three years. Fine as the Monument is as an architectural memorial of the greatest disaster that has befallen the capital, its inscriptions making impossible claims and attributing the Fire to the fury of Papists [2] have been distinctly unfortunate.

London's streets were populated and commerce flowed again in full tide while still churches and towers continued to rise beneath piles of scaffolding. A city of brick replaced a city of timber, but its public edifices and churches were for the larger part of stone. In calm and storm, as year

[1] For list of churches and dates of their construction see Appendix III.
[2] The House of Commons, not to be outdone by the City in its clamour against the Roman Catholics, voted the following resolution on the 10th January, 1680: "That it is the opinion of this House that the City of London was burnt in the year 1666 by the Papists; designing thereby to introduce arbitrary power and popery into this Kingdom." (*House of Commons Journals*, ix, 703.)

succeeded year and one decade followed another, a cease-
less procession of ships, deeply laden, sailed along the
south coast of England to the mouth of the Thames and
up the river, depositing upon its quays the stones of which
were fashioned those structures that to-day are the pride
and glory of the City.   They were quarried at Portland,
in those echoing galleries which, after centuries of use, are
still inexhaustible.   It might well have seemed that Wren
ruled over that vassal land, and willed it to his bidding.

Si monumentum requiris, circumspice.   If you would
see Sir Christopher Wren's monument you must look
around, not alone the vast spaces of his Cathedral, but the
whole vista of the City which his genius has adorned.
The domed church of St. Stephen Walbrook, the unrivalled
steeple of St. Bride's, the tower of St. Mary-le-Bow and
many more, the public buildings which time and fortune
have spared, proclaim his matchless achievement not less
than the greater mass of St. Paul's.   Each building is
stamped with his individuality.   The marvel is that one
brain and hand should have accomplished so much.   London
was fortunate above the experience of all other cities in
that the hour of her greatest calamity should have produced our greatest architect.

The Cathedral was last of the public buildings to be
finished.   On Thanksgiving Day for the Peace of Ryswick,
the 2nd December, 1697, the choir was opened for divine
service.   The Morning Chapel (now St. Dunstan's Chapel)
was ready fifteen months later.   But it was not until 1710
that Wren, then in his seventy-eighth year, witnessed the
full accomplishment of his work, when his son laid the
highest stone of the lantern on the cupola, in the presence
of Mr. Edward Strong, the master mason, and others
employed on the construction.   To but a few of the
onlookers the Great Fire of London was then a memory of
forty-four years ago.

APPENDICES

I. LETTERS FROM RESIDENTS IN LONDON AND CONTEMPORARY ACCOUNTS (ENGLISH AND FOREIGN) DESCRIBING THE GREAT FIRE.

ENGLISH.

ENDORSED

These for his very honor'd Friend, Mr. Henry Griffith, att Benthall Present. Leave this Letter att Mr. Seth Biggs' house, a Draper in Shrewsbury Salop to be speedily conveyed.

DEARE SIR,—Yesterday I received yours of the 6th present. It being left for mee. I hope long before this time you received one from mee, dated about the same time, wherein I gave you in short the sad relacion of our late misfortunes. I suppose you have had itt att large before this time ; had not my beinge out of towne prevented mee I should have given itt you myselfe. Therefore, in fine, be pleased to take notice that I have viewed this sad desolacion, and find the fire, as I then told you, began in Pudding Lane, not far from Billingsgate, in a baker's house, about one or two in the morninge, on Sunday, 2d instant, and the winde full east being very strong. And by such time it had consumed 15 or 16 houses raged soe high that there was no hopes of quenching itt, insoemuch that the only remedy was conceav'd to pull downe severall houses far before the fire, thinking thereby to stop itt, but all in vaine, and then 'twas too late, for in raging soe much and burning soe many wayes and wonderfully against the winde, that before one house could be pull'd down 10 would be burnt, for that that very fire that sett St. Paul's church a burning flew thence into Salisbury Court, in Fleet Street, over the heads of those that were at worke on the houses at Fleetbridge. This caused people to give itt cleerly over, and they began to secure their best goods. Some went to stealing, others to looke on, but all stood to the mercy of an enraged fire, which did in 3 dayes time almost destroy the metropholist of this our Isle, had not God of his

313

infinite mercy stayed the fury thereof, which was done by his
Majesty's and the Duke of York's singular care and paines,
handing the water in bucketts when they stood up to the ancles
in water, and playing the engines for many houres together, as
they did at the Temple and Cripplegate, which people seeing
fell to work with effect, having soe good fellow labourers.

It has burnt all from the Towre to the Temple, and part of
that too along the Thames side, carrying before itt the Custome
House, Billingsgate, London Bridge, Coleharbour, Queenehith,
Baynard's Castle, Black and White Fryers, from east to west.
Northwards itt burnt to Cripple and Mooregate, and something
further to Moor Fields, carrying before itt Cannon and Lumbart
Street, Cornehill, Exchange, Bartholomew Lane, Lothbury,
and most of the buildings towards Moor Fields, Guildhall,
Aldermanbury, Basinghall, and Colman-street.   North-west-
ward it burnt the Poultry, Cheapside, Bread and Friday streets,
Fishstreet, Doctors' Commons, Paul's Church-yard, Newgate
Market, Catteaton street, Wood and Milk streets, Frost [Foster]
Lane, St. Martens to and from Aldersgate, Pye Corner to
Smithfield, Holborn to the bridge, Ludgate-hill, Old Bailey, the
Fleet and Fleet street to the Church, all Shooe and part of
Fetter lanes.   Northeastward, Threadneedle street, Augustine
Fryers, part of Bishopsgate streete, Gratia [Gracechurch] street,
Eastcheape, Fenchurch street, almost to Marke Lane End a
good way past the Church, part of Lime street, Minsing Lane,
Tower street, and most of Marke Lane, together with all lanes,
alleys, streets, and parish churches within this compasse, being
in all burnt 89 : besides St. Paul's church.   And thus have I
given you an account of the sad devastacions, which to relate,
much more to behold, cannot be done without great pitty and
sorrow for the losse thereof and the ruine of its late inhabitants.

And now that wee cry out a plott, a plott, and 'twas treachery
has done this unto us, when alasse 'twas for those personal and
national sinns that this kingdome is guilty of, for their unthank-
fullness for all his mercyes in preserving them during some
years under a tyrannical government, restoreing their king, and
their just liberties, giveing them victory over their enemies at
home and abroad, whereby every man sate peaceably under
his own vine, but this wrought noe good reformacion, wherefore
He stirred up an enemy to warr with us, and brought the plague
upon us, both which I may say have swept away in a short
time some hundreds of thousands, yett did He deliver us from
both, but was noe better rewarded ; wherefore He has brought
this evill upon us, yett cannot many of us be perswaded itt to
be His severe hand upon us.   When, indeed, if all our enemies
at home and abroad had had free liberty and other assistance

to have done itt, they could not have destroyed soe vast a thing in soe short a time without the Almightye's licence. Foolish then are the vain thoughts for men to think that God's mercies are not greater than our enemies' mallice. But I confess several Dutch and French have dureing this time been apprehended, and still are in custody, for being assisting or instrumentall hereunto, by laying traines of powder and casting balls and other fireworks, and some have confest great things, and many will undoubtedly suffer but are not yett tryed. But I have done with this, and I pray that God have done punishing, and then our losse will be gaine. God save the King, and then the city wholly shortly shall be famously rebuilt.

On Sunday sevennight, I dined with cousin John Jones, where I found couzin Edwards and Mr. Stringe, who are both there, but have lost all ; and he hemselfe has extremly suffredd ; he was saying that if you had not disposed of your interest to a house in Gratia street 'twas lost. Somethings of yours that were at Mr. Strings are saved, viz. a little red trunke and some satten, and some other things which I saw there. But for your trunke at our name sakes at Lothbury, it was then lost, being carried into the fields, whence it was stole, but was in hopes making great enquiry after itt to find itt out, and since I have been once to see after itt but could not finde him, and this day I have sent againe, but feare the party will not return till 'twill be too late to send you word, and hoping they have writt to you before now. . . .

The General [Monck] is here, but shortly to goe aboard againe. I have sent you the Gazett, with which I conclude, as thinking I have already been too tedious, for which I humbly beg your pardon, and shall be glad to heare from you, but noe oftener than opportunity and your occations will permitt.

I am, Sir,
Your true Friend, humble Servant
and poor Kinsman,

18th Sept. 1666.   HEN. GRIFFITH.

Little of the city remaynes, save part of Broad and Bishop-gate streete, all Leadenhall street, and some of the adjacent lanes about Algate and Cretchett Fryers.

ENDORSED.   To the Lord Viscount Scudamore, Homme Lacy, near Lincoln, these.

MY LORD,—I suppose your lordship may have heard of this sad judgment that has come upon us by some flying report, though not the particulars, and this goes by the first post.

Being constant with the Duke [of York] I presume to believe none have seen more of it than I have, he being so active and stirring in this business, he being all the day long, from five in the morning till eleven or twelve at night, using all means possible to save the rest of the city and suburbs.   On Tuesday our only hope was to save Fleet Street, and so to Whitehall, by pulling down houses both sides Bridewell Dock [the Fleet River] so to make a broad lane up from the river [Thames] to Holborn Bridge.   The Duke's (? station) was from Fleet Bridge to the river ; Lord Craven, next to the Duke most active in the business, was to come from Holborn Bridge to Fleet Bridge ; the Privy Council to assist him with power, there being a law among the citizens that whoever pulleth down a house shall build it up again, so what was done was by order of the King and Council.

All orders signified nothing ; had not the Duke been present, and forced all people to submit to his orders, by this time I am confident there had not been a house standing near Whitehall. The city, for the first rank, they minded only for their own preservation ; the middle sort so distracted and amazed that they did not know what they did ; the poorer, they minded nothing but pilfering ; so the city abandoned to the fire and thousands believing in Mother Shipton's prophesy, "That London in 'sixty-six should be burnt to ashes."   Sir Kenelm Digby's son, who pretends to prophesy, has said the same thing, and others—a judgment upon the city for their former sins.

The Duke on Tuesday, about twelve o'clock, was environed with fire ; the wind high, blowed such great flakes, and so far, that they fired Salisbury Court and several of the houses between that and Bridewell Dock, so the Duke was forced to fly for it, and had almost been stifled with the heat.   The next hope there was to stop it at Somerset House, it raged so extreme in Fleet Street on both sides and got between us, and at six of the clock to the King's Bench Office at the Temple.   Night coming on, the flames increased by the wind rising, which appeared to us so terrible to see, from the very ditch the shore quite up to the Temple all in flame, and a very great breadth. At ten o'clock at night we left Somerset House, where they began to pull down some houses in hopes to save Whitehall, by pulling down Sir John Denham's buildings, and so up to Charing Cross.   The Queen and Duchess resolved to be gone by six o'clock on Wednesday morning to Hampton Court.   Nothing can be like unto the distraction we were in, but the Day of Judgment.

About eleven of the clock on Tuesday night came several

messengers to the Duke for help, and for the engines, and said that there was some hopes of stopping it; that the wind was got to the south, and had blown the fire upon those houses from the street between the side of the Temple Church; by that means had took off the great rage of the fire at that side, and on the side of the street St. Dunstan's Church gave a check to it. We had not this mercy shown to us alone, but likewise hearts and hands from the people; the soldiers being almost all tired out with continual labour. By six of the clock on Wednesday the Duke was there again, and found the fire almost quenched on both sides of the street; from thence he went to the Rolls, caused all people, men, women and children that were able to work to come, and to those who refused he beat them to it; by this means he got people to other places, as Fetter Lane, which he preserved by the assistance of some brick houses and garden walls; likewise Shoe Lane was preserved by the same way. At Holborn bridge there was my Lord Craven, who gave a check to the fire there, and by noon quenched it. It then broke out again in Cow Lane in Smithfield; so Lord Craven went to assist Sir Richard Brown, who is but a weak man in this business. The Lord Mayor went to Cripplegate, pulled down great store of houses there to stop it, being grown to a great head. The Lords of the Privy Council rid about to every place, to get pipes opened that they may not want water, as the Lord Chamberlain, Lord Ashley and others, so that by Wednesday towards the evening we supposed the fire everywhere quenched excepting that about Cripplegate, which we hoped well of.

No sooner was the Duke come to Whitehall but a new alarm —50,000 French and Dutch in arms, and the Temple on fire again. When we came there we found a great fire occasioned by the carelessness of the Templars, who would not open the gates to let the people in to quench it; told the Duke that unless there was a barrister there they durst not open any door. The Duke found no way of saving the Temple Chapel [Church] and the Hall by the Chapel, but blowing up the Paper house in that court, which experiment, if it had been used at first, might have saved a great many houses. One of the Templars seeing gunpowder brought, came to the Duke and told him it was against the rules and charter of the Temple that any should blow that house with gunpowder, upon which Mr. Germaine, the Duke's Master of the Horse, took a cudgel and beat the young lawyer to the purpose. There is no hopes of knowing who this lawyer is, but the hope that he will bring an action of battery against Mr. Germaine.

About one o'clock the fire was quenched, and saved the

chapel and hall; so the Duke went home to take some rest, not having slept above two or three hours since Sunday night. The next morning, being Thursday, the King went to see how the fire was, and found it over in all places. It burnt down to the very moat of the Tower. They were very fearful of the Tower, carried out all the gunpowder, and brought out all the goldsmiths' money (which was at first carried thither) to Whitehall, above £1,200,000. The King saw all Moorfields filled with goods and people. He told them it was immediate from the hand of God, and no plot; assured them he had examined several himself which were spoken of upon suspicion, and found no reason to suspect anything of that nature; desired them to take no more alarms; he had strength enough to defend them from any enemy, and assured them he would, by the grace of God, live and die with them; and told them he would take a particular care of them all. £500 worth of bread he intends to send them tomorrow, and next day intends to send them as much more, and set out a Proclamation in favour of them. Gresham College is to be the new Exchange, nothing remaining in the old Exchange but the statue of him that built it. There is £25,000 worth of cloth burnt, which will be well for the wool and the poor. The Lord General [Monck] will be here tomorrow, and the fleet sets sail from Portsmouth tomorrow. One of our ships is burnt by the French.

The fire being all within the city, is looked upon as a judgment to the city. Griffin, of the Common Council in Hereford, has lost £1,600 in houses. The Lord Mayor is undone.

My lord,

Your lordship's most obedient servant

WIND. SANDYS.

DUTCH.

Extract uyt een Brief Van seeker particulier goede Vriendt, uyt London geschreven den 10–20 September, 1666.

In the Royal Library, The Hague.

I had hoped to send you this letter last week, but owing to the great fire which has taken place here I have not dared to go out.

On the 2–12 September, Sunday morning, between two and three o'clock, the fire began in a baker's shop in Pudding Lane, between Billingsgate and the Bridge, near Thames Street.

To tell briefly a long story, the whole city of London, as far as her jurisdiction extends, has been burnt out, from the Tower to Temple Bar (of which the greater portion has remained standing). Of the whole city, all that is left is Leadenhall Street, Bishopsgate Street, one half of Lime Street, and Aldersgate. The Dutch Church is among the buildings spared and the Bishop of London's house, and Gresham College, whither the merchants have now transferred the Exchange. Except for these, everything has been burnt to the ground.

Such destruction has never before been seen. This fire was horrible to witness. It burnt five days, from Sunday morning till Thursday at noon. Eighty-four churches were burnt, and not one of them is even in such condition that repairs are possible. St. Paul's was included; it has been so damaged that people can find no place there in which to take shelter and refuge save the vaults. It was marvellous that during this great fire a very strong wind should have prevailed. The wind carried the flames in various directions, and drove them along by the river, which from the fire's start was covered with lighters and boats, all filled with goods which the people had saved out of their houses.

On the first day a vast quantity of merchandise and goods was burnt in Thames Street, for the fire took people by surprise, and they were too much amazed to help themselves. In the afternoon I saw goods being taken out of houses in Lombard Street, and the same in the surrounding streets.

It is impossible to describe the state of confusion into which the whole city was thrown, when people in thousands were left homeless, when provisions could not be got through the streets because the passage was blocked by carts, each person struggling to get away with his own possessions, and letting the fire go its own way. Nothing was done to resist the onslaught of the flames, so the next day the authorities kept the greater number of the carts out of the city, hoping that thereby they would be able to force the people to give help in extinguishing the fire, which had already caused extraordinary damage. Homeless people had piled their goods in the churches, and amongst others in St. Paul's, thinking that in such places they would be safe from the fire, but the flames burnt them all. Many people transferred their goods from place to place three times.

On the third day the authorities again permitted all carts and carriages to enter the city. From that time the panic-stricken people thought only of their own escape, abandoning the city, and many fled also from the outlying parishes.

This day (Tuesday) was the most terrible day of the fire. It burnt so furiously, and the flames spread with such rapidity, that the homeless people could not find shelter. All the surrounding fields were covered with goods, Moorfields, Lincoln's Inn Fields, St. Giles's fields, and the piazza in Covent Garden, and there the poor people camped beside their goods. The King himself, and the Duke of York, took extraordinary measures to stay the advance of the flames, but the fire reached Temple Bar and Holborn. It continued to burn with great vehemence, and the next day was carried to the outlying parishes. Not even with the enthusiasm which the King and the Duke of York infused into the people, and the great diligence they then displayed—not even with the help of half the world, had it been available—could they stem the fire's progress, and it was only conquered with the greatest difficulty.

Many houses were blown up with powder to create a clear space. While the fire burnt, all the King's Guards and the Trained Bands were called up in arms.

The people believed that the Dutch and French had set fire to the city. They said that the conflagration was begun by a Dutch baker, who was bribed to do this work, and that the French went about scattering fireballs in the houses. All foreigners alike were held to be guilty, no discrimination being shown, and many who were well known to be of good character, and upon whom no suspicion could rest, were cast into prison. Amongst them was the brother of Mr. Germius, who has the appearance of a Frenchman, and because of that he was grossly ill-treated. A poor woman walking in Moorfields, who had chickens in her apron, was seized by the mob, who declared that she carried fire-balls, and not only did they violently abuse her, but they beat her with sticks and cut off her breasts. A Dutch baker in Westminster, Riedtveldt, heated his oven to bake bread. The people, seeing smoke issuing from the chimney, cried out that the rogue was setting the town on fire at that end, and they dragged him into the street, severely wounding him, and then beat him nearly to death. The Duke of York happened to pass the house just in time to save the man from being murdered. The mob plundered his house, and the baker is completely ruined. One sees in the city nothing but doorways and chimneys standing amongst ruins. It will be a long time before the people of London forget their wild rage against the foreigners.

ITALIAN.

Relatione esattissima del' Incendio Calamitoso della citta di Londra, Padua, 1666.

In the Public Record Office.

[This somewhat scandalous account of the Great Fire of London was printed in Italian in Padua, but bears internal evidence of Dutch origin. A copy is in the *State Papers (Domestic) Chas. II.,* Vol. 175, No. 164. It was forwarded to Lord Arlington from Venice by Thomas Stanton, who in his accompanying letter says : " The Dutch are busy with their calumnies, and make the people believe that the Fire is a judgment, because, as they allege, four friars of St. Bernard were taken by an English man-of-war, hanged, and their quarters set on the four gates of the city some few days before. The Dutch print weekly the news in Italian, and send copies all over Italy speaking of their great success and power, and representing England as ruined, not only by their victories, but by dissentions at home." The pamphlet fills two and a half pages. The English translation has kindly been made by Mr. J. Parker Hayes.]

London was once the proud theatre of the universe ; now (almost an incinerated corpse) amidst the ruins she bewails alike her own calamities and those of her citizens ; she serves only as a wretched stage for the representation of most unhappy tragedies. She was the executioner of her own King ; she, who presumed to rule not merely over the earth, but over the winds and the waters as well. The Heavens, however, were at length tired of her proud arrogance, and they have shown her that God is the only Master of the elements, by punishing her, as Lucifer was punished, with the torments of fire, and thereby showing her, as in a mirror, how human calamities may proceed from vain ambition.

On the first of this month, a most unhappy day for this nation, the source of all London's miseries burst forth from the house of a baker in a street called Pudding Lane, close to the quay whence the boats leave for Gravesend. The baker's boy having placed some twigs in the oven to dry, about midnight on Saturday they caught fire, setting the whole house ablaze. A strong east wind was blowing at the time. The officers charged with that duty ran up to extinguish the fire, and they advised the Lord Mayor (a young man of little experience) to isolate the flames by pulling down a shop and four houses, by which means the fire could easily have been put out. He answered, " When the houses have been brought down, who shall pay the charge of rebuilding them ? "

This reply discouraged the people. Losing heart (doubtless owing to the Divine will) they abandoned their efforts to combat the fire, which already was proudly devouring everything, and devoted themselves to saving their own most valuable belongings. Meanwhile that superb element Fire was spreading terror in all directions, proving itself unconquerable in a few hours ; and it went on burning fiercely throughout the day and evening, extending along the River Thames towards St. Paul's. It was then too late to stop its progress.

On Monday the wind blew from the same quarter, the ruin resulting was even greater, and finally the great church of St. Paul was itself destroyed. Then the fire began to advance in two directions, eastward along the Thames to the Tower of London, and inland, to the utter desolation of the city. The flames conquered everything, dividing into many local fires, one of which, heading straight against the east wind, entirely destroyed the street of the jewellers (*la strada delli orefici*) called Lombard Street.

On Tuesday the fire entered Fenchurch Street, and passing into Tower Street completely burnt out the Custom House, and travelled as far as The Tower, leaving no vestige of a house standing where the flames had been. But as though frightened by the stronghold of The Tower, the fire stopped beneath its walls, unconquered yet, but unable in that direction to do more harm.

On Wednesday the fire spread as far as Cripplegate, where it worked its way bravely. Another fire, having reduced the Exchange to ashes, spread north, consuming everything on its way up to Moorfields, where the King, the Duke of York, and all the nobles came to see King Charles I. avenged. But moved to pity by the terrible spectacle, they gave themselves an example to the citizens by throwing buckets of water on the fire, exhorting the populace to do the same. The people, who had saved such part of their goods as they had been able to lay hands upon, and neglected what was now past recovery, began, on the King's instigation, to work manfully, and soon the fire was extinguished in that part of the city also.

The flames in due course extended to the very limits of the city at Temple Bar, which was reduced to ashes, all but part of the roof. About Cripplegate the fire raged until Thursday evening, when at length it was extinguished everywhere, and all danger of its spreading farther was at an end. All that survives of this once great city is not as large as a third part of

The Hague. There remain standing, in fact, but two main streets of houses, that is to say, Bishopsgate up to the gate of the same name, and Leadenhall Street from its middle up to the gate. At most, on all sides it is no greater than the length of a musket shot, not counting a few houses along the walls which have been spared.

To one who watched, as from the top of a tower, the spectacle of the city burning, the miseries of this people were appalling. Like madmen, they exerted themselves to save such of their belongings as could most easily be removed, leaving the fire to consume all that remained, and making no effort to stay the flames. Men, women, and children, of all ages and of all ranks, ran through the streets, their backs loaded with their most precious goods; and among them were carried many sick and disabled persons, who had been driven from their houses by the fire. As they ran they made a heart-rending murmur. One would need to have been a Nero to have watched such a spectacle without pity. But amid all their dire distress, not one person turned to Heaven to ask for mercy. Like some Pharaoh of old, hardening his heart when visited by over-whelming calamity, they only cursed their fate, and grew more cruel. Amid this welter of extreme misery, the greatest crimes and most execrable atrocities were committed, par-ticularly against the large numbers of foreigners who dwelt in London, many of whom were murdered. Others saved themselves as best they could from falling into the hands of the infuriated populace. (The Catholic Ambassador on this occasion showed his great humanity by giving shelter to all who sought refuge.) Thefts took place openly during these turbulent days, arms were treacherously seized and as treacherously used, and every kind of false testimony was borne in order that those who had been fortunate enough to save some part of their possessions might be the more easily robbed; and this was the fate, not of foreigners alone, but of Englishmen as well. In short, this Divine retribution has served such miscreants as a cloak beneath which to commit all kinds of iniquity. Pleased be God that evil shall not triumph according to their desires, as is to be feared.

My Lord Monck has been recalled here to restore confidence among the populace by his presence, and he has promised them that he will either die [*i.e.*, in the engagement then hourly ex-pected with the Dutch Fleet] or bring home the value of all that has been burned. But even if he returns with all his ships loaded with silver, he will only be able to restore a part of the damage, which must amount to an incredible sum, as from 14,000 to 16,000 houses have been destroyed, amongst them being the most palatial buildings of the city, all the goods of the East India Company which were stored beneath the Exchange, more than eighty churches, several of which were of extraordinary beauty, such as St. Paul's and others, the Admiralty (*sic*), the Courts of Justice, and a multitude of colleges, hospitals, and other buildings. What now remains is a lamentable spectacle, pitiable to all the world.

Written in London the 24th [N.S.] September, A.D. 1666.

SPANISH.

Relacion Nueva y Verdadera del formidable incendio que ha sucedido en la ciudad de Londres.   Valencia, 1666.

In the Guildhall Library.

[This is one of the most interesting of the foreign accounts of the Great Fire of London, though the facts are so distorted by religious and political prejudice that historically it is of the smallest value. The writer's inaccuracies are so many that it has seemed useless to correct them. The translation was kindly made for me by the late Mr. J. M. Kennedy.]

Briefly describes the flourishing City of London in the year 1666 and proceeds :—

On Sunday, the twelfth of September [New Style] of this present year, at three o'clock in the morning, fire broke out in a blacksmith's forge. The whole house was soon in flames, and the fire extended to the neighbourhood. The result was that in a couple of hours—since the streets were narrow, the wind strong, and most of the houses built of pinewood— the fire, which no human efforts could check, was carried on the wings of the wind over an enormous area. It was carried to the finest street in the city inhabited by the merchants, the street which is called Paternoster Row.

With the dawn of day the news of the disaster spread through the city ; and everybody thought the last hour of the world had come. And all this was but the beginning ; for the flames gathered force in this street and it was not easy to satisfy their appetite. Consternation and terror drove the frightened dwellers from their beds at an early hour ; and they thought themselves lucky to escape with their lives—forgetting what was to them their second life, namely, the life of their shops. This they left to the mercy of the flames, which, in the store of cloths, woollens, and other merchandise found material for their nourishment. So quickly did fortune carry out her designs that those persons who, their eyes dazzled by greed, remained behind for a moment to save their wealth, perished when they found t⁾ ᵗir path cut off by the flames, their eyes now blinded even.   re by the smoke than they had been previously by covetousness. Those people who saw the tempest of fire approaching and endeavoured to remove their possessions to a place of safety were unable to do so : in the first place because the number of people who came to render assistance formed a danger and an impediment rather than a help ; and, in the second place, the fire spread so rapidly that no place which was thought to be safe was so. The sound of the bells noisily warned the parishioners ; but, since these bells were not rung in Catholic churches, their only effect was to make a noise and not to act as a help.

The fire proceeded on its way and soon reached the plazza of St. Paul's, where it attacked the church, one of the most celebrated religious edifices in Europe, renowned for its seven chapels. In each one of these the true faith was formerly preached simultaneously in London, the worshippers in the others being undisturbed thereby. This church is under the patronage of the King, who, with the Lord Mayor, often attends the services of the false faith held there. This is the faith called Puritanism, in which the father of the King wished to die, thereby losing in an instant the glory which he might have won by dying in our true Roman Catholic faith, on that fatal day when the Crown and the scaffold were seen side by side.

Urged on by the steady wind, the fire devoured the majestic fabric of the stately church. At this point the King and his brother appeared on horseback, desirous of bringing some relief to the homeless people scattered about the streets, and wishing also to do something for the safety of the church whither they were called by consideration for their blind religion. Not even the presence of royalty, however, could do more in the midst of that multitude than add to the confusion and the difficulties. The fire was now universal, like Death himself, and respected neither sceptres nor crowns. In the very sight of the King himself it proceeded to crown itself the conqueror of the highest parts of the great building. The flames seized upon the carved timber of which the church was in places composed, licked it up in a twinkling ; and in a few hours left this marvellous building, the labour of many years, a smoking mass of lamentable ruins. No doubt the great Paul, not satisfied with the worship of the false religion which went on within its walls, preferred to see the magnificent edifice sacrificed to the fire rather than left for the veneration of a heretic cult.

Night approached; and the sun disappeared sooner than usual behind the thick clouds and fogs formed by the smoke; but it seemed to the onlookers that the day was returning with all its light, so widely was the fire spreading. The horror, fear, pity, and confusion of that night—to relate them would be the work of days. Think of them : people wandering about the streets because their houses had been burnt, dazed by the thought of the disaster ; the fear of those in the districts towards which the flames were slowly making their way, the wind all the time fanning the flames and bringing the horror closer and keeping the remedy further away.

When Monday morning dawned the fire had gathered further strength, and its ravages now extended over a wide area. It had by this time almost approached the King's Palace. To keep the flames back it occurred to some people to use as a remedy what would at other times have been employed as one of the forces of destruction. Fifty pieces of artillery were brought to bear on the outskirts of the devastated area, the object being to make a sort of fortress, or wall, of the very ruins, so that the onslaught of the flames might be checked, because they had now crept up very near the palace, at that side of it where the apartments of the Queen-Mother Henrietta were situated. It was believed that by this means the fire might be stopped in its course as well as if the wind had turned in the opposite direction. But what happened ? It was observed that, in view of the direction in which the flames were extending, the first building on which they would have had to fasten, and the one nearest to them, was the Roman Catholic Church which was allowed for use of the Queen-Mother and her family and for the celebration of the Holy Sacrament. At this very point the onrush of the flames was arrested : and it is clear and certain that in this way the Almighty (who is Lord of all the elements) wished to rebuke the blindness of those heretics, and to show in what respect he held the sovereign Sacrament of the Altar. A hundred and forty churches of the heretics, including St. Paul's, and extending over thirteen of the principal parishes, were destroyed by the flames ; but at the sight of a Catholic temple the fire acknowledged itself to be conquered. Five-and-fifty thousand houses were left in ruins : it was only at the sight of one of them, one that contained within its walls memories and the worship of our holy faith, that the flaming tempest, which involved so many in disaster, allowed itself to be subdued. Praised be God, who thus showed, and not for the first time, that He could make the flames respect those who loved Him.

An end was finally put to the devastation, but not to its

memory, which must remain throughout the centuries, for it
was one of the greatest fires of the kind which the world has
ever known. The loss of property was estimated at a hundred
millions, and there were some thirty thousand persons who
found themselves wandering about without either house or
home. May God open their eyes to the truth, and enable them
to take a lesson from the destruction of their own hundred and
forty churches and the safety of the one Roman Catholic
temple, the only building that the flames respected. The dead
numbered eight thousand : these were the sick and infirm,
who were buried sooner than they expected amid dust and ashes,
and the covetous ones—those who, in trying to save their
effects, lost them and their own lives—and the daring people
who, while trying to steal, were stolen away by Death.

It was at first thought that this disaster was due to the
malice of some Dutchmen and Frenchmen, who, it was believed,
had managed to set fire to the City, and in consequence many
of these nations were seized and imprisoned. When later it
became evident that the outbreak was purely accidental, the
King ordered that these men should be set at liberty.

It was said that among the ruins of a Puritan church some
men found a stone with a Latin inscription, which, when
deciphered, was found to mean : " When these letters shall be
read, woe on London, for they shall be read by the light of a
fire." Many months before, people said, a pyramid of fire was
observed rising from the sea, which afterwards broke up in
flames and sparks. This lasted a quarter of an hour, and
appeared again in three days. Another portent was the vision
of a deformed monster, who had been born in the city some
days before. He was horrible in shape and colour : part of
him was fiery red and part of him yellow. On his chest was a
human face. He had the legs of an bull, the feet of a man, the
tail of a wolf, the breasts of a goat, the shoulders of a camel, a
long body, and, in place of a head, a kind of tumor with the ears
of a horse. Such monstrous prodigies are permitted by God
to appear to mankind as harbingers of calamities.

In short, it would seem that the disaster just related was a
particular punishment destined by the Almighty ; because
unforeseen casualties preceded it, the rapid currents of air
carried it far and wide when it came, and the ardent tongues of
fire made it known to all. Further, the precautions which had
been taken against fire were found to be useless. . . . Nor was
the solicitude of the King himself of any avail. His Majesty
remained thirty hours on horseback, vainly seeking to arrest
the progress of the flames and to keep them from devouring
the best quarter of the city. He went about the districts in

which the merchants sold silks, and where the silversmiths'
and other shops were situated, powerless while he saw his city
destroyed by fire like the ruined Troy—counting its habitations,
not by houses, but by different fires ; and even more by cinders
than by fires.

And, finally, it was but just that the instrument of this
punishment should have been a blacksmith's forge ; for
London was itself at one time a forge, and, for the sake of
torturing glorious martyrs, manufactured many iron instruments ; and in our age, indeed, the most formidable of them,
namely, the headsman's axe, which—an unheard-of phenomenon
—was dyed with the purple blood of a king.   A forge, then, in
which so many instruments of torture have been wrought, may
well have such punishments wrought for itself ; and let those
who have escaped from this punishment with their lives give
thanks to God ; and (having recognised the true Roman
Church) let them pray to God that he may spare them from a
greater fire, namely, the fire of Hell.

FRENCH.

Extraordinarie   Gazette   du   XV   Octobre,   MDCLXVI,
abridged.

In the Bibliothèque Nationale, Paris.

The people accused the Dutch of being the authors of
their misfortune, and others suspected some fanatical sects
of the English nation, but to tell the truth nobody knows whom
legitimately to blame, nor can it be believed that there are
citizens so vile or enemies so malignant as to resort to an
action of that nature.

However that may be, the conflagration has turned into a
dreadful spectacle one of the most powerful and most flourishing cities, whose inhabitants would now be in the worst possible
state of desolation had it not been for the part that the King of
Great Britain has taken in the calamity.   This Prince, accom-
panied by the Duke of York and the nobility who were in his
entourage, never ceased during the days of the fire to visit
every place, riding on horseback about the City, giving orders
to allay the confusion inevitable from such a calamity, and for
the transport to Whitehall of goods that the inhabitants were
able to save from the voracity of the flames, particularly merchandise and silver that they brought there to deposit in his
Majesty's hands, as in a place of safety.

Moreover, it may be said they could not have found a place of greater security, and the owners have not been slow to recognise that his Majesty has returned to them exactly everything they deposited, with practical testimony of his good-will, and with touching expression of the feelings which his Majesty entertains respecting the public catastrophe, so much so that his Majesty has gained thereby the affection of all his people. It cannot be doubted, after the marks which they have given to him, that their own misfortunes hardly touched them more than the kindness which his Majesty has shown in their interests ; and that henceforward they will have for his Majesty all the tenderness that children ought to have to a good father, as well as the veneration which subjects should have for a Prince who interests himself so greatly in their preservation.

GERMAN.

Kurtze jedoch warhafftiger Relation von dem erschrechkichen Feuer-Brunst welcher den 12, 13, 14, 15 and 16 Septembris die Stadt Londen getroffen. Gescrieben auss Londen, den 20 September, anno 1666.

In Lincoln's Inn Library.

[This brief and sympathetic account of the Fire was written four days after it was subdued. I am indebted to the courtesy of Mr. Etheridge, the Librarian of Lincoln's Inn, for access to it. The pamphlet consists of four pages.]

With the pen alone it is hardly possible to set down an adequate account of the pitiful state of things brought about by the most destructive fire England has ever seen. The fire lasted five days and nights, and raged with such fury that all human means of combating it were unavailing. It began on the night of Sept. 12th, [N·S] about one o'clock, in a baker's shop in Pudding Lane, a narrow passage close by New Fish Street, which leads to the Bridge. This was a closely built district, and most of the houses were of wood, some being coated with pitch and others with plaster. As there was a very strong north-east wind blowing, the flames got the upper hand before daybreak, to such an extent that all attempts made to control them were futile. It might, perhaps, have been possible to confine the fire to smaller dimensions if the houses at first affected could have been isolated ; but the flames obtained complete mastery and raged the whole day, spreading to

Gracechurch Street and thence to Cannon Street, and along the Thames side as far as the Three Cranes in Vintry.

The King and the Duke of York and many other notables were on the spot on the first day of the Fire and the following days, and helped to maintain order ; but they could do nothing to stay its progress. As the inhabitants of the district realized that the flames could not be checked, they seized as much of their property as they could carry, and made off to wherever they could find safety.

On Monday the fire raged even more fiercely, and defied all efforts of the people to limit its ravages. By seven o'clock in the evening the whole neighbourhood by the River Thames as far as Baynard's Castle was burnt out. On the north the fire spread as far as Gracechurch Street, Lombard Street, Cornhill, and Bucklersbury, and so caught the houses built about the Exchange.

Before Tuesday's dawn the Exchange and other buildings in the neighbourhood were burnt. By that night the flames had spread to Fleet Street, and had burnt all the houses as far as St. Dunstan's Church, together with all the buildings lying between the Exchange and the Temple, Crown Court, etc., the whole sweep of which was consumed by the fire, which then deviated from its straight course and turned up Fetter Lane about half-way towards Holborn.

Thus it lasted until Wednesday night. Then a fresh fire broke out in the Temple, and was got under control by about two o'clock on Thursday morning, when it had destroyed the buildings about the cloisters and ignited a portion of the church and the hall.

By Thursday the fire had, for the most part, been overcome—at Temple Church, near Holborn Bridge, at Pie Corner, Aldersgate, Cripplegate, the lower end of Coleman Street, the end of Basinghall Street, the gates at Bishopsgate Street and Fall Street (*sic*) the Standard in Cornhill, the church in Fenchurch Street, Clothworkers' Hall in Mincing Lane, the middle of Mark Lane, and the Tower Dock. And here the destruction came to an end, after the fire had burnt out and destroyed the largest and best part of the city, where most of the merchants lived. In an hour's walk from the Temple to The Tower there is, within the walls, hardly anything left standing ; and without the walls, in Fleet Street and from Holborn to Fleet Bridge, all is in ruins.

In all there were burnt about 12,000 houses and 80 churches, including St. Paul's.

As any one may easily imagine, most of the people had to camp out under the blue sky ; and they presented such an abject appearance, deprived of all means of subsistence, that the cry rose that they should make for the Royal Naval stores, and there provide themselves with what they needed.

The Tower remained standing, after all the houses around it were burnt out, but the flames came up to the very gates.

The fire has wrought so much destruction that a proposal is made that an entirely new city be built on a new plan.

May God Almighty protect all cities and places from such damage and misfortune.

II. OFFICIAL NARRATIVE OF THE GREAT FIRE.

The London Gazette, No. 85, Sept. 3 to 10, 1666.

Sept. 8.—The ordinary course of this paper having been interrupted by a sad and lamentable accident of fire lately hapned in the City of *London :* It hath been thought fit for satisfying the minds of so many of His Majesties good subjects who must needs be concerned for the issue of so great an accident to give this short, but true accompt of it.

On the second instant at one of the clock in the morning there hapned to break out a sad deplorable fire in Pudding Lane, neer New Fish Street, which falling out at that hour of the night, and in a quarter of the town so close built with wooden pitched houses, spread itself so far before day, and with such distraction to the inhabitants and neighbours, that care was not taken for the timely preventing the further diffusion of it, by pulling down houses, as ought to have been ; so that this lamentable fire in a short time became too big to be mastred by any engines or working neer it. It fell out most unhappily too, that a violent easterly wind fomented it, and kept it burning all that day, and the night following, spreading itself up to Gracechurch Street, and downwards from Cannon Street to the water-side as far as the Three Cranes in the Vintrey.

The people in all parts about it distracted by the vastness of it, and their particular care to carry away their goods, many attempts were made to prevent the spreading of it by pulling down houses, and making great intervals, but all in vain, the fire seising upon the timber and rubbish and so continuing itself, even through those spaces, and raging in a bright flame all Monday and Tuesday, notwithstanding His Majesties own, and His Royal Highness's indefatigable and personal pains to apply all possible remedies to prevent it, calling upon and helping the people with their guards ; and a great number of nobility and gentry unweariedly assisting therein, for which they were requited with a thousand blessings from the poor distressed people. By the favour of God the wind slackned a little on Tuesday night and the flames meeting with Brick-buildings at the Temple, by little and little it was observed to lose its force on that side, so that on Wednesday morning we began to hope well, and His Royal Highness never dispairing nor slackning his personal care, wrought so well that day, assisted in some parts by the Lords of the Councel before and behind it, that a stop was put to it at the Temple Church, neer Holborn Bridge, Pie Corner, Aldersgate, Cripplegate, neer the lower end of Coleman Street, at the end of Basinghall Street, by the Postern, at the upper end of Bishopsgate Street and Leadenhall Street, at the Standard in Cornhill, at the Church in Fanchurch Street, neer Clothworkers' Hall in Mincing Lane, at the middle of Mark Lane, and at the Tower Dock.

On Thursday by the blessing of God it was wholly beat down and extinguished. But so as that evening it unhappily burst out again afresh at the Temple, by the falling of some sparks (as is supposed) upon a pile of wooden buildings ; but His Royal Highness, who watched there that whole night in person, by the great labours and diligence used, and especially by applying powder to blow up the houses about it, before day most happily mastered it.

Divers strangers, Dutch and French were, during the fire, apprehended upon suspicion that they contributed mischievously to it, who are all imprisoned, and informations prepared to make a severe inquisition thereupon by my Lord Chief Justice Keeling, assisted by some of the Lords of the Privy Councel, and some principal members of the City, notwithstanding which suspicions, the manner of the burning all along in a train, and so blowen forwards in all its way by strong winds, makes us conclude the whole was the effect of an unhappy chance, or to speak better, the heavy hand of God upon us for our sins, showing us the terrour of his judgment in thus raising the fire, and immediately after his miraculous and never enough to be acknowledged mercy in putting a stop to it when we were in the last despair, and that all attempts for the quenching of it, however industriously pursued, seemed insufficient. His Majesty then sat hourly in Councel, and ever since hath continued making rounds about the City in all parts of it where the danger and mischief was greatest, till this morning [Saturday] that he hath sent His Grace the Duke of Albemarle, whom he hath called for to assist him in this great occasion, to put his happy and successful hand to the finishing of this memorable deliverance.

About the Tower the seasonable orders giving for plucking

down houses to secure the magazins of powder, was more
especially successful, that part being up the wind, notwithstanding which it came almost to the very gates of it, so as by
this early provision the several stores of war lodged in the Tower
were entirely saved : And we have further this infinite cause
particularly to give God thanks, that the fire did not happen
in any of those places where His Majesties naval stores are
kept, so as tho it hath pleased God to visit us with his own
hand, he hath not, by disfurnishing us with the means of
carrying on the war, subjected us to our enemies.

It must be observed, that this fire happened in a part of
the town where tho the commodities were not very rich, yet
they were so bulky that they could not well be removed, so
that the inhabitants of that part where it first began have
sustained very great loss, but by the best enquiry we can make,
the other parts of the town, where the commodities were of
greater value, took the alarum so early, that they saved most of
their goods of value, which possibly may have diminished the
loss, tho some think, that if the whole industry of the inhabitants
had been applyed to the stopping of the fire, and not to the
saving of their particular goods, the success might have been
much better, not only to the publick, but to many of them in
their own particulars.

Through this sad accident it is easie to be imagined how
many persons were necessitated to remove themselves and goods
into the open fields, where they were forced to continue some
time, which could not but work compassion in the beholders,
but His Majesties care was most signal in this occasion, who,
besides his personal pains, was frequent in consulting all wayes
for relieving those distressed persons, which produced so good
effect, as well by His Majesties proclamations, and the orders
issued to the neighbour justices of the peace to encourage the
sending in provisions to the markets, which are publickly
known, as by other directions, that when His Majesty, fearing
lest other orders might not yet have been sufficient, had commanded the victualler of his navy to send bread into Moorefields
for the relief of the poor, which for the more speedy supply he
sent in bisket out of the sea stores ; it was found that the
markets had been already so well supplyed that the people,
being unaccustomed to that kind of bread, declined it, and so
it was returned in great part to His Majesties stores again,
without any use made of it.

And we cannot but observe to the ccnfutation of all His
Majesties enemies, who endeavour to perswade the world abroad
of great parties and disaffection at home against His Majesties
Government ; that a greater instance of the affections of this

city could never be given then hath been now given in this sad and deplorable accident, when if at any time disorder might have been expected from the losses, distraction, and almost desperation of some persons in their private fortunes, thousands of people not having had habitations to cover them. And yet in all this time it hath been so far from any appearance of designs or attempts against His Majesties Government, that His Majesty and his Royal Brother, out of their care to stop and prevent the fire, frequently exposing their persons with very small attendants, in all parts of the town, sometimes even to be intermixed with those who laboured in the business, yet nevertheless there hath not been observed so much as a murmuring word to fall from any, but on the contrary, even those persons whose losses rendred their conditions most desperate, and to be fit objects of others prayers, beholding those frequent instances of His Majesties care of his people, forgot their own misery, and filled the streets with their prayers for His Majesty, whose trouble they seemed to compassionate before their own.

III. CITY CHURCHES IN THE GREAT FIRE.

Below is a full list of City parish churches, numbering 109 in all, that were standing at the time of the Great Fire of London. Those rebuilt by Wren are indicated by a dagger (†). In all cases in the list of " churches destroyed " which are not so distinguished the churches were not rebuilt, the parishes being annexed for ecclesiastical purposes to other parishes.

There was some confusion in numbers after the Fire ; the surveyors' report gives the total burnt in the conflagration as 89, and other authorities 87. It is possible that the surveyors counted the full number in any way affected by the flames, including, say, Allhallows Barking, where the damage was trifling. The number destroyed was 84, and three others were restored after substantial repairs. St. Martin Orgar being left in a ruinous state by the Fire, was repaired in part by the French Protestant congregation for their use.

84 CHURCHES DESTROYED IN THE FIRE.

†Allhallows Bread Street
†Allhallows the More
Allhallows the Less
Allhallows Honey Lane
†Allhallows Lombard Street

†St. Alban Wood Street
St. Andrew Hubbard
†St. Andrew-by-the-
Wardrobe
St. Anne Blackfriars

APPENDIX III

†St. Anne and St. Agnes
†St. Antholin
†St. Augustine
†St. Bartholomew Exchange
†St. Benet Fink
†St. Benet Gracechurch Street
†St. Benet Pauls Wharf
St. Benet Sherehog
St. Botolph Billingsgate
†St. Bride
†Christ Church
†St. Christopher-le-Stocks
†St. Clement Eastcheap
†St. Dionis Backchurch
†St. Dunstan-in-the-East
†St. Edmund King and
Martyr
St. Faith
St. Gabriel Fenchurch
†St. George Botolph Lane
St. Gregory-by-Pauls
Holy Trinity the Less
†St. James Garlickhithe
St. John the Baptist Wal-
brook
St. John the Evangelist
St. John Zachary
†St. Laurence Jewry
St. Laurence Pountney
St. Leonard Eastcheap
St. Leonard Foster Lane
†St. Magnus the Martyr
†St. Margaret Lothbury
St. Margaret Moses
St. Margaret New Fish Street
†St. Margaret Pattens
†St. Martin Ludgate
St. Martin Orgar
St. Martin Pomeroy

St. Martin Vintry
†St. Mary Abchurch
†St. Mary Aldermanbury
†St. Mary Aldermary
St. Mary Bothaw
†St. Mary-le-Bow
St. Mary Colechurch
†St. Mary-at-Hill
St. Mary Magdalen Milk Street
†St. Mary Magdalen Old Fish
Street
St. Mary Mounthaw
†St. Mary Somerset
St. Mary Staining
St. Mary Woolchurch
†St. Matthew Friday Street
†St. Michael Bassishaw
†St. Michael Cornhill
†St. Michael Crooked Lane
†St. Michael Queenhithe
St. Michael le Querne
†St. Michael Paternoster Royal
†St. Michael Wood Street
†St. Mildred Bread Street
†St. Mildred Poultry
St. Nicholas Acon
†St. Nicholas Cole Abbey
St. Nicholas Olave
†St. Olave Jewry
St. Olave Silver Street
St. Pancras Soper Lane
St. Peter Chepe
†St. Peter Cornhill
St. Peter Pauls Wharf
†St. Stephen Coleman Street
†St. Stephen Walbrook
†St. Swithin
St. Thomas the Apostle
†St. Vedast Foster Lane

3 CHURCHES PARTIALLY BURNT AND REPAIRED.

St. Mary Woolnoth St. Peter-le-Poore
St. Sepulchre.

22 CHURCHES LEFT UNHARMED BY THE FIRE.

Allhallows Barking
Allhallows London Wall
Allhallows Staining
St. Alphage London Wall
St. Andrew Holborn
St. Andrew Undershaft
St. Bartholomew-the-Great
St. Bartholomew-the-Less
St. Botolph Aldersgate
St. Botolph Aldgate
St. Botolph Bishopsgate

St. Dunstan-in-the-West
St. Ethelburga
St. Giles Cripplegate
St. Helen Bishopsgate
Holy Trinity Minories
St. James Duke's Place
St. Katherine Coleman
St. Katherine Cree
St. Martin Outwich
St. Olave Hart Street
St. Peter ad Vincula

With few exceptions, Wren's City churches were used for divine worship before the workmen engaged upon their construction had completed their task, and as a consequence considerable confusion exists as to the dates at which they were finished. In some cases, too, the last payments were delayed after the work was done until sufficient money had come in. Elmes's list in his *Sir Christopher Wren and his Times* proves, where it can be tested, to be most inaccurate. The following list gives the dates of the construction of the fifty-one churches as shown in Wren's building accounts preserved at the Bodleian Library. (Cf. Weaver, *Archæologia*, Vol. lxvi, p. 1).

St. Mary-le-Bow, 1670–80 (steeple to 1683); St. Mary-at-Hill, 1670–76; St. Vedast, 1670–73 (steeple 1695); St. Sepulchre, repairs to 1677–1678; St. Christopher-le-Stocks, 1670–75 (taken down to give place to Bank of England); St. Michael Cornhill, 1670–77 (tower 1721); St. Stephen Walbrook, 1672–87; St. Benet Fink, 1670–81 (destroyed in 1843 for the new Royal Exchange); St. Olave Jewry, 1670–79 (destroyed in 1887 under the Union of City Benefices Act); St. Dionis Backchurch, 1670–86 (destroyed 1876 under the above Act); St. George Botolph Lane, 1671–79 (destroyed 1876 under the Act); St. Michael Wood Street, 1670–87 (destroyed under the Act); St. Magnus the Martyr, 1671–87 (steeple 1705); St. Mildred Poultry, 1670–79 (destroyed 1872 under the Act); St. Stephen Coleman, 1674–81; St. Laurence Jewry, 1670–86; St. Nicholas Cole Abbey, 1671–81; St. Michael Queenhithe, 1676–87 (destroyed 1876 under the Act); St. Mary Aldermanbury, 1670–86; St. Swithin, 1677–87; St. Michael Bassishaw, 1676–82 (destroyed under the Act); St. Mary Woolnoth, repairs to 1677; St. Bartholomew Exchange, 1674–86 (removed in 1840 to Moorfields to make way for the Sun Fire Office, and finally destroyed under the Act); St. Anne and St. Agnes,

1676–87 ; St. Bride's, 1670–84 (steeple 1699) ; St. Peter Cornhill, 1677–87 ; St. Antholin Watling Street, 1678–91 (destroyed 1875 under the Act) ; *St Mary Aldermary, 1682 (tower 1711) ; St. Mildred Bread Street, 1681–87 ; *St. Augustine and St. Faith, 1683 (spire 1695) ; St. James Garlickhithe, 1674–87 ; Allhallows the More, 1677–87 (destroyed 1896 under the Act) ; Allhallows Bread Street, 1677–87 ; St. Benet Paul's Wharf (now the Welsh Church), 1677–85 ; St. Martin Ludgate, 1677–87 ; St. Alban Wood Street, 1682–87 ; St. Mary Magdalen Old Fish Street, 1683–87 (injured by fire 1886 and removed) ; St. Benet Gracechurch Street, 1681–87 (destroyed 1867 under the Act) ; St. Matthew Friday Street, 1681–87 (destroyed 1886 under the Act) ; St. Clement Eastcheap, 1683–87 ; St. Mary Abchurch, 1681–87 ; St. Margaret Pattens, 1684–89 ; St. Michael Crooked Lane, 1684–94 (destroyed 1831 for the approach to London Bridge) ; St. Edmund King and Martyr, Lombard Street, 1670–79 ; St. Margaret Lothbury, 1686–93 ; St. Andrew-by-the-Wardrobe, 1685–95 ; Allhallows, Lombard Street, 1686–94 ; St. Michael Paternoster Royal, 1686–94 ; St. Mary Somerset, 1686–94 (destroyed 1872 under the Act, tower left standing) ; St. Dunstan-in-the-East, repairs to 1671 (tower 1699) ; Christ Church Newgate Street, 1677–91.

The two churches marked with an asterisk (*) are not included in Wren's accounts in the Bodleian.

IV. COMPANIES' HALLS BURNT IN THE FIRE.

Forty-four halls of the Livery Companies were burnt in the Great Fire of London. The list overleaf has been compiled from existing records and the picture plan usually known as Hollar's " Exact Surveigh Within the Ruins of London," 1667, which has been reproduced by the London Topographical Society. An original copy in fine state, bearing colour, is in possession of the Sun Fire Office, Threadneedle Street, E.C. It appears from the " Surveigh " that at the time of the Fire Watermen's Hall was also used by the Fruiterers Company, and Glaziers Hall by the Lorimers, these Companies then possessing no halls of their own. " Lorimers Hall, by Moorgate, a hall I had never heard of before," whence Pepys on May 15th, 1668, attended Sir Thomas Teddiman's burial (*Diary*) was accommodation taken after the Fire. Joyners Hall, near the waterside, when the flames overwhelmed it was shared by the Gardeners Company, who were paying £8 a year rent for its use. The Glass Sellers Company had abandoned the use of Joyners Hall in April before the Fire, and met at a tavern. The original

Pinners Hall at Austin Friars, though still standing, was not in use by the Company, the Pinners and Wire Drawers having amalgamated under the name of the Girdlers of London in Elizabeth's reign. Strype has given the number of Companies' Halls destroyed in round numbers as fifty, but this evidently is mere guesswork, for elsewhere in the same volume he says fifty-three. If there were any others than those I have listed, then I have failed to trace them.

The halls burnt in the Great Fire were those of the following Companies :—

HALLS DESTROYED.

Apothecaries	Joyners
Bakers	Masons
Barber Surgeons	Mercers
Blacksmiths	Merchant Taylors
Bowyers	Parish Clerks
Brewers	Paynter Stainers
Broderers	Pewterers
Butchers	Plaisterers
Clothworkers	Plumbers
Coopers	Poulters
Cordwainers	Saddlers
Curriers	Salters
Cutlers	Scriveners
Drapers	Skinners
Dyers	Stationers
Fishmongers	Tallow Chandlers
Founders	Turners
Girdlers	Vintners
Goldsmiths	Watermen
Grocers	Wax Chandlers
Haberdashers	Weavers
Innholders	Woodmongers

HALLS WHICH ESCAPED THE FLAMES.

The following Companies' Halls standing at the time of the Great Fire escaped the flames :—

Armourers	Ironmongers
Bricklayers	Leathersellers
Carpenters	Upholsterers
Cooks	

Glovers Hall is mentioned in a letter as having survived the Fire, but I know nothing of it.

NOTES.

(*) p. 1. PUDDING LANE.

Much ingenuity has been expended upon the origin of the
name " Pudding Lane." Stow's account is that the lane was
so called " because the butchers of Eastcheap have their
scalding houses for hogs there, and their puddings with other
filth of beasts are voided that way to their dung-boats on the
Thames." (*Survey*, ed. 1603, p. 212.) This is inconsequential,
and explains nothing. Simon Ford, a contemporary versifier
of the Great Fire, has this derivation—

> " The *next place* view'd, where the *Flame* began,
>   From *empty'd Tripes* call'd *Pudding-Lane*.
> And ne're (said She) to *greater Honour* rise,
>   Thou *Source* of *Londons Tragedies*."

(*Londons Remains*, 1667.) Originally the place bore the more
picturesque title of Red Rose Lane, from a house sign there,
and Rother Lane, but descriptive names were given quite early
to the mediæval City streets. Cheapside is full of them, with
its Honey Lane Market, Friday Street, Wood Street, Milk
Street, Ironmonger Lane, Old Jewry, and more.

It was " Puddyng Lane " as early as 1372 (Sharpe, *Husting
Wills*, i, 44). The English pudding—the commercialized
article—survives no longer save in the North Country ; but for
centuries it was characteristic English fare. The delicacy
aroused enthusiasm in the breast of M. Misson, a French visitor
to England in the seventeenth century. " Blessed be he that
invented pudding ! " he writes in his *Memoirs and Observations*.
" Ah ! what an excellent thing is an English pudding ! To
' come in pudding time ' is as much as to say, to come in the
most lucky moment in the year. Give an Englishman a
pudding, and he shall think it a noble treat in any part of the
world." I hold with Waterhous (*Short Narrative*, 1667),
rejecting Stow, that Pudding Lane most likely preserves the

fame of " some eminent seller of puddings living of old there,"
and supplying the riverside dwellers, a mute and unknown
English worthy. The lane has survived the changes that
have taken place about the approaches to London Bridge,
and to-day is chiefly occupied by fruit importers and brokers.

(*) p. 13.   OVERCROWDED CITY CHURCHYARDS.

An observant Londoner seeking out these green spots in
the City cannot fail to notice how many of the now disused
churchyards are raised high above the surrounding soil.   I
find this significant passage in the Vestry Minutes of St.
Stephen Coleman Street, when the worst of the Great Plague
had passed over the parish, but it was not yet eliminated.
The date is 26th October, 1665 : " At this general vestry it
was ordered that in regard to the visitation, and that a great
number of bodies had been buried in the churchyard, insomuch
that they began to smell and to annoy the neighbours, it is
therefore ordered that no more be buried in neither of the
churchyards till time convenient, and that the churchyard be
raised with éarth levelled and new paved." There had been
560 deaths in this one parish.

Vincent (*God's Terrible Voice*) writes during the plague :
" The churchyards now are stuffed so full with dead corpses
that they are in many places swelled two or three feet higher
than they were before, and new ground is broken up to bury
the dead."

Early as the reign of Henry VIII. the conditions within
the City were already scandalous.   There is preserved a letter
from the Court of Aldermen to the parishioners of St. John
the Baptist Walbrook, dated the 12th August, 1543, in reply
to a complaint.   The letter says that the inhabitants of the
parish do commonly bury " the corses of their people in the
Churchyard very dangerously for infecion by reason that they
lak roome and lay often times one corse upon another so that
the uppermost of them lyeth not a fte and a half in the yerthe."
They were therefore ordered either to find another ground or
to bury their dead " in the yerth as in other places."

Not wishing to pursue an unsavoury subject too far, I add
a single entry from the records of St. Andrew Holborn, of the
25th Elizabeth, illustrating the extraordinary indifference of
our forefathers to the ghastlier tokens of death : " The great
heap of dead mens bones and sculls that lay unseemly and
offensive at the east end of the church near Shoe Lane were all
this year buried in a pit."

(*) p. 20. MOTHER SHIPTON'S PROPHECY.

It is given in these words in the letter from Wind. Sandys to Viscount Scudamore, written on Sept. 6, 1666 (printed in Appendix I). I have found nothing so definite, however, in *Mother Shipton's Prophesies*, printed in 1641, where the last prophecy reads : " A ship come sayling up the Thames to London—and the master of the ship shall weepe, and the mariners shall aske him why he weepeth, being he hath made so good a voyage, and he shall say, ' Ah, what a goodlie citie this was, none in the world comparable to it ; and now there is scarcely left any house that can let us have drinke for our money.' "

Pepys records that when news of the burning of London reached Prince Rupert at sea, all he said was, that now Shipton's prophecy was out. (*Diary*, 1666, Oct. 20.)

(*) p. 35. EARLY FIRE APPLIANCES.

Reference is made to a fire-squirt placed in a frame by Cyprian Lucus in his *A Treatise named Lucarsolace*, London, 1590—apparently an invention of his own. The " fire engine " used in Nuremberg in 1651 is described by Caspar Schott as having a water cistern, and being operated by twenty-eight men, the contrivance being drawn to a fire by two horses. It is said to have thrown a jet of water to a height of 80 ft., but this probably is gross exaggeration. The water came out, not in a continuous stream, but in repeated jets.

The danger of fire in a city almost wholly timber-built was constantly present to the mediæval authorities, who devised simple protective laws. All London citizens in Edward II.'s reign who dwelt in " great houses " were ordered to keep a ladder, or two, ready and prepared to succour their neighbours in event of fire, and to have in summer-time before their doors a barrel full of water for quenching fire ; this " if it be not a house that has a fountain of its own." Each City Ward, by its reputable men, was under obligation to provide a strong crook of iron, with wooden handle, together with two chains and two strong cords, the ward beadle to have a good horn, loudly sounding (*Liber Albus*, 288–9). The Common Council in 1575 charged every Alderman to see that each parish in his ward should provide leathern buckets at the cost of the inhabitants, to be in readiness for casualty of fire (*Letter Book Y*, fo. 12*b*, Guildhall).

(*) p. 41.   Cloisters of City Churches.

The existence of cloisters attached to mediæval City parish churches seems entirely to have escaped the study of archæologists, which is the more curious as the name frequently occurs in the registers. Unfortunately there is nothing to show exactly what the cloister of Allhallows-the-More was, but that it was a substantial structure is indicated by Stow's description of its state in the last years of the sixteenth century, when it was " foully defaced and ruinated " (*Survey*, ed. 1598, p. 186). This is indicated still more clearly in the case of St. Mary Aldermanbury, " a fayre Church," says Stow, " with a churchyard, and cloister adjoining, in the which cloister is hanged and fastened a shank bone of a man (as is said) very great . . . for it is in length 28 inches and a half of assise. . . . This bone is said to be found amongst the bones of men removed from the charnel house of Paules, or rather from the cloyster of Pauls church, of both which reports I doubt " (*Ibid.*, p. 233). William Harrison, subsequently writing of giants in his " Description of Britain " (Holinshed's *Chronicles*, i, 19) also speaks of this bone åt St. Mary Aldermanbury, and of an image of a man skilfully fashioned to its proportions, being 10 ft. or 11 ft in height, " which is fixt on the east end of the cloister of the same church, not farre from the said bone." The churchwardens when rebuilding after the Fire paid—

" For digging a pit to bury ye bones, 5*s*. 4*d*.
For baskets to carry ye bones to ye pit, 10*d*."

(Accounts, 1672), and possibly the giant's limb bone, a marvel to so many, went in with the rest.

Other churches possessing cloisters were St. Stephen Walbrook, St. Michael Cornhill, St. Mildred Poultry, St. Martin Outwich, and St. Peter Cornhill. Dr. Philip Norman tells me that he has seen a plan of the surroundings of the old church of St. Katherine Cree, on which cloisters were marked. There was a small remaining cloister in 1666 at St. Martin Outwich, which is shown on a plan made before the Fire of London (Clode, *Merchant Taylors*). Therein the name " cloysters " is given to what evidently was a pathway from the street to the church door, bending at right angle, but whether covered or not there is nothing to indicate ; the ground allows no room for the four walks enclosing a lawn of the traditional monastic cloister. Frequent mention occurs of burials—" the 9th day was buryed Samuell the son of Sir William Cowper, Baronet, in the cloyster " (St. Michael Cornhill register, 1666, Oct.).

This tends to support the view that the cloister of a City church was that part of the churchyard traversed by the worshipper, covered as protection from weather in some cases certainly, though in others the covering may have gone. The City churchyards in early times were often large, affording more room for the cloister than the surviving fragments not built over might suggest.

In none of the churches built after the Fire was the cloister repeated, though there is a suggestion of it at St. Michael Cornhill.

(*) p. 52. BURNING OF THE POST OFFICE.

I have committed myself to the statement that the Post Office burnt in the Great Fire of London was in Cloak Lane, Dowgate, after a process of deduction rather than by positive evidence, for I could find no document purporting to give its location in September, 1666. No records at St. Martin's-le-Grand go back so far as the Fire. The assertion made in some histories of our postal service and of London that the burnt-out post-house was in Bishopsgate Street is ruled out by one plain fact. The Fire never reached Bishopsgate Street, and during the night of Sunday, Sept. 2, was far distant from it. The old Post House was in Threadneedle Street, at the lower end by the Stocks, in 1652 ; there is a reference to its being in Cloak Lane before the Fire ; and I have no doubt that it was still there when reached by the flames. The postmaster Hickes's letter, in the State Papers, is conclusive testimony that at one o'clock on the morning of Monday, Sept. 3, when he himself fled, the flames were a few yards distant. At that hour the Fire was flaming up Dowgate. His hasty letter tells that he temporarily re-established the Post House at the Golden Lion in Red Cross Street, by Cripplegate, but unfortunately does not indicate where it was moved from. Nor do the letters among the Duke of Buccleuch's MSS., formerly at Montagu House, London, give the required location.

Immediately the Fire was out the General Post Office was removed from Red Cross Street, first to The Two Black Pillars in Brydges Street, Covent Garden, " till a more convenient place can be found in London " (*Gazette*, Sept. 3–10), and a week later, to Bishopsgate Street, at Sir Samuel Bernardiston's house, where Sir Robert Hanson, Sheriff that year, for a time kept his shrievalty (*Gazette*, Sept. 17–20). It was subsequently established in Lombard Street, where a branch post-office still stands, and early in the nineteenth century was moved to St. Martin's-le-Grand. There was a separate Kentish and

Sussex Post Office, kept before the Fire at the Round House, Love Lane, and after the Fire in a passage out to Tower Hill near the pump in Crutched Friars (*Gazette*, 1666, Oct. 4–8).

(*) p. 53.   POST OFFICE PLANT FOR FORGING LETTERS.

The curious and discreditable business of the secret device employed (till the Great Fire destroyed it) at the Post Office for tampering with and forging letters I have dealt with in detail in *Unknown London*.   Sir Samuel Morland, a clever man but a sad scoundrel, sought to get the practice revived under King William III., but the monarch refused his consent. What the secret was will never be known, for it died with the inventor.   Morland himself claimed that by his process it was possible so to open letters, whether fixed by seal or wafer, that none could detect the tampering, and that copies, even of long letters of eight or ten pages, could be made in as many minutes, the handwriting being so exactly produced in fac-simile that even the writer himself could not distinguish his original letter from the copy ; further, all manner of seals or wafers were reproduced in·exact replica.   So high did Morland place his claims that he suggested that intercepted correspondence of a treasonable nature should be allowed to pass through the post in copies, the originals being withheld till matters were sufficiently ripe for them to be produced to confound the plotters. It is tantalizing not to know the secret.   Unless the process was a chemical one acting upon the ink, one is left to surmise that Morland must have had some prevision of photography two centuries before its time.

(*) p. 55.   SIR THOMAS BLUDWORTH, LORD MAYOR.

The Lord Mayor, Sir Thomas Bludworth, displaced from controlling affairs in the City after the first day of the Fire, has been largely out of the picture.   After occupying the Mayoral chair " in the severest year that ever man had," as he quite correctly said, Bludworth found it desirable to vindicate himself in Common Hall at the election of his successor ; and there is a curious letter of his among the State Papers, addressed to Williamson, Lord Arlington's secretary and the editor of the *London Gazette*.   Bludworth complained that some mention was made in the *Gazette* as if neglect had caused the flames to increase, and he had been prejudiced thereby.   He wished at the publication of his successor to have the character given to

him of being Williamson's friend and servant, so as to assure
distant friends that he was not out of favour until something
was made out against him. He declared that he did not live
by public applause, yet he wished some esteem in the Government, and needed support (*State Papers, Dom.*, 1666-7, p. 167).

No one, in the two and a half centuries that have since
passed, has offered a word in public vindication of this much
harassed official. It was the misfortune of Sir Thomas
Bludworth that he should have been Lord Mayor of London in
this momentous year of London's history. Pepys obviously took
a dislike to the man. He wrote of him in the *Diary* before the
Fire as " a silly man, I think," and after the Fire, " a very
weak man he seems to be ; " and it is almost entirely as Pepys
has drawn him that he has come down to posterity : a back-
boneless person, wringing his hands in the midst of calamity, and
crying, " Lord ! what can I do ? " This probably is a highly
distorted portrait. Pepys seems first to have been brought
into contact with Bludworth over a matter of men pressed in
the City for the Navy, and the Clerk of the Acts was plainly
irritated (*Diary*, 1666, June 30). Bludworth was a stout
Royalist. I judge no man by his funeral sermon—Bludworth's
was most fulsome—but others besides his official panegyrist
have borne testimony to his zealousness in the service of the
King. Even this seemed to have been an additional cause of
offence with Pepys—

> " Going further, I met my late Lord Mayor Bludworth,
> under whom the City was burned. But, Lord ! the silly
> talk this silly fellow had, only how ready he would be to
> part with all his estate in these difficult times to advance
> the King's service, and complaining that now, as every-
> body did lately in the fire, everybody endeavours to save
> himself, and let the whole perish " (*Diary*, 1666, Dec. 1).

The Lord Mayor, we know, might be a terrible fellow in his
own domain in the mediæval age. We know from Harrison
that in Elizabeth's reign, " of a subject there is no public officer
of any city in Europe that may compare in port and countenance with the Lord Mayor of London during the time of his
office." But much had happened since Elizabeth. The Civil
War and the Commonwealth had introduced the London
citizens to persons greater even than the Lord Mayor. The
Restoration courtiers openly flouted the " cits," and decried
with a lofty air of superiority all who engaged in trade and lived
east—circumstances which did not tend to increase either the
dignity or the authority of the Chief Magistrate.

Pepys, used to the absolutism of the Crown, the press gang, and the rest of the powers of autocracy, thought Bludworth a weakling for not asserting his authority in blowing up and pulling down men's houses just as he pleased. " People do all the world over cry out of the simplicity of my Lord Mayor in general ; and more particularly in this business of the fire, laying it all upon him," he wrote on the 7th Sept. while the city's ashes were still hot. It was not in human nature that the owners of 13,000 houses destroyed in the flames should deny themselves the gratification of selecting a scapegoat. But the Lord Mayor's supremacy in the City was hedged about. His work was obstructed by the Aldermen and wealthy merchants, whose anxiety to circumscribe the Fire was no doubt sincere, but who were not the first—often the last—to be content to submit their own houses for sacrifice to the common weal. I am not content to accept Bludworth at Pepys's valuation as a mere fool.

In a MS. account of the Aldermen drawn up for King Charles's information in 1672, and written from a bigoted courtier and Churchman's point of view, there is a reference to Bludworth. This credits him with being " a zealous person in the King's concernments ; willing, though it may be not very able, to do great things " (Beaven, *Aldermen of London*, ii, 186).

Sir Thomas Bludworth, a vintner, and son of an opulent Turkey merchant, was knighted at the Restoration for services to the Royal cause ; was pricked for Sheriff, with Sir William Turner, in 1662—" and so are called, with great honour, the King's Sheriffs " (Pepys's *Diary*, 1662, Aug. 10), and he was one of the Royalist Aldermen appointed (for Aldersgate) by the King's Commissioners when Love and Milner were ejected under the Corporations Act of 1661, which empowered the Commissioners to remove from office in corporations and appoint successors to any whose removal they should deem expedient for the public safety. He was M.P. for Southwark 1660–79, Colonel of the Orange Regiment of the Trained Bands 1660, and Colonel of the Yellow Regiment from 1660 till his death, which occurred in 1682 in Camden House, Maiden Lane, which he had rebuilt after the Great Fire. Master of the Vintners Company in 1665, he gave towards the rebuilding of Vintners Hall £100, and left to the Company two silver bowls and covers which are still in their possession. His daughter married Jeffreys, the Chief Justice and Lord Chancellor of infamous memory, and she became the ancestress of the Earls of Pomfret.

Bludworth's unfortunate remark was long remembered

against him. In a curious MS. poem of ten verses (*State Papers, Domestic, Chas. II.*, vol. 173, No. 136) on the mutability of human affairs and projects, the last line of each stanza being " touch and goe," there is this allusion to the burning of London :—

> Theires nothing fixt beneath the skyes
> London late fyred in ashes lyes
> All though a strong man and a stoute
> Did say at first hee'd pisse it out
> Yet did to such a Blazing grow
> With London twas in ffive dayes spase
> Touch and goe.

(*) p. 57.   PARISH CLERKS COMPANY.

The Parish Clerks were not wholly stripped in the Fire. They saved much of their movable property, among their surviving records being the Bede Roll of the Company, dating back to the reign of Henry VI.   They also possess the ancient pall used at the funerals of deceased members, and two garlands of embroidered crimson velvet, which bear the date 1601.

(*) p. 60.   NEW RIVER WATER SUPPLY.

It is, unfortunately, impossible at this day to plan the distribution of the New River Company's water from Amwell in the City.   A disastrous fire at the New River Company's offices on Christmas Eve, 1769, destroyed their early records. By the courtesy of Mr. G. P. Warner Terry, Statistical Officer of the Metropolitan Water Board, I have been permitted to examine the few charred fragments that survived the fire, but there is nothing, neither accounts nor plans, to indicate how far the distribution extended in the year 1666.

(*) p. 63.   SEVEN CHILDREN PERISH BY FIRE.

Sadder than any other London memorial I know is a tablet placed high on the south wall of St. Peter Cornhill commemorating seven little children, " the whole offspring of James and Mary Woodmason," who were burnt to death on the night of the 8th January, 1782, in their parents' house in Leadenhall Street.   It was the Queen's birthday, a magnificent ball was being given at St. James's Palace in honour of the anniversary, and Mr. Woodmason, who was among the guests,

was called out only to learn that all his children had been consumed in the flames.   Several other persons also perished.
This deplorable occurrence was deeply felt by the Royal Family,
some of whom visited the scene.   In this one accidental fire
in a merchant's dwelling-house more persons lost their lives
than in the flames of the Great Fire of London.

(*) p. 67.   St. John Baptist upon Walbrook.

An old tablet commemorating the church marks the spot,
the letters of which, deeply recut, may be plainly read—

> Before the late
> dreadful fire anno domini
> 1666 here stood the parish
> church of St. John Baptist
> upon Walbrook
> William Wilkinson
> James Whitchurch
> Churchwardens this present
> year anno domini 1671.

The building of the District Railway in 1884 having necessitated
the destruction of the larger part of the churchyard, all the
human remains contained therein were collected and re-interred
in a vault under the little monument that may be seen from
Cloak Lane.

(*) p. 73.   Bishop Lloyd's Story.

Burnet tells with circumstantial detail a story, given to
him by Bishop Lloyd, that the New River water was found to
be cut off when wanted at the Great Fire of London.   One
Grant, a Papist, who was a governor of the New River Company as trustee of the Countess of Clarendon, and therefore
had access to the works at Islington, had gone there on the
Saturday night before the flames broke out, and calling for
the keys, turned all the cocks that were open, stopping the
flow of water ; then went away, carrying the keys with him.
Some hours were lost in sending to Islington, where the door
had to be broken open before the water could be turned on.
Grant denied that he interfered with the cocks, though admitting
that he carried away the keys, but not by design.   The turn-
cock at the works declared that none other than Grant had
access there.   This seems a story very difficult to refute.   But
Maitland (*London*, ed. 1739, p. 291) examining the minute books
of the New River Company, found that only on the 25th Sept.,

1666 (three weeks after the Fire) was John Grant admitted a member of the Company, as trustee for Sir William Backhouse, who died in 1669, and whose widow, afterwards Countess of Clarendon, held no New River Stock until November, 1670.

(*) p. 96. ST. MARY-LE-BOW.

In a sense, this was London's sub-Cathedral, the principal church of a diocese within a diocese, for since very ancient times there had been thirteen City parishes which, though within the diocese of London, were not of it; they acknowledged as their diocesan, not the Bishop of London, but the Archbishop of Canterbury. This curious arrangement was not abolished until 1843. They were called the Archbishop's Peculiars in the City of London, and in the church of Sancta Maria de Arcubus (St. Mary of the Arches) was held the ecclesiastical Court of Arches for all thirteen parishes, the jurisdiction of which ultimately extended over the whole diocese of Canterbury.

It has been commonly asserted that the ancient records of the Court of Arches perished with the church in 1666, but Sir Lewis Dibdin, the present Dean, finds good reason to surmise that their destruction was rather the work of Cromwell's soldiers when quartered in St. Paul's. The Fire can be acquitted of responsibility, for the unbroken series of " processes " which survive date, not from the Fire, but from 1660, when the Court was reconstituted on the Restoration. They form a complete record of everything that happened in an ecclesiastical suit—pleadings, orders, evidence, and sentence—and are of great historical value as pictures of English life and manners in former times.

(*) p. 114. KING CHARLES'S COURAGE AT THE FIRE.

The poets, from Dryden downwards, whom the Great Fire of London inspired to verse, all write in the most laudatory terms of the King's conduct, but the wreath of bays is surely earned by Simon Ford, author of the following fatuous lines :—

> Here *Cæsar* comes, with *Buckets* in His *eyes*
> And *Father* in His *heart*. *Come, come,* he cryes,
> Let's make one *onset more*. The *scatter'd Troupes*
> At his word *rally,* and *retrieve* their *Hopes.*
> The *Rebel-Flames,* they say, felt CHARLES was there ;
> And *sneaking* back, grew *tamer* than they were.
> So that, no doubt, were *Fates* to be *defeated*
> By *man,* the City's *Fate* had been retreated.

But *Loyalty* befriends the *Flames.* Their own
Dangers neglected, thine *affrights.* Alone,
Alone, dear Sir, let's *fall,* they *cry'd aloud,*
And hazard not *three Kingdoms* in a *crowd.*
Long may *King* CHARLES survive his *Cityes Fate*
His *Life,* and all our *Hopes* bear *equal Date.*
Flames can't *undo* us, whiles the *King's secure ;*
He *lost,* though *sav'd* from *flames,* we must be *poor.*
Thus did the *pious Trojan* venture *rather*
All's Treasure to the *City's wrack,* then's *Father !*
His *subjects Love* forc'd *Cæsar* to *withdraw,*
More *griev'd* to *leave* the *Loyalty* he saw.
Next, *Princely* YORK, with *sweat* and *dirt* besmear'd
(More *glorious* thus, then in his *Robes*) appear'd.
He, *Neptune-like,* his *watry Realm* doth *raise,*
And's *Noble Arm* the *spit-floud Engine* swayes :
That *baffled,* next his *Thundring-Canons* spewe
An *armed blaze,* with *Flames, Flames* to *subdue.*
But whom, the *conquer'd Dutch* and *French* did *flie,*
These Foes ('twas *out* of's *Element*) defie.

(*Conflagration of London Poetically Delineated,* 1667.)

(*) p. 115. A LETTER BY SAMUEL PEPYS.

This letter from Samuel Pepys is among the Pepys MSS. at Cambridge—

" SIR,—The fire is now very neere us, as well on our Towre Streete as Fanchurch Street side, and we little hope of our escape but by that remedy, to the want whereof we doe certainly owe the loss of the City, namely, the pulling down of houses in the way of the fire. This way Sir W. Pen and myself have so far concluded upon the practising, that he is gone to Woolwich and Deptford to supply himself with men and necessaries in order to the doeing thereof, in case at his returne our condition be not bettered, and that he meets with his R. H⁸ approbation, which I have thus undertaken to learn of you. Pray please to let me have this night, at whatever hour it is, what his R. H directions are in this particular. Sir J. Minnes and Sir W. Batten having left us, we cannot add, though we are well assured of, their as well as all the neighbourhoods concurrence.—Your obedient Servant

" S. P.

" Sir W. Coventry, Sept. 4, 1666."

(*) p. 124. *The London Gazette.*

But one newspaper was published in London at the time of the Great Fire, a single sheet badly printed on both sides, the *London Gazette*, which seems to have been the property (or at least the perquisite) of Joseph Williamson, Lord Arlington's secretary. Afterwards Sir Joseph, and himself Secretary of State, he was a niggardly person. The many news-letters sent to him as editor add to the interest of the State Papers of the period, among which they got folded. The Fire burnt out the printing office near Baynard's Castle, and the press was again set up in a distant churchyard. Women were the distributors. They complained of the terrible stench from the loosely covered burials of the Plague year, which made it a peril to life to go there for the copies. A Mrs. Andrews took one-third of the entire edition. She had lost all her goods in the Fire, and had no clothes save those on her back, and being a discreet woman deserving encouragement, she was commended for benefaction. Williamson, however, did nothing. The " book-women," as they were called, threatened to leave the work altogether—in short, to strike (Cal. *State Papers, Domestic*, 1666–7, p. 255). As a reminiscence of the earliest days of our oldest newspaper, this is worth recalling.

The imprint of the *Gazette* before the Fire was " Printed by Tho. Newcombe over against Baynard's Castle," but after the issue of Sept. 3, 1666, was simply " London, Printed by Tho. Newcombe."

(*) p. 128.   ST. PAUL'S SCHOOL.

Fears were entertained that St. Paul's school would have to be removed from the Churchyard (Pepys's *Diary*, 1667, May 16); and, indeed, after the Fire a new road from the east of the Cathedral to Cheapside was planned which would have made rebuilding impossible, but the Privy Council, on petition by the Mercers Company, the trustees, directed the Lord Mayor to alter the staking of the road and restore the school land (Guildhall *Journal* 46, fo. 252*b*).

Crouch, in *Londinenses Lacrymæ*, 1666, has a reference to the school in the Fire which may interest Old Paulines :—

> Was't not enough the holy Church had been
> Invaded in her Rites and Discipline ?
> Must her known Fundamentals be baptiz'd
> In purging flames, and *Pauls School* chatechiz'd ?
> She that had long her tardy *Pupills* stripp'd,
> Is now herself with fiery *Scorpions* whipp'd.

(*) p. 128.   LONDON HOUSE, ST. PAUL'S.

The Bishops of London had ceased to reside in the Cathedral precincts a century before the Great Fire.   " The oulde Palace sett lieung and beinge in the church yarde of the cathedrall church of S. Paule," had been conveyed by Bishop Bonner in 1556 to one Thomas Darbieshire.   In 1647, what then remained of the Palace being " all ruinous," including the gate-house, it was pulled down by a successor of his, Richard Coyah.   The property reverted to the Cathedral after the Restoration, and in 1662 the Bishop of London obtained a private Act of Parliament enabling him to lease out the tenements, shops, and warehouses then newly built on the site of his Palace, on condition that he spent at least £5000 in building or acquiring a convenient house for the bishop's use elsewhere.   London House was in Aldersgate Street when the Great Fire of London raged. Henchman, the Bishop of London at the time, died there.   (*See* W. Sparrow Simpson, *Lond. & Midd. Arch. Soc.*, New Ser., i. 13 *et seq.*)

(*) p. 176.   SIR EDMUND BERRY GODFREY CUP.

This souvenir of the Great Fire, of Charles II., and of the ill-fated Sir Edmund Berry Godfrey has a curious history.   The

Earl of Lonsdale tells me that he possesses at Lowther, Penrith, two tankards, one large and one small, which are said to be the originals presented to Sir Edmund Berry Godfrey, and with them he has a parchment record of identity. The Corporation of Sudbury, Suffolk, have a small cup (the third) of identical character, a gift by Sir Gervaise Elwes, in grateful recognition of his representation of that borough in Parliament in the seventeenth century ; and by courtesy of Alderman Baker, I am able to reproduce a print of it. A silver cup (fourth) described as that presented by Charles II. to Sir Edmund Berry Godfrey, was offered at auction in London by Messrs. Debenham, Storr and Sons on the 31st October, 1895, and realized five hundred guineas. At that time a letter appeared in *The Daily Telegraph* from Mr. Walter Lamplugh Brooksbank, stating that he himself had a similar cup (fifth) which had been in possession of his family at least since the days of Thomas Lamplugh,

Archbishop of York, who flourished about 1688.   Since then I have learnt that Mrs. Proctor, of Aberdovey, has a sixth cup.

In the Court Rolls, Warrant Book 68, No. 611, is a warrant, dated the 17th October, 1666, signed by the Earl of Manchester to Sir Gilbert Talbot, Treasurer of His Majesty's Jewel House, to deliver 800 ozs. of white plate as a gift from His Majesty to Sir Edmund Berry Godfrey.   I can only surmise from the existence of so many similar cups, that Sir Edmund Berry Godfrey, highly flattered by this mark of Royal favour, had these smaller replicas of the great tankard made from the silver, and these he presented to friends.

The cup sold by Debenham's is, like the others, a tankard of silver, 6¼ inches in height, with handle and raised lid; its weight is 35 ounces 18 dwts.   On the front are engraved the Royal Arms and the arms of Sir Edmund Berry Godfrey.   On one side, in an oval, is a somewhat crude engraving of the Great Plague, figures bearing coffins to the burial pits, and beneath a Latin inscription relating to the Plague.   Opposite, in a similar oval, is an engraving of London in flames, and a Latin inscription beneath, which translated reads :—

> " A man truly born for his country ; when a terrible fire devastated the City, by the Providence of God, and his own merit, he was safe and illustrious in the midst of the flames.   Afterwards, at the express desire of the King (but deservedly so) Edmund Berry Godfrey was created a Knight, in September, 1666.   For the rest, let the public records speak."

The writer of a letter in the Verney MSS., dated 1666 Sept. 6, describing the Fire says : " Justice Godfrey behaved himself so well at the Temple that the King would have knighted him, but he refused it, so the King has ordered a piece of plate of £50 for him, with his arms upon it, and Ex dono, etc."   Godfrey got both the plate and the knighthood.

(*) p. 192.   " TRUE BILL " AGAINST ROBERT HUBERT.

The " true bill " returned against Robert Hubert, with its endorsements, is among the Old Bailey Sessions Papers, 1666, October Sessions, at the Guildhall.   I am indebted to Miss Ethel Stokes both for deciphering the somewhat illegible Latin text on the parchment and for this excellent translation—

> He puts himself on the country.   Found Guilty. Let him be hanged by the neck until, etc.

London. The jury for our Lord the King present upon
their oath that Robert Hubert, late of London, labourer,
not having the fear of God before his eyes, but moved and
led away by the instigation of the devil, on the 2nd day of
September, 18 Charles II., about the second hour of the
night of that day, with force and arms, etc., in London, to wit,
in the parish of St. Margaret New Fishstreete, in the ward
of Billingsgate, London aforesaid, a fireball by the same
Robert Hubert compounded and made with gunpowder,
brimstone and other combustible materials, and by the
same Robert then and there kindled and fired, then and
there voluntarily, maliciously and feloniously did throw
into the mansion house of one Thomas Farriner the elder,
baker, set and being in Pudding-lane in the parish and
ward aforesaid ; and with the fireball aforesaid by the
same Robert Hubert thus, as aforesaid, kindled and fired,
and thrown into the said mansion house, did then and
there devilishly, feloniously, voluntarily, and of his malice
aforethought set on fire, burn, and wholly destroy not only
the said mansion house of the aforesaid Thomas Farriner,
but also a great number of churches and other mansion
houses and buildings of thousands of lieges and subjects
of our said Lord the King, set and being in the parish and
ward aforesaid, and in the said city of London and the
suburbs thereof, contrary to the peace of our said Lord
the now King, his Crown and dignity.

ROBERT PENNY. JOHN LEWMAN
FRANCIS GUNN
THOMAS FARRINER, senior
HANNA FARRINER
THOMAS DAGGER
[Endorsed outside] True Bill. THOMAS FARRINER, junior.

(*) p. 197. ALARM IN THE COUNTRY.

Curious proceedings at Warwick illustrate the state of
nervous alarm in the country which the Fire of London
occasioned. A boy gathering blackberries saw a man doing
" something " in a ditch. Finding himself observed, the man
hastily put " something " into a bag, and went away. The
boy found at the place a blackish-brown ball, and carried it
straight to the Deputy-Lieutenants, then meeting. The
object had no appearance of anything combustible in it, but
all took it to be an unfinished fireball. The boy described the
man, and repeated his story on oath. All the town took alarm.
A hue and cry was sent out every way to arrest the incendiary

but in vain. All day the town was in tumult, every man standing to arms; the horsed militia kept guard at night. Next day Sir Henry Pickering rode into Warwick with his troop, dismissed the militia, and commanded the townsmen to return home. They peremptorily refused to obey. High words ensued. They told the knight that for all they knew he had a design himself to betray the town. Sir Henry grew angry, and ordered the troop to fire upon the people unless they dispersed. The townsmen dared them to do it, and cocked their loaded muskets in readiness for a fray. Had not the prudence of some of their number prevailed, much mischief had been done. The tempest calmed at last, and the townsmen by degrees dropped home. The Mayor of Warwick declared the object of all the stir to be a fireball. An "ingenious gentleman," however, said it was no such thing (*State Papers* (*Domestic*), 1666-7, p. 127).

(*) p. 212. CLEARANCE AFTER THE FIRE.

An idea of the task which lay before the City householder or owner whose property was in the path of the Fire may be gained from this letter sent out by the Clerk of Christ's Hospital to the many tenants of the Hospital whose homes had been destroyed :—

"October 2, 1666.

"I am commanded by the Governors of Christs Hospitall to send you the precept [from Guildhall] here inclosed; pray forthwith repaire to the ground whereon your house or houses stood, take with you workmen, and let them take the dimensions of every particular Building and ground you held of the said Christ Hospitall, which when you have done and subscribed the same, bring it to the Beadle's booth in the ward where your house or houses stood, and a copy thereof to me at Mr. Hyde's house, Glazier, against the Pump in Little Brittaine, where you shall be sure to hear of him Morning or Evening who is Yrs— WM. PARREY."

(*) p. 221. DAY OF HUMILIATION FOR THE FIRE.

By the statute 18 & 19 Charles II., chap. 7, sec. 28, it was provided "That the said citizens and their successors for all the time to come may retain the memorial of so sad a desolation, and reflect seriously upon their manifold iniquities, which are the unhappy causes of such judgments : Be it further enacted, That the second day of September (unless the same happen to

be a Sunday, and if so, then the next day following) be yearly
for ever hereafter observed as a day of Publick Fasting and
Humiliation within the said City and Liberties thereof, to
implore the mercies of Almighty God upon the said city, to
make devout prayers and supplication unto him, to divert the
like calamity for the time to come."

The special form of prayer, with a hymn instead of the
Venite, Psalms and Lessons, was printed in some of the Oxford
Prayer Books between 1681 and 1683. It was revised under
Archbishop Tenison's authority, and reissued in 1696, with a
different hymn and other changes, and with a collect added
which prayed for the preservation of the City from fire. The
service, of which I possess an original copy, 1666, was reprinted
in a separate form by the King's printers from time to time,
even so recently as 1821, and a Latin version of it is included
in the Latin Prayer Book published by Thomas Parsell, of
which the last edition appeared in 1759.

It was customary for the Lord Mayor and Corporation to
attend St. Paul's Cathedral each year on the anniversary.
The Lord Mayor and Sheriffs went from the Mansion House
in state to St. Paul's, where they were met by the Aldermen,
who had assembled and donned their scarlet gowns in the
Corporation vestry, whereupon the civic procession proceeded
into the choir to hear divine service and a sermon preached
by the Lord Mayor's Chaplain. Afterwards the Lord Mayor
and Aldermen returned to the Mansion House. (Welch,
History of the Monument, pp. 82, 83. A list of some of the
sermons preached on these occasions is given.)

(*) p. 227. PRIVILEGES OF CITY COOKS.

The ancient charter of the Cooks Company gives exemption
to its liverymen from all jury service, on the ground that to take
a cook away from his calling would cause public inconvenience.
Of late years the Courts have constantly refused to uphold
this privilege.

(*) p. 248. JUDGES OF THE FIRE COURT.

Michael Wright's portraits at Guildhall of the Judges who
sat to decide disputes after the Great Fire are of considerable
merit, though as works of art they are not of outstanding
importance. There might have been in their place a collection
of Lely's. The fashionable painter of the King's mistresses
was first offered the commission. Lely's studio was always
attended by waiting sitters, and as he refused to give time to
attend on the Judges in their chambers, Wright got the business

(Walpole's *Anecdotes of Painting*). The names of the Judges are—

Sir John Kelynge.	Sir Christopher Turner.
Sir Matthew Hale.	Sir John Vaughan.
Sir Heneage Finch.	Sir John Archer.
Sir Francis North.	Sir Edward Thurland.
Sir Edward Atkins.	Sir William Morton.
Sir Orlando Bridgeman.	Sir Robert Atkins.
Sir William Ellys.	Sir Timothy Lyttleton.
Sir Edward Turner.	Sir Samuel Brown.
Sir Wadham Windham.	Sir Thomas Twisden.
Sir Richard Rainsford.	Sir William Wylde.
Sir Thomas Tyrell.	Sir Hugh Windham.

(*) p. 273. COMPANIES' HALLS DESTROYED SINCE THE GREAT FIRE.

In view of the large number of Livery Companies' Halls that were built immediately after the Fire of London, it is remarkable that so few of these seventeenth-century fabrics should survive in the City to-day. Poverty and wealth have both contributed to the demolition of the great majority of them; poverty by neglect, and wealth by the natural desire of many Companies, as they became richer last century, to possess more magnificent halls than they were able to erect in the years of penury and strict economy which followed the Fire. Four or five are complete; others retain part of the original structure, the design being much altered and concealed by additions subsequently made; but the larger number have gone altogether, many having been replaced by modern buildings. Those which, having suffered least change, are best representative of types of the seventeenth century gild hall are Apothecaries Hall, Mercers Hall, Brewers Hall, Stationers Hall (the last a brick building cased in Portland stone and enlarged in 1800) and Paynter Stainers Hall. Skinners Hall preserves the massive seventeenth-century staircase.

Fire has been particularly destructive amongst them since the conflagration of 1666. Bakers Hall, in Harp Lane, was burnt down by an extensive fire which began in Thames Street on the 13th January, 1714. Butchers Hall, built after the Great Fire in Pudding Lane, was burnt in 1829. Parish Clerks Hall, re-erected in Silver Street, was very badly damaged by fire in 1844, and has been substantially rebuilt. Pewterers Hall, in Lime Street, then considered a Wren building, was completely destroyed by fire in 1840. Haberdashers Hall

suffered much injury by fire on the 19th September, 1864,
having previously undergone alterations which had defaced
the original work.   Fire also damaged Drapers Hall in 1774,
and it has since been largely remodelled.

The poverty into which so many of the Companies fell
caused the diversion of their Halls to other than gild uses.
Bricklayers Hall, in Leadenhall Street, disused by the Company,
became a Jewish Synagogue.   The old Carpenters Hall, successively utilized as a warehouse and a printing house, was
taken down in 1876.   Joyners Hall, off Upper Thames Street,
has been a warehouse for more than half a century.   Coach-
makers Hall, in Noble Street, was let for an auction room and
afterwards a dancing academy, and Founders Hall for a dissenting chapel and a debating society.   Plaisterers Hall has for
many years been occupied as a warehouse, its ornamental
features having been pretty nearly destroyed.   Weavers Hall
was taken down in 1856 for the erection of offices in Basinghall
Street.   Little of the seventeenth-century work remains
visible in Barber Surgeons Hall ; Inigo Jones's theatre was
demolished in 1783.

Last century the Clothworkers, Curriers, Cutlers, Coach-
makers, Coopers, Fishmongers, Founders, Goldsmiths, Grocers,
Plumbers, Saddlers, and Wax Chandlers all rebuilt their
halls ; the little Cordwainers Hall rebuilt in Cannon Street was
erected in 1788 ; Watermans Hall and Fellowship Porters
Hall, next door neighbours on St. Mary at Hill, are both late
eighteenth-century buildings.

None of the Halls standing at the time of the Great Fire
which escaped the flames survive.   Cooks Hall, outside Aldersgate, perished in a fire in 1771 ; Leathersellers Hall, originally
the refectory of the nuns of St. Helen's, was taken down in
1799 ; Ironmongers Hall in Fenchurch Street, an Elizabethan
structure, gave place to the present hall in 1748.   Pinners Hall,
originally a part of the Augustinian Priory (Austin Friars) is
said to have stood, much altered, till 1798.

You may walk through the City without being made aware
of the existence of a single hall, so sheltered are they, few
offering more than a highly ornamental doorway to attract
the attention of the curious passer-by.   How different is the
case in Flanders, where the ornate halls of the gilds are built
about the sides of the most conspicuous squares !

(*) p. 281.   CITY LAND VALUES.

Few people realize the enormous advance of City land
values of recent years, which makes the 15s. a foot of Restoration

London seem trifling and absurd. Messrs. Farebrother, Ellis & Co., the well-known City estate agents, have kindly made for me the following extracts from their sales books, and the prices will be read with interest to-day—and perhaps with more interest a century hence. They are—

37 *Cornhill.* Freehold of 753 ft. sold in 1901 for £40,800, or £54 per ft.

Corner of Princes Street (now Union Bank). "The Azienda," opposite Mansion House, front strip sold in 1882 to City Corporation at £50 per ft.

53 *Fleet Street.* City Corporation in 1905 took for widening street 228 ft. for £7,500, or £32 per ft.

69 *Cheapside.* 396 ft. freehold sold in 1886 for £14,050, or £35 10s. per ft.

9 *Cornhill.* 776 ft. freehold sold in 1882 for £25,050, or £32 per ft.

24, 25, 26 & 27 *Cornhill.* 2,500 ft. freehold sold in 1893 for £115,500, or £46 per ft.

Savory's, Cornhill. 2,500 ft. freehold sold in 1893 for £155,000, or £62 per ft.

38 *Cheapside.* 260 ft., practically freehold, sold in 1894 for £9,300, or £35 per ft.

24 *Lombard Street.* Land sold in 1878 at £36 13s. 4d. per ft. was valued in 1899 at £50 per ft.

Lombard Street. Post Office site sold in 1897 at £43 per ft.

75 & 76 *Lombard Street.* Land sold about 1888 for £52,500, or £35 per ft.

(*) p. 288. KING CHARLES II. A CITY FREEMAN.

King Charles II. was the only reigning Sovereign who has taken the City freedom. Charles had paid unusual honour to Sir Robert Vyner by dining at his Mayoral Banquet at Guildhall on October 29th, 1674 (the date of the feast and procession was altered to November 9th in the following century). That was, no doubt, the occasion of the incident I have referred to in an early chapter between the two kings—the one who was Royal and the one who was drunk. Charles at the entertainment condescended to accept the freedom, " an unparalleled favour and honour done to the City, beyond the example of all his progenitors," says the *Gazette* account, and the scroll, curiously written on vellum, was presented with much ceremony in the Banqueting House at Whitehall on December 18th following. The description given of the casket goes far to justify Andrew Marvell's denunciation of the City's extravagance, it being " a large square box of massy gold," and hanging dependent from the vellum scroll was the Seal, itself " enclosed in a box of gold set all over with large diamonds, to a considerable value." An address was at the same time presented acknowledging the many transcendent favours the City had received from the Sovereign, " especially in Your late most obliging voluntary Condescention, in taking upon You the Freedom of Your Royal City of London, by which Your Majesty hath raised up this ancient Corporation to that height of Credit which it never yet received from any of Your Majestie. Royal Ancestors " (*London Gazette*, 1674, Dec. 17th to 21st) Such was the hollow testimony borne by the City to the monarch who, two years before, by closing his hands upon the Exchequer and its contents had brought ruin to many prosperous citizens.

(*) p. 298. MEDAL OF THE GREAT FIRE.

Plainly the object of the unknown designer of this medal was to present obverse and reverse with the strongest possible contrast. Pestilence, fire and war, by which God punishes, are seen on one side ; on the other, the removal of the venomous plague, and the blessings of peace and plenty. The following description of the medal is given in " Medallic Illustrations of the History of Great Britain and Ireland to the death of George II." (ed. Franks & Grueber, i, 525) published by the Trustees of the British Museum :—

" *Obverse.* A shrine, enclosing a crucifix, beneath the name of Jehovah, in Hebrew, radiate ; at the sides, cornfield, and vineyard ; before it, on an island, a shepherd feeding his flock and a tranquil river. In the foreground, St. Paul shaking the viper from his hand. *Leg.* Mera Bonitas (Pure goodness). *Reverse.* A city, one half in flames, the other under a storm of hail ; in front, disturbed river, leafless tree, and Death and a warrior contending on horseback. Above the Eye of Providence, comets, and storms of wind. *Leg.* Sic Punit (So He punishes). Ex. MDCLXVI."

(*) p. 300. ST. SEPULCHRE'S CHURCH.

St. Sepulchre's Church is distinguished by its fine mediæval tower and porch with fan vaulting, which happily survived the Great Fire, and are the best of their type in the City. This church is commonly believed to be one of Wren's restorations. The vestry books show plainly that Wren had little, if anything, to do with it beyond his responsibility as architect for rebuilding the City. The churchwardens themselves undertook the repairs as money became available. They made separate agreements with masons, bricklayers, carpenters, smith, plasterer, and plumber; the names of all, and their charges, are preserved in the parish accounts. Disputes arose, and an umpire was appointed. Work done in this piecemeal fashion was not likely to be entirely successful, and Wren appears to have been so little satisfied that there was considerable delay before he would grant the necessary certificates entitling the churchwardens to obtain payments of money from the Commissioners for rebuilding the churches. The bills do not appear in Wren's building accounts, but only the total, " Account of sums received by Dr. William Bell, Minister, £4993 4s."

St. Sepulchre's underwent a thorough restoration in 1880 by Mr. Arthur Billing, who treated the fabric with sympathetic regard for its ancient features. The original Gothic arches within the tower, which had been filled in in 1790 and circular arches inserted, are now restored, and the mouldings and tracery of the windows have been cut as they had existed in the fifteenth century, many fragments having been uncovered in repairing the internal face of the walls.

The church had other associations with Newgate besides Dowe's hand-bell, which is preserved on a bracket against the north wall. For many years the execution cart on its way to Tyburn halted at St. Sepulchre's, the clerk tolled the bell, offered a prayer, and presented the condemned felon with a nosegay. Dowe lies buried at St. Botolph Aldgate. The lines that Dowe was accustomed to recite when he rang his bell outside the barred window of the condemned hold on the nights before executions were these :

> " All you that in the condemned hole do lie,
> Prepare you, for to-morrow you shall die.
> Watch all, and pray, the hour is drawing near
> That you before the Almighty must appear.
>
> Examine well yourselves, in time repent,
> That you may not to eternal flames be sent,
> And when St. Sepulchre's bell in the morning tolls
> The Lord have mercy on your souls."

(*) p. 302. DRYING CLOTHES IN CITY CHURCHYARDS.

Despoiled of their gardens by the growth of the town and everywhere hampered for space, the City housewives seized with avidity upon the opportunities for drying clothes offered to them by the many churchyards left derelict after the Great

Fire. It seems to have been a general practice. The Vestry of St. Michael Crooked Lane sought to put a stop to the desecration, and minutes of the 17th March, 1675, record a resolution " for the prevention of the many inconveniences that have happened by suffering persons to hang upp lynes to dry clothes on the soyle of the church," ordering that henceforward the practice should be stopped, the doors of the ruined church kept locked, and the key retained by the churchwardens. On the other hand, the vestry of St. Pancras Soper Lane, fortified, perhaps, by the belief that cleanliness is next to godliness, could see no wrong in this use of the ground, and formally gave permission to the parishioners (Vestry Minutes, 1629–99, fo. 289) to dry " cloathes " on the site of the destroyed parish church.

I finish a serious book with a note in lighter vein. Prebendary Thomas Jackson, of St. Paul's, in *Good Words*, 1868, August (the article has been reprinted) made ingenious proof that the Great Fire of London never, in fact, happened. The argument developed on the lines of Biblical criticism. Pepys's narrative is circumstantial. Critical examination of this author's writings shows that he was fond of the marvellous, prone to embellish facts with a profusion of ingenious gossip. Serving the Court himself, he exaggerates the personal bravery and engineering skill of the King, and depreciates the acts of the Lord Mayor. Why? Clearly to discredit a free corporation. In this writer we see symptoms of untrustworthiness which throw doubt upon his entire account. Many facts in the Fire narrative, considered together, indicate that it was an allegory, perhaps symbolical of fire-worship. The flames started at the shop of Farynor, a baker. *Farina* is Latin for meal, or flour. *Farinarius* is a meal-man, or dealer in flour. Obviously the word Farynor is a corruption of *farinarius*, not representing any distinct individual. Then the Fire, we are told, started in Pudding Lane and ended at Pie Corner. Enlightened and discerning reasoning must reject such a statement as unhistorical. The existence of the Fire Monument is not questioned. Public monuments, however, often have origins other than those their inscriptions record. Instances are the Arco della Pace, in Milan, raised in honour of Napoleon's victories, which on the Bonapartists' downfall was dedicated to the Congress of Vienna and the Sovereigns of the Holy Alliance; and the Colonne Napoleon at Boulogne. The last, begun to commemorate an invasion of England which never took place, was diverted to honour the Bourbons' return, and to-day shows the statue of the Gallic Conqueror. Such examples justify scepticism in critical minds. Probably the Monument in

London was erected in honour of the Stuart King's return to his throne.   St. Paul's has been cited to support the tradition of a Great Fire.   Applying the principles of Biblical criticism, it seems probable that the present building is a series of reconstructions, outwardly looking new, but containing the older fabric concealed within.   Excavation in Finsbury, Moorfields and elsewhere has revealed no traces of the huts in which the homeless citizens are said to have lived after the Fire.   And so on, till the reader is convinced that there never was a Great Fire of London—or, at least, he ought to be !   The satire is keen.

AUTHORITIES

No attempt has been made to give anything but a working bibliography of contemporary printed books, tracts and records. and manuscripts which deal with the Great Fire of London, The writer gratefully acknowledges his debt to the many modern authors (too many to mention individually) whose works he has consulted, especially those who have written the fine series of histories of the City Companies to be found in the Guildhall Library. Minutes of the City Companies, containing various references, may be inspected with advantage, after permission given. It has not been thought necessary to schedule the records of the City Churches—vestry minutes, churchwardens' accounts, and registers. Most of these are now kept at Guildhall, others at the churches. Some have been printed by the Harleian Society. The volumes of the Domestic State Papers, Charles II., and the Privy Council Registers at the Public Record Office contain much information concerning the means taken to cope with the Fire, and subsequent measures. For the rebuilding of London, the most valuable sources are the Guildhall archives, especially the volumes of the *Journal* and the *Repertory ;* and the surveyors' returns, accounts of relief, receipts from Coal Dues, expenditure on public buildings and the like, which are in the Guildhall Library MSS. For the church building after the Fire, the manuscripts of the Dean and Chapter of St. Paul's and the Tanner MSS. at the Bodleian Library are essential. Various letters sent out from London are in private collections, and for these the published volumes of the Historical Manuscripts Commission are useful. There are Dutch pamphlets of considerable interest in the Royal Library at The Hague.

PRINTED BOOKS, TRACTS, AND BROADSIDES.

A Brief Account of the Maintenances arising by Tithe, Glebe, and other Profits to the several Ministers of the Parish Churches demolished by the late dreadful Fire in London. Broadside. **1670.**

A Protestant Monument Erected to the Immortal Glory of the Whiggs and Dutch. 1713.

A Short and Serious Narrative of London's Fatal Fire . . . as also London's Lamentations on her Regardless Passengers. 1667.

A True and Exact Relation of the Most Dreadful and Remarkable Fires. Broadside. 1666.

A True and Faithfull Account of the several Informations exhibited to the Honourable Committee appointed by the Parliament. 1667.

An Humble Remonstrance to the King and Parliament in behalf of Many Decayed and Decaying Citizens and Families of London occasioned solely by the late Dreadful Fire in that City. By Philanthropus Philagathus. 1675.

An Act of Common Council for the Suppression of Fires. 1668.

An Act [of Common Council] declaring what streets & passages shall be enlarged. 1667.

Atkins' (Edward) Letter. *Archæologia,* xix.

Baildon, W. P. *Records of Lincoln's Inn.*

Birch, H. de Gray. *Historical Charters City of London.*

Burnet, Bishop. *History of His Own Times.*

Clarendon, Edward Hyde, Earl of. *Life.*

Crouch, J. *Londinenses Lacrymae.* 1666.

De-Laune, Thos. *The Present State of London.* 1681.

Dryden, John. *Annus Mirabilis.* 1667.

Dugdale, W. *History of St. Paul's Cathedral.*

England's Warning; or, England's Sorrow for London's Misery. 1667.

Evelyn, John (*See also* under Manuscripts.) *Diary,* ed. by H. B. Wheatley.

> *Fumifugium: or the Inconveniencie of the Aer and Smoak of London Dissipated.* 1661.

Extract uyt een Brief Van seeker particulier goede Vriendt uyt London geschreven den 10–20 Sept., 1666. [Printed in Appendix I.]

Ford, Simon. *Poemata Londinensia, Jam tandem Consummata.* 1667–8. Contains—
  (*a*) *Conflagratio Londinensis* (Latin and English).
  (*b*) *Londini quod Reliquum* (Latin and English).
  (*c*) *Actio in Lond. Incendiarios* (Latin).
  (*d*) *Londini Renascentis Imago* (Latin).
  London's Resurrection (English translation of *d*).

Form of Common Prayer. To be used on Wednesday the Tenth Day of October next [Day of Humiliation]. 1666.

Gazette de France Extraordinaire. 1666, Oct. 15.

Gostello, Walter. *The Coming of God in Mercy, in Vengeance, beginning with Fire, to convert or consume all this so sinful City of London.* 1658.

Griffith's (Henry) Letter. [Printed in Appendix I.]

His Majestie's Declaration to His City of London upon occasion of the late Calamity by the lamentable Fire. 1666.

Hollar's *Exact Surveigh* (London Topographical Society).

House of Commons Journal, Vol. 8.

House of Lords Journal, Vol. 12.

Howel, J. *Londinopolis.* 1657.

Howell's *State Trials.*

Inderwick. *Calendar of Inner Temple Records.*

Jenkinson, Wilberforce. *London Churches before the Great Fire.*

Knight, Valentine. *Proposals of a New Model for Rebuilding London.* Broadside, 1666.

Kurtze jedoch warhafftiger Relation von dem erschrechkichen Feuer-Brunst welcher den 12–16 Septembris die Stadt Londen getroffen. 1666. [Printed in Appendix I.]

Londen Verbrandt. Amsterdam [1666].

Londens Puyn-hoop, oft Godts Handt over de selve, in't verbranden der Stadt, den 12–16 van Herfstnaent, 1666. Amsterdam, 1666. (Another edition printed at Rotterdam.)

London Gazette, 1666, April 30 ; Sept. 3–10 *passim.*

London's Flames. 1679.

London's Lamentations on its Destruction by a Consuming Fire. Broadside, 1666.

Magalotti. *Travels of the Grand Duke Cosmo III.*

Malcolm. *Londinium Redivivum*, Vol. 4, pp. 73-82. (Letters in the Gough collection at Bodleian Library.)

Mayoral Proclamations—

Oct. 10, 1666. *For Clearing the City after the Fire.*

Nov. 3, 1666. *For Punishment of Vagrants and Beggars.*

June 24, 1668. *For Keeping good Night Watches.*

[Oct.] 1668. *For Cleansing of City Streets.*

Marvell, Andrew, Letters to Mayor of Hull (Printed by Grolier Club).

Narrative of the Popish Plot & of the burning of London. [By Captain W. Bedloe.] 1679.

Norman, Philip. *London Churches which escaped the Great Fire*, in " London Topographical Journal."

Observations both Historical and Moral upon the Burning of London. By Rege Sincera, 1667.

Observations on the Proposals of the City to insure houses in cases of fire. Broadside, 1681.

Ondersoek van den Brand van Londen Door ordere des Parlaments van Engelandt. 1667.

Pepys, Samuel. *Diary.* Ed. by H. B. Wheatley.

Proposals Moderately Offered for the full Peopleing and Inhabiting the City of London. By Londinophilos, 1672.

Pyrotechnica Loyolana, Ignatian fireworks; or the fiery Jesuits' temper . . . exposed to publick view, 1667.

Reasons Humbly offered to Parliament for the Abatement of the Proportion of the Assessment upon the City of London. Broadside [1674].

Relacion Nueva y Verdadera del formidable incendio que ha sucedido en la grande ciudad de Londres. Valencia, 1666. [Printed in Appendix I.]

Relatione esattissima del' Incendio Calamitoso della citta di Londra. Padua, 1666. [Printed in Appendix I.]

Rolle, Samuel, *The Burning of London in the year* 1666. *In CX Discources, Meditations, and Contemplations.* 1667. *London's Resurrection, or The Rebuilding of London. In Fifty Discourses.* 1668.

Royal Proclamations, 1666—
   Sept. 5. *For Relief of Public Distress in London.*
   Sept. 5. *For keeping Markets, prevention of tumults, & appointing the meeting of merchants.*
   Sept. 13. *For a General Fast throughout England & Wales, & Charitable Collections.*
   Sept. 26. *For putting off the annual Fair at Gravesend.*
   Nov. 10. *For banishing all Popish Priests and Jesuits.*
   1668, *Sept.* 26. *For a Second Charitable Collection.*
   1669, *May* 4. *Forbidding Transport of Stone from Portland.*
   1670, *Aug.* 19. *For Repressing Disorders and Prevention of Fires.*
   See also, *His Majestie's Declaration to His City of London, etc., infra.*

Rushworth's (John) Letter. *Notes and Queries,* 5th S. v. 307.

Sancroft, Dean. *Lex Ignea : A Sermon Preached before the King, Octob.* 10, 1666.

Sandys' (Wind.) Letter. [Printed in Appendix I.]

Sharpe, R. *London and the Kingdom.*

Smith, William. *De Urbis Londini Incendio Elegia.* 1667.

Statutes of the Realm.

Stillingfleet, Dr. *A Sermon Preached before the Honourable House of Commons, Octob.* 10, 1666.

Stow, John. *A Survey of London,* 1603. Ed. Kingsford.

Taswell, Rev. William. *Autobiography* (Camden Society).

The Burning of London by the Papists : or a Memorial to Protestants on the Second of September. 1714.

Trap ad Crucem ; or the Papists Watchword. 1670.

Victoria County History of London.

Vincent, Thomas. *God's Terrible Voice in the City.* 1667.

Waterhous, Edward. *A Short Narrative of the late Dreadful Fire in London.* 1667.

Weaver, L., " Complete Building Accounts of Wren's City Churches," *Archæologia*, lxvi, 1.

Welch, C. *History of the Monument.*

Wiseman, Samuel. *A Short Description of the Burning of London.* 1666.

Wren, C. *Parentalia.*

Wright, F. *A Poem ; being an Essay on the present ruins in St. Paul's Cathedral.* 1668.

MANUSCRIPTS.

City Corporation Archives (Guildhall, Records Department).

City Accounts. 1667 *passim.*

Fire Decrees, 1667–72, nine vols.

Journal (of the Common Council), vol. 46 *passim.*

Old Bailey Sessions Papers, 1666, Oct.

Repertory (of the Court of Aldermen), vol. 72 *passim.*

Original Letters in Town Clerk's Office, Guildhall.

Joseph Ames to Tho. Pengelly, 1666, Sept. 6.

Duke of Buckingham to ——, 1666, *Sept.*

Lord Mayor of York to Lord Mayor of London, 1666, Sept. 17.

Lords of the Council in Ireland to Lord Mayor, 1666, Sept. 29.

Corporation of Londonderry to Lord Mayor, 1666 [*Oct.*].

Archbishop of Canterbury & others to Lord Mayor, 1666, Oct. 19.

[Above letters by Ames and Duke of Buckingham are printed by Welch, *History of the Monument.*]

Guildhall Library MSS.—

Oliver & Mills' survey and plans made after the Great Fire, 5 vols. MS. 38.

Day books for receipts of money paid for staking out foundations within the ruins of London, 1667 to 1696, 3 vols. MS. 275 to 277.

Posting book of above accounts, MS. 278.

Account of payments for restoration of Guildhall, Newgate, Ludgate, and other public buildings in the City. MS. 184.

Bills and receipts for work done at Guildhall, Newgate, Sessions House, etc., Jan. to Sept. 1667. *MS.* 323.

Account of Moneys received by free gifts and collections for

relief of distress. Payments out of same. 1666–71
MS. 271.

Account as above showing amounts received from each county. MS. 296.

Posting book of money collected for relief. MS. 274.

Orders for payment out of relief, with receipts. MS. 297, 298.

Account of monies received from Coal Duties, and payments therefrom for compensation of ground staked out. 1667–72. *MS.* 273.

Account of payments for expenses of the Court at Clifford's Inn for determining disputes. MS. 360.

John Evelyn's ' *Londinium Redivivum.*' *Proposals concerning rebuilding of the City. MS.* 94 (5).

Bibliothèque Nationale, Paris, *Relation de l'Angleterre en l'année* 1666. *MS. Fr.* 15, 889.

Bodleian Library, Oxford. *Tanner MSS.* and *Rawlinson MSS.*

British Museum, MSS. Department. *Judgments by the Fire Judges, Add. MSS.* 5063 *to* 5103. Has index of parishes.

Harleian MS. 4941, 66ᴇ. *Egerton MS.* 2543, f. 211.

Rugge's *Diurnal, Add. MSS.* 10, 117.

House of Lords MSS. (See *Hist. MSS. Com., 8th Rep.*)

St. Paul's Cathedral, *MSS. of the Dean and Chapter.*

Private Collections. (The page references given are to the published Calendars by the Historical Manuscripts Commission.)

Buccleuch, Duke of, pp. 49–51.
Egmont, Earl of, p. 15.
Hothfield, Lord, p. 85.
Le Fleming, pp. 41–2, 48.
Portland, Duke of, vol. 3, pp. 298, 301–2.
Verney, p. 485.

Public Record Office. *State Papers (Domestic) Chas. II.* (For references see Calendars State Papers (Domestic) 1666, *passim,* especially Mrs. Green's introduction to vol. for 1666–7.)

Privy Council Registers, vol. 59 *passim.*
Treasury Books.

INDEX

St. Mary Somerset, 72, 311, 335, 337
St. Mary Staining, 112, 335
St. Mary Woolchurch, 68–9, 183, 185, 335
St. Mary Woolnoth, 61–2, 177, 183, 184n., 310, 335–6
St. Mary Magdalen, Milk Street, 335
St. Mary Magdalen, Old Fish Street, 86, 300, 306, 335, 337
St. Mary's Spital, 295
St. Matthew, Friday Street, 335, 337
St. Michael Bassishaw, 308, 335–6
St. Michael, Cornhill, 62–3, 276n., 299, 311, 335–6, 342–3
St. Michael, Crooked Lane, 21, 45–6, 50, 306, 335, 337, 362
St. Michael Queenhithe, 72, 306–7, 310, 335–6
St. Michael-le-Querne, 93, 335
St. Michael Paternoster Royal, 57–8, 302, 311, 335, 337
St. Michael, Wood Street, 109, 276n., 300, 335–6
St. Michael's Alley, 62, 305
St. Michael's Lane, 21
St. Mildred, Bread Street, 88, 300, 335, 337
St. Mildred Poultry, 183, 276n., 300, 311, 335–6, 342
St. Nicholas Acon, 68, 335
St. Nicholas Cole Abbey, 86, 309–10, 335–6
St. Nicholas Olave, 86, 335
St. Nicholas Shambles, 144
St. Olave, Hart Street, 2, 167, 175, 336
St. Olave Jewry, 276n., 310, 335–6
St. Olave, Silver Street, 112, 335
St. Pancras, Soper Lane, 299, 302, 306, 335, 362
St. Paul's Cathedral, Old, 3, 7, 19, 64, 128–33, 136n., 221, 226, 237, 259, 313–4, 342, 349; burning of, 92, 130, 133–40, 148, 319, 322, 325; ruins of, 138–40, 173, 177, 180–1, 185, 262, 302–3, 319; Paul's Walk, 131; tombs in, 135–6, 138; misuse under Commonwealth, 132–3; remains of Chapter House, 130; Wren's, 3, 130, 136n., 138, 187, 221, 224, 230–2, 235, 257, 262, 273, 283, 295, 303, 308, 311–2, 356, 363; minor canons of, 308
St. Paul's Churchyard, 128–9, 133, 139, 175, 226, 351; Deanery, 128; School, 128, 237, 351
St. Peter Chepe, 97–8, 335
St. Peter, Cornhill, 63, 307, 335, 337, 342, 347

St. Peter, Paul's Wharf, 86, 335
St. Peter-le-Poore, 103, 335
St. Peter-ad-Vincula, 336
St. Sepulchre, 145–7, 300, 308, 310, 335–6, 360–1
St. Stephen, Coleman Street, 105, 335–6, 340
St. Stephen, Walbrook, 68, 183, 281, 310–12, 335–6, 342
St. Swithin, 13, 70, 300, 335–6
St. Swithin's Lane, 71, 246n.
St. Thomas of Acon College, 8, 88
St. Thomas the Apostle, 302, 307, 335
St. Thomas's Hospital, 145
St. Vedast, Foster Lane, 110, 267n., 310, 335–6
Salisbury Court, 115, 127, 155, 305, 313, 316; Theatre, 5, 148
Salters Company, 8, 71, 300, 338
Sancroft, Dean, 44, 128, 133, 220, 274, 303
Sanctuaries (see Alsatia, Coldharbour, St. Martin-le-Grand)
Sandwich, Edward Montagu, Earl of, 40, 125, 201n.; Countess of, 5
Sandys, Wind., letter by, vii., 115, 170, 315–8, 341
Sanitary Act of 1671, 294
Savoy, 215
Scavengers, rakers, 13, 217, 294
Scotland Yard, 157
Scriveners Company, 112, 272, 338
Scudamore, Lord, letter to, 315–8, 341
Seacole Lane, 149
Seamen at the Fire, 56, 116, 154, 166, 170–1
Seething Lane, 1, 49, 56, 85, 115, 145, 160, 162
Seldon, John, 156
Serjeants Inn, 155–6, 214
Sermons on the Fire, 172, 174
Sessions House, Old Bailey, 127, 214, 224–5, 269
Seymour, historian, 187
Shaftesbury, Earl of, 55, 122, 166, 317
Shakespeare, 2, 42, 50, 69, 82, 95, 109, 125–6, 142, 226
Shambles (see Newgate Shambles)
Sharpe, Dr. R., 107
Sheerness Dockyard, 278, 280
Shene Monastery, 109
Sheriffs, 69, 70n., 109, 211, 214, 267, 269, 343, 356; proposed houses for, 222–3
Shipton, Mother, 20, 316, 341
Shirley, poet, 177
Shoe Lane, 55, 127, 158, 165–6, 169, 227, 233, 317, 340

THE END

DATE DUE
